ACADEMIC SUPERMARKETS

*A Critical Case Study
of a Multiversity*

Philip G. Altbach

Robert S. Laufer

Sheila McVey

Editors

ACADEMIC SUPER MARKETS

Jossey-Bass Inc., Publishers

San Francisco · Washington · London · 1971

ACADEMIC SUPERMARKETS
A Critical Case Study of a Multiversity
Philip G. Altbach, Robert S. Laufer, Sheila McVey, Editors

Copyright © 1971 by Jossey-Bass, Inc., Publishers

Published in Great Britain by
Jossey-Bass, Inc., Publishers
St. George's House
44 Hatton Garden, London E.C. 1

Library of Congress Catalogue Card Number LC 71-173853

International Standard Book Number ISBN 0-87589-109-8

Manufactured in the United States of America

JACKET DESIGN BY WILLI BAUM

FIRST EDITION

Code 7138

THE JOSSEY-BASS
SERIES IN HIGHER EDUCATION

Consulting Editors

JOSEPH AXELROD
*San Francisco State College
and University of California, Berkeley*

MERVIN B. FREEDMAN
*San Francisco State College
and Wright Institute, Berkeley*

PREFACE

That higher education is in a period of stress and transition is news to few people. What is sometimes surprising, however, is the lack of serious and detailed analysis devoted to the challenges which higher education faces in the seventies. *Academic Supermarkets* is presented in an effort to provide this analysis by focusing on a single institution, the University of Wisconsin at Madison. Despite the case study approach of this volume, we feel that the analysis and data presented here have much relevance for other universities and particularly those large and prestigious institutions which have traditionally provided academic leadership. The problems of growth and stabilization, of academic politics, and of increasingly skeptical publics (students, legislatures, trustees, "public opinion") are by no means unique to Wisconsin.

We believe that the case study approach used in *Academic Supermarkets* can provide both the detailed data and the analysis necessary for a thorough understanding of the university in crisis. In the Prologue, we link the specific analysis of Wisconsin with broad aspects of higher education. In some respects, Wisconsin has been in the vanguard of academic turmoil—the rise of unionism among teaching assistants and the 1970 bombing of the Army Mathematics Research Center are examples of the extent of confrontation politics on campus. Yet, most of the problems of the University of Wisconsin are typical of those which higher education faces in a difficult period.

While *Academic Supermarkets* is not intended to provide a complete analysis of the University of Wisconsin, it does deal with the main elements of the academic equation: the power structure of the university—in this category, we include not only the administration of the institution but also such elements as the regents (trustees) and political forces —the faculty, and last (sometimes least as well) the students and teaching assistants. We feel that it is most important to focus attenion on these elements and hope that other aspects of the university will be dealt with later. We have also included material on a number of critical areas of conflict in the university. Specifically, the chapters on research and on women in the university reflect this concern.

Academic Supermarkets is presented with a large dose of modesty, an equal measure of nerve, and several caveats. It is not an exposé of the University of Wisconsin, nor is it a full-scale analysis of an extremely complex institution. We have tried to present a forum for discussion, while not imposing any ideology upon our contributors, and in fairness it must be said that we disagree with the conclusions of a number of them. Some of the authors are critical, a few rather hostile, but all greatly concerned about the future of American higher education and about the University of Wisconsin in particular. We have tried to include discussions and analyses of most of the major issues that have faced the University of Wisconsin in the past few years and to make this volume as comprehensive as possible. We have been quite open concerning both the methodologies and orientations of our authors and have insisted only that all the contributors deal analytically with their subjects. Some of the chapters report fairly traditional research studies based on sociological or other data. Others are more speculative and reflective. A number are a combination of these and other methodologies. We hope this volume provides a beginning at institutional research, for clearly a great deal of research, analysis, and even speculation needs to be done concerning this great multiversity as well as other institutions of higher learning.

The origins of *Academic Supermarkets* date back to a seminar on comparative higher education offered by two of the editors (Altbach and Laufer) and in which the third editor (McVey) was a student in the fall of 1969. We were impressed at that time by the high quality of some of the research papers presented and by the almost complete lack of existing analysis of the University of Wisconsin. Students attempting to do research on various aspects of the Wisconsin situation found many obstacles, such as data which were unavailable from university authorities and the unwillingness of some officials and faculty members to fully discuss aspects of the university. Students also found an absence of background studies from which to work. We were also impressed by the peculiar yet somehow typical situation of the University of Wisconsin. One of the most politically active campuses in the nation, Wisconsin has all the ingredients for crisis: a state university located a mile from the capitol building, a very large and diverse student body, a strong tradition of student political involvement, a substantial graduate school, and a faculty committed to graduate education and research but at the same time faced with a large number of fairly dissatisfied undergraduates and a cumbersome administrative structure. A number of factors, notably the rise of the Teaching Assistants Association as a force on the campus, the great budget crisis, and, most dramatically, the bombing of the Army Mathematics Research Center and its aftermath, make *Academic Supermarkets* a topical book.

A number of important changes are taking place at the University of Wisconsin which are not considered in detail here. Wisconsin, like other major (and minor) institutions of higher education in the United States, is faced with the dual problem of stabilizing or declining enrollments and a general financial squeeze. The implications of this financial crisis are being felt all over the campus in many ways—decreased financial aid for students, freezes on new faculty hiring, cutbacks in office workers, and so forth. In addition, the governor, in a surprise move, has suggested that the University of Wisconsin should be merged with the Wisconsin State University system (eight campuses throughout the state, mostly emphasizing undergraduate programs). If this merger takes place, as seems quite possible given the massive pressure for it despite opposition from the university, it will mean substantial changes in administrative structure. In short, the University of Wisconsin is now in the process of adjusting to the "recession" in higher education. These adjustments will be of major and long-term importance. Thus, while it is unlikely that the Madison campus will be completely transformed, it is in the process of change and the analyses in *Academic Supermarkets* will naturally be affected by these changes.

The lack of material on some key aspects is significant and deserves a note of explanation. One of the major problems of editing *Academic Supermarkets* was securing contributors who were both knowledgeable and willing to write. We found, again and again, that key participants in various events on the campus were, for various reasons, unwilling to set their thoughts on paper. Several individuals were clearly fearful of writing honestly about their experiences. The sanctions against speaking the truth or reporting controversial data must be ended if a full analysis of the crisis of higher education is to be made. It has been jokingly stated to one of the editors that the present book is an exercise in "publishing *and* perishing" for those involved. We shall see,

Our main debt of thanks must go to our contributors. While they disagree, sometimes violently, among themselves, they all have the courage, interest, and analytical detachment to write coherently about an institution and an experience which has meant different things to different people.

November 1971   PHILIP G. ALTBACH
Madison, Wisconsin   ROBERT S. LAUFER
Albany, New York   SHEILA MCVEY

CONTENTS

AUTHORS

PHILIP G. ALTBACH, associate professor of educational policy studies and Indian studies, University of Wisconsin

ROBERT ATWELL, president, Pitzer College

KENNETH M. DOLBEARE, chairman of the Department of Political Science, University of Washington

DAVID EVETT, associate professor of English, Cleveland State College

ROBERT S. LAUFER, assistant professor of sociology, State University of New York at Albany

DURWARD LONG, vice-chancellor, University of Wisconsin Center System

JUDITH LYONS, doctoral candidate, University of Wisconsin

MORGAN LYONS, assistant professor of sociology, Florida State

DONALD J. MC CARTY, dean of the School of Education and professor of educational administration, University of Wisconsin

SHEILA MC VEY, graduate student in educational policy studies, University of Wisconsin

GREGORY J. NIGOSIAN, lecturer in educational policy studies and sociology, University of Wisconsin

MATT POMMER, education writer for the Madison *Capital Times*

ELAINE REUBEN, assistant professor of English, University of Wisconsin

JAMES ROWEN, freelance writer and contributing editor of *Ramparts*

EDWARD T. SILVA, assistant professor of sociology, University of Wisconsin

BERNARD SKLAR, assistant professor of education, University of Southern California

SHLOMO SWIRSKY holds the Ph.D. degree in political science from Michigan State University

STEVEN ZORN, president of the University of Wisconsin Teaching Assistants Association and a graduate student in political science

ACADEMIC
SUPERMARKETS

A Critical Case Study
of a Multiversity

PROLOGUE

●●●●●●●●●●●●●●●●
●●●●●●●●●●●●●●●●
●●●●●●●●●●●●●●●●

THE MULTIVERSITY
IN CRISIS

Philip G. Altbach, Robert S. Laufer, Sheila McVey

●●●●●●●●●●●●●●●●
●●●●●●●●●●●●●●●●
●●●●●●●●●●●●●●●●

The explosion which caused damage of more than a million dollars to several University of Wisconsin buildings and killed a postdoctoral fellow in physics on August 24, 1970, was the culmination of a series of crises on the Madison campus since 1966.[1] The death at Wisconsin was not the first casualty of the academic crisis that developed during the 1960s, but it was different from the tragedies at Berkeley, Kent State, and Jackson State in that the death of Robert Fassnacht was the result of a calculated risk by saboteurs rather than a death stemming from the heat of battle between police and protestors. Perhaps the bombing of the Army Mathematics Research Center (AMRC) made such an impact on the Madison campus, and on the student movement in general, because the incident illustrated the logic of confrontation politics carried to an extreme.

The student left, both at Wisconsin and nationally, was unable to accept this final step in the escalation of protest. Although it had been exposed to brutality and even death throughout the late sixties, the movement balked at the acceptance of terrorism and sabotage. As the national cry of outrage over Kent State and Jackson State indicated,

1

death was beyond the limits of confrontation politics. Although efforts were made by some of the most militant movement spokesmen to justify the "accidental" death of Fassnacht, the movement in general was unable to sustain the contradiction between the moral indignation they felt at the slaying of students at Kent and Jackson State and acceptance of death as a necessary risk of movement tactics, which acceptance of the AMRC bombing would have implied. The organizational paralysis of the student left following the AMRC events illustrates the movement's grappling with its conscience. Of course, the left did not completely reject terrorist tactics. A great deal of ambivalence was apparent in the general reaction— that the AMRC was destroyed was applauded by many, that it had been at the expense of a life was regretted by all, and it was abhorrent enough to contribute to the disintegration of unity within the movement.

It is probably not an exaggeration to say that the bombing, within the context of the student movement, could only have occurred at the type of institution that Clark Kerr has christened the "multiversity." The multiversity is characterized by its variety of interests and purposes; it is a series of communities and activities "held together by a common name, a common governing board, and related purposes." It is more a mechanism than an organic whole, "a series of processes producing a series of results—a mechanism held together by administrative rules and powered by money."[2] Although it was not his intention, Kerr has defined an institution that has lost its sense of community; in the absence of any overriding purpose or goal, the various elements that compose the multiversity engage in constant battle with each other.

The combination of a very large, cosmopolitan student population, a distinguished graduate school, and the tradition of radical student activism at many of the major universities has proved to be a volatile mixture. Furthermore, the growth of militant student activism in the mid-sixties was complicated by a general growth of conservatism in the broader society. Fiscal and enrollment crises in the latter part of the decade heightened tensions between militants and the campus establishment by clearly revealing financial priorities. This combination of factors proved to be more than the traditional means of university governance could handle effectively. The breakdown of university governance is widespread, and the multiversity—California, Columbia, Wisconsin— seems to be hardest hit. Although the attack on the AMRC at Wisconsin was certainly not a typical outcome of the breakdown of academic governance, it graphically symbolizes the dangerous possibilities of the failure of the university to function as a viable community.

The focus of this chapter is on the reasons why the elements of the university community—students, faculty, administration, and governing board—failed to deal effectively with the unprecedented challenges of the sixties. The general type of academic institution with which this paper deals is the multiversity; specific illustrations and analysis are confined to the University of Wisconsin.

Knowledge of the historical, academic, and social context of the multiversity is critical to understanding its current problems. Enormity of physical size is perhaps its most obvious characteristic. Wisconsin, with its multiple campuses, is typical; it is a large state university with four major campuses and seven two-year campuses, and it enrolls 61,546 students. The Madison campus, heart of the institution, has 31,132 students. A host of auxiliary services and research institutes are also part of the academic complex.

The multiversity attained its present size primarily during the years following World War II. The growth was a response to an economy based increasingly on technology; skilled manpower was needed in post-industrial America. The most practical way to secure a reliable source of expertise was through government sponsorship of research in the universities. Thus, the federal government became a major underwriter of higher education. The financial role of government in the multiversity is so great that the prestigious universities of the sixties were referred to as "federal grant universities."[3] The increase of federal spending for research and development provides a rough indication of the major universities' growth rate: In 1940, the universities spent approximately 31 million dollars for scientific research, of which the government contributed half. In 1962, the federal government spent more than a billion dollars for research and development in the universities, or seventy times the amount spent before the war. The total research and development budget nationally increased from 2.7 billion dollars in the late fifties to 16 billion dollars in 1969. With America's acceptance of the intellectual challenge offered by Russia's success with Sputnik, in 1958, the relationship between government and the university seemed to be confirmed, and the early sixties were marked by an extraordinary growth spurt.

Again, the growth of Wisconsin in the early sixties is representative of the rapid expansion in which the multiversity was engaged. During the presidency of Fred Harvey Harrington (1962–1970), growth was a watchword, and no one at the top levels of University of Wisconsin administration foresaw the period of retrenchment now evident throughout American higher education. President Harrington not only expanded enrollments, he also diversified the university into its present parts and added many new programs. Many of these programs were based on "soft" (grant) funds from the federal government and various foundations. With the general economic recession in the late sixties, a number of these programs ran into financial difficulties as both government and foundations became increasingly reluctant to spend money. The only other major financial source available to a public university is, of course, the state. But the people of Wisconsin, as represented by the legislators, were reluctant to pick up the programs formerly funded by outside agencies and were also unwilling to authorize funds for new programs. In addition to the general economic situation, popular resentment against the university, caused mostly by militant student activism, contributed to the taxpayers' unwillingness to give the university the almost unlimited funds it had been able to command earlier in the decade. The present fiscal plights of such state systems as California, Illinois, and New York testify that the problem is general. Nor are financial difficulties confined to public universities. Eminent private multiversities are also experiencing monetary problems. Trustees appear increasingly unwilling to continue expansion, private donors are not giving to institutions with their usual generosity, and endowments are suffering from the recession. Columbia, Chicago, and even Harvard are cases in point.

Wisconsin is perhaps unique in that it is a large university with a substantial commitment to graduate education, but it is located in a relatively poor state. Wisconsin lacks the wealthy urban corporate and industrial centers found in most states with prestigious universities, such as Michigan and California. Thus, the university arouses in the people of the state a mixture of respect for its unquestioned quality and resentment for its high cost. When student agitation combined with a losing football team for several years, the resentment of the public took the upper hand. As one local legislator put it, "Wisconsin is a beer state and cannot afford a champagne university." That the president of the university earns more than the governor and that many professors earn more than senior state officials do not help matters. The university commands statewide attention. The main campus and the state capitol are only a mile apart at either end of State Street, a thoroughfare which has been the scene of many demonstrations and some "trashing" in the past few years. Indeed, the usual route for demonstrations is from the campus to the capitol, and on at least one occasion students invaded the legislative chambers and held lawmakers captive for several hours.

The national crisis of higher education has impinged directly on the University of Wisconsin. This is most dramatically seen in fiscal difficulties and leveling off of enrollments. During the regime of President Harrington, a successful effort was made to attract federal and other outside funds and to quickly expand both enrollments and new programs. Relatively little thought was given to the long-term effects of the sources of funds or of the new academic programs. At the same time, extremely high out-of-state tuitions and the state legislature's quota on non-Wisconsin undergraduates has decreased their proportion in the student body. The leveling off of the birth rate has meant that in-state students have not filled the gap. In 1970 the Madison campus enrollment actually dropped for the first time since World War II, and the budget, which is in part linked to enrollments, suffered.

The financial and enrollment crisis is related to the political difficulties of the University of Wisconsin. President Harrington's effort to build a national university resulted in his neglect of the legislature and of important segments of Wisconsin public opinion. Had Harrington involved the legislature in the planning of the university during the early 1960s and in general treated individual legislators with more respect, the university might have fared better in a period of belt tightening.

The financial problems the multiversity currently faces, which Wisconsin in many ways typifies, are not the only costs of too rapid growth. Another cost of overexpansion, the disappearance of a sense of academic community, stems largely from the expansion and diversification of faculty and was an unforeseen outcome of the transformation of the university into the multiversity. Rapid growth created an enormous institution able to deal with the undergraduate student only on a level of bureaucratic impersonality, since the primary function of the multiversity had changed from teaching to research, from imparting knowledge to producing it. The changing role of America's major universities and the problems which the new orientation to research has brought are reflected in much of the literature on academic reform. Practically all major American universities, beginning in the late sixties, have engaged in major self-studies, although very few have implemented major changes. It is highly significant that almost all these documents have resulted not from the inherent interest of the faculty in reform, but from often frantic efforts by academic communities to deal with the challenges of student activism and disruption. Wisconsin has been typical of this trend and has dutifully appointed a committee to consider each of the crises which have occurred on campus. Several of these efforts have borne fruit, but most have been mere intellectual exercises.

While constantly stressing that the sources of many of the problems faced by the university are to be found in national forces and events, much of the reform literature accepts the breakdown of the intellectual community and the failure of academic governance as a starting point. In other words, although the crises faced by higher education are entwined with forces external to it, the multiversity must also find some means of coping with its unique internal crisis of governance. The solutions offered by the reform literature vary—decentralization, various forms of general education, residential colleges within the multiversity, greater autonomy and freedom for the student in planning his education —but all represent an attempt to correct an institution which has grown so vast, become so impersonal, so highly administered and bureaucratized, so enmeshed in the national economy, that the sense of community necessary to traditional academic governance has been destroyed.

In order to understand the crisis of governance faced by the university, it is necessary to examine the elements of the academic equation within the institution—students, faculty, administration, and regents— that have been critical both to the crisis and to the response which the institution has made. In our attempt to illustrate the problems generally faced by the multiversity, we will rely primarily on our experience and observation at the University of Wisconsin.

Students at Madison have a long tradition of activism and social involvement.[4] The Progressive movement in the early years of the twentieth century relied on student support, and many of its political conventions were held on campus. Madison was a center of student activism in the 1930s and was one of the few bastions of student radicalism during the apathetic 1950s. The student movement, however, has undergone substantial changes since the middle sixties. Although students are very much concerned with broad social issues, especially the war in Vietnam, they are increasingly dissatisfied with the academic environment of the Madison campus.[5] Many undergraduate students have been concerned about large classes, about what they perceive as overly rigid course and other requirements, and, perhaps more importantly, about a university administration which they feel is unresponsive. Various campus surveys indicate that the proportion of dissatisfied students has increased dramatically. For example, distrust of the university administration has increased during the various crises on campus.[6]

The growth of a counter-culture, with its emphasis on rock music and drugs and its general alienation from many of the values of the existing society, has intensified the intellectual and social distance between students and the university. The organized student left, after a short period of attempting to organize around issues of university reform in 1968, has withdrawn from those efforts except for attacks on the institution for its complicity with the Vietnam war or other involvement with the military-industrial complex. Even the Wisconsin Student Association, the elected student government, has moved away from concern with academic reform, largely as a response to the meager results it felt it had achieved through previous involvment in student-faculty committees on various issues. This general dissatisfaction, although not the direct cause of any demonstrations, underlies much student militancy.

Although it is certainly true that the Madison faculty and administration have not given up any of their basic power to students, since the late sixties students—usually token students—have been placed on virtually all the many Madison campus committees. In addition, the university has moved slowly to liberalize regulations concerning dormitories and other aspects of nonacademic life and has, despite hesitation from some Regents and many alumni, moved away from the idea of in loco parentis. Undergraduates, however, generally have not been impressed with this gradual involvement and liberalization. A mass exodus from university-owned dormitories, which has caused something of a fiscal crisis for their management, is an indication of the growing detachment of many students from the whole institutional environment. It is significant that students have, by and large, not been impressed with the fairly modest curricular changes that have been recently made in the College of Letters and Science. In the 1970–1971 academic year, for example, language requirements for most undergraduate degrees were modified, the pass-fail systm was extended, and the grading system was somewhat changed. The overwhelming response from articulate students was that these changes were mere tokenism. Even those relatively moderate students who served on the various curriculum committees which proposed more sweeping changes were dissatisfied with the final outcome.

It is always true, of course, that the majority of students are fairly happy with their academic experience and cause few problems for the authorities. However, available studies, combined with general observation, indicate that the minority of increasingly articulate dissatisfied students is growing rapidly. And on a campus of 31,000 students even a small percentage of dissatisfied students can organize a significant demonstration. The constituency for militant activism during times of crisis in Madison is quite large, especially when police or the National Guard are brought on campus or the administration is perceived by many students to have acted badly. Rallies of close to ten thousand young people are not uncommon during crises, and at least three hundred militant students are constantly active in and around the campus. In addition, Madison has become a center for a large nonstudent youth community of university dropouts and others who come to the area. This community supports a thriving counter-culture in and around the Mifflin Street area which has been the scene of many confrontations with police. The youth culture reflects on the image of the university and is a ready recruiting ground for participants in all types of militant demonstrations.

Graduate students, often ignored in discussions of student activism, have been a particularly important element in crises at the University of Wisconsin.[7] Traditionally, graduate students have been deeply involved in their academic pursuits and socialized to their roles as future professors. Even radical graduate students, and the Madison campus has been a center for such students for several decades, have maintained a commitment to the university and to academic careers. This situation has changed dramatically, and as a result graduate students have become quite important in the crisis at the University of Wisconsin.

The changing self-perception and growing activism of graduate students have a number of causes. Certainly, the overproduction of Ph.D.s which became evident in 1970 in many fields and the resulting difficulty experienced by many new Ph.D.s in finding employment led to dissatisfaction and to decreasing professional commitment. It must be remembered that until the end of the sixties graduates of universities like Wisconsin were not only assured of jobs, but could expect initial appointments at fairly prestigious universities. Now they are lucky to find any employment at all in some fields. The counter-culture has also encroached upon graduate student ranks, and there has been growing rejection of the entire academic career pattern. Radical graduate students, who only a few years ago felt that major commitment was to conduct "radical" research, increasingly reject research altogether; they no longer wish to associate with prestigious universities but prefer working-class students in junior and community colleges. And, of course, the broad political crisis in the country that affects undergraduates also has implications for graduate students. All these factors have produced a new generation of graduate students—one which many professors find it difficult to understand or to work with.

Graduate students have been active in a number of departments —sociology, history, English, mathematics, and several others in the College of Letters and Sciences—in efforts to institute reforms such as changes in preliminary examinations and involvement of students in departmental affairs. These efforts have been largely unsuccessful, although a few departments have made modest changes. In most departments, with the partial exceptions of those cited above, reform efforts have been sporadic, and both undergraduate and graduate students have been unwilling to spend time on committees and in other undramatic work needed to formulate and implement change. In addition, the faculty, for the most part, has been fairly intransigent, and many personal animosities have developed, often to the disadvantage of the graduate students, who depend on faculty members for academic progress and ultimately for their degrees.

The most important manifestation of graduate student discontent is the Teaching Assistants Association.[8] The TAA was established in 1966 by a small group of about 50 of the more than 1,600 graduate students who are employed by the university as teaching assistants, usually in large undergraduate courses. It has been estimated that 68 per cent of freshman and sophomore undergraduate teaching is done by teaching assistants.[9] The TAA grew because of many teaching assistants' discontent over working conditions, lack of involvement in course planning, poor remuneration, and threats by the state legislature to cut out-of-state graduate enrollment and to eliminate the out-of-state tuition scholarships which were automatically granted to assistants. These threats, although never carried out, provided impetus for the TAA, and by February 1969 the TAA claimed a majority of teaching assistants as members and demanded to engage in collective bargaining with the university.

In a still controversial decision, Madison campus Chancellor H. Edwin Young agreed to bargain with the TAA over a contract, and negotiations began in the fall of 1969. The talks continued for four months, and the TAA, feeling that the administration was uninterested in reaching a settlement and also fearing the loss of many members because of its failure to produce results, first suspended negotiations and then called a strike. This strike, which took place in March of 1970, shortly before the Cambodia and Kent State crisis on campus, effectively halted most teaching in the humanities and social sciences for more than a week and affected other parts of the campus as well. Then student support for the strike dwindled, and many undergraduates who had stayed out of classes returned. At the same time, many teaching assistants who were on strike simply could not afford an extended period with no income. The TAA was forced to agree to basically the prestrike contract offer of the university. However, the contract was still unprecedented in Wisconsin history. The TAA gained a substantial measure of job security for its members and also a delineation of working conditions, class size, and other matters. The university made a commitment to joint educational planning by teaching assistants, students, and faculty, but did not spell out mechanisms for implementation. While not meeting the original demands of the TAA, the settlement provided teaching assistants with more power and security than they had previously had.

The TAA has exhibited a combination of the traditional trade union approach to bread and butter issues and more militant concern for social and academic reform. Much of the leadership of the TAA is radical, although the rank and file is probably more interested in the specific gains which the association has won. For the first time, graduate students have been willing to risk the enmity of senior faculty in order to build a union, thus indicating that the commitment to an academic career and to the traditional subservient role of the graduate student is not as widespread as it once was. One result of the existence of the TAA has been a marked deterioration in some departments of relations between graduate students and faculty, and a number of departments are talking seriously of abolishing the teaching assistant system completely. In the summer of 1971, negotiations for a new contract between the Madison campus administration and the TAA took place. With a widespread feeling among faculty against the TAA, due especially to the large number of grievances which the TAA has filed against many departments, and an apparent drop in support for the TAA among some teaching assistants, the outcome of these negotiations is very much in doubt.

These comments indicate that a change has occurred in the student population at the University of Wisconsin, or at least among major segments of that population. Increasing alienation from the academic system and perhaps from the entire employment structure of the society are evident. The pressure of national and international affairs, and especially of the Indochina war, has radicalized many students. Finally, the impact of the counter-culture, as yet generally unanalyzed, has made itself felt in increased alienation. It is clear that not only cosmopolitan students from New York and Chicago, long the scapegoats for campus unrest at Madison, but young people from urban and rural middle-class Wisconsin families are participating in the student movement and are part of the counter-culture in increasingly large numbers.[10]

The faculty is the second key element in Wisconsin's crisis, and, perhaps more than any other element of the university, it has been deeply affected by the events of the crisis years. As one of the major universities in the United States, the Madison campus has traditionally attracted a research-oriented, articulate, and generally competent faculty. It has a first-rate faculty despite comparatively poor salaries (Wisconsin ranks tenth in the Big Ten in salaries and one hundred and fifty-fourth among American universities). The excellence of Wisconsin's faculty is related to what is generally known as the "Wisconsin Idea." This ethos combines the notion of academic autonomy for departments and for individual faculty members with a very large measure of faculty self-government under the very broad aegis of the regents. Faculty power in institutional decision-making may seem to be a poor substitute for monetary reward, but research on faculty militancy consistently shows that professors at major universities are more concerned with wielding effective power within the institution than with attaining higher salaries, although certainly the professoriate is not so altruistic as to reject the latter goal. In point of fact, faculty control over institutional decision-making seems harder to attain than higher salaries. The American Association for Higher Education, in what is probably the most comprehensive survey of various forms of academic governance, estimates that only 25 per cent of institutions of higher education are governed by a system of shared authority between faculty and administration; most of the remaining 75 per cent are either firmly guided or completely dominated by their administrations. Only a few campuses are marked by faculty dominance on a broad range of issues.[11] Thus, Wisconsin's tradition of academic self-governance has been an invaluable aid in securing an excellent faculty in the face of below average remuneration.

Another facet of the Wisconsin Idea stresses commitment to making the university relevant to all elements of the state's population. The Wisconsin Idea dates to the Progressive Era, when the university was intimately involved with the state government and built its reputation for both relevance and scholarly achievement. Hofstadter sees this period at Wisconsin as a foreshadowing of the relationship between the federal government and the academy that became so characteristic of the multiversity in the fifties and sixties.[12] However, in the mid-twentieth century, the scope of the relationship between government and higher education has expanded to a national partnership encompassing all levels of government and permeating all major universities.

Beginning in the late sixties, the Wisconsin Idea has come under major attack, and neither faculty nor administration has been able to restore the balance in terms of morale, power, prestige or, importantly, salaries. The faculty has lost a good deal of its internal autonomy to the regents and, to a degree, to the administration. Its prestige in the state has been substantially diminished, in part because of its "inability" to deal with student radicals. And in a period of financial stringency, highly paid professors who, according to the press and some legislators, spend little time teaching, are naturally the subject of controversy.

Academic governance at Wisconsin underwent substantial change in the sixties, and this has contributed to some degree to the demoralization of the faculty. The faculty more than doubled during the presidency of Fred Harvey Harrington, and academic programs on the Madison campus burgeoned with the addition of many institutes, centers, and other programs. Younger academics, particularly in the social sciences and humanities, who did not share many of the values of their senior colleagues, came into the system. Traditional means of faculty governance came under attack from both internal and external sources. Regents attacked the faculty for not being harsh enough to student protestors and for failing to maintain order on the campus, while students criticized the faculty for its conservatism.

The basis of academic governance at Wisconsin has traditionally rested in the senior faculty, who controlled the important University Committee, the nine-man executive committee which is the voice of the faculty to the adminisration and to other audiences as well. The University Committee, aided by a complex array of other committees dominated by the senior faculty, governed the Madison campus with substantial autonomy and little challenge for decades. In the past, the highest faculty governing body was the entire Madison campus faculty. The monthly faculty meetings were usually attended by a small group of faculty who were especially concerned with specific questions on the agenda or who were members of various committees. This situation changed as the faculty became more heterogeneous and as dramatic crises mea..t the calling of faculty meetings to which more than a thousand came. These factors led to the establishment, in 1970, of the two-hundred-member Faculty Senate which now operates in place of the all-campus faculty meetings. Although the Senate has had the effect of strengthening the power of the senior faculty and especially of the University Committee, which sets the agenda and has a major voice in the conduct of meetings, most of the various factions on the faculty, from radicals to extreme conservatives, are represented on the senate.

The politics and structure of the Madison campus faculty do not differ greatly from those at other major academic institutions. Until the mid 1950s, the faculty constituted a fairly close community with strong loyalty to the institution. The senior faculty, and particularly those professors who had chosen to involve themselves in local campus affairs, dominated the faculty through the University Committee. In a cosmopolitan research-oriented university, the ruling elements of the faculty were more locally-oriented and perhaps less interested in research and in nationally visible scholarship.[13] Junior faculty either used the university as a steppingstone to other jobs or were willing to leave the day-to-day decision-making to their senior colleagues. The regents were content to leave the actual running of the campus to the faculty and its complicated committee structure. A community of interest existed between the research-minded faculty, who were willing to leave the governance of the institution to others, and those who actually did the decision-making.

The situation on campus has changed and the faculty no longer constitutes a homogeneous community. Its response to crisis has generally been without coherent direction and has, in fact, contributed to the institution's malaise. In a period marked by overproduction of doctorates, by student discontent, and by demands for better undergraduate teaching, the traditional research orientation of the Madison faculty has come under attack. The faculty, and especially its senior members, have not been willing to relinquish any of the very real power that professors have over the educational process and over their own professional lives. As was indicated by a national survey of faculty sponsored by the Carnegie Commission, faculty members are notably conservative on issues of university reform and change, with senior faculty holding the most conservative positions.[14] The Wisconsin experience supports these national findings. The usual faculty response to crisis is to appoint a committee to study the matter and, usually, do little to change the status quo. This response is increasingly rejected by both students and Regents, who demand solutions that can be implemented. The faculty, in part with greater knowledge of the intricacies of academic governance and a commitment to Wisconsin's traditional values, and in part as a result of its own vested interests, has refrained from suggesting major changes.

The politics of the Madison campus faculty are significant and, in a sense, somewhat surprising. Despite the existence of a few defined factions within the faculty, there has been little of the bitter infighting or protracted factionalism among the faculty that has been evident at Berkeley or to some extent at Harvard. Despite the fears of some regents and a few administrators, the organized faculty left, grouped around the very small and generally ineffective New University Conference chapter, has little strength and almost no direction. The United Faculty, a union with a membership of about two hundred which is loosely affiliated with the American Federation of Teachers, has experienced some growth, but is not a force on campus. An ad hoc group of liberal faculty, largely drawn from the social science and humanities departments, comes together for common action during crises but has little in common at other times. The mainstream of the faculty is mildly liberal in politics but traditional on matters of academic governance. With relatively few professors actually keeping abreast of the complex and often uninteresting issues involved in campus governance, a small group of senior professors, who are loyal to the institution and have generally been on campus for many years, effectively control the faculty. Their power is based on the support they have from the largely apathetic and generally conservative faculty in such schools as engineering and agriculture and on their involvement in the committee structure.

Despite the lack of political activism among the faculty, there is some discontent. Many junior faculty are unhappy with their lack of power in policy-making and with the general direction of the institution. Worsening conditions on campus, in terms of salaries, teaching conditions, self-image, and autonomy, have demoralized many faculty, and there has been a substantial exodus from a number of departments, notably in the College of Letters and Sciences. Unlike Berkeley, Wisconsin does not seem to have a great deal of holding power in periods of stress.

For the most part, the Madison campus administration, the third factor in the academic equation, represents and reflects the interests of the senior faculty. Most administrators have been Wisconsin faculty members or at least have taken their academic training at Wisconsin. They are usually selected by committees dominated by senior faculty members. For the most part, Wisconsin administrators are professors who have chosen to follow the local academic career pattern and who have given up scholarly productivity and have devoted themselves to academic administration. While styles of administration differ, the close advisors or immediate staff of the chancellor are senior faculty, and very few younger individuals are involved in the top level of academic administration.

The administration, in contrast to the faculty, is concerned to a substantial extent with the maintenance of the University of Wisconsin as an institution. Many administrators, particularly in the crisis-ridden period since 1965, have felt that they are protecting the institution from the ravages of Wisconsin's legislators. This feeling has also been expressed on many occasions by the Board of Regents, who are in closest touch with the opinions of legislators and perhaps also with public opinion. The administration also seems to feel that it is protecting the faculty and, in a sense, the students from harsh treatment by state authorities. This state of mind, while no doubt somewhat justified, has led the top levels of leadership in the university to increasingly conservative public statements and policies in an effort to placate public opinion. Administrative policy seeks to assure the public that the university will remain calm or at least that disruption will be dealt with effectively.

On the Madison campus, the profusion of schools, colleges, programs, and other agencies makes efficient administration difficult, and the implementation of reform is next to impossible because of the complicated decision-making structure and often overlapping jurisdictions. And at the bottom of the system are, of course, the academic departments. The departments have substantial autonomy and tend to be organizationally conservative and quite jealous of their own prerogatives. Reform plans often bog down when they reach the departmental structure.[15]

The Madison campus administration has been under tremendous pressure in recent years and has a difficult time simply responding to recurring crises. Between 1967 and 1970, student agitation and its implications occupied a major portion of the time of academic administrators. In the 1970–1971 academic year, severe budget cuts and an impending merger of the University of Wisconsin and the Wisconsin State University system were imposed on the administration by the state government. In its internal functioning, the administration is severely limited by the immensely complicated system of faculty governance and by the innate conservatism of the senior faculty and of most of the departments. The university is in the unenviable position of being unable to implement change from the top because of internal governance while at the same time no longer having funds to ensure expansion and improvement from the bottom. Thus, administrators live from crisis to crisis with little scope for creativity and growing frustration.[16]

Given these constraints, it is not surprising that the administration has not responded in a very creative manner to any of the crises which it has faced since 1965. Internal and external pressures, in addition to the general establishment orientation of the administration which is ensured by their background and recruitment methods, has meant that crises have been met by short-term compromises, or, more often, by the use of outside force. The general pressures of Madison campus academic administration, the continual balancing of political forces, and the inability to make much headway on educational improvement or reform have caused many to resign. But the nature of decision-making and the general orientation of the senior faculty who have taken administrative posts has remained fairly constant.

The Board of Regents is the fourth factor on campus. It consists of nine individuals appointed by the governor for nine-year terms, plus the superintendent of public instruction.[17] As a result of the appointments of Governor Warren Knowles, a Republican who served during most of the 1960s, the board has developed strong conservative majorities. The composition of the Board of Regents, as is pointed out in Chapter Four, reflects a cross section of the Wisconsin establishment. Most Regents are college-trained, usually at the University of Wisconsin; almost all are Wisconsin-born and have strong ties to the state.[18]

The board members have taken an increasingly activist role.[19] Until the major disruptions of the mid-1960s, the Regents traditionally (with some exceptions during earlier periods of the university's history, such as in the late 1920s) left direct policy-making and administration to the faculty and its administrative officers. But because the faculty has been perceived to have failed to maintain order on campus, the Regents have begun to intervene directly in academic affairs.

According to law, the Regents have final authority over the university and its staff and are empowered to use this authority in almost any way they wish. At Regent initiative, a committee to reexamine the tenure system was established in 1971. The Regents have used study committees on such topics as drugs, student and faculty discipline, buildings, and other subjects to stress their authority and initiative. When these study committees have arrived at conclusions different from those of the faculty, in most cases the Regent opinion has prevailed. This increased involvement and broadened jurisdiction are looked upon with great fear and mistrust by the faculty and administration, which are used to acting autonomously and are quite unhappy with the undebatable loss of power. In 1970 the Regents involved themselves more deeply in faculty affairs by refusing to grant a salary increase to sociology professor Maurice Zeitlin because of their displeasure with his controversial public statements and his antiwar activities. Only after a major campaign by the faculty were the Regents forced to back down on this issue, perhaps indicating that a united stance by the faculty still influences those with formal power in the university. The point, however, was made and it is likely that faculty will be more careful in their statements in order to avoid the ire of the Regents. As the Regents are quite sensitive to the political climate in the state, it is possible that the Republican Regents will moderate their positions in deference to a liberal Democratic governor and to the Democrat-controlled state assembly.

President Harrington did not involve the Regents in his administration, except on the very broadest issues, and as a result they seemed to have been somewhat unaware of some of the new directions in which the university was moving. The Madison campus administration has traditionally attempted, with a good deal of success, to obscure its work so that outside forces could not effectively control the situation. The Regents, the Coordinating Council on Higher Education—a state agency responsible for the allocation of funds to the various public universities and colleges—and the legislature itself have all been somewhat unclear about the nature of the university budget and other aspects of its functioning. And as outside sources of funding disappear and the university must turn increasingly to the state, it is not surprising that both the Regents and state authorities should wish for greater accountability and control over the university.

In order to understand the crisis of academic governance, it is necessary to view the way in which the various components of the multiversity interact. Only by looking at the history of student protest and the institution's response to it can we understand the dynamics of the series of events that culminated in the bombing of AMRC. The question we must ask is why the university community, and especially the students, accepted violence as a legitimate means of conflict resolution. Since violence is a product of a breakdown of legitimate authority, an examination of the means of university governance is the proper beginning.

The legitimacy of academic governance has traditionally been sustained by the myth of the university as a community of scholars. As long as the asumptions on which the myth rested remained unquestioned, authority went unchallenged. The existence of the myth was supported by subscription on the part of the university members to an idea of a diverse community harmoniously united in the pursuit of truth. As long as truth went without need of definition, the consensus upon which the myth depended held. But the pressing social problems of the sixties demanded a clearer definition of ends, and that attempt at definition shattered the myth by revealing the university as an institution composed of a multitude of competing interest groups, each seeking its own end.

As long as a lack of crisis allowed the governing structure to be minimally responsive to the various groups in the community, an uneasy consensus was maintained. However, university government responded to crisis by taking a highly partisan position, and through this stance it showed dissident students and faculty their real impotence. The dissident groups responded by using the tactics they had learned from the struggles of other disenfranchised groups whom they had supported during the sixties—confrontation. In turn, confrontation challenged the credibility of the university government's claim to legitimate authority; in the absence of credibility, the university resorted to coercion. The frequent use of force, which often resulted in violence, completed the polarization of the community.

The administration's decision to use external agencies of social control was not a simple response to student dissent. The decision was the result of the administration's definition of the university when student protest demanded a clear statement of purpose. This definition of the function of the university was to a great extent dictated by the symbiotic relationship that had developed between the university and the larger society in the years following World War II. Institutional relationships between the university and the national government developed in the form of contract research, special institutes, and foundation grants. The implications of this relationship went unquestioned until the Vietnam war turned a significant sector of the university community against the government's foreign policy. When the government failed to respond to early protest against the war, critical students and faculty began to search for the reasons for the government's recalcitrance. Reexamination of government policy in general led many to the conclusion that our domestic economic and political policy was a reflection of foreign policy, that the whole of our society shared in responsibility for the war. The community closest at hand to a large number of critics was the university, and the contribution of the university to the war effort was easily documented by examination of the funding sources for various research enterprises. When students and their supporters demanded that the university sever its connections with governmental and industrial agencies directly linked to the war, the administration refused. In its attempts to justify and defend existing arrangements, the administration revealed its partisan position and began the erosion of its legitimate claim to authority. The adamance of its position led eventually to the use of force, and open coercion destroyed the myth of the community of scholars which, by definition, commands obedience only through rational persuasion.

The administration's decision to use force to maintain order was thus not fully autonomous; it was partly the product of the university's involvement with and dependence on national funds and local government. Also, a significant portion of the faculty favored the use of swift harsh punishment for dissidents. Thus, the administration was pressured by both its external and internal constituencies to use force, yet it was not openly compelled to do so; it had a choice. Admittedly, the choice to seek means other than the use of force would have entailed considerable risks for the survival of the administration, yet there was a possibility of success. Certainly the lesson provided by Berkeley should have warned that employing force was perhaps as dangerous to the long-term stability of the campus as was a search for another means of resolving conflict. If the police had not been utilized at an early stage, thus providing the protestors with a moral basis for their claims that university government was unjust and therefore illegitimate, the administration might have prevented the factionalization of the campus, the profound alienation of students from faculty and administration, of faculty from fellow faculty. There was an alternative to violence, although at the time it was apparently not seen. Undoubtedly, the reason the element of choice was not perceived stemmed from the fact that a choice to abstain from the use of force would have meant a radical reorganization of the university.

Madison's crisis began two years after the Berkeley student revolt. The first disruptive protest took place in 1967 and was concerned with the Vietnam war. The focus was two-fold: opposition to the university's cooperation with the selective service system and opposition to job recruiting by the Dow Chemical Company, manufacturers of napalm. When students occupied a part of the engineering campus in an effort to prevent Dow interviews, the police were called and a number of students were arrested, although no physical confrontation took place and little damage was done. In a move which effectively defused a volatile situation, Chancellor Robben Fleming paid the bail of the arrested students with a personal check for more than a thousand dollars. His action was praised by the faculty and moderate students, but he set several dangerous precedents.

First, he called the police, and a number of arrests occurred. The arrests were peaceful, but the use of police marked the first intervention of an outside agency in campus matters, although Fleming effectively muted the issue of police on campus by bailing out the arrested students.

Second, although his action prevented great hostility between students and administration from developing, he had resolved the crisis by personal imagination, rather than facing the more difficult problem of establishing institutional mechanisms for resolving conflict. Third, he antagonized members of the Board of Regents and of the legislature as well as part of the population of the state by his dramatic gesture, which many perceived as open support of student radicals. Fourth, the faculty, in response to the issue of war-related recruiters on campus, made a policy decision, in a meeting of the whole, to keep the university open to recruiters.

The first large-scale disruption of academic life that involved large numbers of police and the arrest of substantial numbers of students on campus took place in October of 1967, again over the issue of job interviews by the Dow Chemical Company.[20] Fleming had resigned in order to assume the presidency of the University of Michigan and the new chancellor, William Sewell, a liberal sociologist, was confronted with a demonstration more militant than that of the preceding year. In response to the continued escalation of the Vietnam war and to the university's continued, although indirect, support of it, roughly three hundred students had decided to block the passageway in the Commerce Building which led Dow Chemical Company's recruiters to their temporary offices. Thus, the administration was forced to make a decision. Allowing the city police to clear the building meant risking the possibility of violence, police brutality, and polarization of the campus. Allowing the students to remain in the building meant antagonizing the Regents, the legislature, and a considerable segment of the faculty.

Sewell, a former member of the University Committee, was committed to the decision-making system of the university and intimate with those faculty members who controlled the system of faculty self-governance. His commitments to the existing organizational structure prevented him from attempting the difficult search for an alternative. In permitting the use of city police, he gambled that violence could somehow be avoided, and that if violence did in fact occur only the student community would be alienated. In other words, he expected the faculty to be placated by his stand and the alliance between faculty, administration, and Regents to be maintained. However, the violence resulting from the administration's hard-line position was far greater than any part of the university expected; more than fifty protestors and several policemen were injured. Shock and outrage were the dominant reactions on the part of both those who favored the use of force and those who opposed it. In the emergency faculty meeting that followed the protest, the issue of the university's complicity with the federal government's Vietnam policy was obscured by the issue of student brutality compared to police brutality; the issue was transformed into a debate over the basis of internal university governance. Although the majority of the faculty favored the use of force rather than attempts at change, the narrow margin—less than fifty votes out of more than a thousand cast—by which a vote of confidence in the administration was passed gave evidence of serious division within the faculty. Correspondingly, the three-day demonstration held by a significant portion of the student body to protest the treatment of their fellows confirmed expectations of polarization between university authorities and students.

The demonstration also had repercussions in state politics. On the night of the crisis, the Republican-dominated state assembly, then in session, passed a resolution by a vote of ninety-four to five which demanded that the Regents "reevaluate administrative policies of excessive permissiveness in handling student demonstrators." Many other antiuniversity bills were introduced in the following weeks and while only a few passed, the lesson to university administrators, and particularly to the Board of Regents, was clear.

Sewell's handling of the 1967 Dow demonstration was the logical outcome of administration policy. Sewell carried out what he correctly perceived to be the wishes of the dominant forces in university government. This action resulted in a polarization of the university community which called into question both the role of the university in society and the internal mode of governance of the university. The erosion of the university's claim to legitimate authority had begun. After trying unsuccessfully to reconcile the various elements of the university community during the remainder of the 1967–1968 academic year, Sewell admitted failure and resigned. The chancellor had been identified by the community as a partisan official whose primary task was the control of unruly students and dissident faculty. Because Sewell's action during the Dow crisis had so defined the chancellor's role, the next occupant of the office was necessarily a man who would support those elements within the university power structure who demanded maintenance of the existing system of governance and of "law and order"—a large portion of the faculty, the regents, and the legislature.

H. Edwin Young assumed the chancellorship in September, 1968. The next major crisis on the Madison campus came in February, 1969, over the issues raised by the Thirteen Black Demands and corresponded to the national wave of demonstrations related to black studies that year. Following the annual week-long Wisconsin Student Association symposium, devoted to the race question, black students submitted a list of thirteen demands to the university administration. Essentially, they asked for the creation of an Afro-American studies department mainly under student control, the establishment of a black cultural center, the admission of fifteen black students expelled several months earlier from Oshkosh State University, and a substantial increase in the number of black students at the university.[21] (There are only about eight hundred black students on the Madison campus.)

With the support of white radical student groups, the black students called a strike and engaged in militant demonstrations. Initially, the strike did not generate widespread support, so the strikers moved to forcibly prevent students from entering classroom buildings. The administration responded by calling city police to keep academic buildings open. The calling of police had the same effect at the University of Wisconsin as it did at many other universities: The strike won substantially more support. Because of continued disruptions and sporadic acts of vandalism by students, the National Guard was called in on the morning of February 13, 1969. With the National Guard on campus, student support for the strike escalated, and most classes in the College of Letters and Sciences were effectively halted. After a few more days of sporadic demonstrations, some vandalism, and virtual occupation of the university by troops and police, student support for the strike waned, and it was eventually called off by the organizers.

The tactics employed by student demonstrators were indicative of their response to the administration's ready resort to force. Instead of offering themselves as immobile targets for police, the students engaged in hit and run tactics. The police, confronted by agitators indistinguishable from and often hidden by the majority of students, resorted to indiscriminate violence which outraged observers and often provided the catalyst which turned them into demonstrators. The shift from stationary confrontation to guerilla tactics resulted in more severe disruption of the campus and of the surrounding business area and student "ghetto." When the police proved incapable of controlling the situation, Young did not hesitate to call in the National Guard. But increased force only caused more members of the university community to take a stand against the use of outside agents of social control. In the long run, the Black Demands protest confirmed the alienation of the student body from the administration and faculty, heightened divisions within the faculty, and legitimated violence as a means of conflict resolution by introducing outside agents of social control into the initial stages of conflict and by bolstering those forces with the presence of the National Guard.

The immediate results of the Black Demands strike more or less paralleled the aftermath of the Dow demonstrations the previous year. The faculty met in an emergency meeting and, after heated discussion, voted to support the administration's position of not negotiating on or giving in to any of the demands. At the same time, several committees were established to examine the question of a black studies department and related issues. On the initiative of the Regents, several student leaders were suspended or expelled, and a formal investigation of the university was undertaken by the legislature. The student movement, so powerful during the crisis, all but disappeared, and the cooperation between white and black militants, based on white support for the demands and the tactics of the blacks, came to an end.

This crisis, however, produced greater change than the Dow demonstration did, perhaps because minority group protest seemed more legitimate to the university community than did antiwar demonstrations. An Afro-American studies department was established in the College of Letters and Sciences about a year later, and an Afro-American center opened on campus within a semester after the crisis. While the department's structure did not satisfy the demands of the black students for control, it did constitute a substantial university response to the challenge, partly because of the support of Dean Leon Epstein of the College of Letters and Sciences. Although there was some opposition to the concept of a black studies department from conservative faculty, the compromise departmental structure which finally emerged met with no major opposition.

In the spring of 1969, a three-day confrontation between police and students took place in the off-campus student community, the Mifflin Street area. City authorities denied a student request for permission to have a block party. They held the party anyway, and the city police were called in to break it up. Although the Mifflin Street riots were mostly off campus and did not involve confrontation between students and the university, the classic town and gown aspect of the battle identified the immediate community of Madison as being as hostile to and as repressive toward students as were the university authorities. Thus, the difference between city and university administrations was diminished by the use of violence as a means of social control. Through repeated use, violence came to be regarded by both the authorities and the dissident young as a legitimate means of conflict resolution. Furthermore, the use of force by those in positions of authority gave increasing credibility to the militant argument that violence was the only tactic understood by the establishment. Thus, during the 1969–1970 academic year, student protestors and street people came to regard both university and city as representative of an intransigent social order and both were attacked as such in the "trashing" that more and more frequently marked the climax of a demonstration. The student body as a whole, made familiar with violence over a period of years, reacted to this violence with silence. If they did not support it, neither did they condemn it. Violence had become acceptable.

The major campus crisis over the Cambodian invasion in the spring of 1970 was national in scope although it also had some specific local ingredients. The national agitation over Cambodia and Kent State, occurring when the Madison campus was already highly politicized by the recent TAA strike, swiftly and effectively brought academic life to a halt for the rest of the semester. The events on campus followed a familiar pattern, although the intensity was greater than in the past and the numbers of students (and National Guard troops) involved was greater. Another key difference was that, in addition to the Teaching Assistants Association, a large number of the faculty were mobilized in general sympathy with the students. For the first time in a number of years, the isolation of liberal elements of the faculty from the student movement was broken, if only for a short time.

The scenario of protest was similar to that of earlier incidents described above. A student strike, followed by militant demonstrations, some property damage and trashing in the local business area, led to the calling of the National Guard by university officials who otherwise did not speak publicly on the crisis. Classes in many parts of the university, and especially in the College of Letters and Sciences, were cancelled for almost a week. Several schools, including law and nursing, suspended classes for varying periods of time, and, perhaps with the exception of the engineering and agriculture campuses, the university did not function normally for well over a week. Indeed, the combination of the TAA strike and the Cambodia and Kent State crisis meant that the final six weeks of the spring semester of 1970 saw a major disruption of the academic program of the university, although Wisconsin did not officially close nor, with the exception of some revisions in grading patterns, officially change its schedule because of the crisis.

Yet no one was killed. Perhaps death was avoided during the confrontation because both students and police were so familiar with confrontation as a mode of conflict resolution that they had evolved an informal set of rules which marked the limits of acceptable violence, and neither group broke those rules. Despite its intensity, confrontation had taken on a highly ritualized pattern. Students usually engaged police by threatening a war-related facility—for example, the ROTC building or the AMRC—and police responded by dispersing students with gas and physical charges. The student demonstrators were quite aware that they would never reach their stated objective; indeed, it is difficult to imagine what they would have done if they had been allowed to do so—confronting an empty building is hardly as dramatic as waging mock guerilla warfare with the police. The real intent of the students was to so disrupt the university by their struggle with its agents of social control that business as usual would be impossible and the university effectively shut down. Concomitantly, the police made few serious attempts to deal with the mass of students after their initial dispersal. A limit to violence was maintained as long as each group remained in a solid body, and confined its behavior to the ritual pattern of threat and counter-threat. Within these limits, injury to person and property could and did occur on both sides, but death was avoided.

The faculty response to the situation was significant. Close to 300 professors—out of a total faculty of 2,300—signed a statement opposing the United States government's actions, calling for the university to close, and indicating that they would not conduct business as usual during the crisis. Although not quite a strike statement, this was the most radical response taken by Wisconsin faculty members during the various crises. Indeed, the faculty, meeting as a committee of the whole shortly after the signing of the statement, voted to close down the university, thus indicating the depth of their feeling. About 1,200 faculty members attended the meeting, and the resolution passed by a large majority. The university administration, however, did not follow the wishes of the faculty majority, kept the university open, and refused to convene another faculty meeting until the crisis was over and the end of the semester was at hand. The administration, no doubt, breathed a sigh of relief that the legislature was not in session at the time and thus no dramatic outcry was heard and no investigation launched.

As did the other cases discussed here, the Cambodia and Kent State crisis had some lasting impact. For one thing, the Board of Regents after threatening to tighten up discipline for some time, finally set up new procedures to mete out swift justice to student offenders and by-pass the slow processes of the previous faculty-run discipline system. It is significant that the state attorney general was instrumental in devising these new procedures, thus indicating the increased interest of the state government in university affairs. This "incursion" of the Regents into what has traditionally been a function of the faculty is but one example of the increasingly activist role of the Regents.

Many faculty members, particularly younger and more liberal ones, were deeply disillusioned by the crisis and by the response of the university to it. Wisconsin, with its strong tradition of faculty self-government, had long counted on the ethos of faculty power to keep excellent professors in Madison when other institutions offered higher salaries and better conditions. Thus, the tradition of faculty control and perhaps the stability of the faculty were dealt a blow by Regent actions. The student reaction is more difficult to gauge, but it is at least possible that the atmosphere which was created by the whole experience of the Cambodia and Kent State crisis made the bombing of the Army Mathematics Research Center, which occurred only a few months later, acceptable to many non-revolutionary students.

The bombing of the Army Mathematics Research Center not only was one of the most dramatic events at Wisconsin, it had implications for the campus and perhaps for the country at large. While it is fairly clear that the actual bombing was not connected to the radical movement on campus, two of the four individuals who allegedly participated in the event were University of Wisconsin students and former members of the staff of the *Daily Cardinal,* the student newspaper. The reaction of politically minded students on campus was generally mixed, revealing deep sorrow at the loss of life but at the same time showing satisfaction that one of the key issues of the student left, the continued existence of the AMRC, was "solved" by the bombing. (Of course, the question was not in reality solved, since the AMRC simply moved to other quarters and continued to function.) The general campus reaction of shock and helplessness has not yet disappeared.

The bombing threw the radical movement into tactical disarray. Activists found it difficult to deal with the bombing even in terms of "revolutionary" strategy, while the large majority of students, including many sympathetic to the movement, were outraged by the event. Many within the student left disagreed with the action on both tactical and moral grounds. As of this writing, the campus left has not recovered—there have been no successful mass demonstrations and the active political groups do not seem to be functioning effectively. There is no question but that the bombing contributed to the political inactivity of the 1970–1971 academic year on the Madison campus, and perhaps nationally, because of the demoralization and tactical confusion it caused. Many students felt that the bombing was the logical outcome of the confrontation politics of the sixties. Yet the bombing was morally unjustifiable and politically ineffective. Many students withdrew from the movement because of the lack of a clear direction.

Faculty, administration, and Regent response was predictable. The faculty was both outraged and demoralized. There was little they could do to prevent another bombing. Faculty opposition to student radicals, already strong, probably increased. The administration and the Regents merely increased their tendency toward a "law and order" posture in the face of campus problems. For the first time, city police were brought on campus to patrol on a regular basis, and contingency plans for various kinds of disruptions were made.

The University of Wisconsin has obviously been subject to the very serious pressures facing American higher education generally in the sixties. Despite this fact, it is clear that the university has not truly responded to many of the challenges which face it. The symptoms of failure are evident: A faculty senate was organized in 1969–1970 with neither the consultation nor the participation of students, although at other universities, such as Columbia, students were involved in similar changes in governance. Despite a great deal of deliberation and some conflict, no basic reforms in the curriculum have been made, and the administrative structure has remained unaltered, although there are some indications that this situation may be changing. The university has not been able to move far or fast enough to meet demands on it from undergraduate or graduate students, from teaching assistants, or occasionally from junior faculty. While it is very likely that some student demands should be rejected, the University of Wisconsin has met almost none regardless of merit.

Those in charge of the University of Wisconsin—the Regents and the senior faculty and administrators—are certainly not evil men. They are not even, for the most part, incompetent. They are simply locked into an academic system which was formed over a period of almost fifty years and which was solidified during the boom period of the fifties. This system has served the interests of the senior faculty quite well and has permitted the University of Wisconsin to grow and to maintain if not expand its national prestige. But this situation has changed, and it is clear that neither the increasingly radical and dissatisfied students nor the financially troubled state government will continue to support the traditional means of academic governance and orientation of the university.

The political future of the university is unclear. In February of 1971, Governor Lucey, in his budget message to the legislature, called for an amalgamation of the University of Wisconsin system and the Wisconsin State University system under one Board of Regents. Such a shift, which the governor claims will save four million dollars in administrative costs, would have major implications for the Madison campus if implemented and could possibly mean financial disaster. The availability of funds under the new Democratic administration in the state is also unclear, and the prospects seem very dim indeed. Thus, the University of Wisconsin enters the 1970s without direction and in a state of substantial crisis. Budgetary crises have forced administrators to spend much of their time belt tightening while students demand that more attention be given to undergraduate instruction and other expensive proposals. What is more, the will to adapt to what are clearly new situations does not seem to be dramatically evident.

Notes

[1] Portions of this chapter also appear in P. G. Altbach, "The Champagne University in the Beer State: Notes on the Crisis at Wisconsin," in David Riesman (ed.), *Case Studies of Universities in Crisis* (New York: McGraw-Hill, 1972). We are indebted to Matt Pommer, Durward Long, David Riesman, and Verne A. Stadtman for their comments on an earlier draft of this paper.

[2] C. Kerr, *The Uses of the University* (New York: Harper Torchbooks, 1966), pp. 1, 20.

[3] *Ibid.*, Chapter Two.

[4] For a discussion of the history of student activism at the University of Wisconsin, see Chapter Seventeen. The best overall discussion of the history of the University of Wisconsin is M. Curti and V. Carstenson, *The University of Wisconsin: A History, 1848–1925* (Madison: University of Wisconsin Press, 1949), 2 vol.

[5] See M. Mankoff, *The Political Socialization of Student Radicals and Militants in the Wisconsin Student Movement during the 1960's*, unpublished doctoral dissertation, University of Wisconsin, 1970.

[6] M. Lyons, *Campus Reactions to Student Protest*, unpublished doctoral dissertation, University of Wisconsin, 1971, p. 49.

[7] See Chapter Fourteen.

[8] The history and ideology of the TAA are discussed in Chapter Fifteen.

[9] *Report of the Committee on the Teaching Assistant System* (Madison: University of Wisconsin, 1968), p. 21.

[10] See Mankoff for an elaboration of this point. See also M. Mankoff and R. Flacks, "The Changing Social Base of the American Student Movement," *Annals of the American Academy of Political and Social Science*, 1971, *395*, 54–67.

[11] *Faculty Participation in Academic Governance: Report of the AAHE–NEA Task Force on Faculty Representation and Academic Negotiations, Campus Governance Programs* (Washington, D.C.: American Association for Higher Education, 1970).

[12] R. Hofstadter, *Anti-Intellectualism in American Life* (New York: Knopf, 1963), pp. 199–204.

[13] In this respect, the University of Wisconsin conforms to the paradigm developed by A. W. Gouldner in "Cosmopolitans and Locals: Toward an Analysis of Latent Social Roles, I and II," *Administrative Science Quarterly*, 1957–58, *2*, 281–306, 444–480.

[14] S. M. Lipset, "The Politics of Academia," in D. C. Nichols (Ed.), *Perspectives on Campus Tensions* (Washington, D.C.: American Council on Education, 1970), pp. 85–118.

[15] See P. L. Dressel, F. C. Johnson, and P. M. Marcus, *The Confidence Crisis: An Analysis of University Departments* (San Francisco: Jossey-Bass, 1970), for a more detailed discussion of the nature and functions of academic departments in large universities.

[16] The problems of academic administrators are dealt with in Chapters One, Two, and Three.

[17] There is very little written about or by the University of Wisconsin Board of Regents. For two commentaries, from rather different perspectives, see A. DeBardeleben, "The University's External Constituency," in W. Metzger and others, *Dimensions of Academic Freedom* (Urbana, Ill.; University of Illinois Press, 1969), pp. 69–91, and C. Gelatt, *The Regents: Rulers or Rubber Stamps?* (Madison: Board of Regents of the University of Wisconsin, 1969).

[18] The Wisconsin situation conforms generally to the national characteristics of members of academic governing boards which were reported in R. Hartnett, *The New College Trustee: Some Predictions for the 1970s* (Princeton, N.J.: Educational Testing Service, 1970).

[19] See M. Pommer, "Regent Rule at Wisconsin," *Change,* 1970, 2, 27–28.

[20] For a more detailed discussion of the Dow crisis, see D. Long, "Wisconsin: Changing Styles of Administrative Response," in J. Foster and D. Long (Eds.), *Protest!* (New York: Morrow, 1970), pp. 246–270. See also Chapters Seven and Ten of this book.

[21] For a more detailed discussion of the black demands crisis, see Chapter Sixteen.

PART ONE

THE POWER STRUCTURE

It is becoming increasingly clear at the University of Wisconsin, and indeed at other universities, that the role of faculty in the governance of the institution is diminishing at a rapid rate. The faculty has a role, although, as Donald McCarty points out, it is not always a constructive one. This part, then, excludes the faculty from among the elements in the university power structure but includes a mixed bag of other groups and interests. Our intention is to fo-

29

cus on the main elements which affect academic decisions. The chapters in this part by Robert Atwell, McCarty, and Durward Long deal in general terms with some of the problems of academic administration and link the administrators to other elements in the equation—faculty, legislature, Regents. These three chapters indicate that the administrator is by no means a free agent and that he is constrained and influenced by many different elements. Administrators, in fact, often see the faculty as an impediment rather than as an aid to academic reform. These three chapters also contribute to an understanding of the structure and function of the modern multiversity. As Long demonstrates most dramatically, the multiversity is often an unwieldy instrument which not only is difficult to move but is even difficult to understand.

The other chapters in this part deal with specific aspects of the university power structure. Gregory Nigosian provides analysis of the Regents and deals both with their sociopolitical backgrounds and with their reactions to crisis. His analysis clearly links the Regents, at the University of Wisconsin at least, to political currents in the state. Many commentators have looked to the Regents to provide a shield from political interference in academic affairs. But, at Wisconsin, the Regents have been very much a part of the political equation of the university. Matt Pommer provides a useful follow-up for the analysis of the Regents in his discussion of the political context of the university and his description of how various influences in the legislature and the interaction between university officials and political figures affect academic life. One of Pommer's most interesting points concerns the importance of the personalities of the officials involved. The personal relationships between the president of the university and the governor or key Regents or members of the legislature can make a difference in the support the university receives from the state. While Pommer's discussion mainly concerns state institutions, private universities are also affected, although to a lesser degree, by local, state, and national politics.

James Rowen's chapter is a stinging indictment of University of Wisconsin involvement in military-related research. In his analysis of the various ramifications of this involvement, it becomes clear that one of the effects of military-related research was the long and ultimately dramatically destructive campaign by radical students against the Army Mathematics Research Center. For the record, the University of Wisconsin is rather less involved in military-related research than are many major American universities. Nevertheless, the whole question of such research and the political, ethical, and practical questions that it entails are important. Rowen's passionate chapter focuses some attention on these issues. The final chapter in this part is Bernard Sklar's analysis of the 1967

Dow crisis on the Madison campus, a particularly important element in any discussion of the response of the university to crisis. The Dow affair was the first of the major confrontations on the Madison campus and had a continuing and traumatic effect on both students and the faculty.

Perhaps the major finding of Part I is that the power structure of any major university is diffuse, highly complex, and extremely unwieldy. Decision making is at best a difficult process, and the implementation of policy in the academic setting is often even more troublesome than is the making of the policy. The elements which impinge on policy-making at a major university are diverse and at the same time important to understand if there is to be any hope of constructive and planned academic change.

CHAPTER 1

●●●●●●●●●●●●●●●
●●●●●●●●●●●●●●●
●●●●●●●●●●●●●●●

SHIFTS IN THE BALANCE
OF POWER

Robert Atwell

●●●●●●●●●●●●●●●
●●●●●●●●●●●●●●●
●●●●●●●●●●●●●●●

The University of Wisconsin was ill-prepared to respond to the student unrest which began in 1965. The administration and faculty had concentrated their energies on the development of graduate education and research programs and on the construction of facilities for these programs. Although the preceding ten years had seen the most rapid growth in enrollment, both graduate and undergraduate, in the university's history, the maintenance of high quality undergraduate education for this large influx of students was not a matter of high priority for most administrators and faculty members. Indeed, the concern with graduate education and research was so universal that the degradation of undergraduate education seemed to have escaped the notice of many in the university community. The rush for gold in the federal hills was so obsessive—and the university's success was so exhilarating—that little concern was expressed about the extent to which the university's increasing dependence on the federal government might compromise the traditional neutrality of the university.

The administration-faculty relationship was easy and relaxed because virtually all top administrators had been Wisconsin faculty members. Also, it was a period when there was very little of that intense competition for funds that pits administrator against administrator and forces administrators to set priorities among competing faculty claims. The administration during this period was essentially promotional in character, and administrators seemed willing to promote almost anything any faculty member wanted. There were seldom any questions of priority, and hence it was difficult for the administration to antagonize the faculty. State appropriations to meet enrollment growth, although not adequate to prevent the deterioration of student-faculty ratios, were large and permitted reasonable growth in most fields. Established faculty members were absorbed in federal and foundation financed research projects.

Much of the effort of the president during the early and middle 1960s was devoted not only to promotional activities but also to the development of the multiversity system, including the strengthening of the Milwaukee campus and the development of new four-year institutions at Parkside (in the Racine and Kenosha area) and Green Bay. During this period University Extension was created by combining the highly successful and long established agricultural extension activities which had been part of the College of Agriculture with the other extension activities. University Extension was separated from the Madison campus, which I believe has resulted in lessening the generally weak commitment on the part of Madison campus faculty to public service activities.

The internal workings of the university were governed by a labyrinth of faculty committees. There was an occasional student on an unimportant faculty committee, but there was almost no recognition of the desirability of student participation in anything beyond dormitory and social life. Ironically, one of the joint faculty-student committees (significantly, it was a faculty committee to which students had been added) was called the Student Life and Interest Committee (SLIC) which was concerned with housing, social regulations, and related extracurricular matters. The implication was that student life and interests were subsumed within the purview of SLIC and did not extend to the academic side of university life.

The preeminence of the faculty in the running of the university was probably at its height by the mid-1960s. The Regents viewed their role as arranging for the governance of the university—not as exercising the powers of governance themselves—and it was clear that they had great confidence in the president and the faculty. Faculty governance was in the hands of senior faculty members who were in close touch personally and ideologically with top administrators. While the faculty governing mechanisms had all of the appearances of democracy, their basic character was oligarchic. This was due less to any kind of self-conscious despotism than to the indifference of many faculty members to the time-consuming realities of faculty government. Any senior faculty member willing to devote substantial portions of his time to committee work could play a major role in ruling the institution. Increasingly, younger faculty members were also able to play significant roles in faculty government, though they faced special problems.

The basic system of faculty governance and the creation of the multiversity made it very difficult to respond effectively and substantively to student unrest. The structure presumed long, careful, and unemotional consideration of issues, whereas responses to student activism often necessitate the kind of immediate response that can only come from a vigorous and self-confident administration that has the confidence of the faculty. Moreover, the governing structure permitted only minimal student participation and almost no recognition that students have a role to play in decisions on educational matters.

I contend that student unrest has caused a shift of power from faculty to administration and from administration to Regents. The result has been a less democratic and less responsive institution, which is the antithesis of what the student movement is trying to achieve. These assertions will be examined through a discussion of some of the strains placed on the network of relationships among students, faculty, administration, and Regents. These strains include challenges to the faculty hegemony, growing alienation between administration and faculty, challenges to the faculty oligarchy, demands by students for participation in educational questions, the increasing role of the Regents, and the growing bureaucratization of the multiversity.

It was inevitable that faculty domination of the decision-making processes would come under severe challenge. Such challenge came initially from student unrest, but would have come in any event because of the need for better administration of an operation that was costing hundreds of millions of dollars. Outside pressures, from the governor, the Coordinating Council for Higher Education, and the legislature, for a greater sense of priority and for greater accountability in the use of public funds would have inevitably forced the faculty to yield some of its power to the administration. Although pressures other than those directly stemming from student activism would have inevitably had the result of reducing faculty power, I contend that student activism was the major contributor to a shift in the balance of power. The administration was forced to make quick responses to student protest actions and to subsequently ask for ratification by the faculty. As long as administration responses were consistent with the views of a majority of the faculty and as long as they did not involve the use of outside force to quell student disturbances, the administration did not encounter significant opposition.

The lack of opposition is also a tribute to the remarkable skill and acumen of the first chancellor of the Madison campus, Robben W. Fleming. Fleming came to Madison in 1964 from the University of Illinois, where he had been on the law faculty. He was well known to Wisconsin faculty members because he had been on the Madison faculty a number of years before and had taken his law degree in Madison. Fleming was attuned to and in fundamental agreement with the concept of faculty government as practiced at Madison. He combined this faculty point of view with a skillful and pragmatic style in responding to the early student protests on the Madison campus. He consulted widely with faculty members and very clearly had the confidence of a substantial majority of them. This confidence was attributable partly to a skillful handling of situations that arose and partly to the fact that he spent a substantial portion of his time explaining and defending actions and seeking the counsel of his colleagues. He also had a close working relationship with the University Committee. Indeed, despite all the strains that have been placed on administration-faculty relationships during the past five years, there has been a continued close relationship between the chancellor and the University Committee.

However, the various crises of student protest which occurred during the Fleming regime had the effect of shifting power to the administration. The first such crisis was a sit-in during May of 1966 to protest the fact that the university supplied information to draft boards concerning the academic standing of students. The student protestors contended that the supplying of such information constituted complicity with national foreign policy in general and with the war in Vietnam in particular. The evidence of a shift of power from faculty to administration is found mainly in the response to the sit-in rather than in the shift in policy. The students occupied the Administration Building for a period of several days as a means of dramatizing their position and of forcing the university to stop supplying information to draft boards. Despite great pressure from the local police and others in the community, Fleming chose to permit the sit-in to go on rather than to use police action to remove the demonstrators. Fleming defended his action on the grounds that the sit-in was not obstructive. After a few days the students voluntarily left the building, and some modifications were subsequently made in the university policy of supplying information to draft boards. The decision not to end the sit-in by force was solely Fleming's—made against the advice of many of his nonfaculty advisors who were concerned about the possibility of open confrontation between the left and the right if the sit-in was not ended—and it set the tone of the remaining year of the Fleming regime. The decision had widespread support within the university community, but it is clear in retrospect that the flexible response theory of the Fleming administration generated considerable opposition in the state generally and in the legislature in particular.

The second major crisis of the Fleming administration was the protest against campus recruiting activities by the Dow Chemical Company in 1966. The details of this incident are well covered by Long[1] and in Chapter One of this book. Again Fleming set the tone of campus response by writing his personal check to bail the students out of jail. Although this action was widely acclaimed within the university at the time, as a means of avoiding what most probably would otherwise have been a massive police action, there was widespread criticism outside the university.

Following the Dow Chemical Company incident, the faculty addressed itself to the issue of whether corporations should continue to recruit on the campus or whether such recruiting was a secondary function of the university and should therefore take place off the campus. Few questioned that the university has an obligation to carry on its essential functions regardless of controversy; thus, the issue hinged on the importance of recruiting and job placement in the panoply of university activities. In a faculty meeting where the issue was brought to a vote, Chancellor Fleming warned that if the faculty reaffirmed such activities on the campus, he might be obliged to call police to the campus to prevent or remove obstruction. The faculty reaffirmed the continuation of placement activities, but the chancellor's warning proved prophetic because the next fall obstruction of Dow Chemical Company interviews was the occasion for the first massive police action on the campus and the first incident involving injuries to students and police.

In dealing with the faculty on the placement question, Fleming was in some respect simply playing the role of the executive in relation to his legislature. The former carries out the policy of the latter (shall there be placement interviews on the campus), but it is for the executive to determine the strategy and tactics (police action or tolerating nonobstructive sit-ins) for carrying out legislative mandates. In retrospect, however, it seems clear that the real policy issue from the point of view of the university's outside constituency was not whether the university should supply information to draft boards or make its facilities available for corporate recruiting, but what should be the nature of the response to student activism. There is some reason to believe that the university's public would not have been particularly excited had the university (presumably as the result of faculty action) decided to stop supplying information to draft boards and barred corporations from recruiting on the campus. In this sense the public was much more concerned with the phenomenology of protest than with the substantive issues it raised.

The import of this is that the strategy and tactics turned out to be much more fateful for the university than the substantive issues, and strategy was determined largely by Chancellor Fleming. Student action and administration reaction is what has pleased or displeased the outside constituency. It seems clear that a substantial portion of the university's outside constituency and a substantial majority of the 1971 Board of Regents (the Regents at the time were officially supportive, preferring to leave such matters to the administration, but some were privately hostile to Fleming) were in fundamental opposition to the general effort of the Fleming administration to meet student protest reasonably and flexibly and without massive police action.

The Fleming period was marked by a shift in power from the faculty to the administration, because only the administration is in a position to respond to immediate crises. This shift was accompanied by, and to a degree caused, the development of a schism between the administration and the faculty. As the administration became more active and visible, it was blamed by faculty liberals and conservatives alike for the increasing polarization on the campus. The liberals felt that the administration was selling out to the pressures from alumni, Regents, and legislators for a tougher stand on student unrest, while the conservatives felt that not enough was being done to control the dissidents. Both groups abhorred the failure to consult the faculty until after a crisis. The anger and frustration expressed at the faculty meetings which were called to pick up the pieces following a major confrontation probably reflected the increasing realization of the faculty's impotence to deal with the issues of the day, not only because of the need for immediate action rather than interminable faculty meetings but also because of a sense of impotence caused by severe division among the faculty on questions of student unrest.

The schism was very dramativally widened at the beginning of the administration of Chancellor William Sewell. Sewell succeeded Fleming in September 1967, after the latter assumed the presidency of the University of Michigan. Sewell was an internationally renowned sociologist who held an endowed research professorship. Just before being selected as chancellor, he had been elected to the chairmanship of the University Committee, so it is clear that he was in every sense a leader of the established faculty. Sewell had the misfortune to assume the chancellorship at a time when the balance of power within the Regents had shifted from the liberals or moderates to the conservatives. Republican Governor Warren Knowles was a political moderate, but, for reasons still unclear, he appointed Regents who tended to be quite conservative. Knowles did not reappoint Arthur DeBardaleben who was the acknowledged leader of the liberal Regents and a vigorous defender of the university. The conservative ascendancy within the Board of Regents was accompanied by insistence on the part of the Regents that student activism be met with force when it became obstructive and by a generally more active role for the Regents in all phases of university life.

At the same time, student activism was becoming increasingly militant, and thus it was inevitable that escalation on both sides would lead to a major confrontation. That confrontation was the Dow Chemical Company protest at the Commerce Building on October 18, 1967. Previous demonstrations had usually not been obstructive to the point where the activity being protested could not be continued. When obstruction occurred, it was usually dispersed by arrests or the threat of arrests. The administration was not prepared for escalation to the point where an effort to eliminate an obstructive demonstration would lead to violence between demonstrators and police. The administration was, however, under great pressure from Regents and legislators to prevent building takeovers whether obstructive or not. Public patience had worn thin, and thus the administration entered the 1967–1968 year with a great deal of its flexibility or response removed. It was clearly understood that obstructive sit-ins would not be tolerated. Most previous actions had not been obstructive, or had been so for only brief periods. While the number of students and their militance on October 18 was somewhat surprising to the administration, the belief was that the obstructors would permit themselves to be arrested and carried limply to police wagons.

Rather than reacting quickly with a force of men sufficiently large for the occasion, the Madison police, who were called to the campus for the first time, delayed their arrival for a long period and their removal of the obstruction for an even longer period during which the tension and the size of the crowds increased. When police finally entered the building, presumably to arrest the demonstrators without resistance, they were initially repulsed but entered a second time with clubs swinging. Who initiated the violence is still in dispute, but within a short space of time a large number of students and police were injured, tear gas was used to disperse the crowds, and the University of Wisconsin had entered a new phase in the course of student activism.

The faculty, which met the next day, was badly divided but universally shocked and horrified by the violence. The administration barely survived what was tantamount to a vote of no confidence over its handling of the affair. In heated tones, the chancellor reminded the faculty that he had simply carried out its mandate of the previous year that placement interviews should go on. The meeting reflected the polarization within the faculty. The younger professors had much sympathy with student concern over the war and over university complicity with the war machine, and they generally believed the administration had been too harsh in its response. The older faculty generally believed the administration should return the campus to the relatively tranquil pre-1965 period. Sewell's efforts to heal the wounds and bridge the gaps were remarkably successful, involving constant dialogue with all viewpoints and the continual involvement of students and faculty in policy-making, but his efforts could not continue because of increasing pressure from the legislature and the Regents for more repressive acts. The flexible response so characteristic of the Fleming era was no longer possible because of the militance of both left and right. This pressure ultimately led to the resignation of Chancellor Sewell in June, 1968, after only ten months in office.

In September, 1968, H. Edwin Young succeeded Sewell. Young had been a professor of economics at Madison, then chairman of his department, and finally dean of the College of Letters and Science before assuming the presidency of the University of Maine in the fall of 1965. He had just returned to Wisconsin as vice-president in the summer of 1968. He was the most conservative of the three chancellors, and his style of operation was consultation with a limited number of close associates, most of whom were members of the faculty establishment.

The basic administrative philosophies of Fleming and Young were not dissimilar in that both perceived their role as that of mediator. It must be remembered that the more militant tactics of the left and the increasingly hostile public and Regents gave Young much less room for manipulation than had been available to Fleming. Young has not been hesitant to use force where he has believed it necessary to avoid property destruction or personal injury. Given the objectives of avoidance of property destruction and personal injury, his policy has been remarkably successful. The university survived the black student strike in the winter of 1969 and the Cambodian incident in the spring of 1970 without many serious injuries and without massive property destruction on the campus. The use of the National Guard and massive police forces, while it has not contributed to campus harmony, has been successful from the point of view of its limited objectives.

Chancellor Young does not engage, as did his predecessors, in constant dialogue with faculty members of divergent viewpoints, and he is thus further removed from the main body of faculty attitudes. Indeed, the natural divisions of opinion within the faculty may have been widened by his obvious association with more conservative elements within the faculty and by his close association with the Regents. It would be unfair to blame the alienation between a large segment of the faculty and the administration on the chancellor because, in large part, it really reflects the polarization that exists in American society. It would, however, not be unfair to argue that the previously blurred lines between administration and faculty have been sharpened somewhat by events since the late sixties and by the administration's new and close attention to the feelings and desires of the Regents and the legislature. The campus administration has both an internal and an external constituency, and in 1968–1970 it paid much more heed to its external constituency.

A brief case study is illustrative of the schism not only between faculty and administration but also within the faculty. It also points out the importance of faculty dealings with many questions raised by student activism. Following the October 1967 Dow Chemical Company incident, the faculty voted to form a committee (consisting of equal numbers of faculty and students), subsequently known as the Mermin Committee (after its chairman, Samuel Mermin, professor of law), charged with the responsibility for drafting recommendations on the mode of response to obstruction; on the policies and conduct of employment interviews; and on any other matters concerned in the implementation of the principles of the resolution offered by the University Committee on October 23, 1967.

The original plan was for the Mermin Committee to complete its work quickly. However, there was an argument over student membership, with the University Committee insisting that the Wisconsin Student Association should submit a panel of names in excess of the number to be appointed. The students finally won this argument. Because of the fundamental nature of the issues discussed by the committee, the first and most significant of its three reports was not published until March 13, 1968. The fourteen-member committee divided eight to six on its initial recommendations, with five of the seven students being joined by three of the seven faculty in recommending a moratorium on placement interviews on the campus. The issue of the mode of response to obstruction became a debate of in loco parentis within the committee, with the same division as noted above. The majority recommended that (1) there be created a university ombudsman and that the univeresity administration, in consultation with the university community, take immediate steps leading to the establishment of the structure, the delimitation of the power and responsibilities, and the determination of the composition of the university ombudsman; (2) university discipline be imposed only where intentional conduct clearly and seriously impairs access of members of the university community to the educational process, and alternate safeguards to this access are demonstrably inadequate; (3) an individual be suspended from the university only when his behavior and attitude are such as to indicate a continuing threat of impairment of access to the educational process; (4) faculty rules be amended so as to permit the exclusion of students from units and services within the university without necessitating exclusion from the entire university; (5) if some particular behavior is prosecuted in a criminal court, the university shall normally accept the court's judgment as full disposition; [and] (6) in those rare instances in which an individual is liable to the imposition of both university sanctions and those of another authority for some particular behavior, university policy be that he not be forced to contest simultaneously both sets of charges.

The minority of the committee favored sanctions for obstruction or serious impairment of university-run or university-authorized functions as well as of the educational process. The minority spelled out its views on the obstructive circumstances and on the limitations it would place on the use of university sanctions. Both the majority and minority reports were masterfully written and presented in closely reasoned arguments. This seemingly subtle distinction between obstructing the educational process of the university and obstruction of authorized university activity concealed some rather fundamental differences of opinion on the extent to which the university should discipline students instead of relying on the civil and criminal procedures.

The experience of the Mermin Committee is instructive in several respects. The deep divisions within the committee caused the report to lose much of its impact. Neither the minority nor majority position was accepted by faculty, administration, or Regents. By the time the report was issued, events had overtaken the subject to the point where, for example, it was no longer politically possible for the faculty or administration to call a moratorium on placement interviews, as recommended by the majority. Regent impatience with university disciplinary procedures made the majority report unacceptable, and the carefully framed limitations on sanctions suggested by the minority were never adopted as official policy.

The Mermin Report points up both the strengths and weaknesses of faculty governance in responding to crisis situations. The report was learned, indeed eloquent, but given the divisions within the committee, the long period of time which elapsed before the report was issued, and the rush of subsequent events, it was to some degree an exercise in futility. In the final analysis those charged with responsibility for immediate situations that arise—administrators—will respond to those situations by relying primarily on their own wits and the political realities of the moment. In quieter and less polarized times the Mermin Report would have been debated, and the resulting outcome within the faculty would have set basic policy for the campus. By 1968, the balance of power on fundamental questions had shifted to the point where administrators and Regents had assumed prerogatives heretofore reserved to the faculty.

The period between 1965 and 1970 saw not only a shift of power from faculty to administration and Regents but also an upsetting of the balance of power within the faculty. Previously, the university was run by a collection of senior faculty members in alliance with senior administrators, themselves members of the faculty. The growth of the faculty since 1960 has changed the internal composition of the faculty to the point where in many departments, particularly in the College of Letters and Science, the balance between the senior and junior faculty has shifted to the point where the senior faculty can potentially be outvoted by the younger faculty on any given issue. In the humanities and social sciences departments of the College of Letters and Science—and to some lesser degree in other departments of that college and in some of the professional schools such as education and more recently medicine—faculties tend to be divided between liberals and conservatives along age lines. Chairmanships, which at Wisconsin generally involve an election which is theoretically advisory to the dean, tend to go to moderate individuals who are acceptable to all political points of view rather than, as in the past, to those clearly identified with the establishment.

Most challenges to oligarchy have taken place within the affairs of individual departments, but some have been more publicly visible. One of the leading examples of the latter was the controversy over the establishment of the black studies department by action of the faculty in the spring of 1969. The esablishment of the department was recommended by a subcommittee of a chancellor-appointed committee charged with developing programs of Afro-American studies. The subcommittee, under the chairmanship of a very able and hard-working young assistant professor of political science, recommended the creation of a complete department. The parent committee, which was more equally divided between younger and senior faculty members, was split on the issue of a department, with its own faculty and curriculum, or an interdepartmental program which would draw on the resources of existing departments but would not have its own faculty. New departments are seldom created at Wisconsin, both because of the reluctance of established departments to surrender any of their territory and because of a genuine conviction that many new fields are truly interdisciplinary and can best be developed along interdepartmental lines. In this instance the younger faculty members both on the full committee and in the subsequent faculty meeting allied themselves on the side of the department in response to the feelings of the black community that in the academic world the department is the only form of first-class citizenship. In a very emotional and profoundly moving faculty meeting, the faculty accepted the views of its younger people and voted to establish the black studies department. It should be noted that the administration, which remained neutral during the debate, has been very faithful in carrying out the majority viewpoint and has provided generous financial support for the department.

Over the years, younger people have been hesitant to assert themselves in faculty governance, not only because they were in a minority in most departments, but also because they have had to and have wanted to apply themselves to their academic duties. The pressures of the publish or perish system fall most heavily on younger and untenured faculty members and, irrespective of this pressure, many of these people are totally devoted to their field and do not wish to take the time for faculty committee work. Somewhat offsetting these pressures has been the fact that Wisconsin has been in a position to hire the very best of the new Ph.D. crops, and many of these people have been so able that they have very little doubt of their own ability to succeed in the academic system. Consequently, while not being disrespectful, they have been under no particular compulsion to ingratiate themselves with the senior faculty.

A few events in 1970 and 1971 cast considerable doubt on the future of faculty politics. First, the administration cut off the pay of professors who joined in the teaching assistant strike in the spring of 1970. Second, the Regents attempted to reduce the salary increase of a controversial sociologist and subsequently threatened to refuse a Ford Foundation grant for this same individual. While the withholding of the pay of striking professors is defensible to most members of the faculty, the actions in respect to the controversial faculty member were not. However, the effect of both of these actions, other actions of the regents, and some significant losses among the younger faculty, have probably had a dampening effect on the enthusiasm of younger faculty members to take positions at variance with those of the administration or senior faculty colleagues. The black studies issue may well have been the high-water mark of the young turks.

As a result of a feeling on the part of many faculty members that meetings of the full faculty were not proper forums for sober consideration of important questions, given the size of the present faculty, and because some members of the faculty saw an elected representative body as a means for reasserting the supremacy of the establishment, a movement developed in the mid-1960s to establish a faculty senate to conduct most of the business which had previously come before the full faculty. Experience with huge faculty meetings following the 1967 Dow incident, the meetings on the black studies question, and the meetings over the teaching assistants strike convinced a majority of the faculty that an elected body was necessary. The Senate appears to have been structured with sufficient care to calm fears that it would inadequately represent the interests of the younger faculty. However, the genesis of the movement for the Senate is at least in part a reflection of the impotence of the faculty in full assembly to resolve policy issues. The faculty has become too unwieldy to be an effective legislative body.

By 1968, building takeovers and sit-ins in administrative offices over issues of university complicity with the draft system, defense contracts, and placement interviews had temporarily run their course, and students began to turn toward the educational process. This meant, temporarily at least, a shift in the focus of student activism from administration to faculty. Up to this point, student involvement in curriculum and related academic questions was rather limited and included principally some rather inactive student-faculty conference committees which were advisory to the four powerful all-campus divisional committees that passed on promotion to tenure and on all new courses. Individual departments, in a few cases, permitted more student involvement, but the basic pattern was that students were excluded from participation in academic affairs.

In the fall of 1968, students began attending departmental meetings, often uninvited, and began to insist on the right of students to participate in departmental affairs. This movement was limited to a few social science and humanities departments of the College of Letters and Science. The students often found allies in some of the younger faculty members, who would arrange for them to attend meetings or would otherwise defend their interests at faculty meetings, much to the consternation of some of their faculty colleagues. Much of this particular expression of student interest in educational affairs has also run its course, and departments have found ways to conduct much of their business in closed meetings. The Wisconsin Student Association has occasionally pressed for the right to bring matters of student concern to meetings of the faculty, but has not been either effective or sufficiently specific in pushing for such forms of student participation.

The most important developments in student participation in the educational process have been the creation of the Teaching Assistants Association and the subsequent TAA strike in the spring of 1970 (summarized in the Prologue). By 1966, concern over the quality of teaching assistant instruction (particularly in fields where the best students could get more desirable forms of support), over inequalities in the workloads of assistants, and over inadequacies in the supervision and training of assistants led to the appointment by Chancellor Fleming of a committee— known as the Mulvihill Committee after its chairman, Professor Robert

Mulvihill of the Spanish and Portuguese Department—to study the system. Significant among a number of recommendations by the Mulvihill Committee were one that the university guarantee up to four years of support for qualified graduate students making satisfactory progress toward Ph.D. and another that teaching experience be required of every graduate student supported by the university. Partly because of the high cost associated with its recommendations and partly because the chancellorship changed hands shortly after the committee issued its report in the spring of 1967, nothing was ever done, except what individual departments may have done, to implement the recommendations of the Mulvihill Report. But the problems remained and contributed to the rise of the TAA.

The TAA strike had some impact on administration-faculty relationships, for many faculty members believed, generally without justification, that the administration was willing to settle the strike at the expense of faculy departmental prerogatives. Although this view was largely unwarranted, particularly since the administration acted through a bargaining committee comprised largely of faculty members, it seems apparent that the strike drove some wedges into the administration-faculty relationship. These wedges relate to the fact that the terms of employment of graduate assistants had previously been up to the hiring department; campus-wide bargaining has eroded this departmental prerogative. More importantly, the administration clearly implied that teaching assistants had some legitimate grievances over their role in educational planning, and the administration's mere willingness to discuss these issues with the assistants, even without making significant concessions, was viewed by many faculty members as improper. Those faculty members who wished to maintain the existing teaching assistant system—usually those senior professors who benefit most in terms of low teaching loads—believe the administration stepped outside the bounds of its responsibilities.

Meanwhile, the increasingly militant tactics of student radicals, coupled with the conservative appointments to the Regents by Governor Knowles, led the Regents to assume a much more active role in running the university. This more active role was also prompted by pressure from the legislature. Power in the legislature was, until the 1970 elections, in the hands of persons considerably more conservative than the governor. Governor Knowles had been quite sympathetic to university budgetary requests and invariably tried to avoid capitalizing on public hostility to student unrest at the expense of the university. However, key Republican legislators, most notably Assembly Speaker Harold Froellich and most of the Republican majority on the powerful Joint Finance Committee (responsible for the state budget) have punished the university budgetarily, and they have forced the regents to take tough stands on student unrest as the price for financial survival. A number of the Regents believed that some legislative efforts to shift statutory powers of the university governance from the Regents to the legislature would succeed unless the Regents could demonstrate their "good faith" by repressive measures.

Since the 1967–1968 academic year, the Regents have spent countless hours on disciplinary procedures, on the use of police, and on sundry other matters the common denominator of which was an effort to bring law and order to the campus. Increasingly the Regents have insisted on particular courses of action to meet student unrest and have assumed jurisdiction over various disciplinary actions which have followed crises. This turn of events has removed discretion from the administration and has severely limited its options in responding in crisis situations. During this period the Regents have displayed a considerable lack of confidence in the administration and faculty. The administration has been forced to respond to these Regent initiatives. Administrators in higher education are increasingly caught between the irreconcilable positions of internal (students and faculty) and external (governing boards, alumni, legislators, and public) constituencies, and at Wisconsin they have had to be increasingly less responsive to the internal and more responsive to the external constituencies. Some administrators have argued valiantly and at times successfully with Regents to dissuade them from particularly repressive courses of action. However, such arguments take place in private, and the impression of many faculty members is that the administration has simply become the handmaiden of the Regents. Regent committees have taken over areas of concern that were previously within the purview of the faculty.

The faculty has not seriously challenged the ascendancy of the Regents, partly out of a belief that such efforts would be to no avail, partly because of the deep polarization within the faculty on issues of student activism, and partly because of the increasingly cumbersome machinery for communicating between the faculty and the Regents. This machinery takes principally the form of periodically permitting the University Faculty Council to participate in Regents meetings. The UFC is an all-university body composed of representatives of the individual campus University Committees, the executive committees of the faculty. The University Committees are elected by the faculty and have tended to be dominated by conservative senior faculty members. The UFC reflects principally these conservative interests and, additionally, includes a majority of non-Madison faculty. This would be satisfactory in many respects, but, because most of the major issues stemming from student unrest have arisen in Madison (and, to a lesser extent, in Milwaukee), the UFC is not an adequate vehicle for communicating Madison campus faculty problems to the Regents.

Regent power in university governance has very few statutory limitations but I believe that the present phase of Regent activism will soon pass. The legislative power in a great university must ultimately reside in some uneasy coalition of students and faculty, with the Regents arranging for governance rather than exercising it directly. The high level of Regent interference in 1971 is dictated by lack of political or philosophical balance within the Regents, lack of confidence in the administration and faculty, and external pressures. If these factors are no longer as pervasive, the Regents will probably withdraw somewhat.

Moreover, there is a trend to draw the university into the orbit of other state agencies and for the role of the Coordinating Council for Higher Education to expand. The University of Wisconsin is not established in the state constitution, as are some other great state universities such as the University of Michigan, and therefore the university is subject to state regulations in personnel policies, purchasing, printing, and a host of other areas. State budgetary problems and the general bureaucratic jealousy of university independence (and high salaries) on the part of state agency administrators is causing increasing incursions upon the university's freedom to administer its own activities and its own budgets. The tendency to view higher education as a single system with the university being merely one of the constituents of a more powerful Coordinating Council for Higher Education is yet another complicating factor. These various trends will squeeze the role of the Regents from one direction, while the administration, faculty, and students will inevitably push from another.

Note

[1] D. Long, "Wisconsin: Changing Patterns of Administrative Response," in J. Foster and D. Long (Eds.), *Protest!* (New York: Morrow, 1970), pp. 246–270.

CHAPTER 2

●●●●●●●●●●●●●●●●
●●●●●●●●●●●●●●●●
●●●●●●●●●●●●●●●●

REFLECTIONS ON ACADEMIC
ADMINISTRATION

Donald J. McCarty

●●●●●●●●●●●●●●●●
●●●●●●●●●●●●●●●●
●●●●●●●●●●●●●●●●

A number of theorists argue persuasively that the administrative process occurs in substantially the same generalized form in industrial, commercial, civil, educational, military, and hospital organizations.[1] This doctrine[2] implies that broad experience in administration, the ability to mediate conflict, and the skill needed to create cohesion and consensus are minimum imperatives for all administrators; furthermore, it suggests that figures like John Gardner and Ralph Bunche are better qualified to preside over a difficult enterprise like a university than is an illustrious scholar who has had little or no major administrative experience. This idea, to be sure, is anathema to academicians nearly everywhere. The typical professor at the University of Wisconsin is not a deferential person, and he tends to look down on rather than up to those administrators who in other settings might be considered his superiors.

Some Wisconsin professors might admit, if pressed, that a university administrator should have a minimum of competence in such managerial talents as delegation, human relations abilities, and well de-

veloped oral and written communication skills. Most firmly believe at
the same time that university administrators should primarily be academics with solid scholarly and professional credentials; few think that
formal training in administration is required or even desirable. The university does, of necessity, employ professional administrators—specialists
in finance, engineering, architecture, public relations, law, and the like.
These individuals may hold impressive titles (for example, vice-president)
and provide invaluable services to the system; to the faculty member,
however, they are support personnel, only incidental to the academic
process.

The University of Wisconsin, not unlike other great universities,
has followed the British aristocratic tradition: Administration at best is
an art performed by gifted amateurs; at worst, it is a craft meretriciously
practiced by second-class men. The ordinary Wisconsin faculty member
assumes that a professor who has been resolutely screened by a group of
his peers is able to administer effectively the academic affairs of a department, a college, or the entire university. He assumes that there are
sensible and fair mechanisms at hand to remedy the occasional failure
of screening procedures. Real life is somewhat different. Removal of an
administrative misfit is difficult and messy. The law of inertia prevails.
It is not easy to remove an academic administrator at Wisconsin against
his will once he has received the imprimatur of the faculty and is duly
appointed through official channels.

Nevertheless, the University of Wisconsin is organized administratively in a rational manner. There are standard operating procedures for
almost any academic contingency. These structures are traditional and
sacrosanct; changes come slowly and incrementally. In this context, instant solutions to complex problems are not forthcoming. At Wisconsin
it is the faculty who control the curriculum and set educational purposes.
It is they who instruct the students, conduct the research, and contribute
direct services to the public. Any substantial innovations are impossible
without their active consent and participation. In fact, over the years
the faculty has acquired a great deal of power without a commensurate
sense of responsibility. Most faculty members at Wisconsin are intelligent
and humane individuals committed to the scholarly study of their specialty
and dedicated to objectivity and truth. However, very impressive qualities
which distinguish the truly great professor often militate against his ability
to undertake quick action in an emergency. I am convinced that the
faculty lack the time, the information, the inclination, the organization,
and the decisiveness which effective administration requires.

Before 1970, the town meeting approach to governance was paramount at the University of Wisconsin. If the agenda at the monthly faculty meeting was filled with routine, noncontroversial items, a small handful turned out and dutifully rubber-stamped the proceedings. If a controversial issue appeared, large numbers of faculty members assembled; in this emotional setting the showmen on the faculty tended to dominate the sessions. Serious discussion became impossible, and much time was spent in parliamentary maneuvering. Votes were swung by thin margins, providing the administration with a very weak mandate; in fact, the faculty might reverse itself on the same question later on. Meetings were notoriously tension-producing and left many of the faculty frustrated and spent.

Nevertheless, one can conjure up a reasonable defense for our town meeting form of government. Poor attendance at general faculty meetings was often criticized as a clear demonstration of lack of interest, but it did signify that the faculty felt that its concerns were being properly served. The agenda for each meeting was prepared in advance by the secretary of the faculty and included detailed documentation for any action proposed by the administration, faculty committees, or individual faculty members. Protocol did not sanction much deviation from the announced agenda, and this removed the likelihood that a clique could capture enough votes to push through a measure before the faculty as a whole had an opportunity to consider its merits. The system rested on an underlying sense of community; since such a spirit did exist in considerable measure, regular attendance was not needed to indicate approval. In an attempt to overcome the criticisms of the town meeting mechanism, the university has established an elected Faculty Senate. In 1971, its viability still remains to be tested, but its large size (226 plus ex officio members) and its parochial representative base in the several departments do not augur well for sensitive and productive discussions or wise decisions.

Elected and appointed faculty committees are entrusted with major decision-making responsibilities at the University of Wisconsin. The most powerful of these is the University Committee; it reviews most of the key academic matters and it recommends actions to both the faculty and the administration. Only well-known and respected faculty members have been elected to this prestigious office. Since the University Commitee sees its role (in part) as one of keeping the administration in line, and since it performs that role on many occasions, the committee acts fundamentally as the conscience of the faculty. The university has seen fit to implement the work of this and other major committees by providing office space, secretarial staff, permanent files, and the like. The basic intent of these steps was to strengthen faculty operations, although there are some incidental benefits to the administration. A few cynics, however, have been known to refer to the University Committee as an arm of the administration.

Moreover, in the important arena of faculty tenure, campus-wide faculty committees are more or less sovereign. Each professor who aspires to tenure must pass muster through one of four faculty divisional committees, elected by the faculties of the respective divisions. Seldom have tenured professors been released at Wisconsin for any cause. A few have been encouraged to go elsewhere but these informal agreements do not become a matter of public record. In 1971, however, three tenured professors at the University of Wisconsin (Milwaukee) are under formal dismissal charges. It is plain that the university community is no longer willing to support preposterous conduct from tenured professors. If the principle of academic freedom is to be sustained in the face of a disenchanted public, faculty review bodies who take their charge seriously are essential.

Academics have insisted that evidence of research and scholarly productivity be the principal criterion in evaluating candidates for tenure; they assume that in order to communicate ideas and concepts professors should be involved in the creation of knowledge. This is an old and revered tradition and all great universities pay homage to it in one way or another. The upshot is that quality teaching is only a secondary consideration; tenure candidates are rarely labeled as poor teachers. Excellent teaching (as reported by students and colleagues) is hardly the kind of hard evidence which will carry a person through the tough scrutiny of a divisional committee. Service counts for naught; in fact it may have a negative connotation if a case is built around this single criterion. Publish or perish is the order of the day.

My experience on the Honorary Degrees Committee is instructive in helping to explain how faculty committees control most academic decisions. I have served on this particular committee for five years. It has thirty-one members: Sixteen are elected by the divisional faculties, ten are appointed by the chancellor, and five are administrative officials ex officio. The committee meets about twice a year to nominate a small number of distinguished persons, principally scholars, for honorary degrees at the June commencement. These nominations must be approved by a three-fourths vote at a faculty meeting. The chairman ends up doing most of the labor since he has to secure the nominations, chair the discussions, write appropriate praiseworthy statements, and deliver them orally at the June ceremonies. It is a well-established tradition that those eligible for this award are persons with some Wisconsin experience. The members of the committee are conscientious and competent, and they produce a first-rate slate. The Regents eventually approve the final recommendations and may, if they wish, delete names.

Although the Honorary Degrees Committee is not a good illustration of faculty power because it performs a one-time task, it does demonstrate faculty influence on academic matters. The faculty determines who obtains an honorary degree from Wisconsin; its veto power in this respect is absolute. The point to remember is that the university is honeycombed with similar faculty committees, each overseeing a specific matter. Coordination and communication are therefore cumbersome and difficult. The university is not a well-organized bureaucracy with clear lines of authority and responsibility. Not incidentally, most faculty members believe that this open environment is a great strength rather than a weakness.

The administrator best situated to insure that the important missions of the university are implemented is the department chairman. He should be one of the most highly respected professors in the department; when he is not, shudders are felt throughout the entire university structure. It is not the kind of assignment one can do with his left hand while carrying out all the normal professorial duties of teaching, research, and service. At Wisconsin the chairman is elected annually by members of his own department. The election is technically advisory to a dean, but the option to reject a departmental recommendation is rarely exercised. The reasons are obvious—the department is not overjoyed if its choice is ignored, other professors may be reluctant to take over the reins under these less than ideal conditions, and the dean has publicly offended a professor before his colleagues. If intervention is seen as necessary, it is better for the dean to discuss the issue informally with a number of professors in the department before lines have hardened. Needless to say, departments do not wish to be advised in this manner; faculty are likely to interpret the action as an unethical intrusion into departmental affairs.

It is the academic department, not the extensive faculty committee structure, that finally regulates the important levers in a professor's life. The department decides on original appointments, initiates tenure or dismissal proceedings, decides on nonretention of faculty in probationary status, recommends salary increases and promotions, makes teaching assignments, assigns clerical assistance, selects graduate fellows and assistants, and the like. In short, the department's evaluation of a professor is central in determining his success or failure. If the department considers a nontenured professor mediocre, his life at the university will be short. Even a tenured professor cannot escape major penalties (salary consideration is one) if he is downgraded by his departmental colleagues.

Legally, the influence of the department is not quite so complete.

Most of these "powers" must be approved and sanctioned by a dean, elected faculty committees, the chancellor, the president of the university, and ultimately the Regents. Still, in practice, the academic department is almost autonomous. It has the authority of expertise. Who is better placed to judge the competence of a professor than his own peers? Any academic administrator who dares to meddle in this process is destined to have a trying time. Academics may not agree with each other, but they will rally together whenever an outsider challenges their own special prerogatives.

Any privileged class ought to be monitored to some extent, but unfortunately our system is not designed for monitors. The privileges and immunities of the professorship outweigh all other considerations. In fact, the University of Wisconsin is so decentralized in its administrative structure that it must rely for whatever success it achieves on the integrity and good sense of individual professors. Almost all specialists in public administration assert that the operating level is where most decisions should be made. On this one administrative principle, at least, Wisconsin receives high marks. However, the state legislature in particular says the university is too decentralized in its authority, and it urges that there be a single strong leader to make decisions. By tradition, we have gone the other way at Wisconsin, and we condemn the industrial model recommended by the legislature, by some Regents, and by those outsiders who do not seem to understand how a university operates.

The department chairman who speaks for his specialist colleagues ought to be the most talented line officer in the department. Standard bureaucracies would place their most promising executives in these positions. Sometimes we do; more often we do not. The gradual erosion of this position has contributed to a leadership vacuum which has done incomparable harm to the administrative arm of the university. The number of mishandled matters increases, sending more students and other disaffected persons over the head of the department chairman in order to unsnarl their problems.

To understand the delicate nuances of the professor's world one must distinguish between the professor as an individual and as a member of a department. The stars of the academic firmament are those who publish in the journals in which articles are reviewed anonymously by experts and who are nationally prominent in their disciplines; locally we bestow chaired professorships on them. Their high visibility brings them lucrative consultancies, famous fellowship grants, advisory trips to Washington, and numerous other awards. The university would be a sorry place without men of this distinction. But such a person is not likely to accept a department chairmanship where he will be forced to deal with the details of administration—answering departmental mail, approving travel vouchers, adjudicating quarrels among colleagues, supervising preparation of the timetable, submitting endless reports to various authorities, and a melange of other unexciting duties.

The university might well survive the ill effects of its loose structure if it were not for the mammoth size and influence of many departments. Departments frequently act like feudal baronies in their attempts to obtain as large a share as possible of the available resources. Those whose subject matter appeals to external funding sources have been able to expand easily, sometimes irresponsibly; it is no secret that soft money departments open up innumerable opportunities for a professor to serve his own personal ends at the expense of the university. When austerity budgets are put into effect, individuals supported by external (nonstate) funds are not affected. This double standard prevents equal treatment to all professors; those on grants are privileged to continue their activities without limitations while those on state funds are forced to make the sacrifices.

Academic departments, by definition, are discipline-oriented rather than problem-centered; as a result the university has formed a number of institutes and centers to deal with interdisciplinary concerns. These institutes have proliferated so that they almost outnumber the academic departments. Institutes often make it easier to obtain external funding, but they create innumerable complications. Tenured professors attached to an institute are usually paid out of grant funds but they have a position in some department. A mortgage against that department's budget thus exists, and it may be claimed at any time in the future. Institute and center professors may be only peripherally related to a department; therefore, they may not get top consideration for merit salary increases or promotion. In compensation for this possible disadvantage, they generally have access to more graduate assistants, more travel allowances, and more research time. At best, institutes and centers tend to be awkward administrative devices, and seldom are they satisfactorily integrated into the mainstream of university life.

Since many department chairmen see their function as maintenance of the status quo, executive leadership, by default, may have to come from deans and higher administrators. But even here there are problems. Faculty advisory committees are formed to recommend candidates for any important academic line office which becomes vacant. In this sense the faculty chooses all its own administrators. Candidates who emerge from the screening tests are likely to be competent but not necessarily distinguished or imaginative. At Wisconsin all academic deans, all chancellors, the vice-president, and the president hold tenure in some department and are, therefore, legitimately qualified as professors. Nevertheless, acceptance of a high administrative post carries with it the implication that one is deserting a higher calling. Columbia University President William McGill felt obliged to explain carefully why he accepted the presidency: "What would impel a person in full possession of his faculties to take on the responsibilities of a college presidency in these times? Three years ago I was an honest academic. I worked in a rather remote area of mathematical psychology. I was serious about my work and deeply attached to it. Yet in only three years I have formed a similarly deep commitment to what I am about to do. I gave up my work because three years ago I saw that the scholarly tradition I revere, the kind of humane society I want to build, are threatened as they have never been threatened before, at least in my lifetime."[3]

To many of the faculty a dean or a chancellor is something of a pariah, an overpaid and glorified paper shuffler. But publics like the Regents, the state legislature, and the ordinary citizenry expect decisive and tough leadership from these officials and are disenchanted with the methodological niceties and elegant reasoning processes by which academics have traditionally arrived at solutions to problems.

Another grave and discouraging aspect of university administration is its lack of continuity. In the five years I have served as dean of the School of Education, we have had three different chancellors and every vice-chancellor who was here when I arrived has left. No one has stayed long enough to set his own style of leadership; this takes at least five years. How are we as university administrators able to develop a coherent program when our superiors are constantly leaving for better or more pleasurable positions? It requires time to build the mutual confidence between an administrator and his superior which allows the former to take the risk of launching into new projects which are certain to cause static. Experience has taught me that it requires a great deal of energy to engineer a modest program change in a university; it takes immense courage to launch a number of new projects on widely different fronts over a short time span. In fact, if people like myself did not have the security of a tenured professorship, they probably would initiate less than they do now. The condemnation of administrators as pusillanimous seriously oversimplifies the circumstances under which they are forced to labor. Many of the problems administrators have been unable to solve were completely beyond their control and not of their own making. When will it become apparent that it would be more useful to change the system rather than the men who try to make it go?

I admit that I may have exaggerated a bit in describing the low level to which administrators have fallen. It is apparent to me that our administrators still have some room for creative activity in the area of new programs, for the simple reason that they are budgetarily responsible for comparatively large sums of money and are able to exercise some option in expending these funds. What I have related about established departments is accurate, but I think there is some room for administrative maneuver in the area of new funds and new programs and, indeed, new departments. For example, the dean of the College of Letters and Science worked last summer to assemble a new department of black studies. While it is true that the faculty decided to have such a department, it is equally true that the faculty has had very little to do with actually staffing it. This has been the responsibility of the dean.

Students as a group have not been seriously engaged in the governing process of the university. They have been treated as merely temporary clients of the organization. Student government has been viewed as harmless and irrelevant to the central purposes of the university. But it has now become painfully evident that some students, at least, are no longer willing to accept the status of lower participants in university life. That many mature and responsible students have withdrawn from the struggle is obvious. Only a small number (approximately 4,000 of the 33,000 eligible students) generally chose to vote in elections for student body president. Most distressing is the tendency on the part of activist students to uncritically accept the statements of revolutionaries like Abbie Hoffman and Jerry Rubin. These same students adopt demagogic professors as heroes. Very little constructive advice is likely to emerge from these irresponsible professorial models. The antics of those few students who engaged in trashing and bombing (vandalism masquerading as social idealism) are particularly repelling.

I firmly believe that students should have an active part in planning their educational experiences; common sense dictates that the consumer ought to be allowed to express some preferences of his own. Implementation of this idea is not easy; no one seems to know just how to select a representative student. If the Wisconsin Student Association makes the appointment, one can expect the student representative to trade on style rather than substance. If an administrator appoints a student with impeccable credentials, the activist will accuse the administration of cooptation and the student of being a captive pet.

The worst aspect of Wisconsin Student Association appointments is that they produce committee members who represent a fixed position, vote as a block, never listen to or weigh the merits of the evidence, and walk out if the committee judgment is not for them. At the worst, we end up with majority and minority reports, with the students plus a few sympathetic faculty members on one side and the stronger-minded faculty on the other. Occasionally the Wisconsin Student Association makes good appointments; these individuals are likely to be volunteers.

Participation by students on important faculty committees can be valuable, particularly if they are allowed to vote and make motions. I am now serving on the Campus Planning Committee with a very bright student. He consistently comes to meetings prepared, raises very penetrating questions, contributes to the discussions, and does not hesitate to make motions. His presence makes a difference in the quality of the decisions reached. At no time does he evince any tendency to join the establishment. However, he has the courtesy to listen to evidence, weigh its merits, vote accordingly, and accept defeat graciously when his position is not upheld. Serious participation of this type is much more significant than the childish posturing before the microphone or television camera which seems to captivate many young activists. But the prospect that Wisconsin students will choose to seek incremental improvements through such reasonably stable channels does not look promising, even though faculty and administration are eager to share their decision-making power. To the student all our bureaucratic paraphernalia is anachronistic and revolting; likewise the faculty resents the rude behavior and superficial rhetoric engaged in by many student leaders. To paraphrase Pogo, we are ready for the students but are they ready for us?

Since the late sixties, our immediate governing body, the Board of Regents, has assumed a more direct role in academic governance. Under great pressure from the politicians, they have begun to monitor the internal affairs of the university more frequently and with greater impact; they are acting like rulers rather than rubber stamps. Inasmuch as the Regents do not have a permanent staff of their own and can at best give only limited time and attention to the details of university affairs, it is the president of the university who must serve as the chief linke between the faculty and the Regents. Since the president is both the chief executive of the university and the professional advisor to the Board of Regents, and since he is expected to ask his board members for advice and guidance, it is imperative that there be mutual confidence and respect between the Regents and the president.

If the board of regents has genuine confidence in the ability of the president to administer the university, and if the president has faith in the ability and dedication of the Regents, knotty problems are resolved without great difficulty. However, if confidence is absent, there exists no foundation upon which to build improved relationships. In such event, the university must have either a new president or a different Board of Regents. It will almost certainly get a new president. Members of the Board of Regents, by virtue of gubernatorial appointment, are eminently more powerful than the president of the university, who holds his appointment at their pleasure. The resignation of Harrington as president of the University of Wisconsin probably was tendered in response to these pressures.

At lower administrative level, the Board of Regents is unable to tell an academic department how to conduct its affairs. The Regents have access to some strong punitive measures (reducing the salary of an unpopular professor), and they are free to harass their own underlings, the central administration, but there are too many protective layers between the Regents and individual professors to create much anxiety among the regular faculty. The tenured professor will continue to do what he wants to do. I believe that Regents have no greater impact on junior faculty, even during a tight job market. The Regents have many invaluable services to perform on behalf of the university—representing the university to its many external publics, acting as buffer for the president, evaluating the effectivenes of the administration, and securing funds from the legislature. If they carry out these critical responsibilities creditably the university will move forward.

The University of Wisconsin cannot long retain its deserved reputation for excellence without adequate funding. Our professors are already poorly paid in comparison with their Big Ten colleagues. The golden years of the early and middle sixties are behind us, and we have to contend with a miscellany of bureaucrats and politicians who are in a position to use official forms of intimidation in terms of justifications for expenditures of funds, in terms of accounting procedures, and in terms of purpose and mission. The University of Wisconsin has to have its budget reviewed by the Regents, the Coordinating Council for Higher Education, the governor, the Joint Finance Committee of the legislature, and, finally, the legislature as a whole. At each of these review levels, the budget may be reduced no matter how austere and defensible it is. The university does not just compete for state funds with other governmental programs; the various systems of higher education (University of Wisconsin, Wisconsin State Universities, and the Board of Vocational, Technical and Adult Education) all seek the same limited tax dollars. To prevent excessive intersystem competition, the Coordinating Council for Higher Education was formed. The CCHE has had a fairly rocky road; a vote in the Joint Finance Committee of the legislature to abolish CCHE failed by the margin of one vote.

CCHE's role is written in statutory language that, if taken literally, makes it virtual czar of higher education in Wisconsin. In its early history, restricted by a limited staff and probably unsure of itself, CCHE seldom imposed much more than a nominal review of the university's requests.

Under the lash of the state legislature where it had been perceived as an integral part of the education lobby, CCHE began to refuse some of the university's program requests and to make substantial cuts in its proposed budgets. This trend was reversed when CCHE simply forwarded the university's 1971–1973 budget as submitted with only minor modifications. The CCHE staff is so weak that it lacks the ability to insure that its recommendations are approved by its own governing body.

The most fearsome threat to the university's future is not CCHE nor the governor of Wisconsin but the state legislature. This conservative body is well aware of the political climate and cultural ethos of Wisconsin, and it recognizes that the ordinary citizen is angry with the university. Student riots and bombings, reputed light work loads of professors, and the heavy taxes needed to maintain the institution have combined to make the university a popular target for ambitious politicians. The university is vulnerable because it is dependent for funds on sources outside itself. Without doubt the legislature is going to continue its incursions on the university. Legislators are buttressed by expert staff assistance, and they know how to raise hard questions at budget hearings. However, the university still has a huge reservoir of good will throughout the state. It is unlikely that the average Wisconsin native will allow his great university to degenerate into a second-rate institution.

A significant group which is often ignored by analysts of the higher education scene is the alumni. The University of Wisconsin has a very active alumni association; it publishes an interesting journal, its alumni clubs are well organized, and it is well administered. The Wisconsin Alumni Association does its best to explain and defend the university. Nevertheless, too many former students never make contributions to the university and are quick to renounce it when it is in trouble. Our alumni, it seems, are more concerned about the fortunes of the football team than about safeguarding the heart and soul of the university, its academic integrity.

It requires no special clairvoyance to identify the issues which threaten the future of the University of Wisconsin. Predictions about how troublesome issues will be resolved over the short run can be made with considerable certainty. For instance, it appears that the state legislature intends to try to correct what it considers the major deficiency at the university—the breakdown of institutional authority—by reducing state appropriations. Since the university has failed to a greater or lesser degree to satisfy even its internal publics, outside forces can be expected to step in and assert their authority. This response pattern has a familiar ring to it; organizations of all types under stress are subjected to similar pressures. In the long run, however, external interventions are counterproductive;

they do not lead to reorganization of the university. After a measure of order returns, the university must still correct itself; change, if it is to be successful, has to be generated from inside the institution.

Are there any ready answers, or must we sit and watch the gradual attrition of a great university? Most critics offer few concrete proposals for saving it except through punitive measures. I also reject the frequent pleas for participatory democracy, by which is meant that everyone is consulted about everything and no one is charged with the power and responsibility to make decisions. The university is not a utopian community of equals run on pure democratic principles; it is an authoritative institution where professors are expected to know more than students. Presidential commissions, more police on campus, tough administrators, radicalized students, or vindictive legislators are unable to attack the causes of our unhappy condition. It is the faculty which must assert itself; if the faculty insists, as it always has, that it is the central power it ought to exercise its power. Otherwise, others less qualified and less sympathetic to teaching and scholarship will fill the vacuum.

For example, if the faculty were to issue a statement admitting that it has sorely neglected undergraduate education (which is true) and that it is now disposed to make a complete effort to rectify this abuse, the effect would be dramatic. Improving undergraduate education is not all that difficult; we have the knowledge base, but we have expended our energies in other directions. Young undergraduates need to interact with the disciplined scholarship of mature professors. Instead, in their early college years they are exposed almost exclusively to inexperienced teaching assistants who sometimes have debased the importance of teaching by missing classes, joining picket lines, destroying the curriculum (for example, by discussing the Vietnam war in a statistics course), and elevating their own insecurities by masquerading as educational reformers. Undergraduates have a right to be disillusioned and disaffected. When the TAA struck the university in the spring of 1970, it made educational reform the pivotal issue in order to secure support from the undergraduates; at settlement time, typical union concerns such as work load, grievance procedures, and job rights became dominant. Students must realize that discipline is essential if we are to strengthen the university. There need to be rules that are enforced. Society will not tolerate anything less.

More disturbing and ultimately more destructive than student disaffection has been the inability of the faculty to police its own membership. The faculty must realize that there are limits to their freedom; they are like any other member of society in this respect. Protected by tenure, too many professors have been allowed by their colleagues to prostitute the

image of the professoriat by dull teaching, indifferent and sterile service
to the university, mediocre research, and other improprieties which would
be grounds for severe discipline in other professions. We have been too
lenient toward the few who have taken unfair advantage of an honest
professor's deserved freedoms. In 1971, a committee is being formed to
address the matter of faculty responsibility; here is evidence that the
faculty at Wisconsin is awakening to the need for the exercise of initiative
by its responsible segments. The United Faculty, an association formed
principally by younger professors with a reformist bent, has issued a number of position papers. Small in size and unrepresentative, it lacks the
power to shepherd a program of action through the innumerable check
points in our administrative machinery. The major hope for reviving the
institution lies with the stalwarts of the faculty, those hard-working individuals loyal to the institution and proud of their own integrity who
scorn the pettiness of faculty politics.

What kinds of support can the faculty rightfully expect from its
administrators? First, despite mounting pressures from the general public
for strong deans and strong presidents, with courage enough to bear
down on errant professors and anarchistic students, the traditional Wisconsin administrator is the best ally the faculty member has. As a full-
fledged member of the faculty himself, the administrator understands and
appreciates the role of professor, and his position in the hierarchy enables
him to defend the faculty member's interests when necessary and appropriate. Second, most administrators I know would welcome expressions of
interest and concern about how to improve the education of our students;
moreover, they would follow through and try to implement meritorious
ideas. The common complaint of my fellow administrators is the tendency
for the faculty to use its veto power by scuttling reform proposals, whether
offered by the administration or faculty committees. Instead the faculty
should counter with better plans.

The administrator is helpless without the support of the faculty.
Often severely maligned for failing to take intellectual positions on every
isssue which confronts him, the university administrator needs a measure
of respect and sound counsel from his faculty colleagues if he is to survive.
General lack of appreciation of the range and importance of the tasks he
has to perform has eroded the fragile authority which an academic administrator must have if he is to serve his university effectively. The university is being pushed for obvious reasons in the direction of more
affirmative administrative authority. Without such authority the university
cannot prosper.

Too long, perhaps, we have venerated the absent-minded tweedy
apolitical professor (who probably never existed) who romantically spent

his lifetime explicating the works of an obscure poet. At the same time we caricatured the jejune contributions of the pettifogging administrator sometimes humorously and sometimes malevolently. Today's professor is no humble Mr. Chips. He is first of all a dedicated careerist wedded to his discipline; he is more at home with a briefcase on an airplane than with an umbrella on a leisurely stroll around campus. The ablest of administrators are needed to cope with this new breed. Faculty must support the notion that chairmen and deans have a responsibility to control faculty in clearly defined respects; anarchy on campus is no more viable than anarchy on the city streets.

At the University of Wisconsin, we do not need to abolish tenure or make some other dramatic gesture in order to make substantive gains; if the faculty were simply to select better department chairmen and hold them rigorously responsible for performance as administrators rather than as all-purpose academics, the effect on the quality of our administration would be electrifying. Presidents, chancellors, and deans are essentially and properly oriented toward planning and establishing overall priorities. It is the department chairman who works intimately with his faculty colleagues in the day-to-day business of running the university. If he permits his department to degenerate into disorganization, the entire university will be paralyzed.

Notes

1 I have benefited from the sharp criticisms of David Fellman, Charles W. Loomer, and John Palmer of the University of Wisconsin. The biases expressed, however, are entirely my own.

2 E. H. Litchfield, "Notes on a General Theory of Administration," *Administrative Science Qcarterly*, 1956, *1*, 1–29.

3 W. J. McGill, "Commitment to Columbia," *Columbia Forum*, 1970, *13*, 25–26.

CHAPTER 3

●●●●●●●●●●●●●●●●
●●●●●●●●●●●●●●●●
●●●●●●●●●●●●●●●●

FACULTY GOVERNANCE
AND ADMINISTRATION

Durward Long

●●●●●●●●●●●●●●●●
●●●●●●●●●●●●●●●●
●●●●●●●●●●●●●●●●

Since 1900, the University of Wisconsin has developed an image and reputation of prestige and greatness that few institutions ever attain. The university's standing among the world's institutions of higher learning is largely the result of substantive traditions and practices which emphasize academic freedom, an extraordinary degree of faculty governance, and an unwavering commitment to quality and excellence in instruction, research, and public service. These traditions and practices have been influential throughout higher education, perhaps due to Wisconsin's consistently high production of doctorates. Literally thousands of new Ph.D.s from Wisconsin have gone into other colleges and universities to imitate the Wisconsin pattern of governance. The degree to which these graduates have understood that pattern probably varies quite widely. But in the folklore of academe Wisconsin's governance system is synonymous with an ideal of faculty decision-making and administration which has often exceeded the most ambitious standards of national organizations of professors. From this image, an ideal of faculty democracy has emerged and become prominent in higher education.

The University of Wisconsin (enrolling about seventy thousand students) is one of the two large public systems of higher education in the state. The other system, the Wisconsin State Universities, also enrolls about seventy thousand students. Each system is governed by a separate board of regents, and each is composed of several units. The University of Wisconsin consists of six separate organizational units, each administered by a chancellor and each with a somewhat different mission. These units are UW–Madison, UW–Milwaukee, UW Extension, UW Center System, UW–Green Bay, and UW–Parkside. The system is administered by a president and a number of vice-presidents and other support officers. The president is the chief executive officer who is responsible to the governing board, the Board of Regents of the University of Wisconsin, for the total administration of the university.

The administrative structure appears to be clear and forthright. In actuality, however, like that of other universities, the administrative system must be viewed as an integral part of the total governance system. At Wisconsin, that governance system is a complex of faculty organization, precedents, traditions, and values. The faculty governance system also appears on the surface as a unique type of federal system (see Figure 1). A Faculty Assembly of sixty-seven delegates from the six units serves as the "federal" legislative body; a Faculty Council, constituted by categorical membership from each unit faculty's executive committee, serves as the Assembly's executive committee; together these two groups serve as the spokesmen for the whole university faculty. Within each unit the faculty theoretically organizes and governs itself in ways of its choosing— unless it contradicts all-university legislation.

The faculty governance pattern includes the administration as the officials responsible for implementing faculty decisions and policies (see Figure 2). In effect, the administration is viewed as the handmaiden of faculty governance. The theory maintains that administrators (chairmen, deans, vice-chancellors, chancellors, vice-presidents, president) are first among equals, but the faculty in fact rarely regards them in that way. Complicating the structure is the fact that the governing board and the state legislature view the administrative officials as "implementers" of their decisions and policies. Although this is not unique in higher education, the Wisconsin style of interrelationships of these roles of faculty governance and administrative accountability may well be. A review of some of the historical context may contribute to a better understanding of how it came to be.

At the turn of the century, the university's governance structure was fairly simple. Each faculty member of professional rank (assistant professor and higher) was a member of a departmental faculty, a college

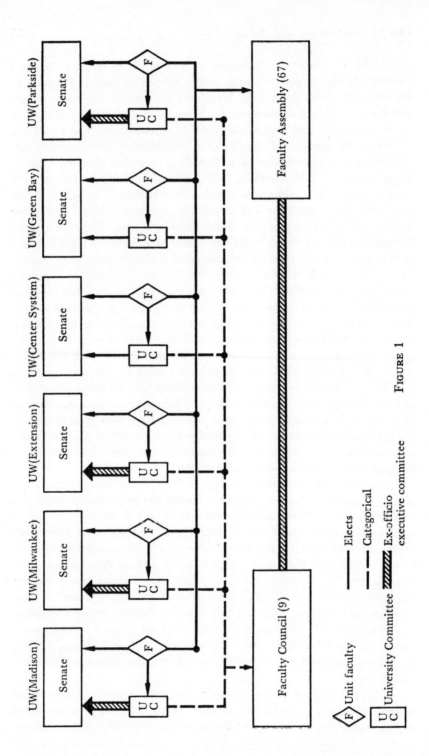

FIGURE 1

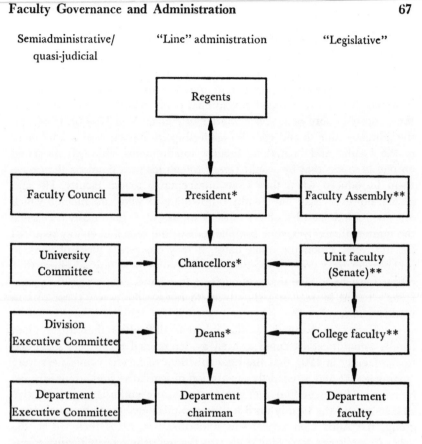

Semiadministrative/   "Line" administration   "Legislative"
quasi-judicial

——— Directive or legislative power

— — "Advisory" relationships

*May appoint special study or administrative committees
**Usually has a number of faculty semiadministrative committees

FIGURE 2

faculty, and the University Faculty. Theoretically at least, each of these faculties dealt with educational matters that pertained to the respective faculty. Each organizational grouping had an administrative officer (chairman, dean, president) responsible for executing policies which had been drawn by the appropriate faculty. In addition to the administrative officer, each department and college and the University Faculty had standing or special committees which often assumed administrative as well as policy-determining functions.

By 1900, the university had already gained some reputation for academic freedom and departmental autonomy. But the institutionalization of many of the values which have become sacred traditions at Wisconsin occurred during the presidency of Charles R. Van Hise (1903–1918). Apparently, Van Hise was a strong leader whose academic experience had led him to some very definite views about meaningful faculty governance. For example, he felt the wisest form of governance was one in which the faculty initiated educational policy which the Regents would then approve more or less as a matter of course. Van Hise believed that the administrator should exercise leadership in making recommendations to the faculty and in making faculty appointments, although he stated on one occasion that he would rather forego his own opinions than have them introduced when they were unacceptable to the faculty. He suggested, however, that "the faculty is unwilling to follow the method which any good administrative officer must, if successful. If the faculty do handle the matters themselves, they complain about the time and energy required for the work. Upon the other hand, if they delegate a piece of work to a chairman or a committee, they are not content as any administrative officer must be to give that committee a free hand, asking only that satisfactory results be secured—they want to reserve the power constantly to modify and regulate."[1]

Van Hise focused on the inherent difficulties that arose when faculty committees executed as well as determined policy. He suggested to the faculty in 1907 that the dual functions of faculty committees were "extravagant" and advised the separation of legislative and administrative functions. His suggestion did not generate any enthusiasm or effective change among the faculty until a state-commissioned study by an external group, the Allen Committee, was undertaken in 1915. Included in the Allen Committee's topics for study was the use of university faculty members' time. Partly in response to the threat of that committee, the faculty appointed a special Committee on Organization of the Faculty. In the report of the latter, it was recommended that the faculty devote its main attention to "policy-determining" and "as far as possible, the determination and execution of matters of administrative routine should be made through committees and representatives." Attempting to clarify the relationship of administrators and faculty in executing policy, the report urged that faculty members be "called upon freely for advice and counsel concerning policies but that the execution of these policies should be entrusted to administrative officials."[2]

Underlining the position that the faculty should determine educational policy, the Committee on Organization of the Faculty recommended that a new standing committee be created to keep the faculty informed of all actions affecting the educational interests and policies of the university in order to bring important educational questions to the faculty. It was also recommended that the president, deans, and the secretary of the faculty serve as the Administrative Committee whose primary responsibility would be to prepare the calendar of faculty meetings and to supervise the execution of such administrative or routine matters which the University Faculty might commit to the secretary of the faculty. The Committee on Organization of the Faculty further recommended that "University Faculty business which shall be chiefly administrative in character whether done by individuals or by committees whom the president shall appoint, shall be performed under the general directions of the secretary of the University Faculty." In effect, the latter officer, rather than deans or the president, became the executive officer of the faculty. The University Committee was created as a watchdog committee over the Board of Visitors and Regents as well as over the deans and the president. The Administrative Committee, at the direction of the secretary of the faculty, set the faculty calendar. The 1916 recommendations of the Committee on Organization of the Faculty were approved, and the institutionalization of dual systems of administration was set. The basic structure and machinery preserving the duality has persisted.

The next significant effort to review the overall governance of the university occurred in 1947–1949. Partly as a result of the postwar deluge of students (enrollment jumped from ten thousand to almost twenty-four thousand in one year), the Regents directed that a study be made of the functions and policies of the university. A faculty Committee on University Functions and Policies was assigned the task. The first part of its report focused on the university's role in the state's educational system; the second part, completed in late 1949, dealt with internal matters. A major section of the second part described the university's committee structure and made recommendations to improve its role in governing the institution. At that date there were forty standing university committees, a substantial number of special or ad hoc university-wide committees, standing and special committees of the several colleges, four divisional committees (for reviewing new courses and tenure promotions), numerous deparmental committees and a variety of interdepartmental and intercollege committees.

Although the study committee pointed out that the "basic objective of dependence upon faculty committees is the preservation of a democratically run university" and the achievement of "monetary economy," it was concerned that committee work diverted "too much faculty energy from instruction and research," that too little attention was "given by the faculty to matters of first-rate university-wide educational policy," and that the structure did not give "younger faculty members and students adequate opportunity" in developing university policies.

The study recommended a reduction in the number of standing

committees, the assumption of repetitive administrative tasks by administrative personnel, and the widening of participation in committee work. It recommended that faculty committees concentrate on policy matters and suggested that "in general" the administrative officers of the university were "experienced educators who can be presumed to possess good judgement on educational questions." The study further exhorted the University Committee to be more active "in considering university educational policies of major importance and reporting thereon to the faculty and the administration," and recommended that the University Committee's powers be interpreted more broadly as they related to initiating studies and recommendations on educational policy.

The 1949 report also found that the office of the secretary of the faculty was a part of the offices of student personnel services, quite contrary to the purposes enunciated by the 1916–1917 committee recommendations, and it suggested that the office be attached to the office of the president and the functions of the secretary be reorganized.[3]

Although the report of the Committee on University Functions and Policies was probably the most thorough substantive internal study of the university, the pattern of governance was improved very little. It is true that faculty committees were reduced in number for a brief time and that certain advice and recommendations concerning interdisciplinary research were followed. The University Committee's role in the scheme of things was strengthened and the office of the secretary of the faculty was made part of the president's office. For a brief period following 1950, there were efforts to distinguish between executing policy (by administrative personnel) and determining policy (by the faculty). But the basic faculty statutes remained as flexible and as unclear as ever on the dual administrative pattern.

The structure of the university in 1950 was very similar to that devised in 1916–1917 despite the changing conditions. Each department was governed by its members; each college was governed by faculty of its several departments, and the whole University Faculty governed in institution-wide matters. In addition to the administrative officers of each organizational unit (chairmen, dean, president) each instructional department or program had an executive committee of tenured members; the University Faculty had the secretary of the faculty as an executive officer and the University Committee as its spokesman. Moreover, each college and the University Faculty had a significant number of standing committees with administrative and semiadministrative functions.

The ambiguities of relationships between the various administrative officers and committees and the faculty bodies which gave them legitimacy might have been tolerable if the university had remained a

single-campus institution as it was in 1950. The dual systems of administration, never resolved in days of lesser size and complexity, continued in
an exaggerated fashion as a multicampus university developed. "Who
governs?" became an even more crucial and more difficult question to
answer.

The first step in the direction of a multiple institution occurred
in 1955 when Wisconsin State College at Milwaukee and University Extension's Milwaukee center were merged to constitute the University of
Wisconsin at Milwaukee. Headed by a provost, the new unit was administratively responsible to the Madison operation, that is, to the president.
Although the state law which enabled the merger prescribed that the new
unit would have the "same degree of self-government by its own faculty
as is vested in other units of the university," in reality mechanisms were
developed which ensured that the Madison system of governance would
be applied in Milwaukee. Ties at the departmental, college, support services, and governance level assured Milwaukee's development along
Madison lines.

Nine years after the Milwaukee merger and well before its full
assimiliation, the university created four additional organizational units.
The Extension Division was separated from Madison and became a new
unit to coordinate and implement all extension activities of all university
units throughout the state. The eleven resident extension centers became
a new system of two-year transfer campuses called the Center System, and
plans were laid for the development of two new degree-granting campuses
to be based on six of the Center Campuses. In 1968, two of the centers,
located in the densely populated area south of Milwaukee, became the
University of Wisconsin at Parkside, and four of the centers, located in
the populated northeast, in and around Green Bay, became the University
of Wisconsin at Green Bay.

The UW–Milwaukee development set a pattern for faculty governance for the new organization. The pattern was drawn from Madison
governance institutions, traditions, and values. The device of a University
Committee, prominent in the Madison scheme, was applied initially by
the creation of an All-University Committee to oversee the development
of the new campuses and units and to set governance patterns for the
entire university. The chairman of each unit's University Committee plus
an additional member from Madison and from Milwaukee constituted the
All-University Committee. Needless to say, Madison's prestige, power, and
institutionalized methods dominated; some would say that the Madison
values and emphasis on the graduate and research function also dominated.

The All-University Committee became the University Faculty

Council in 1966 with three members from Madison, two from Milwaukee, and one each from University Extension and the Center System. Four of the seven were chairmen of the unit University Committees; two extra members from Madison and one additional member from Milwaukee were elected during the early years. With the beginning of Parkside and Green Bay in 1968, the council's membership was increased to nine to include the University Committee chairmen from the two new units. The election of the extra Madison and Milwaukee members was also replaced by a categorical requirement that they too be members of their University Committees. The functions of the council, proposed by the All-University Committee, then endorsed by each unit University Committee and approved by the unit faculties as a university statute, are: to *consider* "questions concerning the educational interests or educational policies of the university"; to *examine* "any actions taken respecting the units by the Board of Regents, Board of Visitors, the various faculty or faculty committees or by any of the other bodies or individuals related to the university"; to *act* as a faculty hearing committee in case of charges; to *consult* "with administrative officers on budget matters"; to *prepare* "the agenda of occasional meetings of the university faculty"; to *report* "annually to the university faculty upon matters transacted during the preceding year"; to *advise* "on procedures which involve the faculty in making nominations for appointments to major administrative positions"; to *advise* "on procedures which involve the faculty in making decisions on the organization or reorganization of interdepartmental or interdisciplinary programs of instruction, research, and service, or the creation of new colleges, schools, or institutes."[4]

The Faculty Council, acting as an all-university faculty executive committee and with the assistance of unit faculties, drew up regulations which created an all-university legislative body, the Faculty Assembly. The total membership of sixty-seven was composed of thirty-eight members from Madison, ten from Milwaukee, ten from University Extension, and three each from the Center System, Parkside, and Green Bay. Madison was given a significant majority (thirty-eight of sixty-seven) and the two graduate campuses maintained an overwhelming dominance (forty-eight of sixty-seven). The assembly was given authority "in matters which concern more than one unit of the university as a whole, on which it is necessary to have a uniform university policy." The words *concern* and *necessary* are not defined. Furthermore, although regulations provide that the assembly has no authority on matters which concern only a single unit faculty, the definition of these "matters" lies with the assembly. In another wonderful sweep of self-interest, the statutes provide that "in case of a conflict of jurisdiction between the University Faculty Assembly and any unit faculty, the decision shall rest with the University Faculty Assembly."

The statutes also provide that the assembly representatives from each unit shall be determined according to the size of its full-time faculty (professorial ranks plus instructors with tenure), but the proportionate formula is not specified in the statutes. Rather, the Faculty Council (as the ex officio executive committee of the assembly) is empowered to recommend the formula to the assembly every three years, and the assembly makes the final decision. A further restrictive, oligarchical provision gives to each University Committee the power to determine the internal apportionment of its assembly members and the method of their election. Such provisions are incredibly antidemocratic and unjust. Furthermore, although the assembly meets only twice a year, a vacancy in a unit's assembly delegation "is filled by a person selected by the appropriate unit University Committee."[5]

The language describing the functions of the University Faculty Council and the authority of the University Faculty Assembly is innocent enough, but like many faculty bodies at Wisconsin, each body becomes its own judiciary and executive in practice. The concept of self-interest which many faculty critics discover in business and government and occasionally among regents and trustees is not perceived by them when analyzing their own governing system. Conversely, in any conflict with administrative review, faculty groups appeal to faculty groups as referees. Administrators have no appeal procedure that offers any basis for objective or equitable judgment.

By the time the assembly was formed, the council had already adopted the Madison governance system as described in the statutes of that campus and slightly modified it into all-university legislation and, in effect, attempted to bring other units into conformity with the Madison mechanisms and style. In the other units, there were fewer senior faculty to exercise the leadership called for in the statutes, and therefore the Madison system was far less democratic in the new units than even in the Madison setting. It is to the credit of the administration and new faculty at Green Bay that they fought the complete imposition of the Madison pattern by developing academic units into "disciplinary concentrations," rather than departments. And it is to Milwaukee's credit that it resisted the council's efforts to force upon it at least one all-university search and screen committee for a Milwaukee deanship. Milwaukee's faculty also rejected the Madison general faculty device for legislating; it created a senate instead. Even Parkside succeeded in deviating slightly from the Madison organizational pattern. But these deviations were minor exceptions.

It is clear that the new units were not permitted to develop their governance and organizational system freely. The seventies probably will be spent by the non-Madison units trying to make practical adjustments to match their needs and conditions. Another tactic they may attempt to employ is the modification of the all-university regulations into more general substantive provisions and less detailed statutes.

A university central administration was created (really simply borrowed from Madison) to administer the new multiversity. Provosts (changed to chancellors in 1966) were to administer the units; they were directly responsible to the president of the university. Like the system of faculty governance, and perhaps as a natural outgrowth of the system, the role of the new central administration was not clarified. Equally neglected was the articulation of specific responsibilities and functions of the chief central administrative officers; who included nine vice-president by 1970. Ambiguous responsibilities and vague relationships between central administrators and unit campus administrators made efficient and effective operation nearly impossible. The nondirective, fragmented, self-defining administrative style traditionally applied at the departmental level was used to construct a central administrative pattern for a multiversity. In that pattern, there was no effort to distinguish between departmental colleagueship and functional relationships required in forming and implementing a variety of administrative tasks in a complex institution.

A confusing type of parallel administration without clear centralized coordination emerged. The central administration was not perceived as a team by the administrative officers in the several units; line and staff responsibilities of central officers were not distinguishable. Some officers who seemed to be presidential staff exercised line sanctions in relation to the several units. For example, the vice-president for business affairs exercised an informal line relationship to the major business officers of the six units; these business officers then exercised similar relationships to business managers within subunits. This and other functional staff or support offices tended to be autonomous from *academic* line administrators. They also tended to be further removed from the jurisdiction and influence of faculty governance and policy than were purely academic line administrators. Policy development seemed to emanate from staff officers of the president and regents and not from the unit chancellors or unit faculties.

The use of all-university committees by central administration is as chaotic as the interrelationships of central officers. On occasion, separate committees appointed by different vice-presidents have duplicated efforts on a single subject. More significantly, direct appointments by a vice-president of unit officers to an all-university committee frequently undercut the process of internal policy development within the units. Overlapping or uncertain jurisdiction is common for these all-university committees. For example, in 1970–1971, there were four committees dealing with computing sciences and equipment and data processing, but these committees had little if any coordination as to jurisdiction, function, or rationale.

Difficulties in administering and governing a multi-campus university are not unique to Wisconsin; thus, a discussion about some of the problems and patterns may prove instructive. One of these difficulties is the degree of uniformity required of all units. Although the University of Wisconsin's several units included more differences than similarities in specific program missions, from the outset the governance and administrative approach did little to allow for or encourage these differences. On the contrary, the approach was designed to bring uniformity in faculty governance and administrative patterns. The pattern, of course, was that of the Madison campus. This approach was a natural one and one which is quite common in higher education. It was assumed that the accomplishments, prestige, and productivity of the Madison campus were as much a result of the pattern of faculty governance and the practice of what might be styled "nonadministration" as of other institutional standards, values, and characteristics.

The Center System, a freshman-sophomore system with campuses and classes of very small size, reflects in microcosm the difficulties of the university in constructing an effective and democratic organization. Unlike Madison in size, mission, and professional opportunities, the Center System provides freshman and sophomore university course work, primarily in Letters and Science, which compares favorably with the same undergraduate work at the Madison campus. The curriculum emphasizes transfer preparation in Letters and Science as well as in the professional Schools of Agriculture, Business Education, Engineering, and Nursing, all of which require most of their freshman and sophomore work in Letters and Science. Despite its separate standing as a unit equal to the other five in determining its own internal affairs, a system of governance and an academic program specifically suited to its particular needs and conditions has been slow in coming, largely because of the dominance of the Madison institutional structures which were imposed on all units.

The administrative pattern followed by the Center System in attempting to develop a system for the several campuses (seven in 1971) within its organization reflects a pattern similar to that used by the university administration in developing a multi-unit institution. Each of the Center Campuses was to be administered by a campus dean (as distinct from a school or college dean) who was directly responsible to the chancellor of the Center System. But the campus deans' responsibility was never articulated or specified, formally or informally. As a result, each campus dean interpreted his role differently from the others, often according to the nature of the issue involved. (University statutes do not distinguish between a campus dean and a college dean.)

The basic operational program of each Center Campus included instruction, public information, student services, and business and administrative management. In an effort to retain systemwide instructional programs, each academic department was organized on a systemwide basis and administered by a chairman. The latter officer, appointed by the chancellor, without Center System faculty consultation in the early periods, was directly responsible to the chancellor. The selection of Madison and University Extension faculty to chair the Center System's academic department by joint appointments removed any prospect of a program unlike that of Madison. Intended to guarantee quality, the approach guaranteed only organizational uniformity.

In this structure, the campus dean occupied an uneasy, unspecified administrative relationship to the chairmen and to the chancellor. The chairmen controlled almost completely the academic programs of each Center Campus and felt little line responsibility to the campus dean, despite the fact that the dean was somehow expected to create a relevant program on his respective campus. In the case of the Center System, however, the academic department imported a "canned" program from the Madison campus with little consideration of the different educational factors and interests in the several communities where Center Campuses were located. Moreover, the organization of departments for instruction in the various disciplines was copied from the Madison campus despite the fact that some departments were so small as to be untenable as administrative units.

The campus dean, in some ways analogous to other university unit administrators, found the public information, student services, and administrative management programs beyond his jurisdiction. Like the academic departments, these programs were developed, structured, and in great measure administered on a systemwide basis by an official in the Center System's central offices in Madison, where they were determined in great measure by the Madison campus structures and functions. This official, like the departmental chairmen, was directly responsible to the chancellor, and only in a formal way did he feel responsible to the campus dean. No one person on each Center Campus was responsible for the development and administration of a program suited to the particular needs of the campus. The campus dean, at best, maintained good personal relations with the local community and its governing boards and assured the faculty of a supply of chalk, parking spaces, offices, and other support services. The systemwide program, developed and administered away from its sites of application, focused on uniformity. The "program" on each campus was whatever grouping of courses and services entrepreneurship could produce. The function of the campus faculty, as a body, was largely undefined. The choice of the administrative structure for the Center System was determined by a pattern elsewhere, and that pattern had little meaning or relevance in the real conditions of the system.

Apart from the larger implications described above, the administrative structure has an impact on the individual faculty member and the practice of faculty governance. The general university statute which makes an instructor a second class citizen in governance has had a more severe implication for the Center System than for the other units. The statutes do not designate instructors as members of the University Faculty. A majority of all faculty committees must be full faculty members; in all units except the Center System, only faculty members can vote in the selection of faculty representatives who give recommendations on promotions to tenure (divisional executive committees); most governance roles and offices are restricted to faculty members.

Partly because of the Madison departments' perception of the Center System, graduate students who needed teaching experience and fiscal support while finishing a dissertation or other graduate degree requirements were recruited for Center System faculty during 1964–1968.[6] Some departments limited the period these former teaching assistants could remain in the Center System to two or three years. As a result, the great majority of the faculty were highly transitory instructors without participatory rights. When an administrator undertook to persuade Center System faculty and their Senate to request a change in university statutes to include instructors among University Faculty, severe opposition developed not only among the senior faculty of the Center System but also among the holders of power in other units of the university. Although the Center System Senate requested a revision of the university statutes to give faculty status to instructors, the Center System representative to the Faculty Council (chairman of the University Committee of the Center System) opposed the senate's position. The Faculty Assembly later approved a Center System provision which permits instructors to vote in choosing divisional executive committee members (who act as a promotional board at Wisconsin), but the move to declare instructors as full faculty was decisively defeated. The stereotype of the instructor as a teaching assistant from the Madison campus was significant in defeating the measure. The discussion also implied that any deviation in participation or structure among the units meant a deterioration in quality.

The fact that few Center System departments had internal participatory structures, such as an executive committee, made even more prominent the second-class status of the instructor. In most departments, recruitment of new faculty and promotions and other advancements for existing faculty were determined by the chairman either alone or in consultation with selected members of the chairman's Madison department. Few of these decisionmakers had personal knowledge of the program or needs of Center Campuses or of the performance of the faculty member concerned. Some chairmen had never been to all Center Campuses by 1968, although they had been chairmen for several years.

As soon as the new unit began its long delayed faculty governance system the Madison influence and involvement began to appear. Promotion committees included non–Center System faculty. When statutes were drafted creating executive committees for Center System departments, they included measures providing for voting members from other units (Madison) who had no appointment in the Center System. The tradition of departmental autonomy permitted the enunciation of faculty recruitment and promotion criteria which failed to give primary support to the teaching mission of the system as established by the administration, the Regents, and the state's Coordinating Council for Higher Education. Furthermore, this autonomy permitted each department to develop specialized courses drawn from a complex, specialized Madison curriculum. The department's concept of autonomy influenced each department to declare its own teaching load standard; in most cases the standard was drawn from graduate institutions. The fact that faculty did not have the same duties (in variety or quantity) as graduate faculty was not considered, nor was the fact that departments with almost identical patterns of instruction had different work load requirements. More than a full year of consultation and discussion was required for most departments to declare that their primary function was teaching, as distinguished from research and public service. Criteria for faculty recruitment and evaluation were then developed, supposedly in support of the objectives. However, the faculty committee responsible for advising the administration on tenure promotions felt free to develop its own criteria in addition to those of recommending departments.

In late 1970, the administration requested the advice of the appropriate faculty committee (the divisional executive committee) on the promotion of four faculty members, one proposed for tenure at rank and three proposed for the rank of associate professor. Each was highly recommended by his department and characterized by the dean as an excellent teacher. The committee recommended advancement for only one of the four, the one who held the doctorate. When requested to give the rationale for the three negative recommendations, the committee stated that those rejected had failed to achieve "academic distinction." Since "academic distinction" is not uniformly clear to all members of the academic community, the administration again requested a statement of criteria or a description or definition of academic distinction to guide administration and departments in future cases. The committee replied that although academic distinction is a kind of superiority which sets one apart it would be presumptuous to try to define it in objective terms. The statement conveyed the impression that each member of the divisional executive committee would make an independent judgment by unarticulated objective criteria and that the latter might change from time to time. In the meantime, departments and administrators would just have to guess what the judgment would be.

Faculty rejection of administrative promulgation of policy for departments, however intense the consultation with departments, is illustrated by Center System administrative efforts to arrive at a rational, equitable teaching load policy over a two-year period, largely in response to inequities among departments and to state political pressures. Surveys of departments, collection and distribution to all departments of statements of practices recommended by all other departments, group and individual consultation with departmental chairmen, and consultation of American Association of University Professors (AAUP) standards became the basis for issuing a suggested systemwide policy according to each department's pattern of instruction (laboratory, lecture, discussion, studio, and so forth). Although the load definition was in most cases drawn from departmental recommendations, the most outspoken proponents of faculty power rejected the administration's right to "officialize" a system work load by official promulgation. Although no graduate teaching or advising was required nor was there significant pressure to perform theoretical or original research, many faculty critics of the teaching expectations standards rejected them on the ground that departmental autonomy was challenged. Again, the Madison mission and program became the basis for faculty judgments, just as it had influenced the administrative organization.

The Madison mold influenced departmental organization, course numbering, titles of courses, disciplinary designation, instructional patterns (large lectures and small discussion groups were used on a campus enrolling a total of three hundred students as compared to Madison's thirty-four thousand), and the nature of the committee system. Instructional areas which include as few as four full-time faculty for the entire system must be organized as a department, with an executive committee and the same administrative paraphernalia as a department of fifty full-time faculty, mainly because the discipline is organized as a departmental unit at Madison.

A recent effort has been made in the Center System to focus on the *substance* of university tradition and standards rather than on the specific patterns of institutional application which may differ according to mission and enrollment and other factors. But different applications of tradition are possible only with the tolerance of the larger units. The fact that the patterns were initially determined by conditions elsewhere adversely affected the educational and administrative strength of the Center System. A study of the development of other non-Madison units might reveal similar lessons. Whether the presumed transfer of the prestige and reputation of Madison more than compensated for the disadvantages of the organizational model will be the subject of intensive dialogue for years to come.

The University of Wisconsin is indeed faculty governed and not administration ridden. In that sense, the institution does conform to its popular image. The statutes which describe the system portray a picture of reasonable checks and balances among faculty legislative groups and administrative officials, a description of responsible review by faculty and administration. The deficiency is not in the emphasis upon faculty governance—that is essential for any institution of any strength and quality. Neither is the major deficiency in the political nature of the Wisconsin system; all governance systems in universities and colleges are basically political. The aspects of Wisconsin's governance system which deserve serious question relate to the kind of governance which results from the institutional structures and from the values undergirding them. Any system of governance which emphasizes departmental autonomy above vital academic program unity, personal and professional interests beyond institutional integrity, and parochial faculty authoritarianism over actual educational needs merits reappraisal.

The Wisconsin system seems to be characterized (not exclusively, but generally) by the concepts of meritocracy, departmental autonomy, individual entrepreneurship, and vague statutes and regulations. First, governance at Wisconsin is meritocratic rather than democratic. Participation is dependent on rank designation and political acumen, and the result is generally an oligarchy based on "meritocratic" criteria. Instructors are not classified as University Faculty, assistant professors do not normally participate in the most important decisions of the department, and generally the more politically inclined associate professors and professors become members of the promotion committees and the university committees. Faculty work loads are often determined by rank. A full professor or associate professor who is under less pressure to do research and publish because he has earned tenure often has fewer teaching obligations than the assistant professors and instructors who are under pressure to publish. An additional aspect of the meritocratic approach is the confusing definition of "peer" judgment which, in the final analysis, makes it whatever the departments declare it. For example, in some cases, only members of the same department are considered peers; in another instance, only faculty members of the same broad disciplinary division (natural sciences, humanities, and so forth) are peers; in yet another case, only tenured faculty in the same college are peers. Never is a dean considered a peer, even when his teaching field is the same as that of the faculty member concerned.

It is difficult to construct a meritocracy without experiencing some of the characteristics of elitism, and the university has not been an exception. Forced to regulate admissions after the World War II deluge, Madison abandoned its historic open-door policy and selected students in the upper half of their high school graduating classes. What started as a policy of expediency to reduce numbers soon became a sacred means to insure quality. The policy was then applied to all non-Madison units, although their missions varied and the spaces available also varied. In the recruitment of faculty and the development of programs, the meritocracy turned to highly selective institutions as sources and in many ways became a follower of other elite institutions rather than a leader in all of higher education. The people's university was changed. Most faculty recruited during the last two decades exhibited an orientation to national and international professional interests, which weakened further the university's contact within the state. Fiscal support from outside the state, amounting to nearly half of the Madison campus budget in the late sixties, gave considerable credence to the view that the university's clientele is greater than the state and that the institution's responsibilities lie beyond the state.

The second characteristic of the Wisconsin system is departmental autonomy, with the promulgation of the expansive interests of the department as ends in themselves. Departmental autonomy achieved supremacy in the second decade of this century, when the Wisconsin faculty was achieving its control of administering policy as well as determining policy. Although the college was the most important unit during the early decades of the century, the department gradually became more important. With the growth of the importance of the department (and more recently of specialties within each department) as the primary decision-making unit as well as the basic educational unit, collegiate unity decreased, departmental colleagueship increased, and academic programs of colleges became a collection of compromises of parochial interests. The results, pronounced at Wisconsin, have been highly developed specialties, research in depth, and disciplinary professionalism, along with what some would argue is a decline and deemphasis of liberal and broad learning.

As the units of decision making became more fragmented and decentralized, the third characteristic of Wisconsin, the practice of individual entrepreneurship, increased. The concept of the "invisible hand," so familiar in laissez faire economic theory, has probably achieved its greatest number of practical adherents in the academic community. It is painfully present at Wisconsin. Scholars there have generally accepted it as a basis for university organization and governance; they seem to sincerely believe that if each academic department or academician strives to advance its or his own self-interest, the sum total of such activity is bound to produce the best possible benefit. Unhampered freedom for each professor to follow his own professional interest, always one of Wisconsin's greatest attractions, has produced the appearance of academic anarchy.

Out of this concept of fairly unrestrained freedom or unstructured freedom emerges what one former high-ranking administrator denoted as "creative tension" in administration. Theoretically, the freedom to be creative in following one's personal professional talents and interests competes with the same application by others to produce creative tension. In practice, however, particularly when applied by members of administrative teams, creative tension is a euphemism for "nobody knows what the hell is going on." Nondirection, inaction, and duplication often are the results.

The three concepts of meritocracy, departmental autonomy, and laissez faire entrepreneurship have produced a governing system which protects and promotes the values on which they are based. Procedure takes priority over educational policy in many instances; in other cases, substantive policy is so ambiguously worded as to defy understanding or application. Ambiguity is the natural result of an obsession with flexibility and an effort by the engineers of the system to make the statutes of the institution as broad as the United States Constitution, overlooking the differences between organic law and statutory implementation.

Statutes describing the jurisdiction and role of faculty committees, units of organization, and administrative officers are quite vague. Administrative, advisory, and policy-making distinctions are rarely clear; legislative, judicial, and executive functions are less specific with each revision of the faculty statutes. Practice indicates, however, that faculty committees expect to exercise all three functions. In fact, many assign their own functions and jurisdiction and, unless challenged, exercise them. In theory, the ambiguity is intended to give the greatest flexibility for changing conditions and situations, but in actuality, particularly in times of stress, it produces the likelihoods of buckpassing, of conflicting jurisdictions, and of losing sight of those who really make a decision. It serves other purposes, too. The tendency of the general faculty (of a college or a campus or the university) is to legislate general procedure (as contrasted with educational policy) in sufficiently ambiguous terms to permit holders of power to apply it to their interest with assurance that equally selective faculty groups will also act as the judiciary to reinforce that power.

Obviously, the power to interpret vague regulations is a final power. As a result, the further removed a faculty decision is from the academic department the more it becomes a loosely worded compromise among parochial interests and the less it resembles educational policy. Such compromises are practically impossible to administer effectively without almost constant consultation and complete agreement with representatives of the department affected. Equity among departments in such a system is impossible and, in fact, "equity" becomes synonymous with endorsing departmental decisions however unlike they are among departments. Measures of program or performance which may be comparable among departments are rejected or rank low in priority even when necessary to justify funding.

Theoretically, the department chairman becomes the key administrator. Such a system places emphasis upon the departmental unit without clear criteria for sustaining or creating a unit and encourages and institutionalizes compartmentalization and fragmentation. Nevertheless, as McCarty points out in Chapter Two, chairmen are rarely effective leaders at Wisconsin. In great measure, this because the system is predicated upon the absence of administrative leadership and upon the "natural" evolution of consensus. The more a chairman becomes an effective leader, the less likely he is to endure. University statutes give the chairman only the functions of a superior secretary, although they provide that the department may give certain additional authority to the chairmen. In fact, however, the real power is held by the department's executive committee, composed only of tenured members.

Administrative review of departmental recommendations and decisions (when they can be distinguished) is generally unacceptable; faculty review is only mildly more palatable. Administrative power to say yes is always present but clear authority to say no is forever absent and must be reestablished in each case. As a result, all but the most foolhardy administrators think more than twice before challenging a faculty or departmental recommendation, however nonrational, expensive, or inequitable it may be. The administrator has few natural or usual allies when his judgment is questioned. On the contrary, his security as an administrator is based more on avoiding judgments that can clearly be traced to him than it is based on sound decision-making. Unless he has retained a tenured departmental affiliation as a retreat, the only sure security he has is to approve all faculty recommendations.

The potential of conflict between departmental faculty and administrators who attempt to achieve equity among several departmental and collegiate units is increased at Wisconsin by a tendency to view the authority of all units and officers as equal. Faculty recommendations and decisions of deans and chancellors are rarely distinguished; on some occasions, there is little distinction among faculty between faculty authority and the Board of Regents' authority. The department's authority to recommend is viewed by faculty as equal to the administrator's authority to review the department's rationale and objective.

It is contended that serious ambiguities, not all of which are new, plague faculty governance and administration at Wisconsin. The system of governance was built for fair weather, presuming general consensus and acceptance of the collegial system. Furthermore, the system was constructed for a single-campus institution in which the senior faculty's authority was rarely challenged. The university has for so long blurred administrative responsibilities and faculty governance that the two can be distinguished by faculty only when things go contrary to their decision. The theoretical base on which the Wisconsin system of governance rests asserts that the faculty is responsible for all policy, and that the administration (consisting of faculty also) exists simply to execute faculty wishes.

The organizational theory declares that the faculty is the legislative, judicial, and executive agency for deciding and executing "educational interests." As one would guess, educational interests have been defined broadly over the years to include a variety of subjects. For example, fees and tuition, out-of-state enrollment, building, parking, in loco parentis, and student discipline have generally been defined by faculty as educational interests. It has been easy to translate "faculty" interests into "educational" interests, and tolerant Boards of Regents did not challenge the interpretations. Not only was there, until the late sixties, an absence of serious conflict with the Regents over these views, there was also the development of precedents which created the impression that the main function of the Regents is to secure public and financial support and to shield the university from attacks on academic freedom. At the same time, the faculty believed that the entire internal operation of the institution lay in its province. Until the mid-1960s, the view was unchallenged, basically because the Regents did not feel political pressures concerning crises at the university and because Regents simply did not wish to take on the battle. Moreover, there have been many Regents who truly accepted the view.

Student protests, fiscal leanness, and changing priorities in higher education have focused on the unresponsiveness and the deficiencies of the organization of the university. The ambiguity of responsibility, the failure to distinguish between recommendations and decisions, the reluctance of faculty legislation to specify functional areas in which purely advisory responsibilities exist and others in which faculty decision-making should be fairly absolute, and the general feeling that no one is in charge has also prompted a change in the role of the Board of Regents. This change, viewed in Chapter One as a gradual reclaiming of authority by the Regents, is a corrective effort which would have been necessary (although it might not have come so quickly) had there been no student protest. Actually, the reclaiming of authority seems to be a first phase in an effort to redistribute authority and to correct a fundamental dichotomy between administrative accountability and faculty decision-making. Faculty committees at Wisconsin have historically attributed to themselves policy-making authority and occasional executive functions to carry out those policies, but the faculty, the governing board, and external agencies have generally held administrators accountable for the consequences.

Another way of interpreting Regent involvement would be to see it as an effort to clarify decision-making in the university and to reinstate administrative review at appropriate levels. The subtle authority structure of consensus is under question and will be gradually replaced by a more formal and more visible power structure. Although the change is in large measure due to a loss of consensus, this new direction is viewed by the older faculty and the oligarchical holders of informal authority as an erosion of faculty authority and as an aggrandizement of administrative authority. Actually, the university is simply experiencing the redistribution of decision-making and review powers that many noneducational institutions have also undergone. Administrative decision-making is becoming less concentrated at the university than it has been since World War II.

Neither the style nor the structure of Wisconsin's governance system stimulates prompt and meaningful response to changing needs. Too often, the style, both of administrative officers and faculty groups, does not promote initiatives for progressive change. The structure is little better. Conditions demanding change have to reach a crisis stage before the system responds. Even then, the style and structure lead first to a bureaucratization of the need. Whatever the issue—student protest, recruiting on campus, student participation in campus governance, discrimination against women—it first must be examined by an appropriate inclusive committee which composes recommendations to a larger group. (Most likely the recommendations include the formation of another semi-administrative committee.) Eventually the response, politicized by the values described above, winds its way through a labyrinth of faculty units. Frequently, the crisis conditions out of which the need for response existed have changed or become complicated by necessary action by the time the faculty response is made. Just as frequently, the response is theoretical rather than substantive.

The final result of the present system of governance and administration at Wisconsin is fragmentation and slow and "political" responses. In an environment which features divisions and subdivisions of academic and operational responsibility, there is little chance for an integrated educational community or for institutional leadership. Often, the more significant the educational and administrative problem, the greater is the tendency for the administration and the faculty not to act.

The University of Wisconsin responds to the needs for broad educational and institutional change very slowly; it responds just as slowly to the need for changes in its governance system. In fact, the three times there were significant discussions of change, the impulse came from outside the faculty. In 1916–1917, the Allen Committee precipitated a study and recommendations; in 1947–1950, the Regents requested an internal review; and in the sixties, expansion to a multi-unit institution provided the impetus to change. In the latter instance, the old Madison system was simply fitted around a larger organization, and the change was really an adjustment.

On the positive side of the ledger, there is no question that the individual faculty member at Wisconsin has an unusually wide latitude and high degree of personal and professional freedom. Academic freedom, particularly in political and social areas, is rightfully highly valued and jealously guarded. Both professional and personal freedom are improved in the Wisconsin system as one advances in rank and in campus political standing. Largely because of these crucial factors, the university has been able to attract and hold outstanding scholars despite a salary scale which is not at all outstanding.

The questions which emerge from a study of Wisconsin's governance system are many. Does the fragmented, decentralized governance system which is based on meritocracy, departmental autonomy, and laissez faire account for the university's greatness? If the academic is inclined to the view that he should be unhampered in developing his own interests and aspirations, can *institutional* responsiveness and integrity be preserved? Can clear and specific descriptions of functional relationships of different groups in the academic community exist in the same institution which promotes the highest professional pursuits of its faculty? Is administrative effectiveness less important than academic ritual?

It appears that Wisconsin's prestige and academic accomplishments particularly in the 1950s and 1960s have been largely due to the professional freedom and the financing of program support, if not of salaries, for its faculty. Only in small measure are they due to its governance structure. Governance participation is very uneven among the various groups within the faculty. Democracy certainly does not exist, and at times the meritocracy takes on the characteristics of an oligarchy. Tenured faculty run the departments with little participation from other members. Academic freedom is less secure for a junior instructor or an administrator than for a full professor, but the required teaching obligations of the former may be greater than those of the latter. Due process is nonexistent for administrators and has only recently come under discussion for faculty at the impulse of court decisions. Non-Madison faculty units have less freedom in their governance than the Madison faculty. Students have only recently been given some small measure of influence in the determination of academic policy, and that small role may have been a political result of protest. This seems to affirm a recent declaration that institutions of higher education change only when they have no other choice or when forced from outside.[7]

I believe that there are strengths and deficiencies in the governance and administration of the University of Wisconsin. The greatest strength is that of protecting academic freedom, but it has failed to expand academic freedom to a greater number of members in the academic community and to the instructional mode and program. An equally crucial strength is the degree to which faculty members may pursue professional interests which are larger than meeting classes and teaching students directly. But it is deficient in that it provides an inadequate balance between institutional interests and individual professional interests and aspirations. The efforts to transfer these positive values to newer units with different missions were motivated by a concern for quality but in so doing, straitjackets were imposed, and different and perhaps more meaningful methods of governance were largely prevented. An obsession with being faculty governed and not administration ridden has stymied effective and efficient administration and discouraged institutional leadership.

Notes

[1] M. Curti and V. Carstensen, *The University of Wisconsin, A History, 1848–1925*, Vol. II (Madison: 1949), p. 44.

[2] *Minutes of the Faculty*, February 14, 1916, Document 21, 1916, pp. 2–4.

[3] Report of the Committee on University Function and Policies, Second Report, November, 1949.

[4] *Laws and Regulations of the University of Wisconsin*, Chapter 5, p. 537.

[5] *Ibid*,

⁶ Faced with declining support for graduate education, some interests on the Madison campus have now (1971) revived their interest in having the Centers formally attached to four-year campuses.

⁷ J. B. Lon Hefferlin, "Ritualism, Privilege, and Reform," in G. K. Smith (Ed.), *The Troubled Campus: Current Issues in Higher Education 1970,* San Francisco: Jossey-Bass, 1970).

CHAPTER 4

REGENTS RESPOND
TO CRISIS

Gregory J. Nigosian

I taught at Madison during 1970–
1971. I arrived following a fatal bombing and, in conversations with colleagues about this event and past disturbances, I heard many theories
about who ran the school and what they were trying to do. Since several
of these theories focused on the Regents, and most recognized them as
an important factor in the balance of power, it seemed that knowledge of
their function would be crucial to any comprehensive understanding of
the university. It was brought to my attention that the Regents kept
virtually verbatim transcripts of their meetings. These records made it
possible for me to look "firsthand," but in retrospect, at the way the Regents had dealt with various issues at several points in time.

Although the Regents' meetings are open to the public, most
people I met and talked with in Madison seemed never to have attended.
Their absence has important epistemological consequences; it means their
knowledge about the Regents is secondhand, at best. In such circumstances, information is probably based on memory of a newspaper editor's
modification of a reporter's attempt to distill an extended (and usually

89

convoluted) discussion by the Regents. This seems a precarious basis for the formulation of accurate theories about the university. This chapter, then, seeks to correct that deficiency. An attempt is made to gain an understanding of the Regents through a series of "retrospective field visits" made feasible by their extraordinarily detailed minutes.[1]

The first thing to remember about the University of Wisconsin and its Board of Regents is that they are creations of the Wisconsin state legislature—literally its progeny. The legislature is the source of authority and money. While the Wisconsin constitution contains a section that refers to "a state university," the University of Wisconsin does not have constitutional status in the sense that we understand that term today: "Provision shall be made by law for the establishment of a state university at or near the seat of the state government, and for connecting with the same, from time to time, such colleges in different parts of the state as the interests of education may require."[2]

The university is, instead, a product of the legislature, the result of "enabling legislation": "There is established in this state at the city of Madison an institution of learning by the name and style of 'The University of Wisconsin.' "[3] To run this university, the legislature created a governing board: "The board of regents and their successors in office shall constitute a body corporate by the name of 'The Regents of the University of Wisconsin,' and shall possess *the powers necessary or convenient to accomplish the objects and perform the duties prescribed by law*."[4] [Emphasis added.]

The composition of this board has changed from time to time; the current structure has been in effect since 1939: "There is created a board of regents of the University of Wisconsin consisting of the state superintendent of public instruction and nine persons, not more than two of whom shall be residents of any one county, appointed for staggered nine year terms."[5]

The legislature has given the Regents extraordinary powers. For example:

The board of regents shall enact laws for the government of the university in all its branches; elect a president and the requisite number of professors, instructors, officers and employees, and fix the salaries and the term of office of each, and *determine the moral and educational qualifications of applicants for admission to the various courses of instruction*.[6] [Emphasis added.]

The board of regents may remove the president or any professors, instructor or officer of the university when, in the judgment of the board of regents, the interests of the university require it.[7] [Emphasis added.]

The immediate government of the several colleges shall be intrusted to their respective faculties; but the board of regents *may regulate the course of instruc-tion and prescribe the books or works to be used in the several courses*.[8] [Em-phasis added.]

While many of these powers are not exercised, it should be noted that the quoted sections are *current* provisions of the Wisconsin statutes.

Though the board seems to have been given considerable power, there is a second factor to bear in mind concerning its relationship to the legislature—"What the legislature giveth, the legislature can also taketh away" and frequently does.

The legislature has reinforced this marionette-like control by its actions in four different areas: enacting specific statutes that deal with various policy matters; specifically restricting the regents from acting in certain areas; reviewing and determining the budget; and, recently, creat-ing an additional level of review between itself and the Regents.

The Wisconsin statutes contain a variety of specific provisions that affect the university and partially delimit the power of the Regents. Most of these provisions are relatively inconsequential. These sections, which occupy most of chapter 36 of the statutes, cover a diverse range of issues, from janitors' salaries (they should be the same as those received by jani-tors at the capitol building, a mile away [36.07]), to scientific investigation (encouraged [36.062]), to ticket scalping (discouraged [36.50]).

More serious in effect are specific restrictions placed on the Re-gents' powers. A major example is the following provision: "No new school or college shall be established unless authorized by the legislature."[9]

Still more serious are the restrictions that result from legislative budget review. Originally, the university was to be supported by the inter-est from the proceeds of the sale of lands given to the state by the federal government.[10] It was not long before such income proved inadequate, and the university was thereafter supported by public funds. The governor is required to "report biennially to the legislature the condition of each of the public institutions . . . which are supported . . . by appropriations . . . with recommendations as he deems proper."[11] And since "no money shall be paid out of the treasury except in pursuance of an appropriation by law"[12] such an appropriation is made by the legislature in the amount and for the purposes it sees fit. Most appropriations are made under the rubric "Education to Advance Individuals and Discover New Knowl-edge."[13] Since the money is appropriated categorically under this main heading, the university comes under budgetary and hence policy review every two years.

Finally, the legislature created a Coordinating Council for Higher Education to supervise the growth and development of the several levels of public higher education in the state (the university system, including the extensions and the centers, the Wisconsin State University system, the vocational schools, and so on). The range of CCHE power has been considerable. For example, the Regents must obey the decisions of CCHE, which can prevent and even rescind certain educational programs. Further, CCHE can override the Regents in determining institutional budgets. However, CCHE has been abolished because of the legislative reorganization of higher education, and its wide powers ended.

It may be that some future, definitive study of this period in the history of the university will indicate that the legislature, not the Regents, was the crucial force in the development of the school. In the short run, though, the Regents seem to have been in a central position in the action surrounding the various student and quasi-student demonstrations of the past several years. It is perhaps best to begin an examination of the Regents' position and power with a look at the composition of the board.

Efforts to describe regents have usually taken one of two approaches. Either the regents are considered as "cases" in national or regional surveys of "the typical regent," and are described in essentially demographic terms,[14] or, regents are viewed as holders and wielders of great economic and political power, who have complex interconnections among each other's companies and enterprises which distort the university's traditional position of neutrality. All of these factors are relevant in this analysis.

There was a substantial membership turnover on the nine-man Board of Regents between June 1966 and February 1969. If we use the party of the governor nominating the board member as our indication of party membership (see Table 1), we see that at the June 1966 meeting, the party complement was six Democrats and three Republicans (plus the non-partisan superintendent of public instruction). In November 1967, the board was comprised of five Democrats and four Republicans. By February, 1969, the membership had shifted to three Democrats and six Republicans.[15]

Table 1 also presents certain demographic information about each of the Regents. Several patterns are notable. First, an overwhelming majority were born in Wisconsin. Second, virtually all have had some higher education, mainly at the University of Wisconsin. Third, more than half the group hold advanced degrees. Fourth, except for one labor leader and one housewife, all are either professionals or businessmen. And fifth, a majority have been residents of the industrialized, eastern part of the state.

Biographies prepared by the University News Service, while presumably not exhaustive, contain a fair amount of information about both

Table 1

Regents	Nominating Governor		Birth Place	Year of Birth	Residence	Higher Education	Occupation	Term of Office (May–April) Except as noted
Robert V. Dahlstrom	Knowles	(R)	Montana	1925	Manitowoc	Idaho (B.S., M.A.), Cornell (Ph.D.)	Chemist, Executive	4/'69–('72)
Arthur DeBardeleben	Nelson	(D)	Wisconsin	1918	Park Falls	UW (B.Ph, Ll.B.)	Lawyer	'59–'68
Ody J. Fish	Knowles	(R)	Minnesota	1925	Hartland	None	Industrialist	'70–('79)
Jacob F. Friedrick	Nelson	(D)	Hungary	1892	Milwaukee	None	Union Leader	'60–'69
Charles D. Gelatt	Knowles	(R)	Wisconsin	1918	LaCrosse	UW (B.A., M.A.; cand. for Ph.D.)	Industrialist	'47–('74)
Kenneth L. Greenquist	Nelson	(D)	Wisconsin	1910	Racine	UW (Ll.B.)	Lawyer	'62–4/'68
James W. Nellen	Knowles	(R)	Wisconsin	1913	De Pere	UW (B.S., M.D.)	Physician	'65–('73)
Maurice B. Pasch	Nelson	(D)	Wisconsin	1910	Madison	UW (B.A., Ll.B.)	Lawyer	'61–'70
Frank J. Pelisek	Knowles	(R)	(——)	1930	Whitefish Bay	UW (B.S., Ll.B.)	Lawyer	'69–('78)
Walter F. Renk	Knowles	(R)	(——)	(——)	Sun Prairie	UW (B.A.)	Farmer, Businessman	'67–('76)
Gilbert C. Rohde	Nelson	(D)	Wisconsin	1914	Greenwood	Wisc. St. Coll. and UW Short Course in Agr.	Farmer, Businessman	'61–'67
Mrs. Caroline T. Sandin	Knowles	(R)	Minnesota	1915	Ashland	St. Peter County T.C.	Housewife, School Bd. Pres.	'68–('77)
Carl E. Steiger	Thompson	(R)	Wisconsin	1896	Oshkosh	UW (Adult Spec. Stu.)	Industrialist	'57–'66
Gordon R. Walker	Knowles	(R)	Wisconsin	1904	Racine	UW (B.A.)	Industrialist	'68–('71)
A. Matt Werner	Reynolds	(D)	Wisconsin	1894	Sheboygan	Marquette (Ll.B.)	Lawyer	'63–3/'69
Bernard C. Ziegler	Knowles	(R)	(——)	1922	West Bend	Darmouth, Northwestern (B.A.)	Industrialist	'66–('75)
Supt. of Public Instruction								
William C. Kahl	Elected		Wisconsin	1908	——	UW (B.A., M.A.)	——	1/'66–
Angus B. Rothwell	Elected		Wisconsin	1905	——	Wis. St. Coll.— Superior (B.A.); Columbia (M.A.)	——	1/'61–1/'66

the political activities and the economic and corporate involvement of the Regents. The information on political activity (see Table 2) indicates that

Table 2. POLITICAL EXPERIENCE OF REGENTS

ROBERT DAHLSTROM	"Active . . . on the state level with the Republican Party . . ."
ARTHUR DEBARDELEBEN	At the University: "a member of the Progressive Club . . ."
ODY FISH	"Active in the Republican Party, Fish was Chairman of the Wisconsin Republican Party from 1965–70, and has held numerous posts, both on the state and national level."
JACOB FRIEDRICK	No information listed.
CHARLES GELATT	No information listed.
KENNETH GREENQUIST	"He was elected to the State Senate as a member of the Progressive Party . . ." He served from 1940–43.
JAMES NELLEN	No information listed.
MAURICE PASCH	"He became acquainted with Philip LaFollette, his instructor in criminal law, was associated with him in his successful campaign for governor, and Mr. Pasch's interest switched to political affairs. . . . When Loomis ran for governor, Mr. Pasch was his campaign manager."
FRANK PELISEK	"A member of the Republican Party since 1952, Mr. Pelisek has been active in Wisconsin governmental affairs during the past several years."
WALTER RENK	No information listed.
GILBERT ROHDE	No information listed.
CAROLINE SANDIN	No information listed.
CARL STEIGER	He "is an active member of the Republican Party and has served as its Winnebago County Chairman, and Finance Chairman. He was Sixth Congressional District delegate pledged to Robert A. Taft at the GOP national convention in 1952 and that year was a residential elector on the Eisenhower-Nixon ticket. He was also an alternate delegate in the years 1956 and 1960."
GORDON WALKER	No information listed.

A. MATT WERNER	He "was a delegate to the Democratic National Convention in 1932 and an alternate in 1940 and 1944 . . ."
BERNARD ZIEGLER	No information listed.
WILLIAM KAHL	No information listed.
ANGUS ROTHWELL	No information listed.

NOTE: As listed on biographies prepared by the UW News Service.

most Regents have had some involvement in partisan politics, but that, for other than Ody Fish, this has not been very intensive. It appears that being a Regent is neither an early step in a political climb, nor a position to which retiring politicians are banished. Rather, it seems to have some element of reward for past service or monetary donation to the party, or friendship with the politicians, or both.

In terms of business involvement, however, the pattern is very different (see Table 3). Here we find extensive past and present activity by

Table 3. DIRECTORSHIPS AND EXECUTIVE POSITIONS
HELD BY UW REGENTS

ROBERT DAHLSTROM	Vice-President, Rahr Bio-Technical Laboratories
ARTHUR DEBARDELEBEN	President, 15th Judicial Circuit Bar Association
ODY FISH	President, Pal-O-Pak Insulation Co. President, Woodland Manufacturing Co. Vice-President, Pal-O-Pak of Canada Director, National Cellulose Insulation Manufacturers Association
JACOB FRIEDRICK	President, Milwaukee County Labor Council
CHARLES GELATT	Board of Trustees and Executive Committee, Northwestern Mutual Life Insurance Co. Board of Trustees, LaCross Trust Co. Board, Wisconsin Manufacturers Association (Chairman of Board and Director, Northern Engraving Co.) (Chairman of Board and Director, Gateway Products Corp.) (Chairman of Board and Director, Aluminum Mills, Inc.) (President and Director, Gelatt Corp.)
KENNETH GREENQUIST	State Commander, American Legion National Executive Committee, American Legion

President, Racine County Bar Association
Counsel, Racine Unified School District

JAMES NELLEN   President, Wisconsin Orthopedic Association
President, Brown County Medical Society
Director, Green Bay Packers Corp.
Member, Citizen's Advisory Committee,
   St. Norbert College

MAURICE PASCH   State Commander, Military Order of World Wars
President, Navy League
State Chairman, Brotherhood Week
Director, Home Savings and Loan, Madison

FRANK PELISEK   President, Multiple Sclerosis Society of
   Milwaukee
(Secretary and Director, Hankscraft Co.)

WALTER RENK   President, William F. Renk & Sons
President, Renk Enterprises
President and Director, Wisconsin Livestock
   Breeders' Association
President and Director, Wisconsin
   4-H Foundation
Director, American Family Insurance Group
Director, First National Bank, Madison
Director, General Telephone Co. of Wisconsin
Director, Wisconsin Power and Light
President, Downtown Rotary, Madison
Chairman, Dane County Red Cross

GILBERT ROHDE   President, Wisconsin Farmers' Union
(Director, Commodity Trading Co.)
(Director, Farmers Union Marketing
   and Processing Association)

CAROLINE SANDIN   President, Ashland Board of Education
President, League of Women Voters, Ashland
President, Tri-County Medical Society Auxiliary

CARL STEIGER   Chairman of Board, Deltox Rug Co.
Chairman of Board, Oshkosh National Bank
Director, Wisconsin National Life Insurance Co.
Director, Bergstrom Paper Co.
Director, Arkwright Mutual Insurance Co.
Member, Oshkosh City Council
President, Oshkosh Community Chest
Director, Oshkosh YMCA
Chairman of Board, St. John's Military
   Academy, Delafield

	Trustee, Ripon College
	Trustee, UW YMCA
	Trustee, UW Foundation
GORDON WALKER	President and Director, Walker Forge, Inc.
	Director, Jacobson Manufacturing Co.
	Director, Wisconsin Metal Products
	Director, First Wisconsin Bankshares Corp.
	Director, American Bank and Trust, Racine
	Director, Kern County Land Co.
	President and Director, Drop Forging Association
	President, Wisconsin Alumni Association
A. MATT WERNER	Editor and Publisher, Sheboygan Press
	Chairman of Board, Press Publishing Co.
	State Director, National Emergency Council
	State Director, Federal Housing Administration
	President and Director, Crystal Lake Crushed Stone Co.
	President and Director, Sheboygan Majestic Theater
	President and Director, Bowler Realty Co.
	President and Director, Bowler Security Co.
	Director, Sheboygan Casket Co.
	Director, Radio Station WHBL
	Director, Commercial Engraving Co.
	Member, Advisory Board, Edgewood College
BERNARD ZIEGLER	Secretary and Director, West Bend Co.
	Director, West Bend Mutual Insurance Co.
	Director, First National Bank, West Bend
	President, West Bend Rotary Club
	(Director, B. C. Ziegler & Co.)

NOTE: Positions listed in parentheses are from the Dun & Bradstreet *Million Dollar Directory, 1971.* All other information is from biographies of the Regents prepared by the University News Service.

the Regents in the running of small and large firms, both their own and others. Reviewing the list of firms mentioned, it is clear that the board does not represent great wealth as, for example, the University of California Board of Regents does.

It is useful to focus on the Regents' response to three student demonstrations generally acknowledged to be the major demonstrations prior to the invasion of Cambodia and the killings at Kent State and Jackson State. It seems reasonable to look at these particular demonstrations as important events during 1966 through 1969. The core of this section utilizes a methodology that is somewhat unusual because data of the kind used here are, apparently, infrequently found. We are doing archival or documentary research, using the minutes of the Regents' meetings. The minutes, while public, do not have wide circulation (in the university, they are distributed down to the deans' level, but not below that); they are intended chiefly for use by the Regents and the administration. It seems unlikely that intentional distortions would be entered, since the original meetings were public. Although some editing has been done in the process of transcribing from tape to paper, I feel confident that a faithful record of the deliberations has been provided.

The antidraft sit-in in 1966 was held by a relatively small group of peaceful students to protest both the giving of class-rank information to the draft board and war-related recruiting on campus. Although a few city policemen were called in, and a number of arrests made, order was maintained and no violence occurred.

The Regents' meeting of Friday, June 10, 1966, was the first one following the sit-in. Since it was also the annual meeting, the first business was the election of officers. The incumbent officers (DeBardeleben, president, and Gelatt, vice-president) were reelected. Other members present were: Friedrick, Greenquist, Nellen, Pasch, Rohde, Warner, and Zeigler. The meeting proceeded with normal business until discussion of the sit-in was introduced by university President Harrington.

Harrington made an opening statement, acknowledging the publicity and the faculty resolutions from Madison and Milwaukee concerning aspects of the university's policy on ranking for selective service. (That policy was not quoted or explained in the minutes.) He indicated that the administration was responding in three ways. First, it was informing Wisconsin's congressional delegation and the White House of the faculties' views. Second, it was establishing a faculty-student committee to study relationships with Selective Service. And third, it was permitting Selective Service testing, and would continue to rank, but "with the understanding that the university is not endorsing the rank-in-class concept." The university would give this rank information to the student, "but will not give it directly to the Selective Service System." Harrington further stated that "there was no need for Regent action on this matter, since it involved no change in Regent policy."

Several Regents then made comments and asked questions. Rohde wondered whether press reports of the sit-in were accurate and was told that in general they were; however, Associated Press was chastised for photos that gave "the impression that [the sit-ins] consisted of curious appearing, poorly dressed students." Friedrick complimented the administration, though he also "granted to the students the right to protest." Nellen (whom we will see later in a more conservative frame of mind) "agreed with the students that the present Selective Service rules and regulations are not right," although he felt that they had to be followed until properly changed. Harrington said he was pleased with the way things worked out. "The sit-in did not disrupt university business . . ." and pointed out that the students "had cleaned up the halls where they had staged their sit-in." He said the university was "well aware of the rights of everyone" but he "did not wish to suggest that protests will cause the university to change its policies." DeBardeleben wondered if there "was something lacking in faculty or Regent policies which resulted in the students' feeling that they had to use this method of protesting." Harrington felt that while student government was strong, some students did not feel adequately represented. Madison Chancellor Fleming felt that the students were trying to dramatize their concern. No action was taken; the meeting recessed and later continued its regular business.

Perhaps the response of the Regents to the first substantial demonstration of the sixties is marked by rational debate as well as defense of and concern for students because the protestors were singularly well-mannered, the issue was deemed legitimate, and the administration's ploys to end the demonstration were successful. In other words, the Regents were dealing with what was to them an isolated incident in which no major crisis had occurred. Yet the dynamics of future protests were hinted at when Harrington, while affirming students' right to protest, assured the Regents that demonstrations would not cause the university to change its policies. Unfortunately, no one gave serious thought to DeBardeleben's question as to whether or not something might be amiss with faculty or Regent policies.

By autumn 1967, the mood of the politically concerned students had become sullen and grave. Distress about the Vietnam war was increasing, and it seemed increasingly unlikely that electoral politics would provide the opportunity to affect the course of the war. Many students were looking for other avenues for effective expression of their concerns. One such avenue opened up for students in Madison when job recruiters for the Dow Chemical Company, the makers of napalm, scheduled appointments. Details of the incident that resulted when the students acted against Dow recruiting have been described and discussed in Chapter Seven, and they need not be repeated here. But as we look at the Regents' meeting following the bloody demonstration, we should try to remember the national mood at the time.

The Dow demonstration occurred October 18, 1967. The first meeting following the demonstration occurred Friday, November 17,

1967. (Note that there was no emergency meeting, as there was to be during the black strike.) Virtually all of the morning and most of the afternoon session were devoted to issues arising from the demonstration and its aftermath.

Summarizing the discussion and action of this meeting is difficult. For example, the record of the morning discussion fills twenty-three single-spaced pages. Much detail must therefore be omitted. But even more difficult to convey is the tone of the meeting, because any coherent description would make it appear far more rational than in fact it was. Regent Greenquist was now president of the board and William Sewell was chancellor of the Madison campus. The other Regents present were: De-Bardeleben, Friedrick, Gelatt, Nellen, Pasch, Renk, Werner, and Ziegler; Regent Kahl was absent.

The meeting began almost normally. President Harrington presented the list of gifts, grants, and contracts, and they were accepted. Vice-President Clodius presented a list of recommendations on fourteen hundred personnel matters, specifically noting that the cases of Evan Stark, graduate research assistant, and Robert Cohen, graduate teaching assistant, were not included in the list. (These two students were singled out because, as we shall see shortly, they were the alleged leaders of the demonstration.) The list of recommendations was accepted. Three fairly large bequests were voted and accepted, with appropriate clucking. Then the meeting fell apart.

President Harrington spoke at length. He first proposed that the order of business be changed to discuss the Report on Student Protests, and then made a "short report." In fact, this was a very long, meandering, and confusing speech. It constantly referred to the rights and powers of the Regents, which might have been an effort to placate and "soften up" the board. Reading the minutes, however, one gets the impression that Harrington was in a daze and did not know quite what to do or say. The main points of his report are summarized below.

He urged everyone to remain calm and not act precipitately, but also pointed out that more employer interviews were scheduled the next Monday. He did not specifically defend either his or Sewell's handling of the current demonstration but stated that the administration had attempted to follow the faculty's insistence that recruiting be allowed on campus, and that it had followed established rules and procedures in suspending fifteen students. He then turned the discussion over to the board, remarking that it would be desirable to discuss the situations with reference to graduate assistants Evan Stark and Robert Cohen. That comment evoked the first of several outbursts of audience laughter noted in the minutes and rebuked by the board president.

The rest of the morning session was a free for all. Many issues were discussed simultaneously. Almost every Regent had something to say about everything, including one another's statements. At some points, several resolutions were on the floor at the same time, and even after votes were taken, the debate on the "resolved" matter continued. Several Regents praised the university's tradition of freedom and the fact that many powers—including student discipline—had been delegated to the faculty. This spirit was dispelled when Ziegler called for action and President Greenquist stepped down to offer the first resolution of the morning, which essentially approved the practice of employee recruiting on campus. Gelatt said job interviews were free speech, and should be allowed. He objected, however, to the phrasing of Greenquist's resolution (it was written in somewhat self-righteous language, speaking of "a willful group of ruthless persons"), and offered a simplified substitute motion which reaffirmed existing policy. Ziegler called the question, which ironically resulted in much more debate.

DeBardeleben thought no action should be taken at the time; then, responding to an earlier suggestion by Nellen that the Regents could retract authorization given before to faculty without regard to disciplinary procedures, said: "The withdrawal of that [delegation of] responsibilities, without proper notice, [is] just as lawless as anything could be." He also thought that since the Regents might hear, on appeal, some of the cases arising out of the demonstration, it was "beyond propriety" to label them "ruthless" in advance. The discussion was now getting warm.

After further debate, during which it became clear that Friedrick was opposed to any action by the Regents at the time, "ruthless" was deleted from the main motion (Greenquist's), which was subsequently passed (with only DeBardeleben and Friedrick against). University policy regarding job interviews was thus reaffirmed.

President Harrington announced that various armed forces interviews would occur on November 20, and "with the cooperation of the City of Madison and Dane County, we will have adequate police force present to keep the peace." The minutes note: "(At this point there was a burst of laughter from the audience, to which President Harrington replied, 'this is not a laughing matter.')"

The next portion of the meeting began with a long period of parliamentary finessing, confused debate, and linguistic bickering over proposed rules for demonstrations, and, generally, tighter security procedures. A complicated resolution that spelled out specific and somewhat harsh measures to be taken against demonstrations and demonstrators was proposed by Renk, but the administration, as represented by Harrington, and several of the more liberal Regents forestalled Renk's proposal with suggestions of their own for a review of disciplinary procedures. Essentially, under the guidance of Harrington, and with the aid of Greenquist, De-Bardeleben and Gelatt, it was voted that the legislature clarify the statutes on regental power to make rules and set penalties, that the administration be *requested* to propose rules regarding demonstrations, and that security and screening procedures for personnel be reviewed. Then, without pause, the true madness of the day began.

Harrington called attention to two cases among the fifteen being considered for expulsion. He took special note of these two because they were also employees of the university. Evan Stark, research assistant in philosophy, had been removed from the payroll. While this would normally be considered a personnel matter and handled in the "personnel package" at the beginning of the monthly meeting, Harrington suggested specific consideration "because this case has attracted such special attention." Stark had left the school, the city, and the state. Pasch moved confirmation of removal, seconded by Nellen and Renk.

DeBardeleben asked why this was being done. Harrington offered two reasons. First, Stark had left campus. "Second, . . . facts that have come to the attention of the administration, which remain to be proved, indicate that his role with respect to the disruption on October 18 was such that he should not be continued as a research assistant. . . . Normally . . . we would favor due process in connection with this case." The last comment elicited snickers and subdued laughter. DeBardeleben asked what the department of philosophy thought, and Sewell, giving his opinion, said since Stark was not a graduate student, he could not be a research assistant. (If that seems a non sequitur, it is at least an accurate rendering of the minutes.) Nellen called the question, and it was voted.

Harrington next recommended "that the Regents consider the termination of Robert Cohen as a teaching assistant in philosophy, with provision for a public hearing before the Regents or a committee thereof, if he desires." His language was nothing if not careful. But then Harrington equivocated. Having made the recommendation, he then explained other, less drastic approaches the Regents might take. They could wait to see if Cohen would be expelled. Or they could refer the matter to the administration, or the chancellor, or the faculty, or Cohen's department. At this point, Harrington somewhat gratuitously pointed out that the department of philosophy appeared to be satisfied with Robert Cohen's work. After several more comments that, in the minutes, appear incoherent, he asked for regental action on the matter. Pasch moved approval of the recommendation and Werner seconded. Greenquist then recognized two people from the floor who wished to make statements. Henry W.

Haslack, Jr., vice-president of the Teaching Assistants Association, charged that Cohen had been recommended for firing without due process. James Villemonte spoke for the University Committee: "The University Committee takes the position that the University of Wisconsin should adhere to due process in form and in spirit in cases involving dismissal of academic staff, in keeping with the procedures outlined in Chapter 10B of University Laws and Regulations, approved by the faculty and the Board of Regents."

Gelatt asked whether the committee was for or against the motion. Villemonte said he did not know; they were, however, for due process, whatever was to be done. Gelatt asked his personal opinion. He replied that he would need to know what the department had said and done, whether the administration had more than hearsay evidence, and whether all proper procedures had been followed. If they had not, he would oppose the motion.

Nellen indicated his understanding of the motion to be that Cohen would be removed from the payroll and then given a hearing. Friedrick, citing Section 10B.09 of University Laws, gave a counter-interpretation, namely, that there would be a hearing first, then removal from payroll. Renk suggested that, according to Section 36.06.2 of Wisconsin statutes, the board could remove anyone they wanted. Sewell joined in and outlined proper academic procedure in such matters. He, in fact, disagreed with Harrington and suggested that the matter should go back to a faculty committee.

Then Gelatt spoke at length. He said he had to oppose Harrington in this case. He spoke about the greatness of the university for the past century, and the relationship between the faculty and the university which made such greatness possible. He recognized that there was a crisis, but felt that the proposed action could not end the crisis; further, it could worsen the relationship with the faculty. DeBardeleben also opposed the motion and supported Gelatt. He questioned whether the Regents, who should have been an appeal board, should be the original hearing board in this case. He also wondered why procedures that had long before been established for such cases were not being followed.

Renk said he agreed that the university had a great reputation; since he did not like the reputation that Cohen was giving it, he therefore supported the motion. Taking up the due process question, Ziegler stated that "we have a rule and have a right to make an exception to that rule any time we see fit, if the affairs of this university are in jeopardy." He declared that this was an emergency; that "people are getting away with permissiveness," that "certain people are using their freedoms to destroy our freedoms." After a number of attempts by Ziegler, Renk, and Nellen to deal more harshly with Cohen, the original Harrington motion to terminate Cohen's employment with provision for a public hearing before the Regents, if he desired, was passed, with only DeBardeleben, Friedrick, and Gelatt opposed. The meeting recessed for lunch, three and one-half hours after it had begun.

When the meeting resumed in the afternoon, Harrington raised the question of "providing a fair hearing." He recommended following usual procedures in such cases. Concerned that some Regents had already formed their opinions on the case, DeBardeleben proposed "that this hearing be heard by the executive committee of the board, excluding that member who has expressed an opinion as to how the hearing should be conducted." Friedrick perfunctorily seconded the motion, Renk and Nellen objected, and, at last, after a voice vote, Greenquist declared that the hearing would be before the executive board.

After a recess and committee meeting, the session resumed, and Renk offered a resolution that essentially fired all those teaching assistants and faculty members who, following the Dow demonstration, either failed to meet their classes or encouraged participation in the strike. He reported student and parent complaints that classes were not held and that teachers were not disciplined. He understood Harrington and Sewell to contend that "these people were under an emotional strain." Renk felt "these people were not immature, and, if they are emotional, we question very much their ability to teach."

Harrington now took the other side. He asked for an understanding of the situation and pointed out that the strike had not been long or effective. Ziegler seconded the Renk motion and Nellen offered his support. Friedrick opposed mass dismissals as both improper and impractical. DeBardeleben objected to the "complete abdication" of tenure rules. Renk defended himself and queried Harrington on the failure to discipline the violators. Gelatt suggested that education was not easily framed in input-output terms: X hours spent in a classroom did not mean X benefits derived. Renk replied, "You cannot turn out educated students if they are not in class." Gelatt pointed out that class attendance was not required in European schools.

Pasch thought it was a simple employment problem—failure to fulfill contract—and supported Renk. DeBardeleben suggested that the Renk policy was "foreign to anything [I have] heard regarding this university." The motion lost, being supported only by Nellen, Pasch, Renk, and Ziegler. And it was over.

Perhaps the most notable feature of the Regents' meeting following the Dow Chemical demonstration was the lack of coherent leadership on the part of the administration. Although both Harrington and Chancellor Sewell were present, Sewell spoke only once and then simply to outline established faculty procedures in dismissal cases. Sewell's reticence is even more surprising in view of the fact that he was deeply implicated in the events of the demonstration, since he, as chancellor, was responsible for the call that first brought city police to the Madison campus. Yet Harrington hardly provided greater leadership. His insistence on regental action in the cases of Cohen and Stark, although he was cognizant of the fact that disciplinary action was delegated by the Regents to the faculty, amounted to abdication of leadership. His position on this matter is even more puzzling when some of the regents themselves—most notably DeBardeleben and Gelatt—felt Harrington's stance represented infringement of faculty rights. In fact, Harrington strongly defended the university only when a portion of the faculty was threatened with en masse dismissal for their participation in a short-lived strike.

The position of the Regents in regard to demonstrations had also changed considerably since the antidraft demonstration. The rights to protest and free speech were not defended on the second occasion. Although the enactment of punitive rules and arbitrary dismissals demanded by the Republican triad of Renk, Ziegler and Nellen was avoided, the remainder of the Regents showed concern exclusively for procedure rather than substance. In fact, the question of the validity of the issues which the students were protesting was not once raised.

The February 14, 1969, meeting of the Regents was held in Milwaukee. The National Guard was occupying the Madison campus. The demonstration going on in Madison followed the week-long, university-approved Wisconsin Student Association Symposium on Black Revolution. Black students, aided by white radicals, called a strike to protest discrimination in admission policies, to demand the creation of a black student center, and to insist on the readmission of ninety-four black students who had been expelled from Oshkosh State University (in Wisconsin) for a similar protest the previous week. (For a more complete discussion of these events see Chapter Sixteen.)

As usual, the meeting began with the acceptance of gifts, grants, and contracts. Then Harrington suggested that, since Chancellor Young was present, the Regents discuss the "difficulties." Chancellor Young spoke at length. First, he discussed events that were averted by police action. He felt that "these policemen and these guardsmen were true heroes, standing out there, being taunted and insulted by people trying to provoke them."

Second, he discussed the black demands. He said many of them were already being implemented by the university and that many of the items demanded "had been discussed over and over again by the standing committees of the faculty," while some others were "purely illegal and unconstitutional."

Third, he discussed power. Young felt that a "small group of students who do not represent all black students" should not disrupt the campus. He suggested (in what was probably not intended to be a patronizing, racist statement) that "if we had no black students on the campus, we would still have difficulties, because there is a determined group of students who are truly revolutionary and say that this is a rotten and corrupt society, and that it ought to be destroyed." Later, he said (presumably about some demands), "we are not setting up segregated facilities." Young has been quoted at length here, because his comments and actions were sanctioned by the Regents.

Ziegler moved to compliment Chancellor Young, though this was expanded to mean the whole administration. The motion also supported "his position in replying to the demands of certain groups" and was seconded by all members of the Board. Pasch hoped "that Chancellor Young would continue to hold the line." The motion was voted. Gelatt hoped, "on behalf of the Regents," that "a reasonable and workable solution could be found in the near future." Renk moved to commend the state officials for their cooperation and support. Nellen said calling the Guard was "judicious" and "a great deterrent." The motion was voted, and the meeting moved on to other business.

However, later in the afternoon, the problem came up again. The Regents departed from their agenda to hear from two Milwaukee students. The first, David Edelman, spoke for Students for Autonomy. He criticized Governor Knowles' "law and order will be maintained at any cost" statement, because he felt that "law is racist and corrupt." He called on the university to meet the Black Student Union demands, remove police and National Guard from the campus, and readmit the suspended Oshkosh students. Then he read a statement condemning regental overruling of administration and faculty decisions and recommendations.

The second student, Miss Marge Kroeger, vice-president of the Milwaukee campus student government, had her comments dramatically underscored by noise from demonstrators outside the building and windows breaking inside the meeting room. She called for dialogue and an understanding of why students were demonstrating around the country that very week. Racism, she said, was one reason: Ninety-four black Oshkosh students had been suspended, but whites who also participated in the same demonstration were not.

President Harrington replied with a lengthy and detailed explanation of admission procedures, why the Oshkosh students could not be treated as a group, and the university decision that no exception from the standard rules could be made "for this semester." (The standard rules prohibited admission of the Oshkosh students to any state school if they were ineligible for admission on one campus.)

Responding to the question on student and faculty power, Gelatt explained that the Wisconsin statutes make the Regents responsible for nearly everything, with only a few provisions for delegation of responsibility. "He noted that the Regents and the administration lean very heavily on the faculty, and depend heavily on the opinions of others in developing policies."

Miss Kroeger made a few concluding remarks, most of which could only be heard with great difficulty, if at all, because of the recurrence of disruptions from outside the building, which included the breaking of a window adjacent to the head of the Regents' meeting table. The meeting moved on to other matters.

Compliments from the Regents to the administration to the contrary, the campus situation worsened, and a special meeting was requested by several members. It occurred in Madison, with all present except Renk. It was called "to discuss discipline of students and non-student disruption, discuss and vote on additional rules, procedures, regulations and policies necessary to maintain order on the campus." Indeed, the meeting of March sixth accomplished all this and more; the board even suspended three students.

The meeting opened with Professor George Bunn explaining that the rules of the university had a loophole—namely, they failed to prevent suspended trouble-making students from coming onto campus. An emergency rule was therefore prepared for addition to the Wisconsin Administrative Code (UW 1.07.19). This rule kept both suspended students, and convicted non-student disruptors off the campus for a year. It was moved by Pasch, seconded by Sandin, and voted. Since this was only an emergency rule, a hearing was called to consider adoption of the rule on a regular basis. The call was moved by Pasch, seconded by Sandin, and voted.

The director of protection and security, Ralph Hanson, then gave a vividly detailed, blow-by-blow account of a chaotic, rampaging demonstration which he witnessed on February 27, and which was the event that prompted the special meeting. This particular burst of violence was essentially a frustrated outburst by a very small group of mainly white radicals which occurred as the black strike lost momentum.

After a discussion, Sandin moved to suspend three of these students, pending hearings, because "the administration of the Madison campus has shown reasonable grounds to cause us to believe that they have participated in both causing the violence on February 27, 1969, and in earlier attempts to disrupt the university." The hearing was set for March 19, 1969. The resolution was passed.

Gelatt then moved to request the administration to consider the feasibility and legality of action that would: require students to agree in writing to obey university rules; improve control of nonstudents on campus; require showing identification to proper authorities; and allow immediate student suspension by the administration, subject to due process. After a discussion which included the state attorney general, the motion was seconded by Werner and passed.

Pasch moved to commend the police, sheriffs, and National Guardsmen, and the motion was passed. Finally, Harrington reported on several bills in the state legislature, which he supported. Most of these dealt with the handling and prevention of demonstrations and the punishing of demonstrators.

A week later, the Regents met again in regular session in Madison. Friedrick, Renk, and Walker were absent. A report on the Black Revolution Symposium was discussed at length. The report had been prepared by Arthur Hove, project specialist in the central administration, though there is no indication of who requested it. One gets the impression that either the Regents or the administration were looking for a scapegoat, because the report talks of the possible connection between the Symposium and the black strike which occurred immediately following it. The Regents' discussion focused on whether university money was used to pay for the Symposium (the chancellor's office had funded a large portion), and particularly whether the chancellor had reviewed the speaker list. He had not.

The discussion then shifted to the report of the Faculty Committee on Human Rights, regarding the suspended Oshkosh students, and a Milwaukee faculty resolution on the same matter. The Faculty Committee report explained in great detail what had happened to the students' applications for readmission at each stage in the admission procedure. The students finally were rejected categorically, but after they had been told they would be considered individually. The problem was that normally, when there is a disciplinary notation on the application (such as suspension for X semesters), officials of both schools discuss the matter. In this case, the suspensions at Oshkosh were not handled by the faculty or the administration—rather, they were initiated and executed by the Regents of the Wisconsin State Universities. Hence, it was a matter between university Regents and state Regents. So an informal poll of Regents was taken, that resulted in rejection of the applications.

Gelatt reminded the board that, according to the Wisconsin statutes (36.06), the Regents "shall determine the moral and educational qualifications of applicants." This meant, he thought, that the Regents could not, on their own, say that moral qualifications could be ignored by admissions offices, because that would put the Regents in violation of the statute. He moved that the Regents reaffirm their informal poll denying exception to standard admission procedures. To make exception and admit them would, he thought, be "a mockery of the actions taken by the Regents of the Wisconsin State Universities."

Gelatt's motion was seconded by Ziegler and voted by all present. Harrington said that the Milwaukee faculty resolution was "not recommended to the Regents by the administration for approval at this time."

Professor Bunn reported on the status of the disciplinary cases. He said that the three students suspended at last week's special meeting had filed a suit in Federal District Court, charging violation of the Fourteenth Amendment due process clause. Judge James Doyle of that court had determined that a fifteen (or more) day suspension was too severe, unless it could be proved that the presence of these students constituted a threat to safety. Bunn "assumed that such a test was likely." The Regents then agreed to have a special meeting later in the month to hear the results of the disciplinary hearing.

The series of meetings in response to the black strike marked a change in regental response to student protest. The most obvious difference was the lack of any debate on the mode of response. Almost all dissension among the Regents as to the proper policy on demonstration had disappeared. Instead, the board presented a united front; punishment and prevention appeared to be the unanimous policy. In sharp contrast to the earlier cases of Cohen and Stark, those students who broke existing rules were promptly expelled and the former scrupulous concern for due process was absent. Instead, the board seemed intent on protecting the university by enactment of strict rules to punish student offenders as well as (futile) attempts to prevent the ubiquitous non- or ex-student agitator from contaminating the campus.

The shift in Regent Gelatt's position represents the shift made by the board as a whole. At the meetings following the black strike, Gelatt himself called for and specified the very rules—spelling out the appropriate steps to take against demonstrators—that he had previously insisted fell in the area of faculty decision making. In other words, the board had ceased to wonder whether it was appropriate for them to take an active role in policy-making in one of the most sensitive aspects of university life. Rather than allowing students and faculty to work out the problems of their community, the Regents, as their commendation of Chancellor Young indicated, had reduced the question to proper deployment of force.

Looking at regental response to these three student demonstrations in this manner has some limitations. Because I have focused only on immediate reactions, I have missed other responses which may prove more important in the long run: the cutback in out-of-state enrollment at both undergraduate and graduate levels by the imposition of a quota on such enrollment and the raising of fees for such students, and the modification of student disciplinary procedures, with a net reduction of student and faculty influence on these procedures.

Comparing the Regents' reactions at three points in time seems to show the following pattern. At first—in 1966—the response was "liberal"; that is, the Regents and the administration were concerned, somewhat accommodating, mildly scolding, and generally unperturbed. In 1967, the reaction was bitter, angry, and spiteful. Both the administration and the Regents expressed their anger and confusion by lashing out, ultimately against only a few students. By 1969, the response was again measured, not because the earlier attitude had been recovered, but because those in power had become more certain of their course of action. That course was one of firmness, increased centralization of authority, and judicious acknowledgment of the "proper procedures" that seem to concern academicians so much.

In some ways, the impact cannot be assessed. Kent State and Jackson State and the bombing of Sterling Hall totally changed the script. The current, perhaps temporary quiet on the campus, the election of a Democratic governor, the appointment of a new university president, and the pending merger of the university with the state university system serve to deflect attention from the issues raised by the demonstrations. Whether the slow building of Democratic strength and proportionate weakening of the Republican hegemony on the board will have a progressive impact is unclear; it may be that the Democrats, finding the Republican course to be the popular one, will join ranks with their erstwhile opponents.

Notes

[1] My thinking concerning the issues in this essay was aided by conversations with P. G. Altbach, R. S. Laufer, S. McVey, Arlene Kaplan Daniels, Theodore Lowi, and others. I am grateful for the assistance provided by Clarke Smith, secretary of the Board of Regents; Robert Foss, assistant director of the UW News Service; and Pat Murphy, administrative assistant with the News Service. These individuals, of course, are in no way responsible for what appears here.
[2] *Wisconsin Constitution,* Article X, Section 6. This and subsequent citations

from the laws and Constitution of Wisconsin are quoted from *Wisconsin Statutes,* *1969,* J. J. Burke and D. T. Thimke (eds.).

[3] *Ibid.,* Statutes, 36.01.

[4] *Ibid.,* Statutes, 36.03.1.

[5] *Ibid.,* Statutes, 15.91.

[6] *Ibid.,* Statutes, 36.06.1.

[7] *Ibid.,* Statutes, 36.06.2.

[8] *Ibid.,* Statutes, 36.12.

[9] *Ibid.,* Statutes, 36.13.9.

[10] *Ibid., Constitution,* Article X, Section 6.

[11] *Ibid.,* Statutes, 14.04.

[12] *Ibid., Constitution,* Article VIII, Section 2.

[13] *Ibid.,* Statutes, 20.285.1.

[14] See R. T. Harnett, *College and University Trustees: Their Backgrounds, Roles, and Educational Attitudes* (Princeton, N.J.: Educational Testing Service, 1969); M. A. Rauh, *The Trusteeship of Colleges and Universities* (New York: McGraw-Hill, 1969), especially Chapter 10.

[15] Because of Werner's resignation in March, 1969, and his immediate replacement by Dahlstrom, the party balance in April 1969 was two Democrates and seven Republicans. But that was to last for only one month, because Friedrick's term expired and he was replaced by Pelisek. So by May 1969, exactly three years from our reference point of May 1966, the board was comprised of one Democrat and eight Republicans.

CHAPTER 5

STATE AND MULTIVERSITY

Matt Pommer

Three men—a university president, a federal judge, and a powerful politician—played key roles in the University of Wisconsin drama of the 1960s. Each came to power through the hand of fate, and the Wisconsin story would have been far different had any of them failed to arrive in power. Their stories tell of the university's relationships to the state government.

Fred Harvey Harrington came to the University of Wisconsin presidency in 1962. He presided over the greatest expansion in the school's history, but was to become the lightning rod for criticism that developed in the wake of student activism in the late 1960s. James Doyle was the second to reach power; he was appointed federal judge for western Wisconsin in 1964. He made his mark as a defender of first amendment rights and due process procedures. He was the man who single-handedly proved to many young activists that all governmental institutions were not corrupt. The last to arrive in power was Harold Froehlich, who won election to the powerful role of speaker of the Wisconsin assembly in 1967. He assumed command of the legislative process, riding herd on the university's finances and the government's relationships with faculty and students.

Harrington led the liberal, expansionist forces that dominated the

112

university during the boom period of the early sixties; Froehlich felt he
represented the people of the state who were opposed to the "foreign"
values for which the university stood; Doyle arbitrated the clash between
university and state through precedent-setting decisions in constitutional
law. Harrington was the central figure at the drama. He had been the
second choice for the university presidency in 1957. The Regents by-
passed him then, by a one-vote margin, and named Conrad Elvehjem to
be the university's thirteenth president to succeed E. B. Fred. The Regents
had effected a compromise by ordering Elvehjem to take Harrington as
his vice-president. But by the summer of 1962 Harrington was preparing
to assume the presidency of the University of Hawaii. Fate intervened
before Harrington formally took over at Hawaii. Working at his Bascom
Hall desk on a humid Friday morning, Elvehjem collapsed and died of a
heart attack. The next day, the Regents placed a transoceanic call to
Harrington, asking him to pick up Elvehjem's reins. Harrington was to
enjoy five years as the master of the university before other forces were
to cloud his star.

One of these forces came into power through the reluctance of
Governor Warren Knowles to enter the fray of Republican politics.
Elected to a second term in 1966, Knowles carried the Republicans back
into power in the assembly. But the party split along moderate-conserva-
tive lines over the key post of assembly speaker. Knowles stood aloof, saying he was part of the executive branch, despite his numerous years in the
legislature. The moderates lost by one vote in the caucus, and Harold
Froehlich took center stage in the state. As speaker, Froehlich wielded
appointive power for the conservatives. The State Building Commission,
the Board of Government Operations, and the Joint Committee on
Finance swung to the right.

The third key figure came to the University of Wisconsin as a
result of the national tragedy in Dallas in November 1963. Doyle had
been a key supporter of Adlai Stevenson in numerous campaigns. When
the federal judgeship in western Wisconsin became vacant, he was supported by Senator Gaylord Nelson and by Doyle's close personal friend,
Miles McMillin, editorial writer for the Madison *Capital Times*. But
President Kennedy had nominated a Sheboygan labor lawyer endorsed by
Robert Kennedy, by Patrick Lucey, the state party chairman, and by
Senator Proxmire. But the Nelson-Proxmire split snarled the confirmation.
After Kennedy was slain in Dallas, President Johnson nominated Doyle,
and the senate confirmed the appointment.

Harrington had become a controversial figure early in his years
at the university. Primarily concerned with the academic status of Wisconsin, he was in office less than three months when he made headlines

with anti–Rose Bowl remarks at a Regents' meeting. He expanded the university administration, first through the use of special assistants and then through the development of the chancellorship system. He ruled the university with the consent of a supporting Board of Regents. This type of administration succeeded in some areas, but failed in the Medical School. Harrington was unable to resolve the bitter political infighting in the medical center which surfaced most notably in the controversy over who was to lead the surgery department.

Equally vexing in the Medical School controversies was the split over how to expand and modernize the plant. Nearly a decade after the fight was started neither the governor nor the legislature has resolved the issue. Many in the Medical School are willing to blame Harrington for the snarls. The indecision came at a time when the federal government was pouring funds into new medical centers. The Wisconsin operation never cashed in on the opportunities. Internal struggles first plagued the plans. Then a legislative committee intervened, and it fell under the sway of a Medical School faction rather than of Harrington. New consultants were hired. Opportunity ebbed away while inflation skyrocketed costs. In addition, Harrington made personal commitments for the university to attempt to build the humanities and social sciences to the national levels already reached by the physical and biological sciences on the Madison campus. In the process the Medical School had to rely more and more on federal and grant money.

The legislators were upset with the way Harrington handled the problem of the new medical school because they had a vested interest in it—most of them were in their later years. When legislators have a personal interest in any project, they are usually unwilling to assign its control to an "expert"; instead they demand an exact account of all details. However, accountability was not part of the Harrington style of administration. Harrington seemed to operate on the principle that the less outsiders knew about expenditures, the easier it was to fund unpopular projects. But in the case of the Medical School, Harrington's usually successful tactic only irritated the legislators who felt that they deserved fuller information.

Among the most influential lobbyists were a small group of the university's most outstanding physicians. Their names have been used in some instances to defeat bills having nothing to do with the Medical School. The best example of this was the argument used by Harvey Dueholm, a Democratic assemblyman, in a debate on a bill to limit numbers of out-of-state students. Dueholm reminded his colleagues that he had been dying of cancer when he went to university hospitals five years earlier. But the university physicians had cured him of cancer. What if these men, as out-of-state undergraduate students, had been denied a premedical education? What if they had never gone through medical school? There were few dry eyes left when he was through. The bill was rejected.

The legislative history of the university is dotted with the works of a handful of men who have wielded great power over the school. The potential of the legislature to effect the policies of a state university is, of course, enormous. Legally, the legislature, as representative of the people, has final authority. Thus, legislative attitudes toward the university are a constant source of tension. One of the forms this tension often takes is a conflict between a local and a national orientation for the university. Those who favor a local orientation argue that the major purpose of the university is to serve the state, that cosmopolitan or foreign elements are a threat to the solid agrarian values of Wisconsin, that academic eminence in no way corresponds with moral eminence. Contrarily, those who favor a national orientation insist on the paramount place of (universal) knowledge in a modern society. Those who have a local orientation are concerned with the disparity between the state colleges and the universities and contend that the two should be equal, regardless of whether or not this injures the academic standing of the university. Conversely, those with a national orientation would keep the university separate and maintain its prestige.

An example of this conflict is provided by a bill which would have required the university to give credit for courses taken in state colleges. The credit transfer issue is one of the most repeated complaints voiced by voters to the legislators. Many Madison faculty apparently think only they can give the proper courses for graduation. In an era of emphasis on graduate education, this pressure for undergraduate "purity" mystifies many lawmakers. Only a friendly request from the university's lobbyist killed the bill in the 1969 session. It cleared the assembly with ease and had more than enough votes in the state senate. But Senator Holger Rasmussen, a Republican who headed the upper house's Education Committee, put it in the bottom drawer of his desk and never called a hearing. The discretion of individual legislators often sets policy for the university.

Committee positions have been the launching pads for other legislators including Republican State Senator Jerris Leonard and Republican Representative John Shabaz. Leonard used his position as chairman of the University Affairs Committee of the State Building Commission to single-handedly delay a substantial expansion program for the university. The reason Leonard gave was opposition to the proposed design of skywalks over streets; the skywalks were only an embellishment on the major building and could have been easily scrapped. But the measures and plan

never came out of his three-man committee. His diligent committee homework paid off—no other legislator spent enough time on the plans to
refute his arguments. The projects remained pigeonholed for several
years while plans were redrawn. The Leonard case is probably the clearest
example of the power of an individual legislator when other members of
an elected body refuse to do their homework on complicated issues. Only
those well-versed in the subjects are willing to tackle the detailed affairs of
government that fail to attract headlines.

Shabaz, a key Froehlich aide, once suggested that a state deficit
could be partially eliminated if all the teaching assistants at the university
had their pay cut in half. The Shabaz bill made the Teaching Assistants
Association a major factor on the Madison Campus. Although the reasoning and strategies employed by Dueholm, Rasmussen, Leonard, and
Shabaz are often obscure, one has grounds for assuming that their actions
were predicated on policy. More often the legislative reaction to the university is malicious or simply unthinking. Once the Republican floor
leader in the state senate assailed the highly paid professors at the University of Wisconsin. Legislators are insecure over their salaries. Many in
both houses and both political parties will argue that no one should make
more than the governor's 25,000 dollars. Their own salaries (then 8,400
dollars) were always a source of bitterness when they reviewed the compensation of university employees. Furthermore, the legislators tended to
think university professors worked only when they were in front of a class.
In one confrontation with university representatives, a Regent asked if
legislators only worked when their house was in session.

Senator Ernest Keppler, the Republican floor leader, reflected this
legislative insecurity when he demanded a list of the highest paid university professors. He read the names and salaries of the university faculty
and assailed the ivory towers in which these men allegedly worked. "How
about Har Gobind Khorana? Anyone know him?" bellowed Keppler. His
associates, either uninformed or bored, did not respond. Newsmen had a
field day. The famed scientist who was to receive the Nobel Prize was
unknown to the men who were attacking the operation of the university.
Some newspapers demanded an apology, while others merely suggested
that the state senate was deficient in its homework. Khorana later moved
his research team to the Massachussets Institute of Technology, although
University of Wisconsin officials claimed that Keppler's slur on the senate
floor had nothing to do with the move.

Like any well-financed special interest group, the university has
lobbyists at work in the state capitol. However, the university is composed
of various heterogeneous interest groups. The more powerful and better

organized of these groups—the Medical School, the athletics department, the central administration—each have their own lobbyists, who sometimes work at cross purposes to one another. A prime example of the several lobbies at work in the legislature was the bill requiring the university to provide athletic scholarships. Only the university medical lobby exhibited more influence in the 1960s than the athletic department. Athletic Director Elroy Hirsch came to the capitol to make the pitch. When the bill ran into trouble, some legislators were told that it would not cost the state any money. With that assurance the bill roared through the legislature, leaving Harrington and the regular lobbying team aghast. The legislature later was to learn that scholarships do indeed cost state funds.

Harrington should not have been too surprised at the trick played on the legislature. He, too, had convinced goodly numbers of people whenever he took to the rostrum. He had led citizens in southeastern and northeastern Wisconsin to believe the university would build new campuses in their home towns. Only Green Bay and rural Kenosha actually got campuses. The sites were selected by four-member committees, on which Harrington was the key member. Citizens of some communities, especially Racine, never forgave Harrington for what they considered a double-cross. However, of Harrington's select team, no one ever doubted the boss' loyalty. The first chancellor of the Madison campus, Robben W. Fleming, praised Harrington's conduct. In those days Harrington was a few steps from Fleming's office. Administrators who were rebuffed by Fleming merely went down the hall and tried to sell Harrington on the same propositions. Fleming was to report that Harrington always shipped them back up the hall to the chancellor's office.

Harrington had moved to Van Hise Hall, leaving Fleming in historic Bascom, when the student disruptions developed. Harrington allowed Fleming a great deal of leeway in dealing with the disruptions. Fleming's gesture of providing bail for arrested students sticks in the throats of right-wing legislators years after the incident. His action was never understood in the legislature or by many Wisconsin Regents.

Outside Wisconsin the action was understood in different ways. The Regents of the University of Minnesota offered Fleming their presidency. The publicity from that offer spurred the Regents of the University of Michigan to offer him their presidency. Fleming's departure for Ann Arbor in 1967 left the key Madison chancellorship for Harrington to fill. The job was initially offered to H. Edwin Young, then president of the University of Maine and a former dean of the College of Letters and Science in Madison. Pressure to fill the job forced Harrington to find a successor to Fleming quickly. Young was unable to leave Maine at that time because of a deadlock over that school's budget. Instead Harrington turned to liberal sociology professor William Sewell, head of the University Committee.

Sewell was greeted with the university's first major violence, the Dow Chemical Company sit-in in the Commerce Building. Sewell and Harrington started out in agreement, but Harrington moved with pressure from the public and the legislators, especially in the dismissal of students involved in the sit-in. Sewell tried to reunite the several bitter factions created on the campus by the demonstration. However, his conciliatory efforts met with little success, and at the end of the academic year he resigned. Young returned from Maine to take first a vice-presidency and then the Madison chancellorship. It was a happy choice for the Regents and the conservative legislators. Despite his reputation as an old school liberal, both the Regents and the legislators admired his toughness on student disruption. Young once told Governor Knowles he would not do the job without massive use of National Guardsmen. Wisconsin became the first school to make major use of troops to quell student demonstrations.

Young's presence in the lobbies of the legislature was able to turn the tide on a number of bills. The most attention was turned on a measure sponsored by Assemblyman Froehlich to remove the campus police force and put all police work under the control of the Madison police chief. Clearly it contained a hint that the university was being permissive or that administrators were keeping the campus police under wraps. Froehlich consistently opposed the university, but his role as speaker meant that much of his attack was carried on behind closed doors with his colleagues. However, the issues he publicly supported were also strongly against the university. For example, he supported one measure that would have stripped tenure from the faculty. The measure failed although only one distinguished former Regent spoke out against it. Arthur DeBardeleben accurately assessed the powerful threat Froehlich posed to the university when he said that the threat to tenure was a blow against the heart of the academic enterprise and that the abolition of tenure would be a breach of faith and contract with the faculty; such legislation would make a shambles of efforts to recruit new faculty members of great ability and promise.

Froelich did succeed in the area in which he had most control— the spending level at the University of Wisconsin. The university suffered severe hardship at the hands of the Joint Committee on Finance. University officials were subjected to abuse from conservatives on the committee. Froehlich was seldom on hand since he was not a member of the committee. But the committee often sought his advice and leadership on

methods to reduce spending at the university. The state senate held out
for more funds for the university, but Froehlich suggested that the dis-
puted funds be placed with the Board of Government Operations for dispersal to the university when enrollments showed the school needed the
additional funds. The senate accepted that idea; it learned too late that
the majority of the board had been appointed by Froehlich and could
manipulate the meaning of the final resolution. They argued that simply
having more students enrolled did not prove a need for money at the
university. Froehlich failed in his attempts to end tenure protection for
faculty members. But his financial efforts succeeded. The university ended
the 1960s in last place in faculty salaries among Big Ten schools.

The third leading character in the university drama, Judge Doyle,
at times stood alone to ensure that the university lived up to its reputation
for fairness. In a number of cases he struck down university rules as unconstitutional, much to the agitation of conservative Regents and of
Froehlich. Doyle's decisions stressed the constitutional rights of students
who were charged with participation in demonstrations. He told a Madison audience:

I choose freedom. I choose an open society. I choose the wellsprings of renewal
in every generation. I choose the First Amendment. . . . We are caught up in
a time of great social ferment. This ferment is reflected in litigation in which
there is a flood of constitutional questions to which the Constitution itself provided no literal answers and on which the Supreme Court of the United States
has not yet spoken. . . . To militant young people who prevent the Secretary
of State from being heard by an audience gathered to hear him, to militant
blacks for whom whitey has nothing to say, the First Amendment is a quaint and
impotent relic of eighteenth century rationalism. To those alarmed by violence
on the campuses and in the streets, to those disgusted by a new sexual era, the
First Amendment is a lit fuse or an instrument of the devil.

Doyle resisted all these challenges to the First Amendment. University issues in his court ranged from Regent rules on loudspeakers to
procedures used before a student could be expelled. He was repeatedly
upheld by the United States Court of Appeals for the Seventh Circuit
and by the United States Supreme Court. As a result of Doyle's judicial
success, Froehlich became a supporter of Everett Dirksen's plan for a
constitutional amendment for the election of federal judges. Froehlich
cited Doyle's decisions in outlining his opinion. Madison citizens appeared
to have a different view of the Doyle name. Twice they elected his wife
to the Madison Board of Education at the height of the controversy over
the judge's decisions.

Doyle's decisions attracted national attention. One of those reviewing the decisions of the western district of Wisconsin was Texas Law

Professor Charles Alan Wright, who wrote in the *Vanderbilt Law Review* that Doyle had emerged as the "protector of the constitutional rights of college students." Wright summarized Doyle's decisions as being undergirded by the basic proposition that students at institutions of higher learning have constitutional rights which the courts must recognize and protect. Wright noted that Doyle's decisions were based on constitutional grounds, implying that he was not merely soft on college students.

Judge Doyle probably had a role in the late 1960s more important than he could imagine. To many he proved that a single principled man could make a difference in events. The university came out of the 1960s with its reputation as a liberal institution only slightly tarnished. The reputation was due to the historical role of the faculty, but its survival reflects the curbing hand of Doyle on the Regents, Fred Harrington, and Harold Froehlich. No university was under more pressure in the sixties. Berkeley did not have a state legislature only a mile away. Columbia students did not invade the halls of the New York legislature. Harrington was bent by the pressure and finally resigned in the spring of 1970. The voters apparently had enough of Froehlich's policies, for they removed the Republican party from control of the assembly and Froehlich nearly lost his own seat. The 1970s moved into full swing with Doyle still enforcing the broad guarantees of the Constitution. He spoke of the nation and campus troubles in a speech, saying, "In such a time, it seems to me, the values of freedom, rooted as ever both in pragmatism and in idealism, shine the more brightly. Pragmatically, in a dangerous universe, the least dangerous alternative is freedom. With developing insight, the human race may survive. Without it, the fates make book against us."[1]

Note

[1] *Capital Times,* March 9, 1971.

CHAPTER 6

●●●●●●●●●●●●●●
●●●●●●●●●●●●●●
●●●●●●●●●●●●●●

POLITICS OF
UNIVERSITY RESEARCH

James Rowen

●●●●●●●●●●●●●●
●●●●●●●●●●●●●●
●●●●●●●●●●●●●●

"The university is partisan to no party or ideology" (Wisconsin Board of Regents, June 1968). A cynic would sneer at that statement; someone with the facts can prove it absurd. Whether the Regents passed this resolution in a moment of conscious delusion or in one of monumental stupidity, it is still false, hiding the highly political nature of the university. An institution which pioneers military weaponry and helps deliver it more efficiently cannot be called neutral. A university cannot help tightly owned, family-run corporations garner a larger share of the market in a system of private enterprise and at the same time be labeled "value-free." In order to understand the nature of the university as well as that of the political system that nurtures it, one must find out who benefits from it. As one Wisconsin businessman put it, "The university is a powerful tool if its knowledge is applied properly. There's nothing you can't get from it."[1] In answering the question of who gets what, it is necessary to examine the relationship of the university to both the miltary and industry.

The myth of university neutrality is easily exploded; the Army

121

Mathematics Research Center provides a dramatic starting point. For example, in August of 1968 a tremendous explosion ripped the Louisiana Army Ammunition Plant in Shreveport. Six workers were killed and nine injured. The plant manufactured and loaded antipersonnel cluster bombs and mines, 155 mm artillery shells, 2.75 in. rocket warheads, and other deadly weapons.[2] In the middle of the war in Vietnam, the army was faced with the supply problem of making up for the loss at the Louisiana plant. Herman F. Karreman was flown from Madison to the Army Edgewood Arsenal in Maryland to offer his advice. He later said, "Part of a plant was wiped out in an explosion and they were interested to find out what was the most economical way to provide the army with the munitions that they will need in the next, say ten to fifteen years."[3] Karreman was one of the ten full-time staff members of the AMRC. The research installation, obtained by the university through competitive bidding in 1955, is contractually required "to provide for the army a source of advice and assistance with respect to the solution of mathematical problems."[4]

It is impossible to beg the question of the university's relationship to the military by a distinction between applied and pure research. The AMRC does not operate in a void; in clear, material ways it manifests the intensely political, value-laden nature of the university. The AMRC is the only center funded by the United States Army for the research and dissemination of mathematics. It is obliged by its contract with the Army Research Office to provide six general services in four areas "in which mathematical research has relevance to problems that exist or are inherent to army operations."[5]

About seventy university professors make up the AMRC staff each year, with slight fluctuations in the number of part-time appointees who also work in other departments, notably mathematics and computer science. The permanent staff of ten faculty members "are specialists in areas of value to the army," who direct "the long-range investigations of AMRC . . . and help select able people for the nonpermanent positions."[6] It is this cadre of army mathematicians which implements the following demands of the contract:

A. To provide a group of highly qualified mathematicians which will: (1) Conduct mathematical research which has relevance to problems that exist or are inherent to army operations, which have emphasis upon long-range investigations, and which is directed towards the discovery of techniques that may have applications to the army's needs; this is research to supplement (not replace) that of existing activities. (2) Provide for the army a source of advice and assistance with respect to the solution of mathematical problems. (3) Upon request, make technical studies of the use of mathematics by army activities, and make recommendations as to the implementation of the conclusions of such studies. (4) Cooperate with army activities in the recruitment of scientific personnel.

B. To provide a facility for stimulating contact between army scientific personnel and other scientists.

C. To create a reservoir of mathematicians that may be called upon by the government for assistance in the event of a national emergency by acquainting mathematicians with the needs of the army and enlisting their work on problems of army interest.

The contract calls for research in four areas of special interest to the army. These are numerical analysis, including the extension of the scientific usefulness of high speed computers; statistics and probability; applied mathematics and analysis; and mathematical research applicable to operations research. The staff of the AMRC fulfills its contractual obligations in various ways besides its day-to-day numerical calisthenics. A sort of Pentagon bellhop service is provided by AMRC to deliver staff experts and papers directly to an interested military base or official. University travel records document the liaison activity between university research and the military.

During fiscal 1968 and fiscal 1969, permanent AMRC member Bernard Harris consulted at Picatinny Arsenal, New Jersey and at Aberdeen Proving Ground, Maryland, gave a series of orientation lectures at the White Sands Missile Range, New Mexico, and attended two army conferences on the design of experiments, research, development, and testing. Another permanent member, Karreman, consulted twice at the Edgewood Arsenal, Maryland, lectured at Fort Belvoir, Virginia, and toured Air Defense centers in Colorado, New Mexico, and Utah. During the tour, according to the AMRC Summary Report for 1968: "Professor Karreman called attention to the availability of AMRC for technical assistance and advice. . . . At the NORAD Center, he discussed the work of the AMRC on the probability of survival of a subterranean target with Lieutenant General Robert Hackett. In answer to requests made during his visits, Professor Karreman upon his return sent information about the activities and capabilities of AMRC and about their in-service educational program to Major General Underwood."[7] In 1966, Karreman, Harris, and AMRC Director Rosser collaborated on an army-initiated study entitled "Probability of Survival of a Subterranean Target Under Intensive Attack," and Karreman brought this information to air force personnel.

Conversely, the AMRC brings army scientists to Sterling Hall for "extended periods. Such visitors are called Research Residents, but in fact can devote their time either to research, or to study with some of

the staff of the AMRC, or to working on an army problem in close cooperation with a staff member of AMRC. . . . Such visits not only help
the Research Resident to increase his mathematical competency but serve
to acquaint the AMRC staff with army problems on a detailed basis."[8]
AMRC is also charged with "stimulating contact"[9] between army personnel and other scientists; this is accomplished through seminars and major
conferences which are held on campus once or twice a year. In this way,
AMRC brings together international military personnel, professors, and
defense contractors. The latest mathematical knowledge is provided to all
interested and accredited parties.

The Conference on Stochastic Optomization and Control in October 1967 illustrates this AMRC operation. The overall topic dealt with the
application of probability theory to the flight of missiles and antimissiles.
There were thirty-nine scientists in attendance who were not connected
with the host university: Five came from White Sands Missile Range, two
came from the Pentagon, and one each attended from Edgewood Arsenal,
Redstone Arsenal, Frankford Arsenal, Army Research and Development
Group (Europe), Army Materiel Command, Army Natick Laboratories,
the Army Research Office, Army Behavioral Science Research, and the
Naval Weapons Center, along with the Chief of Mathematics Branch of
the Office of the Chief of Research and Development, United States
Army.[10] In addition, four scientists from prime military contractors were
there, two from the main developer of the ABM, Bell Laboratories, and
one each from Boeing Air Craft Company and Operations Research,
Inc.[11]

Papers presented at the conference's formal sessions were clearly
oriented toward military operations. Dr. Winston Nelson from Bell Laboratories read a paper detailing the operation of the Spartan-Sprint antiballistic missile system. Another paper, by two scientists from the RAND
Corporation, dealt with the effectiveness of the United States' long-range
bomber program.[12] The military personnel and subjects which dominated
the conference are not isolated instances; all AMRC conferences are
similarly weighted.

Although military subjects predominate in technical reports by
AMRC staff members, references to military applications are deliberately
demilitarized. Scores of these reports are written each year. They consist
of several pages of formulas with a title and sparse prose in mathematical
language, and they conform to the army's demand that AMRC "press
releases, presentations at scientific meetings, and papers should not dis-
close financial details, possible military applications, or the overall army
program in the particular field involved."[13] An instance in which this
regulation was violated demonstrates the army's firm control over its

civilian researchers and the center's necessary obfuscation in reporting its activities.

In December, 1966, the center's director, J. Barkley Rosser, and two permanent staff members, Bernard Harris and Herman Karreman, authored a paper called "The Probability of Survival of a Subterranean Target Under Intensive Attack." It dealt with theoretically shifting conditions of the number and configuration of blasts detonating about a subterranean target area. When the paper was first printed, Rosser recalled, "we must have by chance picked some numerical examples close to those involved in the army's studies. At any rate, the army said that publication of the report with those numerical examples might be a hazard to the safety of the country. We hurriedly collected and burned all pieces of paper with those numerical examples on them. We chose some new ones suitable to the survival of anthills at which rocks are being thrown; and rewrote number 653 with numerical examples based on the anthill numbers. The army had no reservation about this; the report was published in the customary fashion in the open literature. It is freely available to everyone, including even the armies of Russia, Israel, Egypt, et al. I don't see how publication could be more open."[14]

The "revised" paper was sent to General Underwood at the NORAD Air Defense Center and presented at yearly army research conferences. If questioned about the incident, the civilian researchers involved will certainly claim that their academic freedom was not in any way compromised; a change in data description, they would say, in no way violates the integrity of the report. However, this formulation of the issue avoids recognition of the army's exercise of final control.

In keeping with their refusal to acknowledge the army's final authority, Rosser and his staff—like nearly all university faculty under Pentagon contract—continually disclaim any clearly defined military role by claiming that army-initiated projects represent only a small fraction of their time and work. According to the AMRC, open-ended, highly theoretical research arrived at by the prediliction of the individual scholar characterizes the center. This position seems to draw a definitive line between civilian and military as well as between theoretical and applied research. The army's acquiescence to this position is probably based on grounds other than respect for academic freedom. Dwight D. Eisenhower, as chief of staff of the army, authored a general memorandum in 1946 under the title of "Scientific and Technological Resources as Military Assets."

Scientists and industrialists must be given the greatest possible freedom to carry out their research. [Italics his.] The fullest utilization by the army of the civilian resources of the nation cannot be procured merely by prescribing the military characteristics and requirements of certain types of equipment. Scientists and industrialists are more likely to make new and unsuspected contributions to the development of the army if detailed directions are held to a minimum. The solicitation of assistance under these conditions would not only make available to the army talents and experience otherwise beyond our reach, but also establish mutual confidence between ourselves and civilians It would familiarize them with our fundamental problems and strengthen greatly the foundation on which our national security depends.[15]

In other words, the military, as early as 1946, perceived that freedom of personal inquiry would result in what it considered a desirable relationship between the military and the university. Such a relationship ensures that the military's immediate and long-range needs will be met. In the AMRC's case, the emphasis is on both, with day-to-day army problems as well as the frontiers of knowledge being studied. By sponsoring long-range research in areas of relevance (computer development, operations research, and so forth) the army ensures that it will be kept informed of advances in these fields. A researcher who says that he merely does his work and that anyone is welcome to read and use it runs the risk of having a rapacious military absorb it; but an employee working at AMRC knows in advance that the army will have an early crack at his findings. As Rosser once said, "It is very definitely my impression that the work we do is of value to the army. I would say that if it were not useful to the army, the army would stop supporting us."[16]

Despite claims of academic freedom and purely theoretical research, the relationship between the military and the university has produced concrete, practical findings that have been utilized to support a reactionary American foreign policy. The University of Michigan, under Project Michigan, developed sophisticated infrared aerial photography techniques that aided Bolivian troops trained by American special forces to track down Che Guevara. It seems probable that University of Wisconsin's AMRC aided Project Michigan. "By 1966," a researcher wrote, "the Department of Defense decided that Michigan's experience in infrared surveillance technology was sufficiently advanced to permit the transition from theory to practice."[17] At some point between June 1966 and Guevara's death in October 1967, however, the army called upon Wisconsin's AMRC to assist Project Michigan. In AMRC's 1967 Summary Report, "asistance to Project Michigan" is listed in the table of contents' resume of aid to the army. But the entire eight-page section covering fiscal 1967 assistance and advice is censored from the report. In its place is a dry one-paragraph statement from the chairman of the Army Mathematics Steering Commitee declaring that "some of the information con-

cerning these contracts is considered privileged." The exact nature of
AMRC's aid to Project Michigan is unknown and will remain so, since
secret work at the AMRC is protected, by Board of Regents mandate,
from release even to top university officials.[18]

Presumably, some of the eight classified pages deal with AMRC's
aid in the development of heat-seeking, image-amplifying aerial reconnaisance techniques, which resulted in the capture and death of Guevara.
"Che was apparently unaware," said one journalist, "that the United
States had developed aerial reconnaisance techniques which converted
high temperature devices such as camouflaged cooking pots or blacked-out
short wave radio sets into tell-tale liabilities."[19] This aerial reconnaisance
followed Guevara by "seeing" the heat given off by his smokeless "Dien
Bien Phu oven." The value of this kind of research developed at universities under the protections of academic freedom can be measured in
Pentagon body counts.

AMRC is not the only agency at the University of Wisconsin that
engages in military projects. According to the tenets of academic freedom, a University of Wisconsin professor may contract with anyone to provide anything, as long as the faculty member's right to publish the findings
is unimpaired. That means if the Pentagon, for instance, rates a project
"unclassified," between the time the contract is let and the time the in-
vestigator submits his reports, the program, whatever its nature, is permissible under university regulations. In October 1969, two professors in
the Food Research Institute finished a lengthy investigation for the army's
main biological warfare research and development center. Merlin Bergdoll and Concordia Borja's forty-month, 109,000-dollar, "Investigation of
New Types of Staphylococcus Exterotoxin" was carried out for the Biological Center at Fort Detrick, Maryland. The work, according to Bergdoll, involved measuring the effects of new food poisons on monkeys.[20]
When asked what the army might do with the new germs, Bergdoll replied that he would have no qualms if the military used his findings to
develop a new biological weapon. "I wouldn't react adversely to this at
all. . . . You'd rather be incapacitated than shot. . . . This is a more
humane approach." He said that he knew the Russians were working on
such biological weapons and that it was necessary for Americans to have
adequate defenses.[21]

Another chemical and biological warfare project was sponsored by
Edgewood Arsenal, home of chemical warfare research and development.
Edgewood provided Psychology Professor Vincent J. Polidora with more
than two hundred thousand dollars between May 1963 and February
1968 for methods of "Measuring Chemically Induced Behavioral Changes
in Various Mammalian Species." Polidora induced the behavior changes

in monkeys and rats with LSD, amphetamines, tranquilizers, and nerve gases. He even evaluated the performance of a "classified Drug A" brought to Madison by a colonel from Edgewood who never identified the chemical agent.[22] Monkeys and rats were first taught various motor and visual tasks, then were drugged and presented with the opportunity to perform their task. Predictably, the animals were disoriented, and complex tasks were disrupted.

The contract made it clear that Polidora's work was pioneer research aimed at human oriented biological and chemical warfare: "The objective is the development and validation of testing procedures which will be useful in the study of the behavioral effects of drugs in animals. These methods are intended to be used in the prehuman phases of the CRDL [chemical research and development laboratories] incapaciting agent program."[23]

A third Wisconsin chemical and biological warfare project compared the strengths of six of the army's nerve gases. Professor of pharmacy Takeru Higuchi had a three-year contract with Edgewood Arsenal which ended in 1967; he evaluated gases GA, GB, GD, GF, BZ, and VX.[24] Higuchi was issued enough GB gas, developed originally in 1936, to wipe out 180,000 people, or the entire population of Madison.[25]

Along with the army's annual grant for operating the AMRC, which now runs 1.4 million dollars, dozens of additional Defense Department contracts are sought and obtained each year by university faculty members. A study by the University Committee listed thirty-six military projects in progress as of November 12, 1969, excluding the AMRC and its staff of seventy. Of these three dozen programs, seventeen were for the air force, eleven for the navy, and the other eight for the army. The contracts were spread throughout the university in twenty different departments, illustrating the totality of university complicity with the military. Such departments as speech, entomology, veterinary science, anthropology, and journalism, not popularly associated with the military, all had at least one program paid for by the Pentagon.

The breadth of the university's research activities for the armed services can be seen more precisely by examining the Board of Regents' monthly compendium of "Gifts, Grants, and United States Government Contracts" accepted by the university. In June of 1970, the Air Force Systems Engineering Group at Wright-Paterson Air Force Base, Ohio awarded three contracts to university researchers. The Space Science and Engineering Center got a six-month contract, the chemistry department a nine-month agreement, and the department of physiological chemistry a twelve-month contract. Total funding was 87,000 dollars. The Office of Naval Research signed four contracts with Wisconsin scientists in June.

Contracts went to the departments of geology and geophysics, physiology, entomology, and chemistry. Total funding was 71,000 dollars. The department of mechanical engineering received a year's extension on its five-year, 241,000-dollar program funded by the army's Automotive Tank Command in Warren, Michigan. Otto Uychara and Philip Myers were testing the experimental one-cylinder L-141 jeep and other diesel engines.[26] Total funding was 30,000 dollars. The total expenditure by the Pentagon for military projects at the University of Wisconsin in June of 1970 was 188,000 dollars.

A number of quasi-military agencies also made extensive contributions to the university in June 1970. The Atomic Energy Commission added more than 1.7 million dollars for research and the continued operation of a conference and a symposium in experimental physics. The AEC has supported the conference since 1960 at a cost of 12.1 million dollars and the symposium since 1948 at a total cost of 5.7 million dollars. In addition, the National Aeronautics Space Administration signed over 500,000 dollars worth of contracts for research by the meteorology and physics departments, the Space Science and Engineering Center, and the Food Research Institute.

The total military and quasi-military funding is approximately 2.4 million dollars. Other federal agencies, notably the National Science Foundation and the Departments of Health, Education, and Welfare, Agriculture, and Labor, contributed several millions together. Of the approximately 14 million dollars obtained by the university in June 1970 for research, instruction, student aid, and miscellanae, about seventy per cent came from federal agencies. The percentage holds steady from month to month, and is duplicated at most universities like Wisconsin. The sources of the funding explains in great part why I stated earlier that the university serves national purposes.

The question of funding for the initial construction of the Army Mathematics Research Center has not yet been treated, largely because neither the army nor the university provided the money. WARF—the Wisconsin Alumni Research Foundation—provided the installation. WARF is a tax-free foundation founded in 1925 as an unofficial arm of the university by some alumni who were interested in exploiting several patents which the late professor of biochemistry Harry Steenbock secured in the process of Vitamin D irradiation. WARF research later won patents for anticoagulants which WARF-licensed marketers sell as rat poison. Other WARF-licensed items include fertilizer packets sold through S & D Products in Prairie Du Chien, Wisconsin, and "Dariworld" cheese manufactured by Lake to Lake Cooperative, Kiel, Wisconsin.

The foundation's trustees invest WARF's share of these products' profits through a major financial house, Smith Barney and Company, of New York City. Their assets, which include much of the resort area of Wisconsin Dells, were estimated at fifty million dollars in 1961, but current figures are unavailable, as nonstock foundations are not required to make these figures public. Each year, WARF makes a multimillion dollar research and physical plant grant to the university from its investment earnings. Since 1928, WARF has donated more than fifty million dollars to the university, nearly all for the hard sciences, with comparatively small amounts for humanities and housing. As the university wrote in 1967, "WARF has demonstrated in its four decades of existence the practical ability to move knowledge from the laboratory to the production line."[27]

In 1955, WARF donated 1.2 million dollars to the university specifically for the construction of the Army Mathematics Research Center. Much of the foundation's motivation to bring an army research installation to the Madison campus can be traced to the kinds of interests historically represented on WARF's board of trustees. In 1955, WARF trustees directed General Mills, Northwest Bancorporation, Continental Illinois National Bank and Trust Company, Northwestern Mutual Life, Kimberly-Clark, Parker Pen, and dozens of other companies, law firms, stock brokerages, and manufacturers. A current WARF trustee, H. I. Romnes, is chairman of American Telephone and Telegraph, the world's largest monopoly and the parent company of the prime contractor for the Antiballistic Missile Safeguard System (ABM). WARF trustees hold directorships in United States Steel, Kimberly-Clark, Rex Chainbelt, Colgate-Palmolive, Norfolk and Western Railroad, Cities Service, Wisconsin Electric Power, Western Publishing, Ralston Purina, and more than twenty more large firms. WARF trustees also hold directorships in numerous major financial institutions, such as Chemical Bank, New York Trust, Northwestern Mutual Life Insurance Company, Mercantile Trust Company, Dillon, Reed, and Company, Smith Barney and Company, Seamen's Bank for Savings, Mutual Life Insurance Company, and Marshall and Illsly Bank, Milwaukee. In addition, four WARF trustees hold five directorships throughout the First Wisconsin Bankshares Corporation, the state's largest banking system.

WARF has always been run by Wisconsin's most prestigious corporate alumni, men most accurately described as part of the elite of the American ruling class. The national interest is their interest. It is for them, primarily, that the country maintains an efficient and capable military which can be sent to the Dominican Republic or Southeast Asia or Watts against those in rebellion against the American empire. And it is precisely the upgrading of the military's efficiency that is the task of the Army

Mathematics Research Center. For the WARF trustees, who manage large enterprises with subsidiaries and branches scattered throughout the third world, the establishment of the AMRC was a sound investment, and the death of Che Guevara was a quarterly dividend. Students have made the connections.

The university serves yet another master. Getting something for next to nothing has always been the goal of the American entrepreneur, whether he was playing the stock market, paying his workers, buying wholesale, or selling retail. The services of the University of Wisconsin are available to the American businessman to help him garner a larger share of the market. Corporations, industry-wide associations, and foundations grant hundreds of thousands of dollars monthly to the university for projects directly related to improving or inventing products in their field. The anticipated result for the businesses is increase of profit; the consequence for the university is the active refining of the private enterprise system which distributes its benefits unequally.

For the month of June, 1970, corporate America invested 163,000 dollars in forty-three research grants at the University of Wisconsin. A sample shows how a small research grant could lead to an industry-wide breakthrough for a particular company or concern which results in a larger share of the market and the profits for a particular nucleus of stockholders, families, trustees, or executives:

Chemargro Corporation, Kansas City, Missouri, 1,800 dollars "for the support of research in the department of veterinary science from June 1 to December 31, 1970, having for its purpose the evaluation of a chemical compound as an anthelmintic in swine."

Frito-Lay, Inc., Dallas, Texas, 1,000 dollars "for continued support of research on potato genetics in the department of horticulture."

Wisconsin Berry Growers Association, Baileys Harbor, Wisconsin, 600 dollars "for support of research on small fruits, their improvement, culture, handling, to be conducted by the department of horticulture."

Hail Insurance Adjustment and Research Association, Chicago, Illinois, 500 dollars, and Crop Insurance Research Bureau, Inc., Indianapolis, Indiana, 3,500 dollars "for support of research in the department of horticulture for the period March 31, 1970 to February 28, 1971, on the effect of simulated hail injury on growth, yield, and quality of snapbeans."

Stauffer Chemical Co., Mountain View, California, three 500 dollar grants "for support of research in the department of entomology on fruit insect control; support of research relating to weed control in pickling cucumbers—department of horticulture; for support of research on truck crop and potato insects and their control—department of entomology."

Vick Chemical Co., Philadelphia, Pennsylvania, 4,000 dollars "for continued support of an 'Investigation of the Composition, Rate of Production, and the Diffusion Rate of Certain Chemicals in Normal Sebum and Sebum from Acne Patients'—School of Pharmacy."

Borden, Inc., New York, New York, two 2,500 dollar grants to the Food Research Institute, one specifically "for research on detection of staphylococcal enterotoxin [food poison] in foods."

Union Carbide Corporation, New York, New York, 10,000 dollars "for the support of research in the department of mechanical engineering relating to the design and constructtion of an abrasion testing machine."[28]

If these corporations conducted this research with their own trained people, in their own laboratories, on their own taxed property, their total costs would exceed their grants to the university, where the taxpayers provide the researchers, buildings, and equipment.

Corporations also grant funds for scholarships and fellowships earmarked for a graduate student who is assisting a professor or writing a thesis in the company's field. Among the June 1970 corporation grants for student aid were:

Weyerhauser Company Foundation, Tacoma, Washington, 10,000 dollars "for support of a graduate fellowship during 1970–1971 and 1971–1972 in any of the physical sciences where the project is oriented towards the forest products industry."

Caterpillar Tractor Co., Peoria, Illinois, 3,800 dollars for a "fellowship in the department of mechanical engineering."

Stauffer Chemical Co., Mountain View, California, 3,300 dollars "for support of a deserving graduate student in the department of food science during 1970–1971."

Kennecott Copper Corporation, New York, New York, 2,000 dollars for a "scholarship and departmental grant in minerals and metals engineering."[29]

Through is grant, Weyerhauser, for example, first writes off ten thousand dollars that it had donated to its tax-free foundation. Next, it buys the services of a graduate student on a project oriented toward Weyerhauser's own industry. And again, Weyerhauser obtains, very cheaply indeed, the use of some of the world's finest laboratories, computers, libraries, buildings, and professors. The state also subsidizes the corporations by providing rent-free space in public buildings in which to recruit new employees. Through these various benefits, American businesses use the university to strengthen or improve their positions in the marketplace. The entire corporate system, where control and concomitant benefits are held by a few, is thereby reinforced.

On October 18, 1967, the first politically motivated violent confrontation with police on Wisconsin's campus came over the Dow Chemical Company's job recruiting in the Commerce Building. In October, 1969, the antiwar movement on campus evolved into an antiimperialist movement, demanding that the university close down ROTC, AMRC, and the Land Tenure Center, an AID project in Latin America. Throughout the year, major demonstrations and intradepartment pressures were aimed at these programs, often resulting in window-breaking, fire-bombing, arrests, and injuries. A key demand during the student strike in May, 1970, ignited by the invasion of Cambodia, was an end to all military research on campus, and several departments voted to forbid future Defense Department funding in their fields. But until all academics take these first steps and accept some responsibility for ending what the American empire inflicts on people the world over, there will be a student movement pushing in that direction.

Notes

[1] *Knowledge and the Wisconsin Economy* (Madison: University of Wisconsin, 1967), p. 8.

[2] Data supplied by the Information Office, U.S. Army Materiel Command, Alexandria, Va.

[3] *Daily Cardinal*, October 3, 1969.

[4] Department of the Army Contract No. DA-31-124-ARO-D-462, signed by the university, April 26, 1956.

[5] *Ibid.*

[6] *1967 Summary Report of the Mathematics Research Center* (Madison, 1967), p. 3.

[7] Information compiled from the university voucher files, alphabetical listing of expenditures of university funds by university employees.

[8] *1967 Summary* . . . , p. 7.

[9] Army contract cited above.

[10] H. Halperin, J. Rowen, D. Siff, E. Zeidoran, "The Case Against the Army Math Research Center" (Madison, 1970), Appendix B.

[11] *Ibid.*

[12] *Ibid.*

[13] Army Contract cited above.

[14] Public letter from J. Barkley Rosser to Stephen Kleene, chairman of the University Committee, August 19, 1969.

[15] Memorandum from U.S. Army Chief of Staff, General Dwight D. Eisenhower, quoted in S. Melman, *Pentagon Capitalism: The Management of the New Imperialism* (New York: McGraw-Hill, 1970), pp. 232–233.

[16] *Daily Cardinal*, October 3, 1969.

[17] R. Counthill, *The Guardian*, October 12, 1968.

[18] University of Wisconsin Board of Regents, *Minutes*, May 12, 1966.

[19] A. St. George, "How the U.S. Got Che," *True*, April 18, 1968.

[20] *Daily Cardinal*, October 14, 1969.

[21] *Ibid.*

[22] V. J. Polidora, "Methods for Measuring Chemically Induced Behavioral Changes in Various Mammalian Species" (Defense Department Documentation Center, 1968), p. 18.

[23] Vincent Polidora's Edgewood Arsenal Contracts: DA 18-035-AMC 135 (A); DA 18-035-AMC 368 (A); DAAA 15-67-C-0296.

[24] Takeru Higuchi's Edgewood Arsenal Contracts, 1964–1967: DA 18-108-AMC 209 (A); DA 18-035-AMC 721 (A).

[25] S. M. Hersh, "Germ Warfare: For Alma Mater, God and Country," *Ramparts Magazine*, 1969, *8*, 20–28. VX gas slaughtered 6,400 sheep grazing near the Dugway Proving Grounds, Utah, when an army experimental gas ejection nozzle did not shut.

[26] Otto Uyehara and Philip Myers' Army Tank Command Contract: DAA E07-70-c-3336.

[27] *Knowledge and the Wisconsin Economy,* p. 15.

[28] "Gifts, Grants and U.S. Government Contracts" (Madison, 1970).

[29] *Ibid.*

CHAPTER 7

CORPORATE RECRUITMENT ON CAMPUS

Bernard Sklar

Prior to the fall of 1967, Wisconsin had already experienced a certain amount of student unrest.[1] There had been draft sit-ins in the spring of 1966, and the next fall Edward Kennedy had been prevented by student hecklers from delivering a prepared address, largely because he refused to discuss the war in Vietnam. An abortive attempt to confront Dow interviewers on campus occurred in February of 1967 and there was a major confrontation between police and students in the spring of that year over a pedestrian hazard (buses going the wrong way on a major one-way boulevard). All these events should have alerted the university to the fact that students were in earnest about the expression of dissent. Yet as the events of the fall of 1967 amply attest, the campus—students as well as faculty and administration—was not prepared to cope with the meaning of such behavior.

The violent events of October 1967 mark a major turning point in the history of an institution, particularly in terms of the relationship of students toward the university. But to view it only within the limited context of institutional history would be a mistake, for the events at

135

Madison are inextricably bound up with the development of campus life throughout the United States and especially with the disintegration of former styles of student life, administrative behavior, and university governance.

Institutions of higher learning in America, for some forty or fifty years prior to the midsixties, enjoyed a kind of privileged existence. They were an important part of society, in the sense that society valued the activities of universities—training the young for the professions and maintaining a place for scholarship and the liberal arts—but they were apart from it. As George Kateb put it, they were regarded as a "little better or a little less real; higher up, or off to one side."[2] One of the consequences of this social isolation was the development among American academic men of a peculiar sense of their own mission. It was a mixture of high responsibility to moral and ethical goals otherwise abandoned by the mundane world, paternal concern for the social welfare of their immature charges, and single-minded devotion to the pursuit of truth. The fact that there was something anachronistic about a world of scholars devoted to such ideals and a world of students dedicated, it would seem, to something else, did not seem to matter.[3] There was kind of a bargain involved. The university, and in particular the faculty, would go its way and the students would go theirs—as long as the latter did not make it too apparent that they were doing so. For it was the hallmark of this unusual social system that the price of admission to the sanctuary guarded by the faculty was an implicit regard for the faculty's privileges and, more important, for their sensibilities. Students had their place and an important aspect of that place was their manners, manners that were at once obedient, deferential, and respectfully distant.[4]

It is not our purpose here to argue whether those were the proper, most effective (in terms of learning), or "only logical" (in terms of the inherent differences between faculty and students) roles for faculty and students to play.[5] Nor shall we suggest, as some have, that, as a result of student militancy in the late sixties, these manners have been completely altered, for it is apparent that they have not. Rather, it is the purpose of this sociological history to fathom what happens when manners come into conflict with morals. For it is the major assumption of this study that the crisis at Madison in the fall of 1967 was one in which the traditional status and behavior expected by faculty of students came into conflict with purposes and goals that a large number of students felt were higher. It is a classic case of social conflict, growing out of a host of events broader than the campus itself but focusing on the university because of its meaning and place in our society and in the lives of the young.

This chapter is a cultural history, the history of a particular transformation in the way of life of the American university; a particular incident is the vehicle for this study. In reality, the university contains many styles of life or subcultures and many of them seemingly go on as they did before. It is hard to imagine, for example, how laboratory procedures in the physical sciences are affected by changes on campus. Yet in one sense they are changed, for the milieu is different. Students are no longer regarded as the politically neuter, largely infantile creatures, there only to be taught, that they were to a large extent prior to the student revolution. Universities, once privileged sanctuaries, remote from everyday life, now find themselves almost in the center of public concern, subject to daily scrutiny by the press and the legislature and very often confronted with the necessity of calling on the state police or the National Guard to maintain order. All this has happened within the space of a few years; it did not happen at Madison alone, it happened across the country, and the events of one university illuminate and prepare the way, psychologically as well as socially, for the events of another. A history of a particular incident can detail the way in which such transformations come into being. The Dow demonstration of October 1967 serves this purpose admirably, for we can see in the actions and events portrayed the nature of the values, role expectations, and ideological differences that were involved and the path on which they inevitably took all concerned—toward the restructuring of the expectations that people have, particularly at the university, of how students will behave. In doing so we make the assumption, often neglected in conventional history, that the consequences of events, although seemingly political, are, in the long run, more lastingly social.

Each year most students return to the Madison campus in mid-September. But for many, including a number of activists, Madison is a permanent base, and during the summer of 1967 conversations began about the fact that Dow was coming to the campus again that fall. For the student left, much less fragmented than in 1971, the mood was one of heightened militancy. As the underground newspaper *Connections* saw it, "More and more people were beginning to believe that traditional left-liberal politics had become accepted forms, and that new forms and styles were necessary if America was to change."[6]

Dow, of course, was an old enemy. A Dow demonstration the previous winter failed, leaving seventeen students arrested but leading to no tangible results. The 1967 March on Washington to "confront the warmakers" at the Pentagon was scheduled for the weekend following Dow's expected visit, and this gave the recruiter's visit a heightened significance. Although a small group made up of members of Students for a Democratic Society (SDS), the University Community Action party, and Concerned Black Students had discussed tactics and generally agreed on obstruction, the question was far from settled. As *Connections* saw it, "Obstruction appeared to many as a viable tactic; it made sense to physically stop Dow because it was an integral link in the continuation of the war machine, and because it represented corporate America in its most immoral form. . . . To some however, a direct confrontation seemed unwise; they felt that the left was not strong enough to become involved with the police. . . . There were many who were torn and undecided."[7]

The first public expression came on September 21, when both SDS and the Committee to End the War in Vietnam voted to protest. No mention of obstruction was made in the student press which covered these events.[8] The first meeting that publicly discussed obstruction occurred on October 9. The principal argument against obstruction was that the message which the demonstrators were trying to get across would be confused because action was actully being taken against the university. But sentiments were for a show of strength. The "too orderly, too sweet, too nice" demonstration conducted against the CIA the previous spring was cited as meaningless.[9] The idea of protective pickets was also discussed; it was argued that the demonstrators needed protection from agriculture and engineering students who might try to break up the protest. After a long debate the vote was in favor of obstruction.

On October 11 Dean of Student Affairs Joseph F. Kauffman issued a statement in which he said that a repetition of disruptive activity was against the interests of all parts of the university—students, faculty, and administration. He went on to say that the laws and regulations of the university, recently confirmed by the faculty, indicated that if any student were to obstruct scheduled placement interviews or disrupt the operations of the university or organizations using university facilities, the university would not hesitate to invoke university discipline, including disciplinary probation, suspension, or expulsion—whether or not arrests were made. Protest leaders fastened on this statement as a way of attacking the administration and forestalling any action to undermine the movement. In addition, they moved for an injunction against the university on the grounds that the statement was an implied threat to the rights of free speech and assembly. Just one day before the actual confrontation, a decision was handed down indicating that the order could not be granted.

In the student movement, support for obstruction was growing. At an SDS meeting on October 11, Robert Zwicker, a prominent activist, said, "We must assert through our lives and not only ideas that we are agents of liberation." Everything, he said, was obscured in our "one-dimensional society, leaving only one important means of communication, the physical act." Another speaker pointed to the fact that "The system has become immune to demonstrations because it sees it doesn't pose a threat. . . . New tactics or methods would have to be devised, ones which would endanger the structure. Otherwise the demonstration would remain meaningless."[10] The following night, the Committee to End the War in Vietnam endorsed the plans of the planning committee and added its own blast against a "criminal and racist" war. At this point plans called for nonobstructive picketing on October 17, followed by obstruction on the eighteenth. In making this endorsement, however, the committee made it clear "that it was not encouraging its members to obstruct, but merely that it, as an organization, was defending the right of the persons obstructing to do so."[11] The Concerned Law Students that same night took an almost parallel position. The Student Senate, which also met that evening, passed a resolution condemning Kauffman's statement but noted that the senate "in no way either supports or condones" obstruction.[12] Clearly, the student community went only half way in its own commitment to this kind of behavior.

This was evident at a mass meeting held that night. According to the *Cardinal*, "Some felt that a demonstration against Dow could only be meaningful in relating Dow as an active component of the present capitalistic-corporate system of America thus showing that it is the system which needs [to] be changed. Others felt that they should focus on Dow as a furtherer of the war and that it is the war which should be attacked." The truly unresolved question was whether obstruction should in fact take place. There were arguments by a number of people that this would be suicidal in view of the position taken by Kauffman. But Robert Cohen, the activist jailed for his part in the last Dow demonstration, seemed to touch a responsive chord when he said, "I think that we should not back down from Kauffman. He is the reality. You don't react to the reality— you oppose and negate it." Sometime after midnight a vote was taken and the decision once more ratified that peaceful picketing would take place on the seventeenth and obstruction on the next day.[13] As *Connections* saw it, "It was felt that forms of 'simple civil disobedience' had been absorbed into the patterns of society, and that new forms of protest had to be developed." But "The tactics of this general theory were vague." The only thing agreed upon was that demonstrators would link arms to make it harder for police to arrest them. There was no mention of fighting police. In fact, "there was no thinking beyond the arrests, no thinking it necessary to go any further."[14] This statement is, in a way, a testimony that the students still shared the old ethic about how students and the university should behave.

But some students no longer shared it or only partially subscribed to it. The leadership of the demonstration seemed to reflect a new ambivalence in their dealings with the administration. In the past there had generally been some contact maintained through the Office of Student Organization Advisers, headed by Peter Bunn. Robert Swacker, a member of the coordinating committee, initiated such a meeting on October 9, when he applied for a permit to hold a mass meeting on the thirteenth. Bunn reported that Swacker resisted efforts to sound him out on demonstration plans but agreed to return the next day. At that time he was given various policy statements and it was agreed there would be a formal meeting on October 12.[15]

On the eleventh Kauffman issued his statement. Bunn sought out Swacker and asked him to come to his office that afternoon, at which time the statement was given to him. An hour later, Swacker left a note cancelling the next day's meeting. According to Bunn, Swacker appeared in his office on the thirteeenth. He invited Bunn and university police chief Ralph Hanson to attend the mass meeting that night and to bring 250 copies of the new demonstration guidelines. They did so, and the material was accepted, but they were informed, according to Bunn, that "our presence at the meeting was not desired."[16] Late the afternoon of the sixteenth, the day before the protest, Bunn sought Swacker again. Evan Stark, another activist, and Swacker went to Bunn's office where they discussed the guidelines, were warned about obstruction, and talked about the restraining order still in the courts. According to Bunn, Stark requested a meeting with the administration on the seventeenth. The meeting, attended by a number of people from Kauffman's staff and by about a dozen students, proved to be abortive; the students were silent throughout and then left in a body. In speaking of these efforts Kauffman told a select committee of the state senate that "this was . . . a new tactic which we had not faced before, attempts to maintain communication being rejected."[17]

The administration was also occupied with plans for the demonstration itself. A number of meetings between the administration and city officials took place during September and October. Actual planning was left to Kauffman with Hanson assisting him. The general assumption was that, although there might be some obstruction and passive resistance, there would be no violence. One week prior to the demonstration, a decision was made to hire a number of off-duty city policemen to supplement the university force of twenty men.

The day before the demonstration, a group of Concerned Law Students went to Kauffman's office and urged him to retract his statement, saying that it was "tantamount to outright suppression of freedom of speech and denials of procedural due process."[18] During the day the San Francisco Mime Troupe presented a number of performances of their politically-oriented Dow play. That evening a final mass meeting was held.

After much discussion, a decision was reached to have both obstruction and supportive pickets.

Between 9:30 and 10:00 A.M. on Tuesday the seventeenth, about twenty pickets gathered in front of the Commerce Building. Picketing continued throughout the day and engaged about 130 persons at noon. Late in the morning sixteen protestors moved into the building and, without incident, marched in front of the interview rooms. At noon some 400 to 500 people attended a rally in front of the building. Robert Cohen implored the participants to "understand the political reasons for tomorrow's actions before they obstructed," perhaps a reflection of his own training in philosophy, but more probably a testimony to his efforts to legitimize an emerging set of rules for an uncertain group of followers. In describing the events of the day, *Connections* said that they "seemed to most people to be a mere spectacle. It was like any other picket line people had been on. It lacked urgency and immediacy. Most of the campus looked on; it was the left at its traditional best."[19] The *Wisconsin State Journal* detected some of the same dispiritedness but their interpretation, which may have been unusually prescient, was that "throughout Tuesday's demonstration, students seemed only to be preparing themselves for an ordeal with police."[20] That night the San Francisco Mime Troupe performed again. At the close of their performance director R. G. Davis faced the audience and said, "This is your school. If you don't like it, change it. If it won't change, destroy it."[21]

At about 10:30 A.M. on Wednesday the eighteenth, a group estimated by some to be as large as five hundred people formed at the foot of Bascom Hill. Led by members of the Mime Troupe, they marched up the hill in two groups (of obstructors and of supportive pickets). Police Chief Ralph Hanson joined them, but he did not know which building they were going to enter. At about 10:45 the group entered the Commerce Building. No attempt was made to interfere with them, and those obstructing sat down in front of rooms 102 and 104, the doors of which were guarded by several of Hanson's men. In the process, the group (about two hundred at this point) occupied most of the east-west corridor of the building. On the east end is a foyer leading to a north-south corridor and a staircase and landing leading to the second floor. Outside, pickets had begun parading. At this point, Hanson was able to make a path for a faculty member and two of his students from the obstructed office to a classroom. The first fifteen or twenty minutes were peaceful. When Hanson tried making his way back to room 102, however, he found the entrance blocked. He also learned that a student had been restrained from making his way to an interview. Forcing his way through, Hanson asked those blocking the doorway to move. When they did not, he asked them to identify themselves, and, when they refused, warned them of arrest. He then instructed his men to proceed, but the students and blockaders shouted and linked arms, making it impossible to arrest anyone. Sensing new hostility, Hanson called off the arrest.

It was now 11:30 A.M. Blocked inside the room and feeling the situation beyond his control, Hanson called the chancellor to ask for more men. His request was approved, and he put through his request to the city police. He then forced his way out a back exit, meeting hostility as he did, and went to the dean's office. The chancellor was there with members of his staff. There it was decided to give demonstrators every opportunity to leave before asking the police to clear the area. The assumption was that, if arrested, students would go limp and be carried off in small groups.

Shortly after noon, city police began to assemble on an adjacent parking lot. As they put on their riot equipment they were taunted by members of the Mime Troupe and by students. The crowd, estimated at about five hundred at noon, continued to grow as students made their way back and forth to classes. By 1:00 there were about two thousand present. Hanson, seeing the police armed, was assured that offensive equipment would only be used if absolutely necessary. He then entered the Commerce Building and, using his bullhorn, declared an unlawful assembly. The area was jammed with spectators as well as demonstrators and the level of noise—both singing and shouting—was high. It was in a sense a masquerade; students were serious yet uncertain of what were new roles for many of them. The administration was equally serious and uncertain of its own new role.

Hanson returned to the parking lot. It was generally understood that he was in charge. As he later testified, "It was my intention to take these twenty-five or thirty officers and go into that Commerce Building and make my way through to the room 102 which was about seven to ten feet down the corridor. That I was to put myself at the head of this body of police officers and we were going to, we realized that we were going to have to eject some people and move some people aside to do this."[22] Before doing so, Hanson again made several announcements that this was an illegal assembly. At this point there is some doubt about what happened. *Connections* stated that Hanson told the group "the administration had intimated that if the demonstrators would leave the building, Dow would leave the campus."[23] Hanson denied that, but apparently an agreement was made to withdraw the police and have several students talk to the chancellor.

It was approximately 1:15 when the group, which included Evan Stark, arrived at Dean Kauffman's office. Stark demanded that the chancellor put in writing that Dow was going to leave the campus and not return, indicating that he and his colleagues would then try to clear the demonstrators from the building. The chancellor said he was unable to make any such commitments, and the students walked out. A discussion followed with Chief Emery of the city police, who had just arrived. The assumption again was that students would go limp and allow themselves to be carried to police wagons. The idea was to take away as many as the wagon would hold and return until the building was cleared or until most of the demonstrators had left.

The crowd outside the Commerce Building was an orderly one when Hanson entered the building and announced for the third time that this was an unlawful assembly. Leaving the building, he crossed the street to where his men were assembled. Advancing at the head of the column, three of his own unarmed men at his side, Hanson made his way back to the Commerce Building. Apparently there had been a rumor about an agreement with the administration and just as Robert Cohen came to say that this was not so, he saw Hanson and rushed inside shouting, "Here come the cops!"

There was little time for preparation. Those sitting down began locking arms, and some covered their heads or wrapped belts around their hands. Exactly what happened next is uncertain. Hanson, there is no doubt, entered at the head of his column. It is also clear that he was heading directly for the center of a group of students, mostly men, so tightly packed that it was impossible for any of them to move. Apparently this huge crush of people reacted to the oncoming police like a giant spring. Hanson only remembers that, with two other officers, he was thrown clear of the building. Within seconds, and without signal, the police moved in and began clubbing students out of the building. An eye-witness reported that

In the heat of what was really a battle, the nightsticks were the authorities' main weapon. Demonstrators were attacked in the legs, prodded in the stomach, or cracked on the head. Many were bleeding, and all became violently or totally hysterical. Students kicked, tussled with policemen, or went limp, all the while screaming as the authorities wrestled them to the ground and dragged them out of the building. "Shame! Shame! Shame!" the crowd screamed as many of its members dazedly stumbled through the doorway. The demonstrators had clogged the corridors and entranceway in rows, but the policemen broke the ranks and the hallway became a myriad of thumps and scuffles and everpresent screams. It couldn't have been more than ten minutes before the east-west corridor was cleared.[24]

Although initially an observer, Chief Emery was soon inside, and directing the clean-up procedure. No arrests were made nor was any

attempt made to restrain the use of riot sticks. Emery had his men go outside and secure a small perimeter. Hanson rejoined him. The line of
officers outside stretched across the entranceway, no more than twenty
feet from the building and just beyond the parking lot where the staging
area and a police wagon were located.

Outside the screaming increased. The mall became a battleground for the next
two hours. At first the police stood in front of the glass doors, and the crowd
screamed, "Dow Must Go." The police formed a barrier twenty feet from Commerce, and the students, their number about three thousand, shoved against the
line, many with fists raised. Rocks and pebbles, a tomato, sticks, a brick—the
students hurled them at the authorities, screaming epithets and chanting antiwar and antipolice slogans. On three or four occasions, the group jostled with
the line of police before being repulsed by clubs. At one point, students were
pummeled to the ground and a brief scuffle ensued. "Put the clubs down," the
crowd taunted. "Seig Heil! Seig Heil," they chanted, right arms raised.[25]

Several police officers were felled; others were hit by thrown objects.
Six students were arrested and led off to the police wagon. Other students, however, surrounded the van, flattened its tires, broke its windows,
and blocked it with other vehicles. Fearing violence, Emery released the
prisoners, but the crowd refused to disperse, breaking the line from the
perimeter to the staging area. Emery conferred with Hanson and then
radioed for tear gas. It was now almost 2:30. When the gas arrived, its
use proved futile, the wind blowing it away or students shifting their position. Seeing that the situation had not improved, Emery made his decision, with Hanson's approval, to call the sheriff for help. These forces
(about forty men) arrived at about 4:00. With roughly 110 men on
hand it was decided to force the crowd across the street and permit
traffic to begin moving again. This was successful, and some time after
4:30 the crowd began to drift away. By 5:00 the area was clear and most
of the officers were withdrawn. The injured that afternoon included fifty
students and twenty-one officers. Students on the whole did not fare
badly. Among the police, however, two were severely hurt and required
extended hospital treatment.

Thus the drama had come to its unanticipated climax. Both students and the administration had expected a well-established set of responses from each other, with only slight fears that something new might
happen. Instead they experienced the collapse of mutuality and a rupture
in the social fabric binding them together. Obviously, it was the police
that made this occur; however, antecedent postures and provocations had
made it possible. Students simply were not acting in accustomed ways,
and this could only precipitate anger, a sense of outrage, and retribution
from those who felt they knew what student behavior ought to be. But

students (and many of those who supported them), although aware of the unconventional modes of expression they had employed and felt morally bound to employ, were equally outraged by the fact that the university, through the instrument of force, had not acted in the way that it usually did toward them. In the process much of the predemonstration rhetoric was forgotten and the only thing that seemed to matter was that each group felt hurt and maligned by the actions of the other. It was in many respects a family quarrel, with each side feeling great justification in its position and indignation at the behavior of the other. In no other way can one understand what followed the violence that afternoon and the way in which its meaning was ultimately confronted and dealt with.

Throughout the afternoon Chancellor Sewell remained in Kauffman's office. A number of people appealed to him to stop the police action, but he said the matter was out of his hands. That evening he announced that Dow interviews were suspended pending a special meeting of the faculty the next afternoon. He also indicated that the university was "preferring charges against the leaders of the blockade, suspending them from the university, and referring their cases to the student conduct committee." Finally, Sewell stated, "I deeply regret that it was necessary to bring police onto the campus to maintain the operation of the university. This was done only after our officers and staff found it impossible to maintain order. I regret that students and police were injured. This must not be repeated."[26]

Even before the dust had settled, students began gathering in the Social Science Building across from Commerce. Many had been gassed, and discussion rapidly focused around a strike to protest police brutality. Those who tried to broaden the issue to include the university's cooperation with Dow or the war were generally ignored. That evening an estimated five thousand students gathered in front of the university library. *Connections* described the scene: "The rally had to choose between two different proposals. One was to call a strike on the issue of 'cops on campus,' police brutality, and amnesty for the students involved. The second was broader: a strike not only on the issue of keeping police off campus and amnesty." When it became apparent that protest issues (the war and so forth) were going to be submerged in favor of the more immediate civil liberties issue, the radical leadership withdrew. By the end of the evening the movement was in the hands of new leaders, much less radical, yet nonetheless incensed about what had happened on campus that day.

At the same time that students were in the mall, an angry group of about two hundred faculty members were meeting in the Law School. This group, known as the Liberal Caucus, was made up largely of younger, more liberal members of the faculty. Early in the evening word came that the students at the rally were in danger. A vote was taken, and the group walked down the hill to the library, where they joined hands and formed a protective ring around the students. The gesture was met with a roar of approval. But the police were nowhere in sight, and within minutes the members decided to resume their own meeting. The general tone of that meeting was one of anger toward the administration, especially toward the chancellor. The group voted to support the student strike, although it was left up to each individual how he would do so, and a committee was formed to prepare for the next day's faculty meeting.

The state legislature was in session only ten blocks away when it received word of the disorders. By a vote of ninety-four to five the assembly passed a resolution demanding that the Regents of both the University of Wisconsin and the State Universities "reevaluate administrative policies of excessive permissiveness in handling student protestors." Democratic assemblyman Edward Mertz called the students "long-haired, greasy pigs" and demanded that the legislature take over the running of the schools. The resolution was then passed on to the senate. There Assistant Minority Leader Taylor Benson, a Democrat, called for mass expulsions and added, "If there are any faculty members involved, they should be fired." Senator Leland McParland, also a Democrat, in an emotional speech said, "We should shoot them if necessary. I would, because it's insurrection." Other senators pointed out the small number of protestors involved, although calling for strong measures against them. Probably the most controversial statement was made by state Attorney General Bronson LaFollette. He was quoted as saying that the right to protest peacefully at the university had been set back by "police brutality" in breaking up the demonstration. He also indicated he might not defend the university in litigation that could result from such an incident.

The student strike took place on Thursday the nineteenth, but its success was somewhat uneven. The day was one of general disorientation. Even in the agriculture and engineering schools, the talk was about the demonstration. The greatest impact of the strike, however, was felt by the College of Letters and Science, the largest university division, although even there strike participation did not reach the 50 per cent mark some student leaders claimed. An early morning rally attended by two thousand students was addressed by those who talked about the need for violence and by faculty members who tried to focus on the central social and political issues. National Student Association President Ed Schwartz, who had flown in from Washington, told the group that "this was the beginning of a long, hard struggle for the politicization of the students to take over the university in areas directly related to their well-being."[27]

The students, however, seemed to be more concerned with immediate issues, a testimony to the fact that it was their "behavior" that was being challenged. That morning they ratified a resolution calling for no more police on campus, amnesty for all students, teaching assistants, and faculty members involved in the demonstration or strike, and negotiations with the administration to determine what constitutes disruptive behavior and grounds for disciplinary action. Picket lines were set up, but toward the middle of the afternoon protest leaders began to experience difficulty manning them.

A number of teaching assistants refused to meet their classes, but many led them in discussion of what had happened. Among the faculty, discussion of the events was frequent. Heated debate took place in and out of class. Although the beating of students and the use of tear gas on campus had generated a wave of shock and indignation, many students felt the protestors were wrong in what they were trying to do and that they had given the authorities no alternative but to use violence. That day the Wisconsin Civil Liberties Union condemned the "maiming force" used against demonstrators. Chief Emery told the *Wisconsin State Journal* that his officers were "fighting to protect their lives." He described his own surprise at the resistance but pointed out that "this wasn't a typical university crowd at all. This was an organized resistance against law and order and we were overpowered." He also accused coeds of carrying rocks in their tote bags. And he said, "I saw officers standing there, not moving a muscle while being spit on, hit with rocks, and taking the filthy talk the mob threw at them."[28] He was supported by Madison Mayor Otto Festge.

The president of the Madison Police and Fire Commission issued a strong protest to LaFollette's charge of police brutality and suggested that professionals from outside the city led the demonstration. Later La-Follette denied reports that he would not represent the university and said, "The violence which occurred was caused in part by force used by the City of Madison police and by provocation on the part of students. . . . There was brutality on both sides."[29]

At 3:30 that afternoon the faculty met in the Memorial Union. All 1,300 seats were taken and more than a thousand students jammed the large foyer to hear the proceedings over a loudspeaker. It was a tense and emotional meeting. The chancellor, visibly shaken by events, relinquished the chair to Vice-Chancellor Cleary. Before doing so he said, "It is my firm belief that the responsibility for these tragic events rests squarely on those who unlawfully disrupted the functions of the university." He reminded the faculty of its action in adopting and reaffirming legislation in regard to disruption and of the statement by Dean Kauffman about disruption. The police, he said, had acted in a restrained and disciplined manner; students were amply apprised of what was going to happen, and there was no alternative to force. He noted, "I have no great desires for administrative roles nor for power; I love and respect students."

As soon as the chancellor had spoken, the chairman of the University Committee, Professor Cameron, was recognized. Pointing out the necessity for community rules, he said, "We deeply regret this incident and the attendant violence. But in our regret we cannot lose sight of the fact it arose out of planned violation of the rules that were laid down by the faculty for the good of all and that were evident to all. This is not the time for weakness. It is a time to stand firm, a time to hold fast to those principles that we, the faculty, established for the welfare of all members of our academic community." He then read his resolution. "Be it resolved that the faculty upholds the chancellor's action in recognizing his obligation to enforce the mandate of the faculty as expressed in Chapter Eleven of the university regulations."[30]

As the meeting proceeded, the first attempt was made to get the facts straight. Anatole Beck, a mathematics professor and one of the few faculty members to witness the clearing of the corridors by police, pointed out that it would have been "an essentially impossible task" for anyone inside to comply with Hanson's request in the time between his last announcement and the entrance of the police. As for the police, Beck indicated that they met resistance but that they "beat everyone forcefully, viciously, and without restraint."

Earlier, a statement by twelve members of the School of Business had been distributed which said, in part, "The police, Madison and university, carried out the ejection order with noticeable restraint." Professor Ted Finman of the Law School, a leader of the Liberal Caucus, moved that a film of the events be shown. To a number of faculty members it seemed that the liberals were trying to introduce an emotional element. To the liberals it seemed incredible that a group of scholars would not want to see what they felt were the facts. By a vote of 633 to 522 it was decided to see the film.

Philosophy Professor William Hay presented a substitute motion "That the faculty condemns the university's indiscriminate use of violence on the campus on October 18, 1967." The faculty voted that this was not properly a substitute motion. The next move to bring the matter to the floor was made by geneticist Allen Fox. Fox's more conciliatory motion tried to fix responsibility for the violence on a broader basis by saying that "The faculty respects the chancellor's good faith to uphold the rules of the university. Nevertheless, it profoundly regrets the introduction of indiscriminate force during the events of October 18." In response to a question from the floor, the moderator ruled the motion out of order. The decision was appealed, but in the closest vote on any related matter during the evening, he was sustained by 24 votes (484 to 460).

In a final attempt to bring the issue of violence back into the discussion, Professor Stewart Macaulay proposed: "Resolved that the faculty recognizes that the chancellor's actions were taken in good faith pursuant to his understanding of the faculty's mandate. The faculty, however, must condemn the university's indiscriminate use of violence on the campus on October 18, 1967." The issue was thus clearly stated. But to those who saw the issue as one of preserving the integrity of the institution—and as one of how students may act rather than of what they are trying to say— the chancellor was a hero and could not, even indirectly, be condemned. Journalism Professor Scott Cutlip warned the faculty that their failure to support Sewell would only play into the hands of the legislature and the Board of Regents. When the vote on the substitute motion was taken it failed by 67 votes (495 to 562). Then, on the original motion, the faculty voted to sustain the chancellor by a vote of 681 to 378.

A move was then made to suspend Dow interviews for the following day. When a faculty member suggested this be left to the chancellor, Sewell broke his silence to chastise his colleagues for not taking their share of responsibility. "This faculty has already put me in a precarious position in its past actions and here tonight. You haven't had guts enough to admit that my reaction was an exact interpretation of what you intended." He received a standing ovation for his remarks, and the suspension of Dow interviews for the next day was moved and passed. With others still anxious to speak, it was decided to recess until the following Monday afternoon.

Strike activity continued on Friday the twentieth. A midsemester examination period was about to begin, but among the activists sentiment were high. One of those interviewed who expressed views typical of the activists told a reporter, "I'm not a radical. I'm for civil authority. And the police—they're necessary. But the police who came onto this campus Wednesday did something immoral, and I want the administration to take a stand against what they did." Another student told the same reporter, "I think the Dow demonstrators were wrong, but I can't stand by when somebody's head is bashed in."[31] At an afternoon rally it was clear that indignation about the police—and to some extent about the faculty for their failure to condemn the police action—was still the dominant issue. This was partly because the more radical students had withdrawn. (About three hundred students had left the campus for Washington, D.C., and the march against the Pentagon.) At the meeting, which attracted approximately one thousand students, two decisions were made. One concerned a silent march, on Saturday the twenty-first, from the campus to the capitol and to the police station nearby where student demands would be posted. The most important demand would be for no more outside police on campus. There was concern that this be carried out in a dignified manner, the men wearing suits and ties, the girls wearing dresses, and all wearing black armbands. A Sunday afternoon prayer vigil was also discussed.

During the day the state senate voted to set up a bipartisan committee to look into the demonstration. The resolution, which set up a seven-member panel, instructed the committee to inform the university administration and faculty "with respect to the laws and policies of this state and encourage said administration and faculty to vigorously enforce such laws and policies."[32]

Throughout the state the press expressed support for the administration's action. Of the two local papers, *The Capitol Times,* generally the more liberal of the two, was outspoken in its support of the chancellor and suggested that the university be left alone to remedy its problems. *The Wisconsin State Journal* reflected a similar point of view. In addition, it made apparent the growing impatience which many people felt in the face of disruptive student practices. Letters to the editors of both papers were abundant and mostly disapproving. When pressed about what action it was taking, the university simply indicated that thirteen students were suspended and that Robert Cohen and Evan Stark were among them.

Saturday morning approximately three thousand students gathered in front of the library; fear was expressed about hostility from local high school youths as well as from the police. At noon, those who had elected to march, about two thousand in all, began the seven-block walk to the capitol. They were well dressed, many of them wearing black arm bands, and silent as they moved in two columns on either side of the street. Fear of police deterred them from moving to the police station, and their petition was taped to the entrance of the capitol instead. It urged the continuation of the strike, demanded an end to police interference with peaceful demonstrations on campus, and called on the administration to refrain from any action against those who had participated in the demonstration or strike. On Sunday, about three hundred students gathered for the prayer vigil on Bascom Hill. That evening about the same number gathered in Library Mall for a rally. Urged by their leaders to call a temporary end to the strike until the faculty met on Monday, the group voted to do so, although retaining its original demands and holding open the possibility of resuming the boycott of classes.

The faculty was apparently split as a result of its first meeting. The period between its meetings gave it a chance to work out a compromise between those who wanted a firm administration response and those who wished to register their distress at the police action and their support of students. The Liberal Caucus, which had been formed Wednesday night, met on two other occasions over the long weekend. It was an amorphous group, made up of about two hundred younger, liberal members of the faculty, principally in the social sciences, humanities, and law. The work of the caucus was left to a small committee which, like the University Committee, was in continuous session over this long weekend. Early in its development the caucus was joined by three somewhat better established members of the faculty. These faculty members, colleagues of the chancellor, provided a bridge to both the University Committee and the administration. They succeeded in explaining to the University Committee what the Liberal Caucus was trying to do and that it was non-revolutionary, and they helped temper the frustration and anger of militant caucus members by keeping them in touch with central institutional powers and the values they represented.

At their final meeting Sunday night, the leaders of the caucus presented to the nearly two hundred faculty members present the final version of a resolution which the University Committee would present to the faculty on Monday. One of the elements of the resolution called for a joint committee of students and faculty to look into the university's placement policies and into what to do in event of future obstruction. The caucus was also assured of due process for the students involved in disciplinary action. Finally, there was in one of the resolutions a statement that acknowledged the problem of violence. The members of the caucus, placated somewhat by that statement and generally less sanguine about the power of their movement, voted to support the resolution.[33]

On Monday the faculty met at 4:30. The day had been relatively calm. There had been an afternoon rally, but attendance was low. With the boycott of classes suspended and the examination period under way, campus life appeared almost normal. Nonetheless, the action of the faculty was important, and a number of students were standing by to see what would happen. The theater was full and 130 faculty members had to participate in the meeting through closed circuit television. Vice-Chancellor Cleary once more presided. He gave the floor to President Harrington, who expressed his confidence in the chancellor. He told the faculty it had "used its authority well" and appealed to both faculty and students to keep the lines of communication open. Soon afterwards the University Committee was able to place its resolution before the faculty. One or two attempts to seriously alter the motion were defeated. Several alternative motions were withdrawn; the one exception was rapidly voted down. When questions were raised about CIA interviews scheduled that month, President Harrington said that he did not think they would be held unless it was certain violence would not occur. The closing remarks were made by Chancellor Sewell. "These recent days have been very trying for every member of this academic community. . . . No one knows better than I. . . . [But] we must not allow the events of the past days to deter us in our efforts. . . . We must protect the rights of all members of the university and enhance the freest discussion of ideas and vigilant protection of the rights of others. . . . If we do not protect the rights of any individual or group on this campus, we undermine and jeopardize the rights of all."[34]

With this second faculty meeting, the crisis precipitated by the violence on October 18 was, in a sense, brought to a close. There was a student teach-in that night but the momentum seemed to have died out with the faculty's action at this meeting. Lingering effects of the demonstration were visible for some time. The Select Committee of the state senate began hearings which were widely publicized and were broadcast over the radio. Interest was also kept alive through various legal battles. The deliberations of the student-faculty committee appointed to study the problems of placement and the mode of response to confrontation took the better part of the 1967–1968 academic year, and when they finally made their report they did not seem to go very far beyond previous policy.

Thus one may be tempted to say that all was as before. But nothing could be further from the truth, particularly if one views the struggle in sociological terms—that is as a struggle of norms, values, and role expectations—and not simply in ideological ones. For as we tried to indicate, history may stress the political consequences of events but it is often their social ramifications that are more compelling. In this case it is clear that the crisis precipitated by two different sets of manners and, to some extent, of mores, led to an inevitable clash of wills, the results of which can be interpreted as a victory for the administration. But much of what the students represented in their new mode of behavior, if not the specific issues or demands they made, have become an established aspect of university life, not only in Madison but throughout the country. One can see this in the virtual demise of ROTC on the American campus, in the divestment by many universities of their war-related research facilities, and in the new respect students have gained as a political force, so that they are appointed to the governing boards of institutions and consulted on many issues of substance on the campus today.

One must be cautious in not overinterpreting these facts, for it is clear that the results are uneven and that several forces, notably the faculty, have been instrumental in helping accomplish many of these things. However, from the point of view of this analysis, the political victories students have won are not as important as the status they now enjoy. Students at Madison and throughout America are now persons in a way they never were before. If nothing else, the wave of legislation and hardening of administrative attitudes on disruption are a recognition of the fact that students can make a difference. And that new status, which I feel is a permanent attribute of the American university scene, could not have come about unless the old mores themselves had changed. In describing the actions which led up to and followed the events of October 18 at the University of Wisconsin, we have provided what, in the long run, is only a footnote to that process. By reading such history from a sociological point of view, it should be clear just how difficult, complex, and often disruptive such changes in a major set of American manners— the behavior of college students—can be and what they seem to suggest for the university of the future.

Notes

[1] This chapter is adapted from B. Sklar, "Faculty Culture and Community Conflict: A Historical, Political, and Sociological Analysis of the October 18, 1967 Dow Demonstration at the University of Wisconsin," unpublished doctoral dissertation, University of Chicago, 1970.

[2] G. Kateb, "The Campus And Its Critics," *Commentary*, 1969, 40.

[3] Among the many critics who have commented on this phenomenon, none has a more thorough understanding than L. R. Veysey, *The Emergence of the American University* (Chicago: University of Chicago Press, 1965).

[4] For more information on this subject, see E. E. Meyer, Jr., *A Study of Undergraduate Student Faculty Relationship at a Large University,* unpublished doctoral dissertation, University of Wisconsin, 1965.

[5] Commentary on this subject is already voluminous. For example, see J. P. Roche, "On Being an Unfashionable Professor," *New York Times Magazine*, October 18, 1970, p. 30.

[6] *Connections,* November 1–14, 1967.

[7] *Connections,* November 1–14, 1967.

[8] *Daily Cardinal,* September 22, 1967.

[9] *Daily Cardinal,* October 10, 1967.

[10] *Daily Cardinal,* October 12, 1967.

[11] *Daily Cardinal,* October 13, 1967.

[12] *Daily Cardinal,* October 13, 1967.

[13] *Daily Cardinal,* October 14, 1967.

[14] *Connections,* November 1–14, 1967.

[15] J. F. Scotten, *A Report on the Anti-Dow Protests on the Madison Campus of the University of Wisconsin on October 17–18, 1967* (Madison: University of Wisconsin News and Publication Service, 1967), Appendix F.

[16] Scotten.

[17] Wisconsin, Legislature, Senate, Select Senate Committee, *In the Matter of the Investigation of the Select Senate Committee into the Riotous and Unlawful Activities the Week of October 16, 1967 Occurring on the Madison Campus of the University of Wisconsin,* Vol. V, November 1, 1967, p. 70.

[18] Sklar, p. 171.

[19] *Connections,* November 1–4, 1967.
[20] *Wisconsin State Journal,* October 18, 1967.
[21] *Daily Cardinal,* October 19, 1967.
[22] Wisconsin, Legislature, Senate, Select Senate Committee, Vol. VIIA, November 7, 1967, p. 56.
[23] *Connections,* November 1–4, 1967.
[24] *Wisconsin State Journal,* October 19, 1967.
[25] *Wisconsin State Journal,* October 19, 1967.
[26] *Daily Cardinal,* October 19, 1967.
[27] *Daily Cardinal,* October 20, 1967.
[28] *Wisconsin State Journal,* October 20, 1967.
[29] *Capital Times,* October 20, 1967.
[30] All quotes from meeting are in Faculty Document 158, October 23, 1967.
[31] *Capital Times,* October 20, 1967.
[32] *Wisconsin State Journal,* October 21, 1967.
[33] A critical analysis of these events is presented in Chapter Ten.
[34] *Daily Cardinal,* October 24, 1967.

PART TWO

FACULTY

The faculty, without question one of
the key elements of the academic
community, was caught in the up-
heavals of the 1960s. Faculty members, by and large, were not prepared
for the major changes which higher
education has undergone. Ambivalent about the "student revolution,"
confused about changing patterns of
governance, and skeptical about proposed curriculum reforms which
would weaken academic "standards,"
faculty members have all too often

155

been academic conservatives with no clear ideology. In a sense, the great growth of higher education during the fifties caught many faculty members unaware, and no ethos was created to take the place of the previous, much more narrow, conception of the role of the university which existed in pre-World War II higher education.

The chapters in this part exemplify many of the challenges and conflicts which have affected faculty members throughout higher education, particularly at the prestigious universities. Kenneth Dolbeare discusses the declining importance of faculty self-government and the confusion found in most segments of the faculty. This decline has been particularly dramatic at Wisconsin, where traditions of faculty self-government were quite strong. Edward Silva and David Evett discuss the changing roles of faculty members from the perspective of younger academics. Their analyses indicate a deep underlying discontent among many young professors and a generational cleavage among at least some faculty members. Their discussions of the departmental structure reveal that this keystone of academic organization is also in deep trouble. Sheila McVey's departmental case study reinforces the presence of this problem. Bernard Sklar discusses the role of the faculty in a specific event at Wisconsin, the Dow crisis, but his observations have wide relevance. In periods of crisis, although factions often form among faculty members, the faculty as a corporate body has been notably ineffective. Administrators, as a result of faculty inaction or division, have been forced to pick up the pieces, and in many cases this intervention has entrenched their power. The Wisconsin situation is unique, but similar faculty conflict can be seen in other crisis situations at other institutions. Elaine Reuben deals in her chapter with a subject just now coming to the surface in many universities. It is certainly one of importance at Wisconsin and will emerge as a major issue everywhere. The role and situation of women in the university have, until recently, been of only peripheral concern to most academics. Now, with increasing militance among women faculty and graduate students, the issue is becoming a critical one. Reuben clearly shows that the University of Wisconsin is not at all atypical in its response to this issue, and she provides some indication of the depth of the problem.

CHAPTER 8

● ● ● ● ● ● ● ● ● ● ● ● ● ● ●
● ● ● ● ● ● ● ● ● ● ● ● ● ● ●
● ● ● ● ● ● ● ● ● ● ● ● ● ● ●

FACULTY POWER

Kenneth M. Dolbeare

● ● ● ● ● ● ● ● ● ● ● ● ● ●
● ● ● ● ● ● ● ● ● ● ● ● ● ●
● ● ● ● ● ● ● ● ● ● ● ● ● ●

Universities shape both elite and public attitudes and behavior. They are crucial instruments for refining, justifying, and implementing public policy. They are also objects of vast expenditures, keys to individual social mobility, potential sources of challenge to existing societal values and practices, targets of political opportunism and reprisal, and the means by which eight million volatile young adults are each year held out of the labor force in order that they may be better prepared for its future requirements.

The political significance of universities is obvious. But they have not been taken seriously as major political institutions nor analyzed by social scientists as such. There is no apparent reason why they should not be examined in much the same way as other large scale organizations. In some respects, problems of power among their combined populations of up to 50,000 students, faculty, staff, and other supporting personnel may make them more analogous to small cities. In any event, for one intrigued by processes of political change in advanced industrial societies, universities are specially fascinating. Their functions may range from conservative instruments of established values and forces to means of generating radical alternatives and promoting adaptation to new conditions. Within the

157

arena of the university, societal conflicts may be defined as questions of individual deviance or maladjustment and thereby deflected. Or they may be absorbed into an evolving ideological quiescence, or translated into issues of individual aspiration and achievement, or (less often) focused for judgment and action. At least potentially, the university is indeed the cradle of the society's long-term future.

University faculties are often thought to be important factors in determining the actual part played by these institutions within the society. The mythology of academia and the magic of organization charts both appear to place major responsibilities in the hands of faculties. Conservatives too frequently see faculties as the real source of student unorthodoxy. Thus, the actual power, mobilization potential, values and priorities, and general political behavior of faculties are an important component in the larger question of the sociopolitical role of universities. What shapes faculty attitudes and actions? What difference do the latter make in the governance of the university and in the part played by the university in politics, broadly conceived?

I believe that for a variety of reasons faculty are, as collectivities, rather ordinary and more or less conscious agents of the societal status quo. They are usually incapable of (and uninterested in) either supporting or inspiring even the most modest departures from educational practices, let alone societal norms generally. Although individuals may deviate, the main body of the university faculty differs from the mainstream of middle-class politics in only the most marginal ways. And this carries very unfortunate implications for the character and quality of education in universities today.

University of Wisconsin faculty provide a very useful illustration of this basic theme. Wisconsin is a leading American university, and one with a reputation for liberal policies, in part because of the faculty role in shaping its actions. Nevertheless, the faculty is largely powerless—and uninclined—to do anything beyond the bounds of the orthodoxy set for it by the larger society. So many limits are set by outside forces that the faculty could probably do little of an imaginative or change-oriented nature in any event; but because of self-imposed constraints of various kinds, no serious effort is even mounted.

I shall touch upon four different types of constraints that apply to faculty actions. The first category consists of those numerous and powerful limits which flow from the immediate social and political context of the university. These are only marginally subject to faculty control, although they could be in many ways subject to significant faculty influence. The other three categories of constraint, however, are largely or entirely faculty-imposed. Second are those limits inherent in the political sociology of the faculty: the size, composition, motivations, and governing structure of this 2500-member organization. Third are the limits emerging from the ideologies which prevail within this community, and the social control mechanisms which enforce conformity with them. Finally, some limits arise out of the nature of the threats posed by specific issues themselves, as they are perceived by faculty in the context of the other constraints.

I think these limits are applicable to all faculties, and I use the University of Wisconsin as an illustrative case only. In many respects, faculty responsibilities are greater here than elsewhere, and the University is the better for it. But this is what makes analysis of the Wisconsin situation so important. The problems of the universities today are not the fault of specific men, policies, outside agitators, or even rampant antiintellectualism. Instead, they are traceable to the societal setting and political circumstances of academic organizations, and to the "natural" values and behavior of academic men and women under such conditions. In my view, where Wisconsin has failed, all have failed; Wisconsin at least has the distinction of having tried to transcend the limits of structure, values, and circumstance with which higher education is encumbered. The lessons of its experience may enable future faculties to set higher goals, build better, and perhaps even succeed.

Many characteristics of the external environment of the Madison campus are the same as those of other state universities. I shall review them very briefly and try to focus on those which are more or less unique. The Board of Regents, predictably, is made up of appointees selected chiefly for their prominence in the political and economic life of the state. This means that they have little understanding or sensitivity for the character of the education taking place in the university, except as they are fed "principles" or opinion by top administrators.

But their business experience leads them to feel competent to deal intimately with matters of finance, site location, and building design and construction. In an expanding multicampus system, these can be totally absorbing questions—and education may be left to the faculty. The emergence of student unrest and campus disruption in the late 1960s, however, activated the other dimension of sensitivity and perceived competence on the part of members of the board: state politics. Confident of their ability to read the political pulse of the state and convinced of the validity of established values and priorities, the board began to intrude more and more forcefully into preserves formerly left to administrators and faculty. The beginnings of campus unrest, moreover, coincided with the end of major building programs and the unexpected opening of several seats on the board. With new and more conservative membership and continued student outbreaks, board determination to enter the "educational" realm became stronger.

Some members of the board may have been moved by a desire to protect the university against the depredations of those in the legislature and elsewhere in the state who had long perceived the university as an enemy. Smoldering resentments exist in Wisconsin (as elsewhere, no doubt) against the "foreigners" or "outsiders" who introduce cosmopolitanism and unorthodoxy to the state through the university. These focus on faculty and students from New York and Chicago in particular; occasionally it encompasses thinly veiled anti-semitism (as in references to "Brooklyn Indians"). Resentments also exist against the size of the university and the heavy drain on tax revenues that higher education represents.

Wisconsin is not a wealthy state, and it has done more than its share in supporting higher education. The top-heavy nature of the ever-expanding university administrative structure, with a president who earns nearly twice as much as the governor, and dozens of lesser administrators earning three and four times as much as state legislators, could hardly fail to antagonize even some potentially sympathetic legislators. These long-standing resentments were exacerbated by student outbreaks, and successive Republican victories seemed to make them serious threats to the university budget and autonomy. Members of the Board of Regents could well conclude that the long-term needs of the university called for them to act to suppress faculty and student deviance before the legislature did so in even more drastic ways.

These generally familiar features of the contemporary university environment are rendered more acute by some special characteristics of the Madison situation. For example, the university is peculiarly visible within the state. It is located in a rather small (population less than 200,000) and quiet city, and its nearly 50,000 students, faculty, staff, and other personnel (not to mention their dependents) generate heavy impact. Two daily newspapers and three television stations with not much else to report tend to portray university doings with special drama; the university naturally acquires disproportionate emphasis in conversations throughout the state. Legislators are able to make political mileage back home from their eyewitness reports (and occasionally their photographs) of university transgressions. Furthermore, the university is not only located in the same city as the capitol, but is also physically very close to it. The capitol buildings are located a mere half-mile away and have a clear view of the university. The hilltop location of the university and the size of its buildings cause it to dominate the city, and the symbolic consequences are not lost on state officials. Additionally, the traditional route of protest marches from the campus is down State Street to the capitol. Neither legislative nor executive officials can avoid exposure to shouts and chanting even when stringent controls are placed on access to buildings and grounds.

Finally, though it may sound trivial to those unconnected with major universities, it must be noted that the football record of the late 1960s was the worst in Wisconsin's history. Not only did three years of decline culminate in nearly two years without a victory, but the team was clearly inept on the field. Rapid changes of coaches produced no changes in performance. Alumni and university followers throughout the state began to call for reversal of the good-at-protest, lousy-at-football image which they detested; the two most salient features of the university in their minds became linked in this either-or fashion.

No decisions could be taken by a politically sensitive Board of Regents except in the context of these major factors. Nor could administrators fail to be highly sensitive to them; constant public relations efforts to emphasize the "good things" about the university and its contributions to the state testify to administrative concern. And of course faculty members could not fail to be aware of the same forces. But neither administrators nor faculty were helpless in this situation, and what is important to this analysis is the extent to which their self-imposed limitations both allowed this situation to develop and prevented effective action from being taken to defend educational values.

The size, composition, motivations, and governing structure of the Wisconsin faculty are not unique even among major state universities, but they contribute in significant ways to the inability/unwillingness to do more than maintain the status quo. The Madison faculty is large; the number ranges from 2000 to 2500 depending on the year and on what standards are used in classifying part-time, some professional school, and various extension and adjunct members. Because of this size, coupled with the division of the university into schools and colleges, few faculty members are likely to develop real understanding of the special needs and distinctive perceptions of those outside their immediate areas of interest.

The inclusion of so many distinct schools and colleges on the same campus, moreover, means that distinctive enclaves and subcultures develop. Agriculture, for example, engages ever-decreasing numbers of students, almost all of whom come from Wisconsin; its faculty, with fewer students and lower course demands, may be drawn toward administration. Other independent units, such as the business and engineering schools, are similarly populated. But faculty in the College of Letters and Science face a student population more than half of which is from out of state.

In addition, because of their broader graduate focus, they interact with other faculty whose orientations are similarly national in scope.

Perhaps a more important line of cleavage within the faculty is that of age. (See Chapter Twelve of this book for more on age-related differences.) Three categories may be distinguished. The first is made up of those faculty nearing fifty and older, many of whom have been at the university since prior to World War II. They remember the difficulty of obtaining teaching jobs during the Depression and the security and satisfaction of a relatively small and quiet university during those years. This is the model to which they ultimately refer: an intimate institution where paternalism and gentlemanly agreement obviated the necessity for regularized administrative behavior and the extension of due process to students. Attachments to this image and the University of Wisconsin as the embodiment of such comfortable virtues is very strong among such faculty. Incidents of arson and vandalism in the 1960s created physical reactions in some, as if their own property or person had been assaulted. Challenges to established practices and efforts at adaptation were sometimes viewed as rejections of the values so revered and so long bound up with their institution.

The second category consists of those faculty whose formative years were during or soon after World War II and particularly of those in graduate school right after the war. They were formed in the McCarthy era, sensitized by the Cold War, and anxious to get ahead in their new profession. They were also the limited vanguard of what became a wave of additions to the Madison faculty, and they were well socialized into the traditional ways of doing things on campus. Their promotions and tenure were quicker than those of the 1930s, and some tensions existed between them and the older generation; but they were sufficiently few in number and sufficiently anxious to fit in that the university was able to digest them with little problem. Young by comparison, they made up for such handicaps by being conservative in ideology and style.

The final category, made up of those junior faculty joining the university from about 1964 on, included many who proved by contrast totally indigestible. In part the problem was created by their sheer numbers: this was the period of maximum expansion and efforts at self-improvement of American institutions of higher education, and Wisconsin was actively seeking new faculty in all areas. Within eight years, nearly half of the faculty was to consist of men and women in this age group. They simply could not be socialized in the same elaborate way as their predecessors. Their mobility and the extent of opportunities elsewhere created competitive pressures that led to quick promotions and rapidly rising salaries. New faculty fresh out of graduate school were starting at salaries that the older men and women had earned only after decades of service. Moreover, they had none of the institutional loyalty that distinguished their elders. But more important, the new wave of additions had different priorities and different approaches to education itself. They were politically more sensitive, ideologically more iconoclastic, and educationally more experimental. Like their counterparts in freedom rides and sit-ins, they were impatient with established procedures. Continuing and sometimes deep tensions between them and the two earlier generations of faculty were inevitable.

One thing that many faculty in research-oriented universities share, however, is a set of motivations that place research and publication at the forefront. These are the achievements that spell salary raises, mobility, prestige, and success. They are the academic manifestation of the self-interest, individualism, and materialism that characterizes the larger society, and there is no reason to expect faculty to be different from the world around them. The consequences of this individual self-seeking in the university, however, are a disinclination to spend time in matters unrelated to publication or some other income-substitute. Thus, a handful of older men are willingly permitted to do the committee work that determines faculty policies and to govern the faculty itself. And no proposal involving greater investment of faculty time in teaching or other contact with students has a serious chance of success. Attention to graduate students is justifiable, but only because their work lends support to the basic goals; even then, the range to which graduate students can be permitted to stray from a faculty member's own area of expertise or current research is limited.

The governing structure of the university faculty reflects both the evolution of faculty size and these shared motivations. Until 1970, policies were set by meetings of the entire faculty. Predictably, only a minute fraction of the faculty, normally about 150, attended such sessions. These "regulars," drawn chiefly from the ranks of the older men and women, routinely ratified what had been worked out in committees made up of people like themselves. The agenda for such meetings was set by the University Committee whose members were elected by the entire faculty. For a candidate to have a real chance of winning, he would have to have been around the campus, performing a variety of committee chores, for several years before enough faculty would even recognize his name. Only rarely would a man not nominated by the nominating committee (similarly made up of activist elders) be likely to gain election to the University Committee, but few even thought to try. Most faculty perceived university governance and faculty policy-making as such insignificant functions that they could well be left to the activists. When the self-perpetuating cadres of older faculty proved out of touch and out of sympathy with the developments of the late 1960s, however, their hold was too strong for the younger generation to dislodge without substantial expenditures of effort. And, of course, there were many even within this younger group who were unwilling to take time from their more important activities to attend to such matters.

Every organization and every profession develops a set of rationalizing, justifying beliefs or norms that shape expectations, control perceptions, and (often) determine behavior. At least three such ideologies may be identified within the Wisconsin faculty. Among the major state institutions, Wisconsin has pioneered in bringing the intellectual resources of the university to the service of the state—in promoting the agricultural economy, in rewriting the state's statutes, in introducing new legislative ideas, and so forth. In time, the principle of university service to the state has come to be known as the "Wisconsin Idea"; this, in turn, exemplifies the proper means of making use of intellectual resources for enlightened state government.

But what may at first seem desirable may ultimately become destructive. At least some of the thrust behind the Wisconsin Idea was an attempt to sell the legislature on continuing and expanding support for the university. If the university were promoting the state's economy and refining its governmental practices, there would be substantial tangible (principally financial) returns from investing in the university. The Agricultural Extension efforts of the university loomed very large at the outset of this period, but other schools and colleges too began to emphasize their immediate service to the state in various ways. The basis of support for the university therefore became understood in important ways as a visible quid pro quo: budgets and appropriations in exchange for tangible service and measurable aids to the state economy.

A public conditioned to such expectations cannot fail to develop a "what have you done for me lately?" attitude, and (for example) to view the university's proper function as the preparation of young people for jobs in the local economy. Having created such self-justification, the faculty was forced to live with it. Appeals on other grounds, such as the intellectual and critical functions of the university, were simply not understood by any broad segment of the necessary constituency. Perhaps they never are in times of stress, but under these circumstances the chance was even less. Moreover, the faculty itself came to believe in the Wisconsin Idea and found it difficult to understand other fronts on which action might be taken. In effect, they were trapped in their own rhetoric, personally as well as strategically.

Faculty government—this phrase is a common one on the Madison campus, perhaps with greater justification than on most other campuses. It is understood to mean that the faculty has the power to and actually does make the basic rules for university governance, student discipline, and educational practices. Faculty government is a treasured power, and one which is assumed to distinguish Wisconsin from other administratively-run institutions. Hiring, promotion, tenure, and salary matters, as well as course and degree programs, are decided almost entirely by faculty committees; deans of students and others act as agents of faculty policy, as do admissions officers, registrars, and so forth. In the eyes of many faculty, it is faculty government which makes Wisconsin uniquely attractive among state universities.

But the ideology may cloak a reality of more effective control mechanisms than would otherwise be possible. The fact is that faculty government is often mere co-optation. Even its most vigorous and sincere celebrants acknowledge that it carries with it the corollary principle of faculty responsibility. The latter often simply amounts to doing what one thinks the Regents would do before they have a chance to do it. In order to preserve one's independence, in other words, one acts as one anticipates one's superiors would prefer. Animated by such a definition of faculty responsibility, the faculty is likely to do little that strains the bounds of precedent or well-established orthodoxy. At the same time, of course, potentially deviant faculty are subtly brought into line in order that the principle of faculty government not be endangered. The number of occasions on which faculty and Regents have actually disagreed at Wisconsin is very few; in every instance, however, the Regents have proceeded to carry out their wishes. And yet the myth survives.

The characteristics which distinguish men and women of special expertise or experience from laymen are often distilled into the concept of "professionalism." Not only the nature and extent of the knowledge or skill that distinguishes such people, but also their approach (detachment, objectivity) forms part of their professional status. Unfortunately, the concept may be extended still further to include standards of dress, behavior, or even orthodoxies of belief. Disapproval of or disagreement with certain attitudes or actions may then translate into allegations of unprofessional conduct. What one happens to have experienced in the past or to prefer in the present may become the definition of professional. Often the concept is little more than a means of avoiding controversial or value-based actions. But it endures among faculty as an ephemeral standard, to be interpreted and applied by some to the behavior and beliefs of others.

Related to the concept of professionalism is that of neutrality on the part of the university or its faculty. The assertion is that a university is, can be, and should be neutral among the contending forces in the society and world. This is said to be the only way in which academics can retain their objectivity and detachment, and to be essential to the autonomy of the university. Those who seek to use the resources or the status provided by the university in behalf of particular causes are held to be unprofessional and underminers of the neutral stance of the university.

It is hard to see how a university which receives its support from state and federal governments, follows the established values and practices of the society, teaches the orthodox beliefs of the established disciplines, and prepares students for places in an ongoing social and economic order can be anything but a completely nonneutral agent of the present status quo. The only thing remarkable about such status is that many people apparently define total integration with the surrounding society as neutrality. Socially and politically, of course, the status quo is suffused with differentials of power and value preference and the wholly nonneutral societal structures and practices reflecting the existing pattern of power and preferences. The university, by avoiding any expressions at odds with such power, values, and structures, is at least implicitly endorsing them—and not being neutral at all. And yet the myth persists that only those who challenge the accepted and seek to divert the university's resources in other directions are being nonneutral. When the university sponsors research for the armed forces, for example, it is neutral; when (if) it rhetorically condemns an act of foreign policy, however, it is nonneutral. Academic freedom may become the principle under which a variety of nonneutral acts are undertaken.

This curious extension of professionalism and one-sided neutrality quite clearly has the effect of justifying and requiring quiescence and orthodoxy on the part of the faculty. Nor are such pressures merely admonitions. Because they are real in the minds of many senior faculty, they are supported by the tenure- and promotion-granting processes of the university. A junior faculty member who oversteps the bounds of professionalism as it is understood by the senior members of his department may well find that it is a sufficient reason for denying him status, or even retention or promotion, and deviant senior members may find the same with respect to salary increments. Should a department support its member in cases of this kind, the individual could still be turned back by the senior faculty sitting on school- or unit-wide review committees. Much of the social control that takes place in the university setting is peer-group control, subtle rather than blatant. As such, of course, it is essentially self-imposed restraint.

Many issues have agitated the campuses of the nation in the last five years. They cover a wide range of matters, some local and unique to particular institutions and others broadly shared among all universities—such as the reaction to the Cambodian excursion. But the threats perceived by faculty may be organized into some rough categories and considered in those terms. Most easily recognized are the threats posed to established societal values. In this respect, faculty perceptions are much like other relatively favored middle-class citizens: they see challenges to the capitalist economic system, to familiar habits of dress, materialist values, work-oriented ethic, and established political structures. They do not welcome change in these respects any more than other middle-class people, and they are exposed to relatively clear insight into what is happening within this generation. The alternatives, in many faculty eyes, are repression or revolution. If these are the choices, many of them appear to have concluded, then let us end the war in Vietnam so we can get about the repression efficiently. Granting that this response is more characteristic of the oldest faculty members, especially in the science, engineering, business, agriculture, and medical schools, it is still representative of a substantial fraction of the faculty.

Others react to the kinds of issues that have become familiar in the last few years in terms of threats to the established role of the university. And these issues have played a part in the changing social function of universities. Instead of training rising elites only, the university is now becoming a more egalitarian institution. Black studies programs and departments raise the elite-egalitarian conflict acutely: they accept the validity of a subculture and its standards, emphasizing group social and intellectual development rather than the intellectual and professional values and standards of the dominant population. For many, this represents perversion of the university as an intellectual arena. Open admissions proposals, or decreasing selectivity of any kind, pose similar threats. Faculty steeped in the research and graduate student training ethos of prestigious universities find it almost impossible to adapt to these pressures.

But perhaps most poignant of all the threats perceived, and most crucial to faculty reaction, is the sense of personal threat and insecurity that many faculty have developed. This is only rarely a real concern for physical safety, except in isolated cases. Most often it is an ego-involved psychic insecurity growing out of a sensed incapacity to deal with today's students amid today's academic conditions. It is, after all, a somewhat arrogant act to go before large audiences and purport to be a source of knowledge and insight whose words must be respectfully transcribed as nearly verbatim as possible. Moreover, it is an act which makes one terribly vulnerable: factual or interpretive errors can easily be made, and/or one's very intellectual or personal qualities put up for general judgment and possible rejection. Spreading one's brains out on the lectern for students to casually pick over and probably sweep aside three times a week can be a debilitating challenge. Most faculty therefore develop defenses that will enable them to undergo these pressures with a minimum of ego-threat. Some become highly authoritarian, occasionally using grades rigidly as a means of forcing students to toe the mark; others develop the attitude that students are ignorant, emotional, diverted, and so forth and therefore incapable of making valid judgments anyhow.

But it is becoming harder and harder to maintain these defenses. There are more and more students in classes; they are more challenging in the classroom; they have new and threatening ideas in their heads; they are far less respectful of authority; and they are resentful of the use of grades as a club. Many older faculty are simply incapable of understanding or coping with these conditions, and they feel personally threatened by them in the most fundamental ways. Their reaction is the understandable but unfortunate one of clinging desperately to every vestige of the old ways, in hopes that they can delay the bursting of the dam past the day of their retirement, or simply that they can hold on to as much of the past as possible.

This defensiveness is by no means limited to senior faculty. It extends in some instances to even the most "progressive" junior faculty. At Wisconsin, for example, some junior faculty had begun to build membership in a local chapter of the AFT, and were beginning to use it as a substantial lever in faculty politics. When the teaching assistants unionized, however, and demanded (among other things) the right to participate in the shaping of courses, the AFT local split seriously on this question. As faculty, many members could not entertain the prospect of sharing their profesional prerogatives with graduate students. When it came down to an issue involving the substance of education, in other words, the junior faculty reacted much like their seniors in resorting to traditional defenses.

The unstated premise behind the analysis here presented is that the conditions of academic life and the societally-created natural motivations and priorities of faculty militate against effective education. Accepting the various constraints here described, in most cases willingly and even enthusiastically, faculty have not seen the many facets of the problem of education. They have seen teaching, even graduate teaching, as the transmission of a commodity; whether facts or methods, this commodity is seen as packageable and capable of being passed from one mind to another (or at least to the notebook which serves as the representative of the latter). Faculty have not seen education as a process in which students become independent thinkers, capable of critical analysis of the society around them. They have not been willing to invest in the trial and error tactics of adjusting educational methods to the rapidly changing perceptions and experience of the new generation of students. And they have not sought to insist upon the necessity of maintaining some responsible ratio between number of students and number and teaching effort of faculty.

If there is one failure to be singled out, it is this one. For the most part, faculty have not seen education in any terms except those the society sets for it—vocationalism, adaptation to the ongoing society and economy and their needs, and the means to mobility and status. They have thus become hopelessly mired in outmoded methods and assumptions, to which they cling out of fear of what might take their place. And they have permitted their institutions to become trapped in the destructive crossfire of frustrated students and resentful older men of power.

CHAPTER 9

●●●●●●●●●●●●●●●
●●●●●●●●●●●●●●●
●●●●●●●●●●●●●●●

FACULTY IMAGES OF
POWER AND KNOWLEDGE

Edward T. Silva

●●●●●●●●●●●●●●●
●●●●●●●●●●●●●●●
●●●●●●●●●●●●●●●

Out of my participation and observations as an assistant professor in the department of sociology, I have constructed a mapping of this department, the university, and their mutual environment. This exercise in social cartography is, of course, personal and subjective, but not unique. Rather, it is one shared in broad outline by many of those new to the University of Wisconsin at this time. The central idea of this mapping is a paradox. Coming of age in the multiversity is grasping the paradox that at the very heart of the educational institutions of a technically developed, formally democratic society, power is structured along lines more appropriate to an earlier autocratic epoch.

Deviance and Control

One evening during the summer of 1968 I received a phone call from my department chairman. A very important faculty meeting would be held the next day. At the meeting, I learned that the fellow in the office next to mine had decided not to file grades with the central administration for students in his first level statistics course. I did not know the non-filer, an assistant professor, at all well, nor did I have much stake in the questions around grades. As a graduate teaching assistant, I had both sat in on question-drafting sessions and had graded hour and final exams using these questions. From the drafting sessions I knew that the five or six people teaching the same course often have very different senses of what constitutes a reasonable test of course competence. I also learned that whatever you ask elicits from students an enormous range of responses. Most answers indicate only the vaguest understanding of the material, and at the end of a grading session one is necessarily convinced that what went on in the classroom was not educational in any transmission sense of the term. However, rather than dealing with why that might have been so, the task usually becomes one of deciding who gets what grade. In this process, the understandings of both student and faculty triumph over absolute standards. Relatively superficial, vague, and trivial analysis is accepted as, and becomes, the average standard by which student performance is judged. At the same time the sheer fact of giving and receiving a grade implies that some definable amount of learning went on in the course. This upholds the image of all participants as being involved in an educational process, whether they are or not.

Given these experiences with grading, experiences that I believed were shared by all of my colleagues, I expected that we would turn to a discussion of the social functions of grading. We did. But the discussion revolved about the social *utility* of grades, or their equivalents. How else would the university award scholarships, compute class standings, grant honors, and so on? In all, about two dozen specific social uses of grades were given. Many of these social uses seemed to involve convenience rather than necessity. As the discussion created an avalanche of institutional functions that must not be disturbed, it became clear that the social issues involved were to be buried in a consensus not to disturb those who found grades useful, including ourselves.

If the resort to social utility arguments seemed a collective evasion of the points that the non-filer wanted to raise, at least they were publicly put forward and discussible on their merits. Another set of arguments, often informally advanced, was more elusive. It was said that the non-filer had violated the norms of "good colleagueship" by acting unilaterally. The idea here was that a department is run by sharing ideas and opinions so that a consensus emerges. This is a notion of the department as a community of scholars, united in the search for the truth about certain phenomena, and sharing mutual understanding and respect for one another's wishes and needs. Without minimizing the degree of shared respect and affection among ourselves, it is clear that departmental consensus was subjected to certain structural limits. In particular, such consensus is limited by the by-laws of the university which provide for two levels of decision-making within the department. The executive committee is composed of all tenured members and is responsible for personnel and budget matters, while the departmental committee, made up of all but instructors, lecturers, and teaching assistants, is charged with questions of educational and administrative policy. Since tenured professors are members of both committees, the possibilities of executive committee understandings coloring and structuring the issues in departmental meetings are enormous.

It is not important to argue whether or not a formal executive committee consensus was reached to state the non-grading case in "social utility" and "colleagueship" terms in order to avoid educational issues. Quite the contrary. It seems much more likely that participants in the executive committee's deliberations over a number of years have articulated and fostered attitudes and values that disclaimed any interest in what went on in the classroom, as long as it was not organizationally troublesome. Consider, for example, the overt hiring and tenure criteria. The executive committee has tried over the last decade to hire "the most promising" sociologists and to encourage them to secure sufficient resources to fulfill that promise by publishing "significant" work, that is, work that is methodologically and substantively fashionable, and perhaps, as some say, "big business."[1] To the extent that our department encouraged such work, it developed a staff with skills that had little carry over to the undergraduate classroom. Indeed, since the careers of nontenured staff members were dependent upon such work, the classroom was necessarily deemphasized. In a pragmatic way, a curious empirical understanding of education evolved, one that saw students as passive note and exam takers and teachers as passive lecturers and graders within a context that is research dominated. This pragmatic philosophy, rarely verbally articulated, did not hold that faculty members must publish or perish, where perish meant being let go to waste away at some academic Siberia. Rather it specified that we must both publish and perish, by emphasizing fashionably specialized research at the frontier and the foundation, and deemphasizing teaching in the classroom. Educational philosophy in this context is simply not discussible because there are no terms of discourse available. Where research is the lingua franca of the realm, all other tongues are unintelligible.

In such an environment, "colleagueship" is the acceptance of these values as one's primary ethical premise. Not only is such research way ahead of whatever is in second place, but anything that disturbs its flow is morally reprehensible. Therefore, the raising of educational issues in a manner which requires the department to answer the many users of grades is a clearly disruptive issue, as it distracts all the department from their business at hand. Thus the arguments of "social utility" and "a lack of colleagueship" are intertwined. When a challenge to the department's ethos of specialized, supported publication and educational perishment was presented, these values were simply reasserted. The matter of not filing grades was taken care of by action of the departmental committee, action structured no doubt by executive committee consensus. An exam was written for the course by two faculty members, without the approval of those teaching the course, and graded by teaching assistants. With the fall term, two separate series of events flowed from this response: a number of colleagues offered symbolic support to the non-filer, and the executive committee failed to renew his appointment.

The symbolic actions offered on the grading issue were remarkable in that they emerged in a totally uncoordinated way. Apparently without collaboration six (of fifty) sociologists announced to their classes that some modification in grading was going to occur in their classes. For example, in the only case involving a tenured faculty member, a class of four hundred students, after discussion, voted everyone an A. In another case, students were to formulate their course goals and to evaluate their own movement toward these goals as the term progressed. In the end, their grades would be up to them. In all six actions, students were given significant access to the process by which they received grades.

At this point, some unusual patterns developed in the way some colleagues related to these grading innovators. For example, the department chairman would stop by and chat. Most often, these conversations became Dutch uncle affairs—offers of a senior colleague's advice and a repetition of the issues raised in the first instance of nonfiling of grades— with three differences. First, great stress was placed on the necessity for integration of the department and the college, with special mention of the possibility that all this deviance might well lead to a major loss of resources for the department. Second, these deviations were thought to be a reflection of "social isolation," or some other psychological problem, and some counseling was offered. Third, those completing degrees within the department were warned to "be good team players" so that letters of recommendation could be wholehearted in their praise. In brief, organizational heat was applied to the bottoms of all the grading deviants.

Within three weeks, substantial retrenchments occurred. The sole tenured deviant read a two-page recantation at the next departmental meeting. This effectively removed the possibility of a firmly and authentically committed friendly voice within the secretly meeting executive committee, and matters seemed to reach a point of equilibrium. The arm-twisting continued at low level, and none of the innovations approached the taboo of not filing. Meanwhile, the enterprising college newspaper began reporting on all sorts of grading and teaching innovations in other departments. This made it clear to us that the university administration was faced by deviance in many departments and would not be able to isolate ours. This effectively undermined the argument that the innovators were endangering departmental resources. Given this condition of perceived equilibrium, it was something of a shock when the executive committee moved dramatically beyond the mere formal specification of grading and grade-filing as normal and required classroom behavior by firing the non-filer and unilaterally revising the agreement renewals of the other nontenured faculty.

Of the ten nontenured members of the sociology faculty who were hired in 1967, two were not renewed, and the term of renewal for the other eight was unexpectedly reduced from three to two years. The executive committee's decision was communicated by a brief letter to each concerned faculty member. Among the faculty, discussion of this case was handled in two ways. First, given that the action was a sensitive one to raise between senior and junior faculty, the issue was discussed mostly at arms length if at all. Hence, a heavy curtain of public silence fell: only in the most trusted senior-junior contexts was the drape lifted. Second, many of the nontenured faculty did not seem to realize that there were collective dimensions to their executive committee's action. This last point cannot be overemphasized, for each of these sociologists is by temperament and training sensitive to exactly such dimensions.

By the end of January the basic facts of the executive committee's class action were in hand, and attempts at redress by the junior faculty began. There were three distinct phases to these attempts. For several weeks, we discussed the situation formally with the chairman and informally with friendly tenured staff. From these conversations it appeared that the two firings or nonrenewals were based on vague, but firmly held, opinions that the two faculty showed little promise of "high level" scholarship, had published little, and should not be a part of the department. This seemed puzzling since most of the rest of us had published little since arriving in Madison, and since at least some of the publications of tenured faculty seemed without scholarly promise. The objective basis of the evaluation thus seemed obscure. At last, it came to two questions. Are sixteen months enough time to make what is essentially a tenure decision? If so, then is it not obligatory for the department to make the basis of these decisions crystal clear to all involved, especially the nontenured faculty?

Once these issues emerged a series of junior faculty meetings were held to grasp and possibly act upon this matter. The dynamics of these meetings were extraordinary. Two factions emerged, factions whose membership changed both within and across meetings, yet whose current members took consistent and enduring positions. One was a "solidarity" group which spoke as peers of the fired sociologists, taking the position that all were vulnerable to what they saw as arbitrary actions of the executive committee. The other faction, the "Missouri" clan, were unable to define their seniors as capricious. For them, if the stated reason for dismissal was lack of promise, then it must be so. If renewal was for two years, so, too, it must be. The aim of the solidarity group in these meetings was to find a mechanism by which the executive committee could be approached and apprised of their shock and concern. The tactic of the Missouri faction was to continually raise questions on the validity of the solidarity group's interpretations. Guesses as to the reasons for membership in each faction are hazardous. Yet my guess is that when one felt particularly dependent upon the executive committee, or most attuned to its apparent political position, one was a Missouri. This consistent structural cleavage, existing in spite of changing membership, reveals varying perceptions and sensitivities of the tenured faculty's collective tolerance and power. We all knew that the executive committee could and would use its power as it saw fit, and yet our individual experiences within the academic arena had taught us that appeals to the powerful were possible and effective. Our power etiquette predilections were ultimately insurmountable. Our meetings went on for four months. Finally we decided to invite the department chairman to meet with us.

The meeting with the chairman was instructive. He seized the occasion, talking virtually non-stop for more than an hour. It was a discourse on how all the committees of the department and the university try hard to do their jobs and interlock to shape up the system, and if one wanted to do something one could as long as the rules were followed and seniors were consulted. The audacity of the performance was matched only by the withering of the petitioners' collective sense that their shared definition of at least some of their problems was real.

Whether or not the chairman intended to constrain and inhibit his nontenured colleagues in immaterial. He was presenting the official view of the decision-making processes in our department and university as his own because it was his own, perhaps as a result of his participation in it. As he spoke he revealed the sincerity with which he held his views, and in that sincerity the essence of power's inherent corrosiveness. Power corrupts because it undermines the capability to perceive and empathize with those who are affected by its exercise while constructing an empty edifice of participatory rationalization with which to sincerely screen out the words and pictures sent from those so affected.

At this point, some of the more regular solidarity faction members prepared a memo linking together the firings, the renewals, and the overly broad powers of the executive committee. This draft memo, prepared for faculty-wide distribution in the first month of school (1969), was delayed by the emergence of what came to be styled the first "X Affair."

On Monday, September 15, 1969, the chairman of the department found a discrepancy in the payroll. An associate professor, "X," author of a standard work in his field and several other books, a continually articulate public spokesman and organizer against the Vietnam adventure (and, incidentally, the tenured participant in grading innovation), was not to receive his recommended salary increase, an increase recommended by the department, college, and university administrations—this by unilateral action of the Board of Regents. The faculty response was immediate and widespread. On September 22, 1969, the department meeting of rural and general sociology overwhelmingly supported executive committee resolutions which expressed deep concern with what was considered an attack on the freedom of expression. In a publicly distributed resolution, these faculties held that: "The question is . . . why [Professor X] was singled out for such a penalty. The issue from the point of view of the university as a whole is that of a threat to academic freedom. We conclude that the Regents' action was prejudicial to free inquiry and public dissent." Attempts were made to mobilize other departments in support of a demand that X's raise be restored. On October 17, 1969, upon appeal from the University Committee, and with the support of thirty-odd departments whose faculties adopted similar resolutions, as well as the less formal but real support of other department chairmen, the Regents retreated and accepted the original salary recommendation.

While there is no doubt in my mind that the Regents' actions were correctly perceived by many faculty members as a clear and present danger to expression, the case also involves an instance of attack by the Regents on the autonomy of the executive committee as a device of senior faculty power. Therefore, from the point of view of nontenured faculty, here was a case of inter-elite conflict. Accordingly, it is somewhat instructive to speculate as to why the junior faculty closed ranks with their seniors. Was it a response to the issue of academic freedom? Certainly not in the broadest sense of the term, for what was at stake was an academic freedom hostile, for example, to grading innovation, and operating, in the words of another observer, in ways "subtle, hidden, tricky, and difficult to cope with . . . [and] very difficult to prove precisely." If it was academic freedom, it was freedom from the Regents that was being supported, not freedom from the secretly meeting executive committee. In his choice of masters, a reasonable man selects those who may better appreciate his service, and nontenured faculty must always, I suppose, choose their tenured counterparts rather than Regents. What surprises reason is that the selection occurs with almost no public acknowledgment of the options.

There then occurred what I believe was an almost public acknowledgment of these options of subservience. After the Regents capitulated, the already drafted memo from the "solidarity" nontenured group was distributed to the entire faculty. It asked for discussion and action on the questions of renewal, dismissal, and the broad powers of the executive committee. The official responses to this memo were personal letters from the chairman after the next executive committee meeting reporting the addition of another year to all the renewals. No public discussion of tenure, or the two firings, or even the power of the executive committee occurred. Even a request for copies of the minutes of executive committee meetings was unanswered. It seems plausible that if the first X Affair had not occurred when it did, even this one-year addition would not have been granted. To believe otherwise leaves the timing of this executive committee action a mystery, or requires the assumption that the executive committee was not previously aware of the details of the issue. To believe this explanation, we must assume that the chairman, who was very aware, did not discuss it with his fellow executive committee members at the time of our meeting. This is unthinkable.

Or is it? Could the executive committee possibly have been unaware of the details of the issue? Is it possible from the materials on publishing and perishing to argue this position? Perhaps the department exists not so much as a community of scholars with shared interests, but as a disorganized and anomic division of laborers driven by individualistic compulsions and fantasies of competitive, sponsored production. If so, then it is possible to think of the tenured faculty as inattentive to the day-to-day events occurring within their department. Second, there is no reason to believe that something like the solidarity-Missouri cleavage is not operant within the tenured ranks. Certainly, the social science literature is filled with typologies that might help identify the basis of such a cleavage.[2] (See Chapter Twelve of this book.) Third, in noting the corrosive effects of power upon its exercisers, it is both inconsistent and inhumane to stigmatize all members of the executive committee simply on the basis of their shared social location. Therefore, it is morally and sociologically correct to put the matter hypothetically, and to move on to see what other data may be developed to resolve the interpretation.

In summary, these episodes may be hypothetically related as a series of actions and reactions which describe the uses of power by the departmental executive committee to control deviation by nontenured members of the department. First, a nontenured member decided not to file grades. Then, in reaction, the departmental meeting, reflecting values fostered by the executive committee's prior actions, removed the grades from his control. Second, in an uncoordinated way, a few grading innovations occurred in symbolic opposition to the value of research publication and educational perishment. After some personal attempts at influencing these deviants, the firing of two faculty and unilateral altering of employment agreements occurred. This was in apparent reaction to the broadening of grading deviation. Third, after the demonstration of junior-senior staff solidarity in the conflict between the Regents and the senior staff, and upon a public petition, the contractual agreements of those nontenured faculty who were not fired were extended to their original length. While it is not possible for me to demonstrate the reality of the connections hypothetically stated here, it is possible to show self-interested outcomes from executive committee actions. To the degree that such additional analysis is plausible, then the surface plausibility of the social control argument detailed above is enhanced.

Self-Interest and Power

As noted above, some members of my department, especially tenured ones, reject in drift and detail the hypothesis of action and reaction traced above. From one point of view, this merely confirms the analysis: for their rejection of this interpretation provides us with yet another sincere instance of an ideology, one that serves the psychological function of decreasing the power exerciser's ability to empathize with those whom they attempt to control. Happily, however, we may move beyond an honest difference in opinion to some clear indicators of the uses of power on the part of tenured faculty in my department: the structure of deference, labor, and material reward.

First, the senior members of the department inescapably suffer from what another cultural worker, a long-time editor of a liberal journal of opinion, calls "Buyer's Disease." "When you are in a position to buy something other people want to sell—in my case manuscripts or chances at a job—you are treated with a deference beyond your deserts. When you leave your editorial chair—or as a buyer of anything, anywhere—and people no longer have any material reason to cater to you, it can be a traumatic experience."[3] Although many members of my department are wonderfully sensitive to these market dynamics and try to compensate for them, it is really a structural rather than a psychological matter and is simply unavoidable. The tacit acceptance of Buyer's Disease within the department is nicely captured by the tradition which makes the newest member of the department committee its secretary. He takes and dis-

tributes committee meeting minutes although he is, by virtue of his newness, clearly the most unacquainted with the names and issues he must
tick into those minutes. In this simple inefficiency, we see symbolized
the structural demand for deference. Interestingly, the exclusive executive
committee uses a similar newness criterion to get its minutes taken.

It is important to add that Buyer's Disease requires a comple-
mentary illness among the nontenured staff. "Seller's Malaise" involves
the propensity to respond a little overenthusiastically to senior faculty
concerns over the lunch table, the work table, the cocktail table, and the
dinner table. This propensity might well be a major skill developed within
our educational institutions. And is it not part and parcel of the middle-
class ethos nurturing the bulk of our students and staff, encouraging them
to make friends and influence people, to school themselves for better
paying jobs, and to seek after the powerful with smiles and wares, including themselves, for sale. In fighting against this structural situation
in good faith, although we may win battles, the outcome of the war, for
most of us, is a foregone conclusion. In spite of ourselves, we share
Buyer's-Seller's Disease.

Second, not only do the tenured faculty finally accept the proffered
deference of the junior staff, but they, through their participation in the
secret executive committee meetings, benefit in interesting material ways
from that committee's creation, or tolerance, of an exploitive division of
labor and reward within the department. Academic departments are
productive organizations. They produce credits which students use to
gain education certificates, and research, which industrial, political, and
philanthropic organizations use to their own advantage. In their productive activities, academic departments procure and expend resources.

As the department produces student credits and sponsored research, it brings into the university funds beyond the costs expended in
salaries. Students, of course, pay tuition, and it is possible to estimate their
payments for their credits taken within the department. For example, although the annual figure varies, within the period 1964–1968, tuition
payments for sociology courses totaled 130 per cent of salary costs. Sponsored research payments typically run 150 per cent of salary costs, plus
expenses. This money beyond salary costs goes into a general university
fund and helps pay for faculty fringe benefits as well as overhead and supporting services: plant, maintenance, heating, and so on. Although it is
difficult to settle the matter precisely, it is arguable that these monies beyond faculty salaries fully support the department's productive investment, and indeed contribute to the costs of smaller departments.

If the executive committee is as self-consciously powerful as we
have suggested above, then we should see its power expressed in the

Table 4. Departmental Division of Labor, Tuition and Reward, Academic Year 1967–1968

	Department	Tenured Faculty		Nontenured Faculty	
Credit Hours Taught	33,051	8,744	(.26)	24,308	(.74)
Undergraduate credit hours taught	28,372.2	6,349	(.22)	22,023	(.78)
Graduate credit hours	4,679	2,395	(.51)	2,285	(.49)
Tuition Estimates Total	$640,027.4	$194,396.5	(.30)	$445,630.9	(.70)
Undergraduate share	461,198.8	103,308.5		358,812.7	
Graduate share	177,906.3	91,088.0		86,818.2	
Division of Labor within Department					
Faculty instruction positions	34.45	17.33		17.15	
Faculty research positions	6.67	4.00		2.67	
Average Salary	12,704.7	16,616.7		9,909.2	

NOTE: All figures are computed from official university records held by the archives and registrar. Salaries and proportion of time in instruction or research are found in the university budget. Credit hours computed from time-schedules and credit hour reports. Tuition estimates are based on fifteen-hour semester loads for undergrads and twelve-hour loads for graduate students, and estimates of the proportion of students paying in-state tuition. Assistant professors, instructors, and lecturers, but not teaching assistants, are nontenured faculty. Some faculty hold joint appointment, and the nonsociology proportion is not included in these computations.

work and reward structure of the department. Tenured faculty, who held 50 per cent of the teaching posts in the academic year 1967–1968, taught about one-half of the 4679 graduate credit hours produced by the department, but only about one-quarter of the 28,372 undergraduate credit hours. The much greater teaching load of the nontenured faculty produced more than twice the tuition revenue paid by students of the department (70 per cent:30 per cent). Although the nontenured faculty teach more students, and therefore produce more tuition revenues for the university, their seniors were paid about 80 per cent more, on the average (see Table 4). Why are senior salaries higher? Of course, they are better known, perhaps due to their greater accomplishments, which yields them fame and the lever most useful for salary advancement: research and job offers from other departments. Still, there is no doubt that one who teaches fewer undergraduates simply has more time within which to demonstrate competence and gain fame. Indeed, in most academic departments the most rewarding position, careerwise, is either not to teach at all, thus being able to devote all your energies to research, or to run an empire with sponsored research funds paying you to teach a few graduate students how to do whatever you are currently doing and, perhaps, having them share your work.

Since the department's executive committee collectively allocates salary money, recruits and promotes faculty members, and generally permits the exploitive division of labor and reward described, it seems perfectly plausible and consistent that its members participate, some reluctantly, some tacitly, and some with vigor, in the deviation controlling events described above. It must be added that the results of the processes described go far beyond social control or the objective work exploitation of the nontenured faculty. First, when sales deference dominates social relationships, the quality of comity evaporates from departmental life. Second, when sales deference and work exploitation permeate superior-subordinate relationships, then subordinates, like the bicycle rider of authoritarian personality lore, kick at the bottom while bending at the top. It does not take much imagination to see that the grading system provides a ready channel for this. Finally, when deference hangs as a cloud in the air, the ability to see clearly the new frontiers of knowledge is weak, for honest criticism and new ideas are unsought and unseen.

Structural Context

Although the department executive committee secretly controls the carrots and sticks of academic careers, it is not without its own problems. Its power is limited. Beyond the internal limits of character and personality differences, differences that might parallel those among the nontenured staff and similarly prevent collective action, external limits exist as a result of the department's location within the university. As we have seen in the case of Professor X, elements in both the university and society occasionally seek to limit the committee's power. What is true in crisis is true in day-to-day life. Since the central function of the committee is to define and protect academic careers, it must deal continuously with those in its environment who can offer or deny to it the stuff from which academic careers are manufactured.

In order to create academic careers in the contemporary multiversity, departments must be able to allow faculty to pursue research that is fundable (research that someone outside the department is willing to pay for; the alternative is paying expenses out of pocket), to remove the quality of classroom teaching from serious analysis, and to protect the executive committee's power to distribute carrots and sticks. The concepts of academic freedom and academic tenure are the principles legitimizing departmental career construction, and their substance is what is gained in dealings with the higher levels of university administration. In order to gain the academic freedom and academic tenure with which to create their academic careers, the department offers to the college the labor of its nontenured staff, and to the plant managing campus and central administrations it offers its lack of moral and intellectual criticism. We can examine these exchanges by interpreting the way the department is integrated into its social context. This analysis proceeds by intuition, inference, and implication since I have not been party or participant to the exchanges I believe to exist in this area. Although I know the imagery seems reasonable to many sharing my position, readers should consider these remarks hypothetical and testable within their own lives.

Departments are part of a college or school. Administratively, the chairman, as nominal agent of the department at large but more likely as spokesman for the values of the executive committee, deals with the dean. These interchanges necessarily have to do with the relative claims of the department on college and university resources. Probably, these claims vary with the dean's and the executive committee's thinking about the past and future of the department, particularly its fame within its field. Such departmental glory, as well as academic careers, depends in large part on the salaries and employment benefits available to tenured faculty. However, the substance of these conversations finds the ears of the executive committee but not the rest of the department. This administrative arrangement links the executive committee into the formal reward structure of the university, creating a high probability that the needs of the senior staff will be met and a low probability that the problems of the junior staff will be dealt with. For example, trying to teach large under-graduate classes is one of the central working problems of nontenured staff. There is an obvious and significant qualitiative difference between discussing an idea with 15 students and with 150 students. Since few executive committee members are enamored of teaching ideas to under-graduates in small classes, the possibility of forcefully raising this question with the dean is remote. To the extent that the senior faculty is struc-turally insensitive to such problems and fails to raise them with the dean-ship, while raising their own salaries and the conditions of their pro-fessorial status and allowing the department's junior faculty to bear up as best they can with the administration's notion of a decent-sized class and other working conditions, then the senior staff may be said to ex-change the labor of their junior for their own salary and social honor increments. The exact terms of this trade are suggested in Table 4.

When departments deal with deans, they come into contact with the lowest reaches of an extensive bureaucracy. In their negotiations with this bureaucracy they gain control over academic careers. But in exchange, the tenured faculty seem to avert their minds from the broader implica-tions of the university's role in society. To the extent that this is true, then, the question becomes how do administrators at the top of this bureaucracy define university-society relationships? The general answer seems to be that university administrations act as plant managers for both the producers and consumers of knowledge. As plant managers, these administrators accept the world as given and assert that the university is apolitical in its organizational posture. But acceptance of the world as given in fact aligns the university with whatever organized interests exist in society at large. In fact, as plant managers, administrations facilitate and encourage the production and consumption of knowledge to serve vested interests in two distinct ways. In doing so, they legitimize the uni-versity's very existence, its claims upon the public budget, and the careers of all concerned.

First, the university produces knowledge and information that is useful to manufacturers, agri-businessmen and other commercial enter-prises, as well as foundations and governments. This is why these organiza-tions provide the University of Wisconsin with well over 60 per cent of the biennial budget funds. To these users, the university is an extension, without the costs, of their own production plants. Because their research questions would not be answered as cheaply or as competently if the university did not exist, it is in their interest to keep the university going as is, for to do so keeps their research flowing. Since the university can-not continue to exist as it is now without 60 per cent of its biennial resources, and the simplest way to retain these resources is to continue the production of the desired research, the interpenetration of interests is clear.

A second service of the university is the maintenance of the social myth of meritocracy. According to this myth, American education is available to almost everyone able to benefit from it. One's level of education is therefore a mark of one's intellectual merit. Accordingly, the myth concludes, the rewards available in society—money, power, prestige— should, and do, go to those with the highest educational degrees. Although it is clear that those with university diplomas get more of what society has to offer, it is incorrect to interpret these benefits as rewards for demonstrated merit. For there is a relation between university attendance and the social class of the student's family. For example, in a 1961 national study of eleventh graders, 87 per cent of those boys in the highest quartile of measurable academic skills who were also in the highest socioeconomic quartile went on to college. Of their peers in this highest quartile of testable academic performance, only 42 per cent of those from families in the lowest socioeconomic quartile went to college. What is true for the brightest holds even truer for the less academically competent. Within every quartile of measurable academic ability those from richer families are much more likely to enter a four-year college than those from poorer families (see Table 5). From studies like this, a clearer picture of the relationship between class structure and higher education emerges. Universities, especialy those of national reputation, easily succumb to the process of class ghettoization, particularly in the undergraduate programs.

In servicing the material and ideological needs of those with vested interests in society, the administrators are facilitating brokers between these interests and a busy, strangely silent and uncritical faculty. Ordinarily this decade-old linkage of department chairmen, executive committee, deans, top management, and knowledge consumers hung together easily enough. When changes in resources and the expectations of exchange occurred they passed along the linkage, aided in some degree by the campus faculty meeting. This meeting, open to all faculty members, allowed expressions of dissent as well as support for the structure of exchange that had developed between the university and society. With the political crises of Dow, 1967; the black strike, 1969; and the TAA strike, 1970 (reported elsewhere in this volume), raucous faculty meetings indexed their widespread uncertainty that the tacit exchanges that had previously integrated the university were operating as they had bargained. During the Kent State–Cambodia situation, the faculty, meeting in a committee of the whole, found a limit to this structure of exchange. It voted to close the university. For its part, the university administration

Table 5. MEASURED ABILITY AND THE EMPIRICAL PROBABILITY
OF ENTRY INTO FOUR-YEAR COLLEGES BY CLASS AND SEX

		Socio-Economic Quartiles				
	Low	1	2	3	4	High
Academic Ability Quartiles	1	.06/.07	.12/.07	.13/.05	.26/.20	
	2	.13/.08	.15/.09	.29/.20	.36/.33	
	3	.25/.18	.34/.23	.45/.36	.65/.55	
	4	.48/.34	.70/.67	.73/.67	.87/.82	
	High					

NOTE: The left probability in each entry is for males; the right, females. The socioeconomic index combines a large number of social class indicators, such as parental occupation, income level, type and character of housing, and so on. The academic ability rankings are also composites of tests of verbal, mathematical, and other school skills.

SOURCE: J. C. Flanagan and W. Cooley, *Project Talent: One Year Follow-Up Studies* (Pittsburgh: University of Pittsburgh, School of Education, 1966), Tables 5.3, 5.4.

found the vote uncompelling and kept the institution open in name only. Perhaps in retribution, the faculties of some colleges voted to permit grading innovations of a most interesting sort: grades on limited portions of the semester's work were allowed full semester's weight, and across-the-board pass-fail marks were permitted.

The administration's refusal to officially close the university suggests that their ability to respond to the faculty has its own limits. One source of constraint is the knowledge and class clienteles described above, clienteles which demand that the university remain open. Another source is found in the rapidly emerging state fiscal crisis. How is this crisis related to the refusal of the university administration to close down at the request of its faculty? We would expect the crisis to lead to some strange bed-partners, and it seems that there does exist a relationship of convenience between the university administration and law enforcement agencies. If such a relationship exists, it is, once again, one of exchange. If exchange takes place between the administration and law agencies, what commodities are being traded? Administration and police use each other in different ways to enhance their own resource procurement capabilities. Both depend upon the state for their resources. Both in fact compete with each other for pieces of the same tax pie. Both legitimize their claims to tax monies by stressing their capacities to produce certain desirable, yet undefinable, goods. The university legitimizes its share of state funds by assuring material progress, while the police create public order. Of course, both sets of claims are somewhat true and somewhat false. The university does supply an environment within which industrial corporations and others can obtain research findings quickly and cheaply. Inasmuch as the contribution of the findings to progress, material and otherwise, usually depends upon the sponsor's will rather than the university's desires, what is assured is that the university will be mute when the use decision is made. For their part, the police try to solve crimes and assist the respectful law-abider in everyday life. But they are clearly dealing with the symptoms, not the well-springs of the public order. Thus, when order occurs, they cannot claim it. And, of course, in times of disorder their contribution is often counterproductive.

The police's stake in this exchange is seen if we first pose a simple question. Why are police agencies moving in on campus as forcefully as they have? Certainly campus protest, aside from the rhetoric, has not been particularly violent in any usual sense of the term. Indeed, the destruction of physical property and the use of force had been minimal until the large-scale introduction of lawmen. If large-scale police movement onto the campus is not violence-related, what other reason draws them there? It is most probably the desire to increase their power by increasing their resources. When crime is in the air and on the mount, then the police chief can come to the budget table and demand more than his usual share of the available funds. The growth of multiversities has created both ungovernable communities and administrators who lack the patience and skill to deal with students on their own terms. It is these administrators, time and again, who have resorted to violence technicians to solve the political problems of the university and preserve their own legitimacy. College town police have reacted with joy and speed at the possibilities of tax-farming the situation and perhaps expressing some town-gown hostilities.

As the administration thought about responding to the faculty's demand that the doors be shut, I believe that the administration had to consider not only its well-established clientele in the economy, in the polity, and in the class system, but, in addition, its state agency bedfellows, and their competitors for tax monies. Closing the school would have meant a rupture in this exchange relationship, one mutually profitable to both parties.

Power and Knowledge

In this essay I have tried to explore the paradox of educational institutions in technically developed, formally democratic societies whose power-structure is more appropriate to an earlier, autocratic epoch. The experience of the new and untenured faculty member is somewhat unusual as he confronts this autocratic power. The freshly-minted Ph.D. is at a pinnacle of personal and technical knowledge. At the same time he has never quite participated in the processes of academic politics. Like others who move up fairly organized career ladders, he has had some smattering of secondary insight into the politics of his profession. But it is well not to talk too strongly or certainly about technical training sites as agencies of professional socialization. Without participatory exposure, the models available for emulation must seem as meaningful as Easter Island statues. Still, the case of academic training and the first faculty post may well involve more than the sheer lack of participatory exposure. It may involve the unusual situation that the new Ph.D. is, by his very nature, extremely dangerous to his tenured colleagues, collectively considered.

By definition, the new Ph.D. knows more about some scholarly matter than anyone has ever known. In the best of cases, by his labor and by standing upon the work of those who toiled before him, he has advanced man's collective ability to rationally control his destiny, his experience has been one of individual and collective success. He has captured and possessed an intellectual problem and has felt the power of his mind at work, turning and pushing the problem until its solution yielded. From his mentors he has received certification of this experience. But his experience of knowledge as power, coming as it does at the end of his period of technical training, is an extremely dangerous one. Should such knowledge-as-power flow unregulated around social space, who knows to what disorderly use it could be put? It is important that his personal experience of power be constrained as tightly as possible. As one comes of age in academe, an initial period of organizational powerlessness seems to have been designed to constrain those new Ph.D.s who might want to extend their personal experience of power into an alternative structural form. The initiation into organizational powerlessness necessarily serves the vested self-interests of the tenured faculty, the university administration, their clients, and their bedfellows.

But constraint involves both a constrainer and a constrainee. As dangerous as the new Ph.D. experience is to the tenured members of the department, how much more is it to the new faculty member himself? How will he integrate the experience of knowledge-as-power into his prior experiences as knowledge participant? If he has experienced power as the unearned validation of his parents' class position, then perhaps the experience will be converted into yet another commodity flowing into his life from a beneficent social system. Or if he has climbed the ladder

with self-conscious attention to task and meaning, how contradictory
the experience of Ph.D. as self-power is to the degradation of sterile
requirements, be they inappropriate languages, methods, or statistics.
Here the danger is being personally immobilized by the contradiction of
Ph.D. as simultaneous subjugation and self-actualization. Whether the
new faculty member experiences himself as a class benefactor or as immobilized, he is a sitting duck for the latent and structural constraint
probable in academe.[4]

Yet one can choose not to be a sitting duck, and it is possible that
nontenured assistant professors can contribute significantly to the restructuring of the university. It is important to see that the constraining
structures press upon him with only the weight of the energies of those
who benefit most directly and self-consciously from these arrangements.
Most of the exchanges described above are tacit and, much more important, illegitimate. The selling of nontenured labor to the colleges to
gain salary increases cannot be justified within a community of scholars.
The interlocking of class system and higher education casts doubt on the
validity of the university's claim to public funding. As these and the other
illegitimate arrangements are exposed, the heat of public scorn and outrage may be buffered with new twists and turns in the structure of academic mystification. Yet, given the fiscal crisis of the state, the heat can
only increase and must act to awaken those who now tacitly associate
their interests with the present structure. With their awakening, the
present structure must fail for simple lack of energy.

Why should we expect the awakening of the tenured faculty of
the University of Wisconsin and other multiversities? Simply because we
know they have all at least once experienced knowledge as self-power.
Further, we know they valued this experience or they would not have
entered the university. It is their demonstrated commitment to this
valued experience that is to be deduced from their entry and continuance
in academe. This shared and valued experience is a central avenue into
the souls of all within any one department, and it is therefore a central
element in the about-to-begin dialogue on the uses and abuses of the
university.

I suggest that the opening line of the dialogue is this: Have we
spent all that time in the libraries and the laboratories, late nights and
early mornings, only to give away the fruits of our labor, our knowledge,
to those within our profession and without who think money is the measure of all things? It is time that we asked our colleagues to think back
to their doctoral experience and forward to the experience we collectively
create for our students. Are we training people to be bought and sold
as some of us have been? Or are we willing to teach them what we

have all learned: that knowledge is power as self-experience? Our task must be to create the conditions within which our students can re-experience what we learned.[5]

In this dialogue, nontenured faculty are uniquely positioned. They are close enough to the primordial doctoral experience to still taste it, and they are not yet implicated in the structure of tacit exchanges that is the multiversity. From this juncture will flow the moral leverage to wrench the multiversity from its present position of tacit servitude to its historic function of continuing the intellectual traditions that liberate men.

Notes

[1] R. A. Nisbet uses the term "higher capitalism" to describe the sponsored research arrangement usual to the multiversity. See his *The Degradation of the Academic Dogma* (New York: Basic Books, 1970). For commentary on fashions in American sociology see P. A. Sorokin, *Fads and Foibles in American Sociology* (Chicago: Regnery, 1956).

[2] See, for example, C. W. Mills, *The Sociological Imagination* (New York: Oxford, 1959).

[3] B. Bliven, *Five Million Words Later* (New York: John Day, 1971). The journal is *The New Republic*. For other recent accounts of the process see N. Podhoretz, *Making It* (New York: Bantam Books, 1967) and G. Talese, *The Kingdom and the Power* (New York: Bantam Books, 1970), dealing with the situation at *Commentary* and *The New York Times*, respectively.

[4] In spite of constraint structure, untenured faculty have some power bases. For a theoretical discussion, see D. Mechanic, "Sources of Power of Lower Participants in Complex Organizations," *Administrative Science Quarterly*, 1962–1963, 7, 349–364.

[5] Although the dialogue is only beginning, it is already possible to see that at least one structural change is imperative. At least in sociology, research which is not teachable to undergraduates should be out of bounds for academic departments. If the knowledge being developed is unpresentable to those majoring in the field, then it must be sufficiently distant from the structure of the discipline to be illegitimate at face. It is not unreasonable to require those who claim to be participants within an intellectual tradition to show their departmental colleagues, peers and pupils, the relationship between their work and that tradition.

CHAPTER 10

●●●●●●●●●●●●●●●
●●●●●●●●●●●●●●●
●●●●●●●●●●●●●●●

ANATOMY OF
FACULTY CONFLICT

Bernard Sklar

●●●●●●●●●●●●●●●
●●●●●●●●●●●●●●●
●●●●●●●●●●●●●●●

The reaction of the faculty to a crisis in institutional life is of crucial importance to understanding the modern university.[1] Not only does such an analysis yield valuable insights into the structure of the university and its governance, it tells us much about the impact of outside forces on the academic environment. Most important, such study reveals an increasingly vital aspect of faculty culture, and that is the nature of the faculty as a political body. This chapter is a study of faculty response to the first major crisis on campus—the October 1967 Dow demonstration and the violence it provoked (see Chapter Seven). The mode of analysis is largely sociological, the attempt being to provide a sense of the structures involved, their relationship to each other and the academic body as a whole. The data were gathered by a variety of field methods, including a number of open-ended interviews with the people involved.

In terms of ideological structure, the faculty can be divided into five groupings (see Figure 3).[2] On the far left there is a small group of radical faculty members, no more than a dozen at most.

190

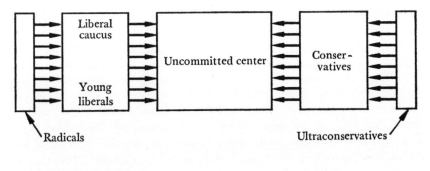

——▶ Lines of Influence

FIGURE 3. *Ideological Map of the Campus*

Just to the right of these men is a group of two or perhaps three
hundred young liberal faculty members who came together to form the
Liberal Caucus and who were largely recruited from the social sciences,
humanities and, to some extent, law. In the middle are the vast majority
of the slightly over eleven hundred voting members of the faculty. The
bulk of them might be described as liberal "non-Left" middle-class. To
their right are the conservatives. They came largely from agriculture,
engineering, and the other professional schools, although one or two will
be found in virtually every department. The sciences generally harbor
their share of conservatives, too, but are by no means solid in this regard.
Finally, within the professional schools, particularly engineering and agriculture, will also be found a very small group of ultraconservatives, many
of whom attributed the events of October 1967 to a Communist conspiracy. In terms of this analysis, it will be necessary to convert this
ideological structure into a decision-making apparatus in order to indicate how the two major centers of action in these events—the University
Committee and the Liberal Caucus—brought their influence to bear on
the various ideological blocks within the faculty.

Perhaps the most interesting and most easily misunderstood aspects of what happened are reflected in the actions of the Liberal Caucus.
Not a group in a continuing sense, it met only three times and there
were never more than two hundred persons present. Nevertheless, the
group represented a distinct body of opinion, and there is no question
that it functioned as a body throughout the crisis. The group's origin
was a result of the occupation of the Commerce Building and subsequent police action. A number of young liberal faculty members
who had been present decided that something had to be done. Using a
Faculty for Peace phone list, they alerted members to a meeting that
night in the law school. Emotions were high when they met. There was

indignation at the use of riot sticks and tear gas, anger at the administration, and a determination to express this through militant action. To some extent the call for a strike,[3] which was voted on and passed, served this purpose, but it certainly did not represent the full extent or the real content of what ultimately became the Liberal Caucus program.

Although the group as such had never met before, virtually everyone was from the "Hill"—Bascom Hill—the area of the campus where the humanities and the social sciences are concentrated. With the exception of one or two men, there was no one at the meeting who could be called a senior man or an established member of the faculty. There were a few representatives of the recognized campus Left present. Although these men had more prestige in general, they did not offer any leadership. For one thing they were a trifle older and somewhat removed from the mood of the present group in regard to political power. They did not feel, for example, as remote from the centers of influence as the young liberals did. There was also a difference in political style. The older members had learned to coexist with their less liberal colleagues and were much more accepting of traditional methods for gaining influence. Although the radicals had a recognized place in the Liberal Caucus, they too could offer little leadership, partially because of their personal style, which was somewhat anarchic and typically less subject to group discipline. Their political style, too, was generally unacceptable because of the risk-taking and demands they tended to advocate.

The members were generally young and just starting their careers; politics had a limited place in their busy, professionally-oriented lives. As among liberals generally, issues had different effects upon them, sometimes winning their wholehearted support, but most often only gaining their approval and perhaps a willingness to exert a limited amount of effort. The actual work was delegated to a small group of six to eight, at times as many as ten, individuals. These men, unlike the others, were immersed in the events, and for them it was an exhausting experience.

Just after the first meeting of the Caucus and while emotions were still high, the position of the group was fairly militant. Although never truly radical, the presence of radical members gave it that appearance to those outside. In a sense, of course, they were outside the established structure, a structure which nominally included all the faculty but which was dominated by senior men devoted to the prevailing academic and social norms. Angry at the administration, and distrustful of those who were supposed to reflect their interests, the group set out to expose the police brutality which they felt would be obscured by charges against the students, and to frame a series of resolutions which would establish the administration's responsibility for the police action. To accomplish

the first part of this task, one of the members put together a handout
of eyewitness accounts to be passed out at the faculty meeting scheduled
for the next day. At the same time a copy of a five-minute videotape
of the police action was obtained from one of the local TV stations.
Meanwhile, several members of the Caucus prepared a series of resolutions, also to be presented at the faculty meeting.

Out of inexperience, and what some later felt was naivete, and
also because of the loose organization of the group, the results of their
efforts at the faculty meeting were far from successful. Although they
had developed an elaborate strategy, it was impossible for them to control many of their own members, particularly the radicals. They were
also unprepared for the fact that the University Committee would present its own resolution first, and that this resolution would tend to
dominate the discussion. When the motion was made to show their film,
a battle developed, and only by the narrowest of margins did the motion
pass. This was a blow to this highly-charged and idealistic young faculty
group. To most observers, however, the meeting was dominated by the
sentiments, accusations, and statements of the young liberals. When the
faculty finally voted two-to-one in favor of the University Committee's
resolution supporting the administration, it was evident that the faculty
was severely split. In that respect the Liberal Caucus had been successful,
for one of their implicit goals was not to have the established mode of
faculty thought and action adopted without major dissent.

But they had not "won," and once the first wave of emotion had
passed, most of the members of the caucus were left with serious doubts
about their purpose. The question of police violence, as well as the police
presence on campus, was still an issue; yet, the fact that a demand for
wholesale condemnation of the students had not, as anticipated, arisen
blunted their anger. At the same time, there was still some question about
treatment of the leaders of the demonstration. Finally, the campus was
still upset, a student strike was in progress, and there were threats of
reaction from the state legislature.

Perhaps no other group was in a position to focus faculty anxiety
and concern more broadly than the University Committee. On the
Madison campus the University Committee occupies the central seat of
faculty power. To some degree this statement is an exaggeration, for the
committee is by and large an advisory body. Nevertheless, it is in a position to exercise great influence. Elected by the faculty, its function, as
outlined by university statute, is broad and encompasses the whole range
of faculty interests and concerns. In an institution where the faculty has
long prided itself in its decision-making powers such a mandate can be
exercised with a great deal of effect.

In the normal course of events the monthly meetings of the faculty were poorly attended and what was required for the successful conduct of its business was a meticulous understanding of the peculiarities of various pieces of legislation. Even though it was the chancellor's job to chair the meetings, it was the University Committee that sifted through the relevant questions and prepared the agenda. More important, in the processes of screening and considering various questions, members of the University Committee acquired the authority that grew out of their knowledge of these matters. Thus, when it came to a crisis of these proportions, with administrative leadership clearly in question, the members of the University Committee were in a position to exercise a leadership role. But it was not a role they were prepared to handle. The Committee is not an executive body. It meets on a regular basis, but usually to consider questions of a long-term nature and not those requiring executive action. Thus, when violence broke out, the members of the committee, like most of the faculty, were not only caught by surprise but were equally unprepared to deal with the situation.

The committee was typically made up of senior, well-established faculty members. All but one were over fifty. As one of the members admitted, it is "almost a fact of life that you can't get a real young faculty member elected, because nobody knows him." They also have a tendency to be representative of the more conservative departments. Their average length of service on the faculty was 19.5 years, which together with their age and their willingness to serve in an extraordinarily demanding post suggests a group whose members have not only great institutional loyalty but regard themselves as no longer mobile. It should also be pointed out that the ties these men have with their colleagues—in their own departments as well as others—are such that they know and communicate almost exclusively with other well-established senior men.

When word of violence spread across the campus during the afternoon of the Dow demonstration, it was natural for those who knew or felt they could communicate with members of the University Committee to do so. It was the only recognized body that had a representative function, and in practice, it was fairly open. It was rarely the case, however, that junior men, particularly the young liberals, made such calls. The conservative make-up of the University Committee, together with the built-in lines of separation between senior and junior men, all tended to make it more likely that those who made such contact felt that the students had widely overstepped their rights or found the disruption of established university routine a provocative issue. It was also in the nature of those making the calls to urge the members of the committee to take some kind of action to solidify the faculty on the side of law and order and not, as in the case of the Liberal Caucus, to condemn the violence or express concern about the rights of free speech or dissent. One of the members of the University Committee described the calls he got in this fashion: "There was certainly a strong feeling that nothing should be done to interfere with the pattern of industrial interviews . . . and that the university would absolutely have to provide for having these interviews take place in an orderly fashion. [There was also] concern that it shouldn't happen again." Once the chancellor had decided to call a faculty meeting for the next day, it seemed clear that the committee had to go into session and frame a resolution that would reflect the solidarity of the faculty and its support of the chancellor.

There seemed to be no question about this among the committee members at the time. It was not done out of loyalty to the chancellor, although he had been a member of the committee only the year before, but more as a response to the prevailing ideology of the members, to their obvious commitments to established practice and the existing order, and to the fact, quite readily acknowledged by some, that they were in touch with only one segment, although obviously an important one, of the faculty. A number of the committee members were actually critical of the chancellor and felt that the violence could have been avoided with a more adroit handling of the situation. But with the institution in a state of paralysis, they felt there was no alternative but to condemn the behavior of its disloyal sons and bring the full weight of the faculty to bear against them.

It was with some surprise, then, that the members of the University Committee found themselves with a serious division within the faculty at the meeting held the next day. Most of them were prepared for some dissent, but to find almost four hundred members of the faculty ready to support what would have been a vote of censure of the administration was without precedent. For a majority of the professors, one of whom defined the job of the University Committee as that of helping "the faculty reach a consensus when important issues come up," this was a serious blow. Whatever the issues might have been, it did not seem possible to leave them unresolved in this fashion.

The position of the University Committee was fairly conservative though certainly not reactionary. Although there had been one or two attempts at the faculty meeting to make a case for "student brutality," or against student anarchy, the general attitude of the faculty was not punitive. Rather there seemed to be a desire to maintain order and condemn disruption. On this point a large segment of the faculty seemed united, although they felt the need to find some way to bridge the differences which now seemed to divide the faculty. The result of these feelings was a flurry of meetings or caucuses across the broad non-liberal sector of the faculty. Usually this concern was expressed by a call to one of the members of the University Committee. These calls, as one member put it, were typically of two kinds: "They wanted to talk to us," which reflected a desire to know what was happening as well as to influence any decisions that might be made or "They wanted to know what to do," which was a kind of generalized offer of assistance.

Committee members were unprepared for this pressure to function as a sounding board, information center, and action agency. But the nature of the crisis and, to a degree, the personality of the chancellor forced an almost inevitable change in the University Committee's role. The chancellor, who had held his post for less than five weeks (and who had been ill for two of those weeks), was essentially an academic man. In contrast to his predecessor, Robben Fleming, who had actively engaged in trying to mold faculty opinion, Sewell sought to "win" it, to lead by example rather than by force of personality. In addition, it was quite clear to everyone that the events of October 18 had severely shaken him. In an interview he described himself at that time as being "as close to a state of shock as a man can be." Not that he was incapacitated, for he communicated with key figures throughout the crisis, but the combined effect of his own temperament, personal inclinations, and the events themselves led to his personal withdrawal and that of his office from the center of the stage during this period.

It was this vacuum that the University Committee had to fill. Not only did the committee have to carry out their normal function, they also found that they had to lead the faculty to some kind of agreement. This was a function they neither relished nor were prepared for, as it involved, in addition to an enormous burden in time and energy, a number of essentially difficult if not disagreeable tasks. There was nothing in their personal experience, for example, that could help them in coping with highly emotional issues, often with angry and stubborn men on the faculty, and at times with recalcitrant and equally angry students involved in a strike against the institution.

Their primary concern, however, and the bulk of their energies were taken up with efforts to coordinate the various pressures brought to bear on them and to reach some kind of compromise that the bulk of the faculty would accept at its next meeting (the first faculty meeting had ended in adjournment). One of the expedients employed was to have the caucuses with which they were in contact place their ideas or suggestions in the form of a statement or resolution. When individual faculty members called they were asked to join one of these groups or offer whatever ideas they had in the form of a resolution.

Thus, throughout this period between the first faculty meeting and the second on October 23, different lines of communication were maintained with various groups or individuals; that is, with one exception, and that exception was the Liberal Caucus (see Figure 4).

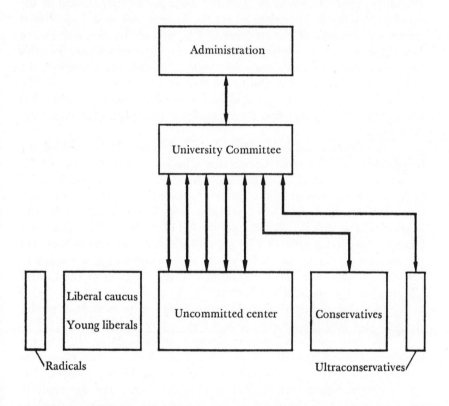

Lines of communication

FIGURE 4

In terms of the Liberal Caucus something entirely different was involved. The leadership or spokesmen for this group were virtually unknown to the University Committee. Where members of the University Committee were aware of particular individuals whom they identified with this group—largely, although not entirely the campus radicals—

they had a very negative impression. They felt these men were irrational or irresponsible and that there was no way they could or should deal with them directly.

This attitude was in part a difference in style. The young liberals, and particularly the radicals among them, often appeared to be excessively emotional, or if not emotional then abrasive in their attacks on established policy or tradition. This had been particularly evident at the faculty meeting on Thursday, where the longest and most impassioned speeches in support of the students had been made by two well-known campus radicals. For a number of those on the University Committee this kind of rhetoric was particularly disagreeable; it made them hostile to the individuals involved. They also found the remarks of young liberals like Caucus leader Paul Samson,[4] who had accused the faculty during that meeting of lack of guts when they denied any police brutality, extremely distasteful.

But it was not only this question of style which troubled the members of the University Committee. The young liberals and radicals seemed to represent a point of view which was in direct conflict with their own, for it seemed to the University Committee that they were not only trying to upset established tradition but also involve the university in political acts that would endanger the life of the institution. The latter was in large part a reflection of the radicals' pronouncements that tied the campus events to the wider world of university-corporate relations and the Vietnam war. To a certain extent, the members of the Liberal Caucus, like the students involved in the demonstration, were regarded as enemies of the institution, and the tendency was to exclude or punish them as they had the students at the first faculty meeting.

As time went on, however, it became increasingly clear to the members of the University Committee, particularly as they came into contact with those who knew the members of the Liberal Caucus, that such a posture was unrealistic. This was not only because of the relatively large number of dissidents, but also because the committee's goal of maintaining a united faculty required some kind of compromise with those in the opposition. It was not immediately apparent just how they could reach this broad group which, at this point, they did not even identify as keyed into the activities of the Liberal Caucus. To them the Liberal Caucus appeared to be another group with whose membership and purposes however they were unacquainted.

From its very beginnings, the Liberal Caucus represented the loosest kind of coalition. Its leadership structure was self-assumed. Art Lang, who chaired the first meeting, was in his early thirties and had been a member of the economics department for five years. Only recently appointed as associate professor (tenure is assumed with this step), Lang had been involved with students from the time of the draft sit-in in May 1966. He and a friend, Paul Samson, formed the nucleus of leadership within the Caucus. Samson, who was in his mid-thirties, was entering his fourth year on campus and was a full professor in the law school. He was active in Democratic politics in addition to the Faculty for Peace group. With his encouragement another member of the law school faculty and a full professor, Bob Krug, was brought into leadership. At the second meeting of the Caucus on Friday afternoon, two others— Alexander Adze and Arthur Hill—were formally designated to the steering committee of the Caucus. Adze, a full professor in computer sciences, had been at the university since 1964. In his late thirties and a radical of sorts, Adze had almost single-handedly organized a local protest against a "wrong way" bus lane (regarded as a pedestrian hazard) the previous spring. Hill was a physicist in his early thirties, an associate professor, and had been on the campus since 1960.

When the Liberal Caucus met on Friday afternoon there were about sixty faculty members present. The mood of the group was one of discouragement. As one of those present put it: "There was a letdown over Friday and Saturday after [the first faculty] meeting had been held and everybody let their blast go. The concern was: What's gonna happen now? There were a number of motions up, everybody was excited, but it appeared that nothing was going to happen." It was understood that motions would be worked up for the next faculty meeting on Monday afternoon and that the Caucus would meet on Sunday to ratify any decisions that were made. If one examines the record of this Friday meeting, one gets a sense of the dead end to which the Caucus members had come. This, together with a persistent sense of alienation, is brought home in the remarks of one of the members who was asked to describe that meeting several months later. "I don't remember any feeling that there should be a rebuilding of the consensus, rapprochement, so on. I remember rather a sense of frustration at not having won the vote, a sense of achievement at having come very close—the Macaulay Motion—and scaring the establishment. I didn't have any sense of any further obligation or goal that I was likely to realize."

It is not surprising then to realize that someone had to play an intermediary role between these two groups. In this case it was not a single individual but a group of persons—Robert Ross, Richard Aldrich, and Melvin Mattick—who, somewhat informally at first, took on the task of communicating with and negotiating between the University Committee and the Liberal Caucus. This intermediary role evolved spontaneously out of the circumstances surrounding both the individuals and the situation. The three were very close personal friends as well as colleagues of the chancellor. Aldrich, in his mid-forties, is well-known in his field and at the time was editor of an important journal. He had been at Wisconsin for eleven years. Robert Ross, in his fifties, was the oldest of the three and had been a member of the faculty since 1951—a soft-spoken, benign individual, he had a reputation for institutional know-how and working behind the scenes. Melvin Mattick was a rising star within his department and had direct links with the younger generation within the Caucus, just as Ross had ties to those on the University Committee.

It was common, both before and after these events, to hear these three referred to as Sewell's "Kitchen Cabinet." All three were liberal and in sympathy with many of the objectives of the Liberal Caucus. (One of the ironies of the situation was that the chancellor, generally acknowledged as a liberal for his antiwar stand, was, by his action in calling the police, identified with and applauded by those on the right.) Aldrich had himself been very upset by the events outside the Commerce Building and tried to persuade Sewell to call off the police. He also attended the initial meeting of the Liberal Caucus and spoke against the police action and in support of the faculty strike. It was in this way, in fact, that he and the others became involved in the events and were able to use their contact with the chancellor to effect a bridge between the Liberal Caucus and the established wing of the faculty (see Figure 5).

Before anything like a rapprochement could be worked out, however, it was necessary for the University Committee to overcome the feeling that the Liberal Caucus, or at least its leadership, was dominated by unreasonable men. A careful examination of the Liberal Caucus makes it apparent that this group was far from radical. There is also evidence that once the initial faculty meeting had been held, an increasing awareness developed on the part of the members of the Liberal Caucus that the radicals were giving the caucus a bad name. As one of the members put it: "I was also concerned that the . . . meeting might be identified with a radical orientation; especially because people like Roger Jacobs and Felix Festing were making the longest and most impassioned speeches. Somehow the discussion by a lot of other people was getting lost in the shuffle." This was not a repudiation of the radicals, but rather a way of indicating the general tendency of this group to see itself as a force trying to mitigate the effects of both extreme left and extreme right. The same individual goes on to say: "I was not concerned that the radicals not make their voice heard but I was concerned that there be some not quite radical group, but still liberal group, if you will, that

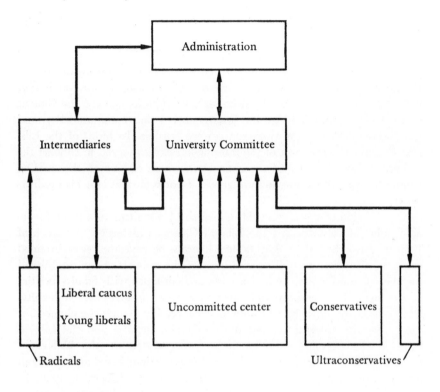

➤ Lines of communication

FIGURE 5

got itself organized and came up with a constructive motion that could pass. My real fear at the time was that the motions that might be submitted would be radical in both extremes."

At the same time, if communication with the University Committee were to take place, it was essential that members of the Liberal Caucus overcome the sense of antipathy that they had for the administration. The administration—and this inevitably came to mean the chancellor—was seen as being either clumsy or as having an unerring sense for what would provoke the greatest student antagonism. These attitudes made it difficult for either side to deal with the other, and the intermediaries performed their most important service in helping to reconcile them. For notwithstanding the fact that their primary function was as go-betweens on particular issues, they conveyed much more than substantive matters in their contacts with either side.

In terms of the University Committee it seems that the three successfully conveyed the impression that, first, they were not dealing with any of the more radical members of the caucus and that, second, those who were conducting the affairs of the Liberal Caucus were, by and large, simply men who had different convictions. This process of "taking the horns off the devil" did not take place immediately, nor was it ever entirely accomplished, but the deep-seated antipathy toward the Caucus was sufficiently modified by the intermediaries that communication and negotiations between the two groups were possible. In terms of the Liberal Caucus, the presence of the intermediaries also served to convert the feelings of hostility toward the chancellor, whom no one on the steering committee actually knew, to indulgence, if not sympathy, for his predicament.

The job of converting the University Committee to a more favorable point of view toward the Liberal Caucus was largely the work of Ross. If somewhat older than typical liberals, he nevertheless maintained contacts with them as well as with some of the radicals. As an established member of the faculty, he had a wide acquaintance with faculty politics and enjoyed the friendship and esteem of a broad spectrum of the faculty. Throughout the crisis he was able to move readily among the chancellor, the University Committee and the established faculty, and the Liberal Caucus. His energies, however, were concentrated on the University Committee with whom he was able to discuss various issues and to whom he was able to convey many of the concerns of the Liberal Caucus. In the process he was not only able to communicate the substance of various proposals ultimately woven into a general resolution, but also the impression that the Liberal Caucus was a legitimate (i.e., non-radical) group with a point of view that was particularly important.

The job of working with the Liberal Caucus was largely in the hands of Aldrich. More than either Ross or Mattick, he was deeply committed to what the Liberal Caucus was doing. Like Ross and Mattick, however, he was also in touch with the chancellor and was motivated by a desire to help resolve a situation that had placed their colleague and the institution in great jeopardy. The most important contribution Aldrich made was in helping the Liberal Caucus overcome its antagonism toward the chancellor. In many ways it was not difficult, but here, too, this was not entirely accomplished nor accomplished uniformly throughout the group.

It was generally clear to the members of the Caucus that Sewell was basically liberal and that his temperament was not well suited to some of the more ruthless aspects of the administrative role. In addition, it was becoming increasingly clear that Sewell might quit under the pressure of events and that in many respects he was the lesser of two evils. As one of the members of the Liberal Caucus put it: "Although there was some discussion originally about what Sewell's role was, we began to feel, especially with [the] legislative body . . . on their high horses that Sewell was probably better than anyone who would be replacing him. . . . The general consensus that was reached very immediately was, if Sewell quits, and it quickly became a concern that he might quit, not that we might ask him to leave, but that he might quit, then we might really get someone extremely conservative who'd come in and essentially be an iron hand on the faculty." When to all this was added the presence of Aldrich, who could bring vividly to their attention the anguish of the chancellor in the face of circumstances he personally abhorred, it was almost impossible for the members of the Caucus to maintain their original posture toward him and the administration he headed.

While pointing out the importance of the intermediaries, it should be stressed that they were not the only link between the Liberal Caucus and the University Committee. Art Lang, for example, one of the principal figures of the Liberal Caucus, communicated with his department chairman, who was on the University Committee. Although the intermediaries helped develop the link between the two groups and in many ways continued to maintain it, eventually that channel was also used to keep the two groups "formally" informed of each other's position.

While these efforts were going on, the situation within the institution remained critical. The student strike continued throughout the weekend and the feeling persisted that the faculty had to resolve its differences if the institution was to regain its balance. To some observers this might seem an exaggerated statement of the importance of faculty opinion, inasmuch as the Regents and ultimately the state legislature had a more powerful voice in the government of the institution. Yet it cannot be denied that everyone was watching to see what the faculty would do: the students, the legislature, the press, and the people of Wisconsin. But more important, in view of the focus of this analysis, faculty members themselves felt that their role in the decisions and judgments was important, perhaps crucial.

Throughout the weekend, the University Committee and the Liberal Caucus were busy with their separate constituencies and their differing problems of organization, communication, and political pressure. University Committee members, in addition to nearly continuous sessions, were individually meeting and talking with other groups and individuals in the center and on the right. As a result, by Saturday, the University Committee was able to define four areas in which they felt there was substantial agreement (in addition to implicit support for the administration; on this the University Committee assumed there was no room for discussion). First was the question of violence: "Everyone," as one member of the University Committee put it, "was united on the 'no role for violence' issue." Second, the question of interview policy. Although the faculty had an established policy in regard to job interviewing on campus, the feeling was, as one faculty member put it, "that we ought to look into this business again." Third, the "mode of response," a realization on the part of the faculty that a decision had to be made about how the university should deal with confrontation should it occur again. Finally, there was agreement that a committee should be established to consider the questions of mode of response and employment interviews. It was also generally agreed students should serve on such a committee although there was a question about their numbers and who would actually control such a committee.

The Liberal Caucus, instead of having a number of groups or individuals with whom to communicate, was still in the process of defining its own area of influence. After a lightly-attended Friday afternoon meeting, most of the energy of the Caucus went into broadening its list of potential members and getting them to turn out for the meeting that Sunday night. In addition to this organizational effort, there was an effort to define the issues within the caucus. Unlike the University Committee, the focus of the Liberal Caucus was largely on the question of violence. "We wanted to make sure that there was a strong statement to the effect that we deplored what had happened, felt that it was unnecessary and that . . . we wanted machinery set in motion that would implement this desire to see that things like this will never happen [again]." The question of support for the administration, which had split the faculty originally, was no longer an issue. Time and the efforts of the intermediaries had done their work.

Time, as well as discussion, had also served to soften—if not eliminate—a number of the other issues. Reflecting on this matter, one member of the Caucus stated: "It seemed to me that the issues . . . were pretty clearly drawn and there was nothing to be gained by going into a long discourse on whether the students were breaking the law. Clearly they were. There was nothing to be gained [by discussion] about whether or not people got beat up. Clearly they were. There was nothing to be gained [by discussion] about whether or not the cops also got hurt. Clearly they were." Somewhat more subtle distinctions were now involved, for, as this same individual pointed out, many of the ideological conflicts that might have divided the faculty simply were not present within the Caucus membership.

No one liked the fact the cops were here and that kept coming up. . . . I don't know anyone who spoke for the war, not one person. . . . So it wasn't a division between the conservatives . . . versus the liberals; it wasn't a separation between anti- and pro-war faculty, and it wasn't really a separation between people who wanted firm control on campus versus people who wanted to give the students . . . a freer hand; and it wasn't a separation, really, between people who were opposed to free speech and people who were in favor of free speech. It was a much closer distinction than that, but it was very strongly felt.

And to a degree this statement accurately reflects the status of faculty discussion at this time. The first faculty meeting had demonstrated the unwillingness of any significant number of faculty members to support the war or applaud the police. No one at any time really debated the right of students to protest but neither did they contend that they had unlimited rights to such protest. The real issues were quite different and much more fundamental: "There [was] a whole complex of issues here. Is the Vietnam war right or wrong? To what extent should Dow be permitted to go on campus? When you have an issue you feel very strongly about, what steps do you take to express this? What response should the community make? The university and the ctiy?" Needless to say these were not issues which a single faculty meeting in the midst of an institutional crisis could solve. Yet the members of the caucus felt that they needed to be discussed and for that reason a committee to look into the "mode of response" question and interview policy had direct appeal to them just as it did (if for other reasons) to the rest of the faculty.

The remaining question that provided much of the focus for zero-hour negotiations between the Liberal Caucus and the University Committee concerned the way the faculty would recognize and deal with the question of violence. This question had in many ways displaced the other issues. Police violence had provided the impetus for the student strike and had become the focal point for a wide-ranging debate within the faculty. For some, it was seen only as a question of police brutality. For others, it was really the violence of the confrontation and the violence against the police which were the issue. Yet the fact remained that students had gotten hurt, and a great deal seemed to depend on the resolution of this general question. As one caucus member saw it, it was really a question of just deserts versus unjust deserts. "There were people [in the faculty] who felt that the students asked for it and they got it . . . that it's bad that it happened and things of that sort, but they asked for it. And another group of the faculty felt . . . well maybe they were asking for it but they got a lot more than they should." For the members of the caucus there was no question about how this should be resolved: violence, and that meant police violence, had to be condemned.

By Sunday morning the University Committee had received the

drafts of a number of resolutions, all of which reflected the issues just enumerated. These had all been discussed within the committee and in many cases with representatives of the various groups which had produced them. At some point during this period the three intermediaries, with Bill Carnes, an administrator and close friend of the chancellor, put together a resolution and presented it to the University Committee. It reflected what they knew the Liberal Caucus wanted, particularly in regard to the question of violence, what they felt the chancellor wanted in the way of a general consensus, and what they felt the bulk of the faculty who supported institutional order would "buy."

It was not until late Sunday afternoon that Ross, in a telephone conversation with a member of the University Committee, was able to get what he was assured was the final draft of their resolution. It was essentially the resolution the four had submitted. Aldrich duplicated it and prepared a set of remarks to present to the Liberal Caucus that evening. The whole operation, he admitted afterwards, "was the neatest trick of the week," and reflected an enormous expenditure of energy on the part of the three intermediaries, not only in getting the resolution out of the committee but in obtaining its acceptance by the caucus as well.

When the Liberal Caucus met that evening they could see the results of their organizational efforts. There were at least two hundred people present and they seemed to represent a wider spectrum of the faculty. When Aldrich presented the resolution, it met almost no opposition. What concern there was seemed to focus on the "force and violence" statement and a number of peripheral issues. Aldrich's resolution, which with one minor deletion was approved by the faculty the next day, read as follows: "That the faculty deeply regrets the series of circumstances which resulted in violence on this campus on October 18, 1967, and expresses its grave concern about the damage such occurrences do to the integrity of a university community. We affirm our resolve to join in partnership with students and administration to make every possible effort to ensure that this university can, without recourse to force and violence, carry on its activities in an orderly way, and guarantee the rights of every member of the university community." Attached to this resolution was the motion: "That the faculty support the decision of the University Committee to form immediately an ad hoc committee consisting of equal numbers of faculty and student members, charged with the responsibility of drafting recommendations on the mode of response to obstruction, on policies and conduct of employment interviews, and on any other matters concerned in the implementation of the principles of the resolution offered by the University Committee on October 23, 1967." Prior to the resolution an announcement was made that the thirteen students singled out for discipline were not being kept from attending class until their cases were heard before the Student Conduct Committee. There had been some fear about the summary expulsion of these students, and the announcement—a guarantee of due process—resolved what might have been the only remaining issue separating the caucus from the rest of the faculty.

In his presentation Aldrich stressed the pressure being placed on the chancellor from the legislature and public to condemn the actions of the students. He indicated that Sewell was resisting these pressures "forthrightly," but the implication was that he could not do so without the support of a united faculty. He also indicated the sentiment of Sewell and others that something had to be done to "revise the policy of employment interviews in order to avoid further confrontations."[5] Finally, he pointed out that both the chancellor and the University Committee "felt that there was a strong need to recommend legislation to the faculty that is passable"; that is, that had some chance of being accepted by the bulk of the faculty.

The discussion that followed was varied. There were still those who felt a more militant stand was essential as well as those who supported such demands as amnesty for the students up for discipline, but the caucus was basically unsympathetic to these considerations. The mood was one of reason and restraint—at least that was what the leadership seemed to convey—and it was mirrored by the failure of the group to ratify any effort to broaden the issue or deal with the more controversial aspects of the problem. Thus, for example, when someone raised a question about the upcoming CIA interviews, the feeling was that if the group pressed for their suspension they would only tie the chancellor's hands:

Lang [who was acting as chairman that evening] said the best thing to do is not to introduce specific legislation [calling for the suspension of CIA or other interviews] because there were a lot of people who felt that you were denying free speech, free access to students to things like CIA if you didn't let them come and interview on campus. And Lang was saying he felt there was enough support for this attitude on campus that specific legislation might fail, in which case the chancellor would be *duty bound* to have the interviews. His point was that if you give the chancellor a little bit of room then . . . he can decide as things develop. [Emphasis in the original.]

There was, as this passage indicates, a growing awareness within the group of political feasibility—an attitude that had been almost entirely absent from the initial gathering. To some extent this must be credited to the effect of experience. But it must also be seen as the result of strong and persistent efforts on the part of the leadership to create for the caucus a viable basis for success in the struggle that lay ahead. Thus at one point, when challenged by a student not to "sweep the issues under the rug," the point was made that "the protestors don't have to worry about majority opinion. They don't have to care whether the rest of the campus or the faculty agrees with them or not, but we do; we, this body." And at another point, when confronted with the fact that the resolution offered very little in terms of the original issues, one of the leaders pointed out that "this kind of legislation is something that provides us with some means of action. If we get more oppressive legislation then there is nothing we can do."

The point seemed to be that the group had to deal realistically with the situation, that they were in fact in a good position, and that more could be gained by trying to work for the proper "interpretation" (implementation and manipulation) of those motions than by trying to force through their own. When the vote on the proposed motion was taken, only ten of the nearly two hundred people present voted against it. Privately, pressures were brought to bear on the most disputatious members, particularly the radicals, to temper any move they might make at the meeting the next day. They were also encouraged not to speak for the resolution because it was felt this would alienate some who might otherwise support it.

In the meantime the University Committee, in an effort to strengthen the chances for passage of this resolution, made an effort to contact all those groups they had been in touch with (estimates range from ten to twenty). Everyone who had a resolution pending before the faculty was also contacted and asked to withdraw in favor of the University Committee. The results were apparent the next day. Not only were the radicals largely silent, but with only one exception all pending resolutions were withdrawn. Passage was accomplished with a minimum of debate and with what was described as only token opposition. The breach in the academic community had been healed, for the present at least, and the general effect of this statement of solidarity and resolve to study the issues was one of calming the atmosphere generally.

The purpose of this analysis has been to develop an understanding of the actual forces at work within the situation and how they helped the faculty to arrive at the position just described. From a purely historical point of view this is the last "great consensus" this faculty has achieved, at least on issues such as these. What has happened since at Wisconsin, as at most large universities in America, is that the major divisions adumbrated here have become more pronounced and their effects more pervasive. But in describing these events we have prepared a basis for understanding the effects of student political action on the faculty and what this means in terms of the development of the faculty as a self-conscious, ideologically divided political body in its own right.

Notes

[1] This chapter is adapted from B. Sklar, "Faculty Culture and Community Conflict: A Historical, Political, and Sociological Analysis of the October 18, 1967, Dow Demonstration at the University of Wisconsin," unpublished doctoral dissertation, University of Chicago, 1970.

[2] I am indebted to K. M. Dolbeare for first introducing me to this scheme and for our many conversations about its implications in regard to the Madison conflict.

[3] To many the strike only represented a "gesture," because it was left up to the individual to decide whether he would attend class and lead his students in a discussion of the events or not attend at all.

[4] The names of those participating in these behind-the-scenes activities are fictitious.

[5] This and other quotations are taken from a tape-recorded interview with a member of the Liberal Caucus who took the minutes for this meeting. It is the only meeting for which a written record exists.

CHAPTER 11

●●●●●●●●●●●●●●●
●●●●●●●●●●●●●●●
●●●●●●●●●●●●●●●

WOMEN IN THE MULTIVERSITY

Elaine Reuben

●●●●●●●●●●●●●●●
●●●●●●●●●●●●●●●
●●●●●●●●●●●●●●●

"Of the fifty-five departments in the College of Letters and Science represented, twenty-seven departments have no women as instructors, assistant professors, associate professors, or full professors; a half-time lecturer is the sole female of teaching rank in these departments. Eleven of these twenty-seven departments employ women in nonfaculty professional, scientific, and specialist positions only, while the remaining sixteen employ no academic women at all." These 1969–1970 figures, from the *Interim Report on Study of the Status of Academic Women* (Madison Campus, Letters and Science Sample), prepared for the University Faculty Council by the Central University Office of Planning and Analysis, confirmed and called some attention to what women had already known: there are not very many of us in the faculty, and most of us stand at the bottom of the hierarchy.

In the sample there are 10 female full professors, 2.5 per cent of the 392 faculty at that rank; 9 female associate professors, 5 per cent of the 169 at that rank; 30 female assistant professors, 11 per cent of the 271 at that rank; and 13 female instructors, 35 per cent of the 38 who may never be promoted. We not only get paid less than men of equivalent rank, but, as the report comments, "in general, for women, there is a positive correlation between increase in rank and increased discrepancy in dollar differential," so that those ten female full professors are paid an average of 3,744 dollars less than their male counterparts, the associates 1,158 dollars less, the assistants 219 dollars less, and instructors 363 dollars less.

Commenting on the report to *The Wisconsin State Journal* (January 10, 1971), Assistant Vice-President Edwin Cammack said, "More intensive research would be needed to determine the reasons for the salary differentials to find out if indeed there is unjustified discrimination." Women would reject the hypothesis that the discrimination against them might be justified and would recognize that the pattern evident in the report repeats that at other universities and in the labor force in general.

The full report on the status of academic women at the University of Wisconsin, covering all campuses, was made available in precis in March 1971. It indicates that, with few exceptions, women throughout the university system are not distributed across academic levels as are their male colleagues, but are concentrated in the lower academic positions; paralleling the patterns shown in the Letters and Science interim study, women's mean salaries, with few exceptions, are lower than men's, and the unfavorable dollar differential increases as the academic level rises.

The percentage of women holding instruction-oriented appointments varies from unit to unit. On the Madison campus there are thirty-nine women professors, twenty-three associate professors, sixty assistant professors, and thirty-six instructors; these figures represent, respectively, 4.8 per cent, 6.8 per cent, 11.5 per cent and 50.5 per cent of these ranks, percentages lower, except at the instructor level, than for public universities nationwide, where they are 5.4 per cent, 10.4 per cent, 14.8 per cent and 30.5 per cent. The situation of women at Madison is inseparable from the situation of women in America. The status of women in the university has only recently become a topic to be considered in anthologies such as this one, as an increased awareness of the oppression of women throughout American society has been created by and within a growing women's liberation movement.

The special problems of women, in the university and outside it, may be seen as essentially one problem; Betty Friedan, in *The Feminine Mystique*,[1] called it "the problem that has no name . . . a strange discrepancy between the reality of our lives as women and the image to which we were trying to conform." Many other female voices have spoken out since, or have been heard again from the past, in deeply felt outrage and in increasingly sophisticated analyses, understanding and beginning to struggle against the ways in which the limited role assigned to women prevents their being full persons and is used to buttress institutional and interpersonal discrimination and exploitation.

The women's liberation movement began to be visible in Madison during 1969. By the fall of that year, a number of small groups had been formed, some a result of developments on the student left, others the outgrowths of a YWCA conference; one was the continuation of a meeting called by graduate women in the department of English concerned about discrimination in the academic job market. Most women involved were students, although some staff and faculty women, faculty and student wives, and women from the Madison community joined one group or another. During the first semester the focus of these various groups was largely educational—the personal, supportive discussions the movement calls consciousness raising, the sale of literature, and participation in both formal and informal opportunities to speak about job discrimination, causes and effects of sex role stereotypes, child care and alternatives to the nuclear family, and the struggle for women's right to control their own bodies.

The Wisconsin state legislature provided one opportunity for local women to speak out at its hearing on a bill proposing to make giving birth to an illegitimate child a felony. The presence of vocal women speeded the recess of that hearing and the death of the bill in committee. Many women present at the hearing were then involved in the formation of a Women's Counseling Service, to provide information and assistance to women in need of contraceptives or abortions. They understood that the vindictiveness of the bill was such that it would eventually have been quashed by embarrassed legislators without pressure from women. They understood also, however, that this attack, directed primarily at welfare recipients in the wake of their growing militancy, was only a bizarre extension of both law and custom affecting all women in the community: If fornication is a felony, if abortion is unavailable, and if the sale of contraceptives to unmarried women is forbidden, as it is in Wisconsin, it can only follow, according to male logic, that women who dare to be sexual beings without the permission of the state should be punished.

Those who speak for the University of Wisconsin, like most Wisconsin legislators, would be unwilling to officially formulate this position with quite such harsh clarity. Their silence, however, supports it, and as women affiliated with the Counseling Service discovered in their confrontations with the university hospital and its policies, that silence cannot be explained simply in terms of the pressure of law and public opinion. In March 1970, a three-judge federal panel ruled that the Wissonsin statute prohibiting abortion of an unquickened fetus was unconstitutional. Some hospitals in the state took this ruling as reason enough to open up their policies, although the decision was being appealed to the United States Supreme Court and the possibility of harassment prosecutions, particularly in an election year, remained. The university hospital, however, not only continued to require psychiatric certification for abortion—a woman would have to (pretend to) be crazy not to want a child —but actually cut down on the number of beds available for the procedure.

In October 1970 the Supreme Court refused to hear the state's appeal, thus upholding the panel's ruling; in March 1971 the university hospital had yet to act, despite unofficial indications that a clinic would eventually be established. The university hospital and the student health service continue to provide neither contraceptives nor abortion assistance to women who need them, nor has the university's prestige been used to help create a climate in which positive change would be possible; such prestige has been used in other states with repressive laws.

While publicity about the Women's Counseling Service was still in the word-of-mouth stage, its clients were mostly women associated with the university community, as were its counselors. During its first year the service was able to become semipublic, receiving calls and referrals from a variety of groups within the community and around the state; many of those it helps are still, however, university women, now occasionally (quietly) referred by the health service.

The Counseling Service story is illustrative of a larger pattern: The special problems faced by women at the university are related to those confronting all women; the university accepts the status quo. By refusing to meet the needs of even its own women, the university places a substantial burden on those seeking to use its services and helps perpetuate the problems of women in society. One local doctor, active in the campaign for changed attitudes and practices, insisted to his audiences, "If it were men who needed these services they would be available." A woman, writing about the Harvard Health Center, said (as she might of Wisconsin's), "Male chauvinism affects medical policy by its implicit assumption that the female reproductive apparatus is an 'extra' that may be optionally omitted from consideration of the body's problems" (*How Harvard Rules Women*, New University Conference, 1970).

Medical care is a particularly appropriate instance of the special problems of women in the university because it is nonacademic, in both the strict and the popular senses of that term—it is a concern outside the classroom, part of the reality of our lives as women, which the institution ignores but which must be dealt with if women are to function fully within the academic world. The developing women's movement is avoiding the trap of asking for equality which is only academic and is unembarrassedly demanding both equal and specific rights. As one movement document puts it:

Equal rights means all those "rights" that men are supposed to have: the right to work, to organize for equal pay, promotions, better conditions, equal (and *not* separate) education. Specific rights means those rights women must have if they are to be equal in other areas: free, adequate child care, abortions, birth control for young women from puberty, self defense, desegregation of all institutions (schools, unions, jobs). It is not so much an academic question of what is correct theory as an inescapable empirical fact: women must fight their conditions just to participate in the movement.[2]

Most of the time, in a posture of neutrality which objectively discriminates against women, the university ignores women's special needs. When the University of Wisconsin does acknowledge women as a class and offers courses and services for women, these programs are usually aimed at helping women in their traditional roles rather than extending their horizons. Thus, for example, under the category of Self-Improvement, University Extension has, for a number of years, offered a widely advertised course titled "Managing Yourself: Your Role as an Executive's Wife." The description in the fall 1970 catalogue reads:

As an executive's wife, besides being a mother, wife, homemaker, community volunteer, and career woman, you must also be a hostess *par excellence,* an amateur psychiatrist, an accomplished country hopper, a home settler, and an instant interior decorator—not to mention the necessity of being an accomplished chauffeur. The course includes the art of listening, psychological demands, dressing for your role, communication, community relations, bridging the generation gap, entertaining employees and the boss, and attending trade shows.

One wishes it were possible to believe that this paragraph were intended as a parody of the feminine mystique. Unfortunately, this is a perfectly straightforward exposition of what the university, objectively if not officially, presents as woman's role and of what corporations are willing to pay to have taught.

During the spring term of 1970 some campus women challenged this presentation in several symbolic confrontations that were minor but not trivial events in the history of Wisconsin women's challenge to a limiting image: one occurred at the handball courts, one at the "Bridal Fair," and one at "Women's Day." The battle of the handball courts was waged, and won, by a determined woman who refused to accept the university's established policy of segregating athletic facilities by sex; the newer and more complete facilities were for the men, of course. After several skirmishes on the site she took the matter to the university's Human Rights Committee, where conferences with the athletic department brought about a policy reversal without the court action she threatened; although physical education classes still basically teach men to be athletic and women to be graceful, both sexes (now segregated only faculty/student/staff) may use athletic facilities during nonclass hours. The other two episodes were not so clear in their outcome. Both involved groups, rather than an individual, and both posed a political challenge to university practices in which it was not just a woman or women discriminated against, but women being cast for their (supporting) role.

University policy is quite strict, and is growing stricter, in insisting that only registered student groups and academic departments are entitled to the use of meeting room facilities and that only approved organizations may sell or solicit funds on university property. Yet, under the auspices of the Wisconsin Union, and therefore with the full prestige of the university, local merchants were invited to the Union to present a "Bridal Fair"; the event was publicized so that girls and their mothers from the Madison community might attend, to be entertained and counseled on their trousseau shopping. An ad hoc guerrilla theatre group of women from various women's liberation groups also attended. Their intention was to challenge this commercialized celebration of marriage as woman's highest attainment; they were asked to leave, and, although the request seemed personally embarrassing for the employee in charge, his official threat of forcible ejection or arrest was understood.

Within a month such an arrest was to take place, not in the Union but next door in the Wisconsin Center, headquarters of the Wisconsin Alumni Association. Twice yearly the association, again with full prestige of the university, presents a "Women's Day," to which all women in the state are invited. In practice the audience, numbering about five hundred, are older, upper-middle-class women, some of whom come long distances for the event. On this occasion a women's liberation group asked for permission to set up a table in the lobby of the center, at which they might sell and distribute movement literature, information about the situation of women at the university, and analyses of the implications of this pseudocultural Ladies Day, offered to women who have already, so to speak, been through the Bridal Fair and the course in executive wifery. As one of their publications put it:

Mommy heals Daddy's wounds, and Women put the bandages on society's sores. For both purposes, auxiliary organizations, like Wisconsin Dames (graduate wives) and the University League (faculty wives), offer lessons in flower arranging and opportunities for volunteer work. . . . These gracious lady roles (the ones women are so well suited for) are essentially conservative, helping to maintain the status quo in a society which cannot provide decent work or proper services for its citizens.[3]

Other leaflets pointed out the class bias of the program and the absence of any reference to women's needs in a program planned for them.

Permission for the table was granted in an atmosphere alternating between outright hostility and unconvincing geniality; the official response to the request, by representatives of the association and the center, was most consistently somewhere between, "These women *like* being women and are perfectly happy with the program provided for them," and *"These* women . . ." The table was set up, but the lobby was filled with plainclothes police and university staff, keeping all but the most intrepid guests from contact with the unwelcome visitors who wanted to talk to them. Whether because of conspiracy or confusion, members of the group had found it impossible to obtain tickets for the lectures which made up the program for the morning. One of the four (male) speakers, however, had agreed beforehand to allow representatives of the group to use part of his time, to speak about their presence at the event and their challenge to its assumptions.

"But apparently the administration is clamping down," he was quoted in the next day's *Wisconsin State Journal* (April 22, 1970), "and is afraid of them." The administration's fearful clampdown resulted in the forcible ejection of the group's representatives from the meeting room and an arrest for disorderly conduct. Moments later, a young female employee of the university's Bureau of Audio-Visual Instruction, who had been sent to show a film in another meeting room, was dismissed, and BAVI was requested to send a male projectionist for the Women's Day film; the director of the Center feared, he said, that *she* would be disruptive. BAVI complied.

Earlier in the spring the Wisconsin Center had hosted a conference of mathematicians; a disruption of that event by students protesting the university's sponsorship of the Army Math Research Center led to the arrest of two female students. This episode was cited by informal apologists for the official overreaction to the presence of the women's liberation group. The explanation was unconvincing to the women involved, who had experienced a clearly articulated opposition to what they represented, coupled with an overwhelming concern that the image of the Alumni Association and its program not be tarnished by any criticism; unsuccessful attempts were even made to retaliate against the female reporter who had covered the newsworthy aspects of the day.

The university did not comment on the event, or the issues raised, but Women's Days continue and the chancellor himself appeared as the luncheon speaker for the next program in October 1970. Sympathies may have tended to the women, but power still remained with the powers-which-are, and women were not yet sufficiently organized to make a challenge which would be more than symbolic.

At about this time a women's caucus within the Teaching Assistant Association and an embryonic secretaries' union, the Organization of University Office Workers, began to organize, influenced by women's liberation activities to some degree, but developing out of their own particular situations on the campus. The TAA women were originally mobilized during the union's membership drive, to deal with the "women's departments," where little support for the union had been found. Those who went on recruiting trips (in dance, home economics, and related arts) discovered that women in these departments did not feel themselves truly a part of the university and were thus not interested in the union's activities. TAA women realized in the process of these meetings that the union itself had little concern for the special problems of its actual or potential female membership and that in fact its own structure and attitudes were nearly as male dominated as those of the university.

The pattern of women being used to support a cause which did not support them is hardly new; what was new was the organization of a TAA women's caucus during the period before the TAA strike. It brought the male chauvinism of the union to the attention of a general membership meeting; one result was an effort, sincere if somewhat feeble and self-conscious, to include women more conspicuously in public leadership roles. (In the next union election more women ran, and were elected, largely because of this combination of pressure and encouragement.)

The caucus, with the support or at least the acceptance of the union, defined its membership to include wives of teaching assistants as well as female teaching assistants, asserting these women's real connection with the university and making vivid, within the union, the tracking mechanism which sends men to graduate school and their wives to typing jobs to help support them while they study. Institutional policies, including the absence of day care facilities and administrative procedures which make part-time study, admission past "normal age," and the transfer of credits difficult, are cogs in that tracking mechanism.

The women's caucus brought such issues to the union's discussion of proposed contract demands; no provision in that first contract deals with them directly, and the general clause on discrimination was watered down in bargaining to a pious affirmation of mutual good will between the union and the university, but it may yet be possible for the TAA to be an agent in confronting some of the special problems of women in the university. As the union continues to struggle with its own priorities, at least informal contact is maintained between women teaching assistants and those who are organizing in other sectors of the university's employed female population.

Many Wisconsin student wives work at the university; the Placement Office advertises year-round on campus bulletin boards that clerical jobs are available for them, and, since Madison's economy is essentially the university and state government, anything other than clerical work is hard to find. Many single women come, or remain after graduation, to work for the university, partly, one imagines, because of a notion that this is an interesting place to work; many discover otherwise, but, whether married or single, the university has a constantly replenished source of cheap labor. They, too, are women in the university. Although some of the secretaries who attended early meetings called to discuss their grievances were reluctant to identify with women's liberation, many discussions focused on women's issues: day care, maternity leave, and the secretary as sexpot-office wife syndrome.

The syndrome has various components: being expected to make coffee and run what amount to personal errands for faculty and administrators; being expected to be cheerful and conversational when the boss wants to talk and respectfully quiet when he does not; being expected to do responsible work for which no credit is given, or work for which not enough time is allotted, or work beyond the original job description; being expected to dress "like a lady." All these demands can be seen as aspects of a caste relationship; they also bear a strong resemblance to the woman's role, traditionally defined.

The question of dress has been dealt with variously by various departments; a growing determination by women—linked perhaps to the change in fashion dictates—is making staff dress regulations almost unenforceable. In one office the entire secretarial staff wore pants to work in response to a memo saying that only graduate assistants were allowed to, and the memo was rescinded.

When a representative of the university's personnel office who came to speak with the staff women was asked about the policy on maternity leave, he explained that no such leave was permissible, not even by accumulation of sick leave; it came out in the discussion that men, however, were allowed to accumulate sick leave so they might help at home while their wives were in the hospital. By this time in their history the women were sensitive to the fact that the representatives of Local 171 of the Wisconsin State Employees Association who met with them were men and were presumably satisfied with the present policy. As for day care facilities, there are simply none to be had, except by whatever private arrangements women can make.

The office workers' grievances are not limited specifically to women's issues, of course, but it seems likely that, as they press for changes, the women's movement will be an ally. A brief alliance of this sort was first made on August 26, 1970, Women's Strike Day, when movement women leafletted at the Memorial Library on invitation from civil service women there who were afraid to be personally conspicuous but were quite aware that their particular grievances were connected to the sexual hierarchy in that realm of the university. Women are 84 per cent of the permanent, full-time, nonstudent employees of the library, but only 23 per cent of those with faculty rank, with only one associate and no full professors.

The older, more conservative constituents of the Organization of University Office Workers (OUOW) tend to identify themselves as employees of the state, rather than of the university, and continue to be ill at ease with a vocal women's liberation perspective; such a perspective, however, should become increasingly respectable when the Wisconsin Bureau of Personnel's survey on the utilization of minority groups in state civil service is finally released. This report, undertaken at the urging of the Governor's Commission on the Status of Women, will, according to preliminary indications, reveal serious inequities in the status of civil service women in regard to pay, promotion, and fringe benefits. (Data have been collected, but until the new gubernatorial administration resets its compilation as a priority there seems to be neither staff nor funds to produce the full report.) In the state civil service at large women compose approximately half of the work force but are almost nonexistent at the administrative level, predominating in service and clerical work. One instance of an institutionalized, if inadvertent, mechanism of discrimination is the state policy of providing points toward promotion for military service, thereby giving most men an advantage over most women.

The 1970 Annual Report of the Human Rights Committee for the University of Wisconsin, Madison, provides figures which repeat this now familiar pyramid pattern for university staff women: of 178 employees classified as officials and managers, 16 are female; of 1,706 employees classified as office and clerical, 1,568 are female.[4] The report includes representative complaints alleging discrimination on the basis of sex and suggests, in its summary observations, that there is some substance in the claims that women are discriminated against in admisssion and financial support, as well as in employment and promotion procedures. As this sort of data becomes more widely available within the university community, and as women continue to become more aware of the institutional nature of their personal dilemmas and less afraid to speak out about them, some changes in the status quo can be anticipated, but they are unlikely to be significant changes unless the full dimensions of the special problems of women are confronted.

As long, for example, as men are socially perceived as doers and women as helpers it is difficult to change the practice of (men) hiring men as administrative assistants and women who do the same job as secretaries. This sort of conflict between ascribed roles and women's needs and potential was demonstrated by two episodes at the end of the spring term, during the Madison campus' response to the events of May 1970—Cambodia, Kent State, and the student strike.

At the huge faculty meeting called "to discuss the situation" the only female speaker was a representative of the School of Nursing. The noise level rose in the Stock Pavillion, as it so often does when a woman rises to speak in public, and not everyone heard her say that the entire School of Nursing, students, faculty, and administrators, had met and decided to suspend classes while working together in response to the national situation and in reevaluation of their own program; she urged similar action for other schools and departments. What was probably the most reasoned yet the most radical event of that moment was virtually unnoticed; it had, after all, come from women, nurses and not doctors.

What was noticed, and resented quite out of proportion to the expectation of the participants, was the response of a group of faculty wives who, with their children, maintained a week-long picket at various ROTC installations on the campus. When their presence was not seen as a joke it was often seen as somehow unwomanly; all too few of the male passersby were able to relate to it as a serious political statement. The academic year ended, for women, somewhat on this note. Women were not yet prepared to press their demands against the university, and without pressure the university was not going to change. During the summer, however, a procedure for applying pressure was initiated which may prove to be an effective aid to the women's struggle and has already provided a means for different women's groups on the campus to work together.

On July 5, 1970, a formal complaint against the University of Wisconsin was filed with the Secretary of Labor, under Executive Order 11246 as amended by Executive Order 11375; this presidential order, which applies to all federal contractors, specifically forbids discrimination against women in all aspects of employment activity and requires that employers "take affirmative action" to counteract discriminatory barriers and to remedy the effects of past discrimination. Such actions include, but are not limited to, employment, upgrading, demotion, transfer, recruitment, lay-off or termination, rates of pay and other forms of compensation, and selection for training.

The complaint against the University of Wisconsin was filed by representatives of the Women's Equity Action League (WEAL), which had filed similar suits against other educational institutions; the charge of discrimination was based on the number of faculty women at each academic rank compared with the number of men at that rank in various departments. The data, WEAL said, "show a shocking absence of women on the faculty, even in those departments where women receive substantial numbers of doctorates. . . . In history, women earn 13 per cent of the doctorates, yet the history department, which even has an endowment to hire a woman, has not yet hired a woman at all among its sixty faculty members. In art education, women earn 34 per cent of the doctorates, yet in the department of art in the School of Education there is only one woman among the faculty of thirty-six."

The university's first public response to the complaint might be summarized as, "We don't have a problem, and if we do we're working on it." In *The Wisconsin State Journal* (July 25, 1970) it was reported:

University President Fred Harvey Harrington conceded Friday that "it is true, of course, that our faculty includes fewer women in full professorships than we would like. It's true also that among our civil service employees, the bulk of our women employees are not at the highest administrative level." He reported, however, that "Wisconsin compares well" with other universities and he cited "definite efforts" here to improve the place of women in the faculty and student body. While emphasizing "we'd like it better if there were more" women in top jobs, Harrington said that nevertheless "a substantial number of the university's most distinguished people" are women. He specified as illustrations Full Professors Helen White of the English department; Elizabeth McCoy, bacteriology; Germaine Bree, humanities; and Maxine Bennett, surgery. (Miss White died June 7, 1967.) Wisconsin, he said, also has done better than its competitors in training young women in its professional schools and in putting women like Martha Peterson, former dean of students who now heads Barnard College, and Kay Clarenbach, a co-founder of the National Organization for Women, in jobs where they have contributed to increased national awareness of the need for educating women. (Dr. Clarenbach is ranked as an extension specialist in family living.) The university also has set aside its Depression days policy against "nepotism"—in this case giving jobs to husband and wife, he said. The "significant number" of husband-wife teams he cited include Vice-President Robert Taylor and his wife Fannie, as associate professor with the Arts Council; biochemistry professor Frank Strong and his wife Dorothy, a full professor of food sciences, and psychology Professor Harry Harlow and his wife Margaret, recently promoted from project associate to full professor of educational psychology.

President Harrington can, perhaps, be forgiven the natural tendency of the administrator to say very little impressively, but the incredible pau-

city of his response to or understanding of the problems which the
WEAL suit focused is symptomatic of those problems. Even the reporter
sensed some of the ironies of his remarks, and those who know the campus recognized how fully evasive they were.

The Department of Health, Education, and Welfare is the agency
responsible for the enforcement of the executive order in colleges and
universities. When a complaint is filed, HEW is called upon to conduct a
compliance review, with on-site visit and interviews, and where patterns
of discrimination are found to require from the university specific, pro-
grammatic commitment for its correction: failure to be in, or moving
towards, compliance, could result in the withholding of federal contracts.

HEW conducted a preliminary review for the University of Wisconsin July 27–31, 1970. The university did not make the fact of that
summer visit public at the time and has not yet made the text of the
HEW report or the university's response public, but those women who
have seen it (unofficially) found that it confirmed the charges which led
to the WEAL complaint and indicated the university's unpreparedness
to affect the structural basis of women's situation.

As news of the suit, the compliance review, and the report came
to the attention of faculty women in the fall of 1970, inquiries were
made of university representatives as to why women, at whatever level
of employment, had not been consulted. One response offered was that
there was no way in which to consult women, and certainly no organized
group to speak for faculty women; in November, at a gathering attended
by "legal faculty" (of professorial rank) and women in those other categories where women are numerous (instructors, lecturers, specialists), an
Association of Faculty Women was created, whose temporary steering
committee then formally requested from Acting President Clodius public
access to the HEW report. Clodius, while "appreciative" of the AFW's
interest, and claiming to be eager to share in cooperative efforts to increase opportunities for women in teaching, research, and administration,
replied that he did not feel free to release the report. The AFW then began negotiating directly with HEW, and by the time of the second review visit in January 1971, the faculty women and the OUOW were
both prepared to call large meetings and provide to the investigators
case study complaints which they had gathered.

From this point on the history of the relationships between the
university, HEW, and university women is a complicated one, not yet
completed. Its details may be less important, though, than the fact that
more and more women are now participating, formally or informally, with
the administration and with each other, in determining to shape the im-

plementation of affirmative action on the status of women in the university.

To make such participation possible, the AFW, working with other groups, is investigating and beginning to prepare reports and position papers on such substantive topics as faculty and administrative recruitment, pay, and promotion; student admissions and financial aid; curriculum; health services; fringe benefits; and enabling services such as child care, housing, placement, and counselling. Without engaging in major research projects, women are confirming the patterns which most of them have experienced; they are also suggesting the steps necessary for change.

Whatever the university's stated policy on nepotism, for example, refusal to hire or promote faculty wives seems to be common. Academic appointments and promotions are difficult to rationalize in any case, and it is always more difficult to explain what did not happen than what did. Nevertheless, there are, within the AFW membership, women who have been refused employment, or only allowed to function professionally in adjacent, nontenure positions, and many of them are faculty wives. There is, in fact, evidence that at the level of policy implementation there remain strong prejudices against hiring wives in full-time, nonexploitive positions. Policy statements from the administration, without real evidence of determination that they be implemented and education about why they have not been in the past, are inadequate to break down the power of an Old Boys' Club.

The double bind women experience, of course, makes it little easier for single women to advance in academic life; they will, "after all," get married, and thus become a bad risk! The accumulated prejudices against women who survive in academia long enough to be considered for appointment or promotion result in the sort of figures quoted at the beginning of this essay. In no departments outside of "women's fields" are women present in the faculty in proportion to the number of female graduate students, or in proportion to the numbers of degrees granted, and in no departments are they not clustered disproportionately in the lowest ranks. Lower salaries and inequities in health and retirement benefits profit the university, although in long-term effect they are also harmful to male employees. The ideology which sustains such practices involves the image of woman: Since she is not seen as a self-supporting individual, even when she is, one can justify (or not need to justify) less than equitable compensation; if the woman accepts the image, she will not complain.

The university educates women to accept this image. Literature courses glorify the myths of womanhood, sociology courses accept the traditional roles, psychology courses assume them. Female students can graduate from this university (and others) without ever having had a female professor or seen a woman on a university committee or in any position of responsibility.

When the Career Placement Services office presents its annual report on B.A./B.S. graduates, it explains the fact that the salary average for men is less than the national figure by pointing to the number of men who have gone into educational services and governmental activity; the summary statement on women's salaries makes no apology for the fact that educational institutions (i.e. women's work in the primary and secondary schools) are low-paying, nor does it "explain" why the average salaries for women in all fields are lower than men's. The report never comments on what its data clearly indicate, that women are channeled into low-pay, low-status jobs: the same degree does not mean the same opportunities for men and women, not even at the beginning of career life.

And then the paucity of professional women is used as evidence that women "fail," presumably because they are not serious or not equipped to make it in a man's world. The figures need to be reinterpreted to stress discrimination, not dropping out; frustration, not failure; prejudice, not pusillanimity. Women are beginning to make that sort of reinterpretation, and to complain and organize. With the formation of the Association of Faculty Women the spectrum of organized women on the campus is now complete, although female students have as yet to relate as specifically to their student role. Each group has its own concerns, but the overlaps are understood because the same problems face all women: There are so few of us at the top because there are so many at the bottom, fulfilling women's roles.

Groups continue to form, and topics to be brought out for discussion. Female graduate students have joined together to teach a course in the untaught history of women, for women; female law students (roughly 7 per cent of the law school) are insisting that the law school not allow placement interviews to firms which will not hire women. Undergraduate women understand that the Regents' reinstatement of curfews for freshman women is an insult, though they have not been able to reverse the ruling, and many women were quick to note (though again less able to change) the fact that the much touted 1971 Symposium could not seem to find more than two or three women, on or off the campus, to invite as speakers.

When President Harrington said that the University of Wisconsin "compares well" with other universities in its dealings with women he was not wrong, he was simply using an unacceptable standard of comparison; it would, perhaps, have been more meaningful to say that things are just as bad here as elsewhere. The situation of women at the University of Wisconsin is not really different in kind from that in other institutions, though some are moving more creatively to change.

In elite schools, which cling harder to the cloistered academic life-style, the contradictions between being a student or professor and being a woman are more obvious; at a school like Wisconsin, which attempts to combine the functions of an elite, national university and a service-oriented state university, they can be harder to see. The sheer number of female students in the university makes it harder to see, as one walks around the campus, that the experience of being in the university presents special problems for women: The undergraduate is literally harassed out of science or engineering; the graduate student's advisor (if she can find one) constantly questions her motivations until she, too, begins to question; the faculty woman discovers that she must be twice as good to be taken seriously and that a personal life is often the price to be paid for a professional one.

As the complexity of "the woman question" is becoming increasingly evident, the University of Wisconsin is only slowly looking for, or finding, ways to deal with it. President Weaver's responses to the subject have appeared to understand it as a matter of employee relations. While some of his administrative proposals for correcting inequities, though made under the pressure of the impending HEW report, are to be commended, there has, as yet, been little change in the prevailing atmosphere, in which it was possible, earlier in the term, for a UW (Parkside) administrator to announce that a young female professor who had just had a baby could no longer be counted upon to be a productive scholar and should not be retained. Chancellor Young has appointed a part-time staff person and a faculty-student-staff committee to deal with the status of women on the Madison campus, and its work promises to be productive in the future. In the same month the committee began, the engineering school, in which women are conspicuously absent, selected "princesses" to decorate its annual exposition, and the Regents turned down a student-faculty-administration proposal for coed dorms in terms reminiscent of their decision in 1970 to lock up women undergraduates.

Some impact has been made, through the intersection of official, top-down, pronouncements of policy and unofficial, bottom-up, expressions of anger and concern; it appears that there will be a few women next year in departments which have not previously hired women, and that some of the most glaring cases of salary or rank inequity will be rectified. However, on the level of equity alone (redressing the financial exploitation of women presently employed) to fully face the question of what ending discrimination would require would be to deal, and in a time of financial crisis, with values and priorities in a more than rhetorical fashion. It will cost money, and it ultimately may cost the pain and tension of social revolution.

Many, though not all, women who have begun to struggle for equality have come to feel that the terms of the game are inhuman ones, and that they must be changed to allow women, and men, to function productively as people, not just as employees. This may be a hard distinction to make, in the language presently being used in the university, but it might mean, for example, that the sort of work into which women have been channeled, which is generally people rather than product oriented, *is* valuable, and should be regarded socially. It might mean that nonexploitive part-time work for both men and women would allow them both to be productive professionals and part of their families, although the competitive race for professional advancement might have to be reevaluated. It might mean active recruitment, rather than passive acceptance, of husband and wife teams, or the hiring of one's own graduate women, which would challenge present standards and attitudes.

In the first phase of the struggle for equality, women are likely only to insist that they can do a job as well as men. More women are coming to insist that differences in life patterns should be respected, not denied, so that, for example, as long as child care remains primarily a woman's responsibility the university should accept, as a social responsibility, an obligation to make it possible for her to fulfill both her responsibility to the child and her responsibility to herself, whether through providing day-care facilities or allowing late careers or extending the period of time in which a professional is evaluated.

As the university does its studies to see if the discrimination against women is justified, it will be necessary to define standards which have never been defined, to examine procedures and practices which have not before been scrutinized. Women are becoming rightly cynical of closed channels and representative committees which do not serve their needs or represent their interests, and they may bring a new kind of constituency politics to the university, as has already been the case elsewhere. If class barriers, whether faculty/staff/student or university/working class, begin to be overcome by women working together, there could occur the sort of general opening up of the university which would affect every sphere from grading to course content to degree requirements to the function of the secretarial staff in a department.

We are still a long way from the truly liberated university, however, and are still in a period in which women are losing ground even by traditional standards. When President Emeritus E. B. Fred surveyed the situation of women at Wisconsin in 1960 the numbers of female faculty at each rank were lower, but the percentages were higher than they are today. Today the consciousness of women is higher, however, and while the special problems of women cannot be solved in the university alone, the struggle has begun on many fronts, and here as well.

Notes

[1] B. Friedan, *The Feminine Mystique* (New York: Norton, 1963).
[2] K. MacAfee and M. Wood, "Bread and Roses," in E. H. Altbach (Ed.), *From Feminism to Liberation* (Cambridge, Mass.: Schenkman, 1971), p. 36.
[3] Women's Research Group, *Women at Wisconsin* (Madison: Women's Research Group, 1970), p. 2.
[4] *University of Wisconsin Faculty Document 10,* October, 1970.

CHAPTER 12

●●●●●●●●●●●●●●●
●●●●●●●●●●●●●●●
●●●●●●●●●●●●●●●

DEPARTMENTAL CLASHES

Sheila McVey

●●●●●●●●●●●●●●●
●●●●●●●●●●●●●●●
●●●●●●●●●●●●●●●

In their classic study of higher education as an academic marketplace, Caplow and McGee comment that, "to the sociologist, the department is perhaps the most interesting component of the university, because of the extraordinary involvement and commitment of its members."[1] The importance of the department stems from its structural position as the basic organizational unit of intellectual activity in the university. Perhaps because of its centrality, the academic department has been the focus of bitter conflict among faculty members during the recent, crisis ridden years experienced by the university. In many ways, this conflict is a reflection of the broader tensions that have made the campus a place of strife. However, conflict among faculty members at the departmental level tends to center more specifically on academic issues and their relationship to social problems. The essential question that confronts the faculty member is how to define the role of academic man in a chaotic society that depends on the university for many of its needs.

During the 1950s the model of the academic man cherished by faculty members was that of the august professional, eminent in his field of specialization, an unfailing source of wisdom in councils of state and conferences of the business world, a neutral arbitrator in the profane world of politics.[2] The key to the professor's entry into the social milieu beyond the university was seen as technical expertise, and thus the role of the faculty member as professional dominated. Currently, this image is undergoing critical scrutiny by a new generation of academics, and the result is often conflict between intellectual generations over the definition of the academic man's role in society.

The ages of the participants in the struggle, and the historical moment at which they were socialized into their profession in many cases seem to determine the way in which a faculty member will define his role as academic in society. However, a number of factors qualify the effect of age—for example, the discipline to which the faculty member belongs, the internal stage of development of that discipline, the political ideology of the professor, and the state of the wider political, social, and economic scene. But age and historical moment of socialization seem to serve as the most accurate general indicator of the position a faculty member will take in defining his role.[3] Therefore, the concept of conflict between intellectual generations is a useful analytic tool to use in the examination of strife within academic departments.

This paper is an attempt to illustrate the way in which the struggle between intellectual generations operates in a department rent by conflict—the English department at the University of Wisconsin. The struggle is essentially over who will shape the future of the discipline at Wisconsin. In the early and mid-1960s an unprecedented number of junior faculty were recruited to the department in order to cope with the great influx of students. Among the ranks of these untenured professors were men who did not share the consensus that generally prevailed within the senior ranks about what a department of English should be. The divergent views of the younger men became apparent in their response to a number of issues. During the tumultuous student demonstrations that began in 1967, they often sided with the students, not only on principle but also on tactics. In 1968, when student criticism turned from the larger society toward the university in the form of student departmental associations demanding radical educational reform, these men, already identified as dissidents, retained their allegiance to the students. In 1969, they supported the English teaching assistants who demanded autonomy in the courses they taught.

As the position of this small but extremely noticeable group of untenured faculty became clearer, tensions within the department heightened, the spectrum of issues effected grew wider, and most people were forced to choose sides. When a prominent member of the dissident group, James Martin, was dismissed before the usual probationary period had elapsed, the conflict crystallized. Many of the junior faculty who had previously refrained from commitment vociferously attacked the senior faculty for violating the canons of academic freedom; in turn, the senior faculty accused their juniors of conduct unbecoming to professional scholars. Each perceived the other's charges as unwarranted and irrelevant; any meaningful dialogue had ceased.

At this point, the academic year of 1969–1970, the present study was undertaken. It is based on a series of open-ended interviews with department members on problems of the discipline. Some of the questions in the interview schedule dealt with James Martin's dismissal. The original plan of the study had called for interviews with half of the seventy-six members of the department. However, Martin brought a court case against the department in order to contend the grounds of his dismissal in early 1970, and the interviews were halted after twenty had been completed because the faculty feared that the material involved might be subpoenaed. That Martin felt compelled to resort to external authority to obtain an unbiased judgment on his case is testimony to the bitter internal conflict that rends the department.

The present study is thus incomplete and therefore suggestive rather than definitive. However, the twenty interviews completed are true to the original conception of the study in that they are representative of the main academic ranks. At the time of the study, the department was composed of seventy-six members—twenty-four full professors, sixteen associates, twenty-six assistants, two lecturers, two visiting professors, two visiting lecturers, and five instructors. Interviews were given to twenty randomly selected department members; seven were full professors, four associates, eight assistants, and one instructor.[4]

The department belongs to what Caplow and McGee call the "major league."[5] Its senior members quite clearly fall into what Laufer terms the "expert scholar" or most prestigious academic category; they are primarily concerned with their specialty, both in the classroom and in their emphasis on research.[6] Selection of junior members is based on their promise to become expert-scholars. Members of the department are generally recruited from what Bell calls the "elite circle" of highly rated graduate schools.[7]

Before dealing with conflict between intellectual generations, it is necessary to understand the anomalous position held by a humanities department in the multiversity. The primary goal of an institution like the University of Wisconsin is the production of knowledge, and the most prized professional rewards are available only to those in the sciences because they alone produce the kind of knowledge valued by an advanced industrial society. Although they pay tribute to the same gods that are worshipped in the temples of science—research, professionalism, and publication—the humanities departments are categorically excluded from the altars of prestige in the institution because their subject matter denies the methodology of science.

Rather than attempting to emulate the ideals held by science departments and professional schools—research and service—humanities departments should strive toward goals more in keeping with their subject matter. By definition, a humanities department holds in trust for future generations the main traditions of Western civilization. The time-honored academic task of such a department is scholarship, the exegesis and elaboration of a set of received or classical texts as well as the major commentaries upon them.[8] Teaching is traditionally viewed as central to the humanities because, "in the humanities, knowledge is *concentric;* one moves within many different circles of meaning in the effort to attain, if ever, an understanding of a text and an experience."[9] Thus, the very structure of knowledge upholds the centuries-old emphasis on the role of teacher in the humanities, as this kind of understanding is best gained by a close, affective relationship between teacher and student.

At the University of Wisconsin, however, the priorities of science and professionalism are more generally accepted than the aspirations traditionally associated with a humanities department. But the humanist is aware that he plays Janus, and the precarious balance between the roles of researcher and teacher is presently threatened by the students' demand that he tip the scale in favor of the latter role.

Because humanists are historically obligated to value the role of teacher, even the most ambitious researchers cannot lightly shrug off their classroom duties. But there are varying degrees of commitment, and these degrees are often, although certainly not always, determined by age or generation. Three model types are discernible—the oldest members of the department, or the "aristocratic humanists" ("some of whom antedate the New Critics," as one junior professor remarked) who range in age from their mid-fifties to mid-sixties; the middle-aged faculty or the "institutional liberals," who are roughly between thirty-five and fifty-five years old; and the younger professors, or "moral critics," who are generally under thirty-five. Rather than carefully defining each type, a very brief sketch will be presented and the characteristics of the different groups more fully delineated by their reactions to the issues later discussed.

The aristocratic humanists have a tripartite concept of their role as academician; they emphasize equally teaching, service to the department, and scholarly research. They have an intense loyalty to the department and, through it, the university, hold an attitude of noblesse oblige toward undergraduates, treat their graduate students as apprentices, and generally make noteworthy contributions to the community of scholars. They yearn for the vanished community of closely-knit academics that they remember from their early years at Wisconsin and are resentful of the increasing bureaucratic impersonality of the university, the rampant professionalism of many of their colleagues, and the unseemly behavior of the students.

The institutional liberals pay lip-service to the dual roles of teacher and researcher, but their practical emphasis is on research. The department commands little of their loyalty and the "profession" is honored instead. They are often critical of and many times cynical about the institution, but they never question its ultimate legitimacy or denigrate its ideal value. Graduate students are looked upon as valuable assets; undergraduates who are not English majors are regarded with apprehension. They view the late fifties and early sixties as the golden age of academe and greatly resent the many recent encroachments on their professionalism.

The moral critics are sincerely concerned about teaching at the undergraduate level and regard this function as their primary duty. Neither the department nor the profession claims their adherence, and the institution is viewed as corrupt. Their life-style in many instances more closely resembles that of their undergraduate students than that of their colleagues, and they feel in no way obligated to take on the professional mode of conduct that binds their seniors together. They feel it is their right to reshape the goals of the university and are hostile to all those who stand in their way.

Of the twenty faculty members interviewed, seven were classified as moral critics (five junior, one associate, and one full professor), eight as institutional liberals (three junior, three associate, and two full), and five as aristocratic humanists (one junior and four full). Distinctions between tenured academic ranks are not significant; in other words, associate and full professors are not analytically separate categories because there is little or no substantive difference between the rights and privileges of the two ranks. Associate professors tend to fall into the institutional liberal group because they are generally younger than full professors. Personal observation confirms that the proportion of each age group in a given category is probably representative of the department as a whole. However, it should be kept in mind that age is not the sole determinant of the group into which a given faculty member will fall, although it unquestionably has strong predictive value.

In dynamic terms, the three groups do not often function as

separate entities. Usually the aristocratic humanists and institutional liberals form a coalition and, as a result, the tenured faculty present a united front to the small groups of juniors, the moral critics. As the divisions within the academic ranks mentioned above indicate, tenure and age are not the only determinants of allegiance; a fairly large number (four) of untenured faculty side with the tenured, while a smaller number (two) of senior faculty side with the junior. Again, observation of the department as a whole suggests that these proportions are representative, but this judgment is impressionistic. Nonetheless, struggles in the department essentially pit those who have power against those who are trying to win it for themselves and others. And to the winner goes the right to determine the future shape of the department.

At first glance, it would seem that there should be no doubt over the outcome of the battle; the coalition of aristocratic humanists and institutional liberals dominates both numerically and structurally. More junior faculty members are apt to adhere to their seniors' position than the reverse, and the executive committee, composed only of tenured faculty, makes all major decisions. Moreover, the prevailing ethos held by those in power is an intense professionalism. However, it is precisely this professionalism that presents the moral critics with an ethical Achilles heel. As mentioned previously, a research orientation contradicts the traditional function of a humanities department, and the institutional liberals are often uncomfortable when confronted with their repudiation of the past, while at the same time they are well aware of the tenuous nature of their claim to a legitimate professional status. The very vigor with which they defend their position implies its inherent weakness.

A quick look at the historical moment of the initial professional experience of each group illuminates the generational dimension of these conflicting claims. Most of the numerically dominant group, the institutional liberals, were in graduate school after World War II but before 1960. This was the period during which the professional scientist dominated the rapidly expanding university. Contrarily, the aristocratic humanist almost always received his graduate training before World War II in the period prior to government subsidy of university scientists. At that time, the tradition of scholarship associated with the humanities could at least hold its own with scientific methodology. After the war, the "hard" sciences completely obscured the humanities, and as a result the English faculty socialized into their profession during this period felt obligated to ape the methods of science. The result was a defensive professionalism, and a rigid insistence on the necessity of research and publication. Currently, the spectacle made by the use of sophisticated scientific technology against barely mechanized nations, plus the growing belief that technology abuses humanity, has caused a reappraisal of the high regard for science, and the moral critics reflect this attitude.

Despite the insistent claims to professional status voiced so loudly by the institutional liberals, there is a lack of any clear agreement within the discipline as to what constitutes proper methodology. When asked to define the methodology most commonly used in literary research, many respondents seemed to have great difficulty with the question, and no two listed the same number or types of methods. Only two of the twenty faculty interviewed presented an organized schema capable of encompassing the various methods named. Using their methodological classification, we can categorize the host of approaches to literature listed by the others: "[The main methodologies are] scholarly, in the sense of digging up facts with regard to literature; textual, which is the technical study of manuscripts; critical, which is the analysis of literature as art." Into the category of scholarship fall historical criticism and the study of literature in relation to other disciplines. Textual study covers the discovery of new texts, editorial work, and linguistic analysis. Criticism envelops numerous approaches: New Criticism, interpretive, comparative, Freudian, Marxist, mythic, aesthetics. With the exception of the historical method, and perhaps the New Criticism, there is no agreed upon approach to the study of literature.

An institutional liberal voiced the feelings of inferiority called up by a comparison of his work to that of the scientists. This statement, which reflects a sentiment held by many, illuminates the tensions created within a humanities department when it accepts the research orientation of a multiversity and agrees to compete with externally imposed standards. "This [English literature] is in sharp contrast to exciting scientific research, which has a sense of going somewhere in particular. I don't see this in English. This is bound to make it seem pointless to others, and in a sense it is pointless. There is no aim for English scholarship, no end point for scholarship as a whole or, in most cases, even for specific projects. Often the aim is say what you think. This cannot be conceived of like finding a cure for cancer, or discovering DNA."

Even though many are aware of the lack of methodology in their discipline, the majority still insist that research is perhaps their most necessary function. Again, the importance that faculty place upon research is in some respects determined by generation. This is most clearly revealed when goals are discussed. Everyone agrees that the present goals of the department are "publishing, primarily; second, production of Ph.D.s; and third, teaching," but there are great differences of opinion when a reordering of existing goals is discussed.

The aristocratic humanists identify two ideal goals, excellent professional training and the preservation of the Western tradition. Research belongs to the graduate level, and quality rather than quantity receives special emphasis: "Research . . . is a way of making teaching better, research [that] is done as passionately as the artist, and as precisely as the scientist. I'm not talking about crap!" Another senior professor puts the matter more strongly: "Damned to the lowest reaches of hell be any man who sends out nonsense to fatten his bibliography." Research is also thought to enhance one's ability as a teacher: "It's possible to be a good teacher without publishing, but the teacher's hardest problem is to stay alive. The very best people I've known in teaching are alive across the board." Perpetuation of Western culture through teaching is the reason that the undergraduate college exists. "The goal is . . . I want to quote Matthew Arnold . . . and his definition of culture: 'Culture is the best that has been said and thought in the world' by anybody at any time in any language." The traditional functions of a humanities department are strongly believed in: "We are committed by the nature of our profession to the belief that one must have an education in the humanities and not merely in the practical subjects. The greater the breadth a man has in literature, art, music and history, the richer person he is, and this, I suppose, is the primary goal of education." Yet each of the aristocratic humanists adds a cautionary note:

We [are] keeping the tradition of the free mind. . . . If you start trying to make immediate and relevant everything that you read and teach, if you try to bring it always into a political context, it means playing the game of an authoritarian government . . . Man's got to see his whole long tradition . . . if you lose that power, you're going to lose yourself every other way.

I think that it [tradition] is more valuable basically than some of the things that people get tremendously excited about for a short time. This is probably a . . . product of my age. I'm old enough to have a longer view than the person who is very close to the activity that he is involved in. . . . I may be just fooling myself, but I don't think so.

The aristocratic humanists, then, accept the existing goals of the department, although they stress particular aspects of these goals. Teaching is seen as the necessary vehicle by which the Western tradition is transmitted. It is almost a missionary act; teachers are able and therefore obligated to instruct young acolytes in the myths and mysteries of culture. However, all perception of the past is selective, and aristocratic humanists are not exempt from this generalization. They stress a tradition of humanistic individualism, and demand that the past they venerate be preserved intact. Any attempts at modification by the uninitiated are perceived as heretical. Thus, contemporary politics are anathema because they stress submergence of the individual in collective action and attack the cultural myths that legitimate the status quo. Like the moral critics, the aristocratic humanists believe in the importance of teaching, but their abhorrence of the political implications which the moral critics feel are inherent in the act of teaching causes them to side more often than not with the institutional liberals.

The institutional liberals, on the other hand, emphasize the need of the professional to educate fellow professionals, thereby contributing to the advancement of knowledge. "You see I also believe that we exist not only for students . . . but we also teach our colleagues. . . . No one who hasn't published anything should be advanced unless you are dealing with an experimental school . . . which is a kind of informal, structureless program where students come in, sit on the floor and discuss anything they want. . . . This has its value. People who want that can have it." Publication also brings the professor intimations of immortality: "It is essential for teachers to keep learning. I also think as I get older that you could argue that there is a social obligation involved. By the time you're teaching grad students at the University of Wisconsin, you are presumably an expert. It's a shame, if not an irresponsibility, to do something with that which is not more permanent than simply flinging words out before a class."

When undergraduates are mentioned, it is conceded that English attracts a large number of students uncommitted to any particular branch of knowledge and that an effort should be made to offer them an opportunity for personal exploration. However, the rationale provided stresses the need for the discipline to direct students into acceptable channels. "We get students who have not made decisions about life, and I might say that these are the most intelligent, analytic, and the most creative minds. . . . I think it essential for the English department to provide a favorable environment for those minds. . . . If we don't give them this opportunity, our society will lose one of its most valuable natural resources."

Criticism of the department's goal is often made and usually involves an idea of balance: "An English department should be humane, I suppose. I don't think we necessarily succeed. When grad students are overemphasized it becomes a technician's profession rather than a generalist's. Surely a balance should be maintained between specialized knowledge and the humanists role, and I don't think the department has succeeded in reaching the mean." When suggestions for reform are offered, they never involve a resetting of priorities. Instead, token changes are suggested—"the manipulation of the orthodox structure would help, and a greater flexibility in the teaching role." In other words, the institutional liberals direct the greater part of their attention to other members of their profession. Undergraduates are regarded as a commodity to be manipulated into socially productive roles. Criticism of the existing set of goals is half-hearted and made with the express intention of preserving a balance rather than altering the scale by which priorities are weighed. Nor does the image of teacher figure highly in the institutional liberal's professional conception of himself.

The moral critics express greater discontent with the department's goals; in the words of one junior professor, "I think the goals are incestuous, and the product will be the extinction of the human race." Their analysis of present priorities mocks many of the claims made by their seniors as to goals.

The department by and large exists to perpetuate itself. We are individually and corporately concerned with turning out imitations of ourselves. The positive view has us sustaining tradition, but in fact we're hostile to anything that looks abrasive and rocks the boat.

English was fundamentally devised as an imitation of the successful scientific pattern. In this country, they tried to make a scientific study of humane things.

The alternatives they offer threaten the professionalism that is so much a part of the older faculty's identity:

I think the goals of English studies . . . should serve the people. Literature should remind people of what their potentials are . . . it should thrill them. It should move them. . . . Everywhere [literature] should be seeking to affix itself to those social movements which are seeking to liberate people's lives.

Traditional literature is didactic; it persuades to a moral end. Modern literature is too. Only a small percentage of literature is literature for its own sake. Therefore, criticism of didactic literature should be didactic. Literature is concerned with moral behavior, and not to study it in this way is bad. Literature is a moral imperative, yet we analyze it, talk about it, and totally disassociate it from the fundamental raison d'être of literature.

The introduction of passion into the study of literature defies the canons of professionalism; in an age of relativism, morality is a subjective concern, which taints the necessary objectivity of the scholar. Thus, any pedagogical theory that holds that the teacher's attitude is the most important element in the process of instruction—"Finally, it comes down to the teacher, the books and the students. It's an attitude as much as anything else. I guess I'd call that attitude love"—threatens the precarious professional identity of the senior man.

However, the emphasis that the moral critic places on subjectivity and intensity in teaching does not automatically abnegate the necessity of publishing.

Publishing militates against teaching, although the two shouldn't be separated. If you're in the middle of a book, you have a strong temptation to hand out last year's lecture notes, no matter how bad they might be . . . [but] there is a disinterested quest for knowledge involved which is our responsibility to continue.

The danger of research is that it's narrow. It's a myth that better research makes better teachers. It's a disaster that we choose because it gives you a little world in which you can be master . . . and a sense of power and authority. . . . [So] I do not believe fully in pure scholarship . . . [because] . . . I see no conspicuous effort to relate pure scholarship to the problems of being a human being.

In other words, even that group which is sincerely committed to teaching for the undergraduate cannot outrightly deny the validity of research. In the words of a junior professor: "The socialization process begins early. . . . You fall into habits which are professionalized in graduate school, and this is very powerful. This is enforced by men whom you admire because of their worth, their charm, their intelligence. It is a 'mighty engine' of conformity."

In summary, the aristocratic humanists are in full accord with the present goals of the department—publishing, professional training for graduate students, and teaching. Each should be sought after equally, because the three are inextricably entwined. Research keeps the teacher alive in the graduate classroom, and teaching undergraduates assures that the Western tradition will survive. The institutional liberals stress their relationship to their fellow academicians above all else, and publication, the primary professional act, becomes their highest priority. Other aspects of departmental duties—teaching undergraduates and service— are constraints to be borne stoically. The moral critics value the more affective aspects of the teacher's role, and in so doing, denigrate professionalism. However, even they still grudgingly acknowledge the importance of the research function.

The dispute over the Freshman English program was a departmental matter that illustrates more concretely the ways in which these groups differ from each other. The mandatory year of English composition for freshmen was taught by teaching assistants with only minimal supervision from the faculty. The course became an issue when the teaching assistants demanded that their roles as autonomous teachers be recognized, and all pretense of supervision dropped. In response to such insubordinate behavior on the part of graduate students, some of the senior members called for the course to be cut out of the curriculum. Abandoning the program meant a substantial cut-back in the amount of support that could be offered to graduate students since teaching assistantships were almost the sole means of funding students; it also meant repudiating the traditional service that the English department rendered the rest of the university by teaching the student body to read and write. The decision, then, had many long-range policy implications.

Because the senior faculty feared the vocal lobby of students in support of the teaching assistants, an attempt was made to bar them from attending the meeting at which the deciding vote was taken. Traditionally, faculty meetings have been closed, but Wisconsin state statutes hold that all university matters other than personnel are open to the public. At the time, however, the practical application of this statute was unclear. As a result, the department stationed a university policeman at the door in order to enforce its definition of the situation. A number of younger professors walked out in protest, and the decision to drop Freshman English was made without their vote. However, the Teaching Assistants Association took the matter to court and at a hearing the judge indicated that the issue was public. The English department reheld the meeting in order to comply with the law, and the previous decision prevailed. The final decision indicated the superior strength of the senior faculty.

The institutional liberals provided the official rationale for dropping the course and stood solidly behind it: "Freshman English was dropped because it was part of a national trend. Students are better prepared in composition—not that they write beautifully, but they have reached that level of skill where you can't deal with them positively. Unless you are a very skilled teacher it is hard to improve style. And the TAs are not capable." They refused to recognize that animosity toward the assistants on the part of senior faculty members had anything to do with the decision. "Those who are teaching Freshman English now will not lose their jobs [next year]. So I don't feel that the TAs are a factor in the decision. I think that the decision was based largely on an historical situation, as Mr. Kramer said. Not being in Freshman English, and not having the facts at my fingertips, I can only take his word for it. He is an expert."

The rationalization for dropping the course is two-pronged: elevating the decision to the arena of national educational policy lifts the issue above the local level and prevents the faculty from being accused of personal prejudice against the teaching assistants; raising the issue to one of professional competency legitimates the faculty's right to make the final decision. In other words, not only do expertise and professionalism provide the rationale for dropping the course, but they are also major goals to be achieved by making a negative decision. Removing the course rid the department of perpetual embarrassment to their professional pride. "I myself voted to drop the program because I thought it was a terrible course. . . . I felt the course was inappropriate for a genuine college curriculum." The heart of the matter is that "they [other departments] think the English department exists to teach grammar and writing while 90 per cent of us are trained for literature and only tangentially concerned with a service. It would be better to call it a department of literature than of English."

In a sense, the aristocratic humanists, see the issue more clearly. They realize that in part the dispute over Freshman English arose because the senior faculty shirked their duty. "If it is going to be run in a school, the English department has got to commit itself . . . teach Freshman English itself as at Berkeley, where all the faculty teaches it at least once a year." Perhaps they have such a strong conception of duty because their professional socialization provided for service to the department. "I've taught Freshman English myself for years. When I was brought here first I was put at the head of one of the three types of Freshman English that were being experimented with in 1939." Another veteran also insists that the course is part of the department: "The idea is that they're getting enough in high school, but the point is that it's still part of our business." Yet, despite all the admonitions about duty, they strongly resent any suggestion that something was amiss in the decision to drop the course. "The situation . . . is perfectly sound so far as I can see. Those are all perfectly honest people, and nobody is trying to pull the wool over anybody's eyes." And when it comes to designating who is going to teach Freshman English, statements are extremely vague: "People are going to have to continue to write . . . perhaps sophomore English." Or substitutions are suggested that range from a general disciplinary orientation to expression of satisfaction with the present writing clinic which serves as a remedial program for a small percentage of the freshman class. While the aristocratic humanists feel strongly about departmental duty, they would prefer that someone else actually performed it.

The moral critics generally supported the TAs claims to autonomy. Perhaps they sided with the teaching assistants because they realized the issue was a test of the limits of the senior faculty's control over the department. To grant the assistants autonomy would deny the need of a professional ethic; research could no longer be defined as a necessary adjunct of the teaching function. If research was not deemed central to the task of teaching, then the moral critics' attacks on professionalism would be validated, and the way would be cleared for them to demand a standard other than publication for promotion.

Thus, the moral critics reacted by accusing the senior members of the department of harsh retaliation against the rebellious teaching assistants: "It was only at the point when the TAs demanded the right to also be responsible for the decisions controlling the course that . . . the department . . . cut back . . . Freshman English. . . . It was another blatant and naked example of professional . . . venality." Another junior faculty member said: "One of the reasons they're dropping [Freshman English] is to get rid of annoying graduate students. . . . The senior members felt that they were no longer in charge of the course. The TAs wanted to deviate from the syllabus and the older members said you can't have autonomy on the part of the people who aren't certified." The moral critics also expressed concern for the one group that was never consulted, the students: "But simply to eliminate Freshman English as a course, not to teach it any more, to pay no attention to the students' ability to write . . . that's not a national trend. Nor is it realistic to say that students come in better prepared than they used to be. If anything, they come in worse prepared."

In summary, the institutional liberals refuse to recognize any personal animosity toward teaching assistants, and they disguise what is essentially a challenge to the legitimacy of professional control with talk of competence, credentials, and national trends. In fact, they seem delighted to be rid of a task which diminished their professional pride. The aristocratic humanists speak highly of duties they would have others accomplish, and more or less blindly defend the integrity of the department. The moral critics recognize that their collective interests coincide with those of the powerless assistants and therefore defend them. They do voice concern about the student, but it should be remembered that it is the teaching assistant whom they want to teach him. In other words, reasons vary greatly, but nobody really wants to assume the tedious task of teaching freshman composition.

Any consideration of conflict in an organization must examine the means by which the dominant group attempts to maintain social control. In the academic world, tenure marks the division between the powerful and the powerless. In theory, the tenure system is governed by meritocratic principles—quality publication is rewarded with promotion. The personal or political should not intervene in a professional decision. Because tenure is the major mechanism of social control, the way in which the various groups view the validity of this selection method should reveal the way in which each group defines its collective interests.

The moral critics agree that a meritocratic principle is desirable because they are the objects of judgment; they have most to gain from the articulation of a clearly defined set of standards. Although they are insistent about the necessity of a principled guide for tenure decisions, they hotly contest the propriety of the standards that presently prevail. Rather than using scholarly publication within the field of specialization as the sole criterion for evaluating performance, they want teaching and literary publication (novels, drama, poetry, criticism of contemporary literature) to weigh in the decision.

Perhaps their demands for new standards would not be so strident if they were not unanimous in their belief that the present criteria for promotion are a sham. In practice, they feel the standard is selectively applied, and this perception fosters a condemnation of the whole system.

The standards of this department are extremely uneven and unpredictable. I would almost go so far as to say there are no standards. It's very capricious and the standards are applied or not applied according to who's up and to what kind of gut feeling his immediate superiors have toward him. . . . Very often you discover that most people who end up voting yes or no on any given individual haven't the slightest idea of what he's doing or why it's worth anything.

Generally speaking, the assumption is that a person is promoted with a book. It is a tradition, like paying lip service to democracy. I think more people who make decisions . . . [must be] forced to recognize they make those decisions much more on the basis of prejudice than on really sound, rational [grounds]. . . . the profession of traditional standards becomes a form of hypocrisy. And consequently one's respect for people who should be deserving of that factor simply disintegrates.

The objective value of publication as a means of gauging performance is often demeaned: "I don't believe an English professor is a good professor unless he's a good teacher. And I think you can make judgments, evaluate teaching. . . . We're just resistive—publication is also a wildly subjective way of evaluating." The insistence on scholarly publications in a department of literature evokes bitter criticism: "It is said that you need a book to be promoted here. But a book of fiction is not considered a book. The only writers of literature we have in the department are guests. They are not on the staff. . . . Writing a novel . . . doesn't count."

Contrarily, the institutional liberals accept publication as a test of merit in the promotion process, given the status and purpose of the department.

This is a major league department. On the last survey of its kind we rated sixth nationally.[10] You come here and you know you're going to do research. It's taken for granted that you'll do teaching competently . . . [but] produc[ing] a body of publications, this is the determining factor.

The English department at an institution like Wisconsin depends for its reputation nationally . . . on the quality and to some extent quantity of the publication of its members. This is simply a fact of life in America.

The institutional liberals have no illusions about the manner in which the relative importance of teaching and publishing are weighed in the promotion process. "I think that a really good publisher will be advanced even if he is a mediocre teacher. That is, realistically speaking, I would certainly claim that if it were a choice of promoting someone here . . . who is an exemplary teacher, a superb teacher, and someone who is a mediocre teacher but who has published . . . the nod would definitely go to the man who had published." Quality of production is always praised at the expense of quantity, but in fact quantity—or at least the format associated with quantity—does weigh heavily in promotion considerations. "A book is more important than a large number of articles. . . . Even a tiny book is more valuable than articles." Despite the almost universal acceptance of meritocratic standards of promotion, it is acknowledged that publication constitutes only a necessary condition for tenure. "It is publish or perish, with this qualification. Publishing does not insure promotion, but nonpublishing does insure dismissal." Ultimately, the matter comes down to something called "professional judgment."

In the abstract . . . I don't believe there can be any objective criteria or any mechanical procedure which alone can determine promotion. In the end the decision comes to an evaluation of the man's quality of mind . . . character . . . intelligence, ability . . . Therefore, for promotional review to be successful, the executive committee has to be able to make these professional judgments. It comes down to professional judgment. Either the executive committee has it, or it . . . hasn't.

Both the institutional liberals and the moral critics make essentially the same analysis of the current system: publication is the official standard by which promotion is judged, and it is supposed to be governed by a complicated set of rules, involving quality, production and potential, but in fact the final decision is made on the executive committee's evaluation of the man and how he fits into their image of the department. The difference in their attitude stems from the willingness of the institutional liberals to pay lip service to a debased principle in order to protect their means of social control, while the moral critics demand that the principle be upheld or changed.

Like the institutional liberals, the aristocratic humanists accept the department's mechanism of promotion. However, they feel that the granting or withholding of tenure is an absolute and unquestionable right vested in the corporate body of the executive committee. To malign the tenure process is to slander the senior faculty. "How you judge is arrived at over a long period of time and . . . cases. This is not a matter of charges, it is the result of combined judgment at work over a long period of time." Faculty tenure decisions are an important part of the Wisconsin tradition. "That is one of the things that is always appreciated at the University of Wisconsin. The faculty has more control over these things than in other places. Therefore, I think the chance of human fallibility is less." Recent tendencies toward formalization of the process are regarded with suspicion. "There's a tendency toward greater legalism, to having everything spelled out in rules and regulations. The more this is done, the more the letter becomes important, and the further away you get from things of value. The only thing of any value is trust, and this is disappearing."

The way in which each of the groups views the tenure process is consistent with its position in the power structure of the department. The moral critics seem to take the official standards of promotion most seriously; at least they express most chagrin when these are violated. How much of their indignation is anxiety over their own ability to pass muster and how much is sincere criticism of a corrupt system is not easily determined. The fact that the moral critics disagree with even the ideal standard for a tenure judgment suggests that they see the issue in a wider perspective than the personal.

Although the institutional liberals profess to believe in the validity of publication as the test of promotion, they are willing to concede that some tenure decisions are made on a personal level. Moreover, they feel it is acceptable for them to use the promotion mechanism to screen out those who might mar their image of the department. This violation of professional principle is tolerated because they have generally made a major commitment to the department and the discipline and realize that they must share it for an indefinite and perhaps lengthy period of time with the persons to whom they give tenure. Yet, even though the personal factor is often weighty, promotion is usually not granted without considering the gross amount of publications. Because publication of some sort usually figures in promotion, it is easy for the institutional liberals to uphold publicly the myth of "publish or perish" as the standard for tenure, thereby undercutting criticism from below or outside.

The aristocratic humanists agree with the institutional liberals in considering tenure a matter of judgment. However, they do not even pay lip service to the idea of meritocratic decisions. Rather, they feel that tenure is a privilege, not a right, and they are the only ones with authority to bestow it.

The preceding discussion of the promotion process has been abstract, uncomplicated by departmental tensions and generational conflicts. An examination of a specific case will more clearly illustrate the way in which the process works. James Martin was a popular teacher and a controversial and outspoken moral critic of Marxist persuasion whose case was decided in the fall of 1969. The decision involved a departure from the usual promotion process. Normally, a junior member comes into the department on what is called a three year "up or out" track. At the beginning of his second year, he is given a pro forma review, which almost automatically extends his probationary period to a total of four years. The extension could be denied only if the person in question proves "obviously unsatisfactory." At the beginning of his third year a tenure decision is made: the junior faculty member is either promoted or told that his contract will be terminated at the end of his fourth year. The extra year is given in order that another job may be found. Contrary to this customary procedure, James Martin was denied an extension at the beginning of his second year and was told he would have to leave at the end of his third year. The normal process had only the status of an agreement and was not bound by formal contract, so the department was not legally obligated to retain him. Like tenure decisions, extensions are decided upon in closed sessions of the executive committee, which consists of all the senior or tenured faculty. Thus, no public apology for their actions is necessary.

The decision at the beginning of the second year obviously meant that all pretense of rendering judgment on Martin's scholarly capacity was dropped; a man cannot be expected to publish a significant amount of work one year out of graduate school. The decision, then, was made on other than professional grounds. Because the firing was so questionable, a movement to make the decision into an academic freedom case developed. Academic freedom, however, is a widely misunderstood concept, and it has no legal status whatsoever.[11]

The academic freedom proffered to the professor at first glance seems a broad right; he is free to conduct research and publish the results, to teach his subject, and to speak freely as a citizen. However, the American Association of University Professors makes each of these clauses dependent upon a condition. Research and publication are contingent upon adequate performance of "other duties"; controversial subjects which bear no relation to the field of specialization are not to be introduced in the classroom; in the exercise of the citizen's prerogative of free speech, the faculty member must clearly separate himself from his institution and, in addition, reflect the responsibility and restraint appropriate to his professional role.[12] Moreover, this narrow and somewhat nebulous freedom applies, in effect, only to tenured faculty members because it is not meant to provide a criterion for promotion; it only governs cases in which a professor is dismissed after he has received tenure. Thus, a tenure decision, by definition, does not fall within the purview of academic freedom. The rules governing academic freedom were made for self-protection by professors who already had tenure; they wanted to prevent both attacks from outside the guild and palace revolutions on the part of untenured academics.

The moral critics who felt Martin's dismissal involved a violation of academic freedom were thus mistaken. However, their interpretation is indicative of their perception of the case. Entering academe after the McCarthy era and during a period when the professor was held in high esteem, they accepted their right to freedom and saw the accompanying "responsibilities" as archaic constrictions of their professional role. At the same time, they attempted to extend the somewhat limited definition generally held in academe of the professional's role. They perceive the dichotomy between the professional and the political as a categorical convenience held by their elders in order to make their decisions appear to be governed by rule rather than whim. In many cases, the moral critics feel it is impossible to separate passionate personal commitment from the study of literature, to view the act of teaching as limited to the classroom and bound by a particular text, to enforce what they feel is an artificial separation between the world of the scholar and the sphere of political man. Thus, they are attempting a fusion of the personal, the professional, and the political man.

Yet the moral critics seem unaware of the difficulty their position poses for a system of evaluation that is purportedly based on meritocratic principles. They do not ask that the system, which they perceived in practice as failing to operate strictly according to merit, be changed to accommodate the reality. Instead they demand that the professional criteria be upheld, and seem to ignore the fact that the professional standard applies to only one aspect of the personal, political, and professional roles they want to fuse publicly.

The moral critics, then, perceived Martin's dismissal as political, as a violation of academic freedom. More importantly, they saw the case in terms of the conflict between generations in the department. To them, Martin's fate was determined by the longer standing battle over the future of the department.

The firing was partly personal. Some people simply don't like Martin. But it was also political. . . . Martin tried to relate literature to life. His politics are partly a response to his understanding of literature. . . . Martin had an idea [that] education could be very different from theirs, a concept of the university that is different, and a different concept of society. This is a threat to senior English professors. But finally, they believe in what they're doing. There is malice, but it is largely self-deception. I think they're wrong. . . . There is no question that education is a failure. Milton says education is to repair the Fall. But education is doing very little to make men better. Nothing could be lost from trying something different. We are the most educated people that ever existed, but we are no nearer to being human.

Martin symbolized the antagonism the junior faculty felt for their seniors.

Martin's firing sharpened my perceptions of the department. Martin is an affront to the whole genteel tradition. He's a walking insult to the Harvard ideal of the 1890s which still has a lot of cut. In Martin's case, the whole thing is complicated in three ways. The first is personality. He is abrasive. The second is ideology. He would make a better object if he weren't a doctrinaire Marxist. . . . Third, it is the political situation in the department at the present time. He reaped all the ill will of four years of agitation by students, TAs, and junior faculty. They felt they had to strike out at something, and he was in the way. He thumbs his nose at all the traditional assumptions of the department, and I think one way or another he tells some of them that they are moribund.

His dismissal was seen as the culmination of all the tensions in the department.

The senior members of the department who have most at stake in the status quo are very frightened indeed. They are frightened of everything from the TAA, to the junior faculty [member] who doesn't accept their way of doing things, to the administration which seems to be uninterested in the humanities, to the Regents who seem equally uninterested. They're just scared to death, and they don't want somebody around who is something of a lightning rod. Martin's politics, coupled with this fear on the part of a lot of people . . . crystallized around the question of his extension.

The institutional liberals also realized that the future of the department is at stake, but they do not put the matter so boldly. Perhaps they played down some aspects of Martin's case because acknowledgment of the full dimension of the conflict would force them to make a closer examination of their conduct. More precisely, open admission of the actual grounds of conflict—facing the charge that the senior faculty violated the professional standard of promotion by introducing the personal and political into the decision—would have put them in the uncomfortable position of publicly justifying their tolerance of a particularistic application of a supposedly universal principle. They avoided such an admission by indicating that Martin knew the unwritten rules of the game, and if he wanted to win he should have played by them. Reluctance to face the ambiguity of their position allowed them to ignore the apparent contradiction of the moral critics' charges; they did not take them to task for demanding an apolitical judgment on a man who openly avowed that politics are inseparable from academics. Their self-protective understanding of the issue prevented them from taking into account the full implications of the case. However, they did express a fear that the reality of the situation may be changing, that perhaps there is a new game played by rules of which they are unaware.

A junior professor in the institutional liberal camp saw more clearly than his senior colleagues what the question of Martin's firing implied. Perhaps his perception was sharpened by the ambiguity of his position.

This bears on the question of whether I am loyal to my assistant professor colleagues, the nontenured faculty, or whether I'm loyal to the department. . . . I think it was unjustified because it involved a one-year extension and therefore should have gone through unless he was absolutely delinquent, and he wasn't. But he called it upon himself by his outspokenness. . . . He knows he's not going to get tenure if he proceeds the way he did. So I don't think the big hue and cry over his renewal was really justified. I don't consider myself a radical but a simple liberal, not too much to the left. I don't think politics should absorb people the way it does around here. I don't think politics should be in classes. Politics should be separate.

The tenured professors were usually more circumspect:

Martin is symptomatic of the kind of problem that this department will have to come to terms with. . . . The question concern[ed] not his competence as a classroom teacher, but his discharging of professional responsibilities. Rather obviously, being a good classroom teacher means more than being good in the classroom. . . . It is symptomatic because Martin is an outspoken activist which is a breakdown of the conventional academic role of neutrality. . . . In other words, he is a new breed.

Martin threatened the professional identity of the tenured faculty, and he was punished for it. Effort to justify an unprofessional decision is external rather than internal, as an internal explanation would call for a more realistic reckoning. The political forces beyond the department are often mentioned.

I don't see any professional reason for the decision taken against him. I'm not saying he was ousted from the department in a sinister manner. But I do think he was the victim of an executive committee that made a decision on other than professional grounds . . . Martin did not fit the executive committee's image of itself, or their image of the department. "He wouldn't fit in, you know"— that was the kind of comment. That's a nice way of putting it. [But] the English department is under pressure on a national level. . . . The public thinks we're a staging ground for revolution.

The aristocratic humanists were somewhat embarrassed by the repercussions of the Martin decision. They avoided the conflictful aspects of the case by defending their right as a body to make whatever decision they felt was correct. The criteria by which such a decision is made are not open to any discussion no matter how oblique but are rather based upon an unspoken gentleman's agreement among themselves.

This is not, [as] popular interpretation suggests, a political issue. . . . I would defend the executive committee's right to make a judgment even if I would take issue with the way in which they made their judgment. . . . The notion that the executive committee is prejudiced by personal or political considerations is simply not tolerated. Once in a while you get some signs of prejudice in [a promotion decision] but usually prejudice is very easy to spot because it is accompanied by emotion. And also we don't live in a vacuum. We know when there are personal animosities . . . so that [in] the chance to give a man a fair deal . . . I think we're as close to that kind of system as we can get. I've seen it work for many years and I don't think we've done many injustices. I think in the case of Martin a very careful judgment was made, but that is all I will say.

Another professor came close to facing the reality of his feeling, but backed away at the last moment. "There is a lot to be said. . . . In some ways I respect Martin a great deal . . . I guess I don't. I would, judging by what evidence I can get, say that he is probably an excellent classroom teacher of a peculiar sort. I guess I would have to say that he is less impressive in other ways. This is the most accurate and tactful way I can put it."

The moral critics were the only group that heavily stressed the conflict called up by the Martin case. Because they were convinced of the injustice of the decision, they dwelled on the contradiction between principle and practice. They based their description of the decision as unjust on the fact that it was obviously impossible to judge Martin's professional competence in one year. At the same time, they attacked the professional standard as an inadequate criterion for tenure decisions. In other words, the existing standards were better than an absence of standards, but even more desirable would be a radically new criterion of judgment which would encompass the whole man and his various roles. Yet, in their vague allusions to such a standard, they did not clearly work out the relationship of the professional and the political role.

The institutional liberals did not squarely face the antagonisms generated by Martin's dismissal since this enabled them to avoid dealing with the grounds of their tolerance of a breach of principle. To acknowledge a particularistic application of the tenure standard would have forced them to recognize the legitimacy of the moral critics' accusations and open the whole tenure process to scrutiny, thereby undercutting their major mechanism of control. The aristocratic humanists refused to deal with the conflict engendered by the case because to do so would have called into question the judgment of the executive committee. They believed it was the prerogative of the committee to exercise its power as it saw fit and that the use of this right was not open to public debate.

In summary, the main purpose of both academic freedom and the tenure system is to preserve the vested interests in the department. More specifically, tenure is granted or denied with an eye to preserving the present professional identity of the department and to retaining the prerogatives of rank. The tenured faculty, while not a monolithic group, are nevertheless united on all important decisions—on dropping Freshman English, on the necessity of the tenure system, on dismissing Martin, on perceiving the junior faculty as a threat.

The junior faculty have refused to accept their seniors' rather limited definition of the discipline. They are attempting to turn the department toward what they feel is a more truly humane course. They would abandon professionalism for passion and honor the role of teacher above that of researcher. In short, the senior faculty are perfectly correct when they see their juniors as a threat.

Apparently the senior faculty have seized on the promotion process as the most potent means of punishing their juniors. One senior faculty member suggests that the promotion process provides an opportunity to vent long nourished resentments, and that if the wider economic and political scene remains propitious, those who cloud the department's image of itself will be ousted: "The reason for the presence of the radicals is that many of them came in during a period of expansion and would not have been hired otherwise. But now we're in a period of contraction, and the radicals will be the first to go." And indeed, this seems to be the strategy employed by the executive committee. Seventeen junior professors came up for tenure decisions in the autumn of 1970 and none was granted tenure. Several of the decisions were outright terminations but the majority were postponements of decisions. By dismissing those who did not fit in within their image of the department and delaying decisions on others, the senior faculty warned the untenured faculty that defiance of their professional image would not be tolerated, while at the same time they protected the manpower needs of the department.

That the decisions were a punitive action against those they felt were deviant among the junior faculty and not a consideration of scholarly merit was demonstrated by an open hearing requested by two of the junior professors. One had published several substantial articles in his own field and in areas outside his specialization and was of a decidedly activist left-wing political persuasion; the other had published both articles and a book in his own field and had not made himself particularly noticeable on the campus political scene but had supported the moral critics on departmental matters. The differences in their publication records would presumably call for a separate evaluation of each man, yet they were both dismissed by exactly the same vote, which suggests that attitude toward the department is the crucial factor.

In conclusion, the struggle which took place in the English department can perhaps best be understood as conflict between intellectual generations. However, it must be understood that this is not a simple clash between men of different ages, but a struggle over the definition of the appropriate role of the academic man in society. The dominant image of the academic as professional—which is underpinned by concepts of value-free knowledge, the neutrality of the academic man, the necessity of rigorous specialization, and the importance of the expert to society—is under attack.

Notes

[1] T. Caplow and R. J. McGee, *The Academic Marketplace* (New York: Basic Books, 1958), p. 22.

[2] See D. Bell, *The Reforming of General Education* (Garden City, N.Y.: Anchor Books, 1968) for a more scholarly rendition of this portrait of the professor. pp. 4–5.

[3] See S. M. Lipset, "The Politics of Academics," in D. Nichols (ed.), *Perspectives on Campus Tensions* (Washington, D.C.: American Council on Education, 1970), pp. 85–118, for a succinct statement of the effects of age on faculty members.

[4] Several professors at the senior level were excluded because their major concern was teacher education, while the chairman and James Martin were specifically included because of the light they were able to shed on some of the more hotly-debated issues.

[5] Caplow and McGee, *op. cit.*

[6] R. S. Laufer, *Higher Education in Post-Industrial Society: Innovation and Conflict in American Higher Education*, (Brandeis University: 1971), unpublished doctoral dissertation. The designation "expert-scholar" is part of a typology of faculty role systems: the expert scholar, who reflects the dominant role of research and the discipline; the classroom teacher-scholar, who focuses on both the student and research within his discipline; the expert-teacher who focuses on the student through a disciplinary perspective; and the classroom teacher-teacher, who focuses primarily on the student.

[7] Bell, *op. cit.*, p. 9.

[8] R. P. Wolff, *The Ideal of the University*, (Boston: Beacon Press, 1969), pp. 4–5.

⁹ Bell, *op. cit.*, p. 177.

¹⁰ In the next rating of this kind, the department dropped from sixth to eleventh. See K. D. Roose, C. J. Anderson, *A Rating of Graduate Programs,* (Washington, D.C.: American Council on Education, 1970), p. 40.

¹¹ W. P. Metzger, *Academic Freedom in the Age of the University* (New York: Columbia University Press, 1955), p. 200.

¹² L. Joughlin (Ed.), *Academic Freedom and Tenure: A Handbook of the American Association of University Professors,* (Madison: University of Wisconsin Press, 1969), pp. 35–36.

CHAPTER 13

●●●●●●●●●●●●●●●
●●●●●●●●●●●●●●●●
●●●●●●●●●●●●●●●●

TRAVAIL OF A
DEPARTMENT

David Evett

●●●●●●●●●●●●●●●
●●●●●●●●●●●●●●●●
●●●●●●●●●●●●●●●●

I do not mean to talk about the English department at the University of Wisconsin as though it were a microcosm of the university as a whole, to say nothing of American academia as a whole. I doubt that any department in any university can be legitimately so designated. At the same time, I think it is proper to say that during my service in it (1965–1970) nearly all the wide band of problems afflicting the University of Wisconsin in particular, and the American university in general, found some form of expression in the life of the department. Contention between students and faculty, between faculty and faculty, between faculty and administration, between students and administration, between the university and the larger community—we felt them all. It was a hectic, if interesting, time and for that reason alone is worth considering. I must at the outset renounce any claim to scientific authority or even absolute historical accuracy; as a participant in the situation and most of the events I will discuss, I can claim no more than the intention to be as fair and true as possible.[1] As an analyst of those events, I can hope for no more than some measure of applicability beyond the immediate Wisconsin situation.

Let me begin with a brief description of the department's structure. Formal power in the department is divided among three interlocking agencies: the departmental committee; the executive committee; the chairman. The departmental committee, whose membership includes all persons holding regular teaching appointments (professors, associate and assistant professors, and, recently, instructors), is the official policy-making body of the department (although naturally much of the routine work is done by the various standing subcommittees and by the various executive personnel). For many years, this committee was a largely ceremonial body, meeting a few times a year to rubber-stamp decisions already made. Lately, however, thanks mainly to pressure exerted by younger faculty, it has claimed a growing share of departmental power, and has met ever more often for ever longer and more acrimonious debates. The executive committee, consisting of all tenured faculty (full and associate professors), enjoys most of the actual power in the department by virtue of its control over matters of budget and personnel, and until fairly recently made most departmental policy. The chairman has little independent authority in principle; in practice, he exercises as much as his own strength of character, his executive committee, his dean, and his faculty will allow him. He is appointed annually, for not more than three consecutive years, by the dean of the college. Normally, the dean follows the recommendation of the department, expressed through secret nominations submitted by members of the department. Practices vary here, but in the English department there is customarily some discreet advance canvassing, then a department meeting during which nominations are made and straw ballots taken, then a final ballot, the results of which are sent to the dean.

Such was the pattern in the spring of 1965. But there was a difference between that election and preceding ones. It has been said that the dean let it be known that he would refuse to name as chairman any of the handful of exceptionally energetic and forceful scholars of international reputation who had been circulating the chairmanship among themselves for three decades. Whether or not this assertion is true, the new chairman that year was a relative newcomer to the university and the English department. His three-year period in office was not unmarked by turbulence (as an easy index, I might note that in 1965–1966 the departmental committee met four times, in 1966–1967 seven times, in 1967–1968 twelve times). Among the events of the period I would single out one: the formation, during December 1965, of a junior faculty caucus (assistant professors and instructors, plus, later on, one or two recently promoted associates), which met irregularly but frequently during my time at Wisconsin to air mutual grievances, formulate proposals and positions (some quite far-reaching and ambitious), evaluate possible chairmen with an eye to junior faculty interests, consult with students, and otherwise engage in departmental politics.

This caucus played some informal part in the next election, in April 1968. The big issue that year was intramural: educational reform and student power. The atmosphere on campus was generally tense. During the preliminary canvassing two distinct candidates emerged, both full professors, one of them associated with the old regime, the other identified with the junior staff, a maverick (though also a former assistant dean). The issues were supposed to include such matters as student participation in departmental decision making, curricular reform, and relative priorities of teaching and research in questions of promotion. The final ballot was a near tie. The dean, correctly interpreting this fact as evidence of a major departmental rift, and unwilling to name a chairman who lacked a clear mandate, interviewed a number of members of the department and then named a third, compromise figure, again a newcomer to the department, not clearly associated with either camp.

During that year, an ad hoc committee of the department had been attacking the thorny problem of Freshman English. Morale among the students in the course had never been very good. Among the graduate students, who had come to do almost all the actual teaching of the course, it was plummeting: nearly all of them wanted to teach literature, not expository writing; nearly all of them balked at the regimentation they had to endure by following a syllabus and a calendar handed down from above by the director of the course. The ad hoc committee's decision to reduce Freshman English from two semesters to one for most students was therefore universally applauded, especially since a way was found to provide alternative and attractive work for most of the teaching assistants: the format of the first half of the required sophomore literature course was altered from lecture to discussion-section and the course was handed over to the teaching assistants. Furthermore, in a significant departure from previous methods, the policy-making responsibility for these courses was vested in two committees which included teaching assistants as voting members, admitting them for the first time directly into the decision-making process. This development was symptomatic. During the same general period, the junior faculty caucus proposed a new structure for the department's principal standing committee, which gave students and junior staff a voice in curricular policy. Furthermore, a new committee on teaching was proposed, which likewise included student members and which was promoted as a way to counterbalance the built-in institutional bias toward research at the expense of teaching. Finally, graduate and undergraduate student-faculty liaison committees were proposed. These committees were somewhat weakened by amendment during departmental debate, but they were instituted—although, as it turned out, their actual contributions to departmental activity during the next year or two were not great, giving rise to accusations of tokenism and co-optation.

It was against this background of innovations in curriculum, stance, and organization that the new chairman appointed new members of the ad hoc committee to continue their overhaul of the department's undergraduate offerings by attacking the major. The old program was the object of increasingly vocal dissatisfaction among an increasing number of both students and faculty. Even the most conservative members of the department had to concede that the requirements had been established at a time when the university and the department were smaller and less complicated and that therefore a period of self-scrutiny was probably in order. The committee as appointed seemed young enough and brassy enough to come up with something interesting.[2] And within a few months, the committee did bring to the departmental committee a fairly innovative proposal, which substituted for the former distribution requirements a series of three five-credit "super surveys" incorporating opportunities for individual and small-group independent study, increased instructor-student contact, and other pedagogical desiderata. But the proposal was savagely assailed in the department meeting; it managed, one way or another, to offend nearly everybody. For another year, the committee floundered about, considering and then rejecting a great variety of ideas. In the spring of 1969 it proposed to the department a few relatively minor modifications in the old program, which were duly accepted, leaving the major essentially unchanged. At the same time, however, a significant new policy was adopted, which by limiting the size of most upper-level courses both improved the student-instructor ratio and cut back employment opportunities for teaching assistants, who had done much of the grading and discusssion leading for the upper-level surveys.

In the meantime, relations on the campus and in the department had been deteriorating. The long series of extramurally-focused protests sapped departmental energies, of course, and colored virtually all discourse between faculty members and students during 1968, 1969, and 1970. It appeared that in the eyes of the more conservative members of the faculty, any innovative proposal (whether it was overtly political or not) came wreathed with the red streamers of the Students for a Democratic Society and the Young Socialist Alliance, and that, in the eyes of the radical left, any faculty or administration resistance bespoke black fascism. Vietnam, student power, ROTC, required courses, the Army Mathematics Research Center, relevance, pot, parietal hours, the National Guard, Bobby Seale grew weekly more intertwined, grew at length into a Gordian knot for which there seemed (and seems) to be no solution but the sword. And the confusions on the campus were certainly exacerbated by political and economic developments in the nation and especially in the state, as an increasingly conservative state legislature and Board of Regents responded to campus disorder and inflation alike by budget cuts, real and threatened, with consequences that have still not fully declared themselves. The pattern of responses to each new campus crisis was much the same. After an initial shock, at some extraordinary meeting the departmental committee would make some united effort, try to find a unanimous reaction (usually by involving a study committee). But the debate would be sometimes intemperate, and the aftermath a period of bickering. The net result was that each new episode seemed to increase the distance between the department's conservative and radical poles and the futility—or impotence—of the moderates (who tended to be the younger members of the executive committee).

In this atmosphere of growing confusion and hostility there rose up the Teaching Assistants' Association, proclaiming a new era in university and department organization. The union movement has been creeping slowly but steadily into academia for some time, but resistance to faculty unionism has been very strong, not only from administrators but also from professors (including many earnest supporters of union activity in other lines of work), since the union concept contradicts the highly individualistic image they have of themselves. Teaching assistants are of course academic amphibians—more than students, less than professors, but still professionals. Hence the appearance of the TAA did indeed constitute a significant innovation. The new look, however, was not really in labor relations (or so I judge). The goals of the TAA seem to be those of most unions—better pay, shorter hours, better working conditions, better job security, more control over one's working situation. These material questions have been and will be negotiable, especially in a profession where dollars and cents, though by no means insignificant, do not as yet constitute articles of religion. But in ways that I will note later, the union provoked strong suspicion, resentment, even open hostility, among some members of the faculty, and equally strong expressions of support from others.

The president and other leaders of the TAA, and one of the largest contingents of its members, came from the English department. The effect on department events of their participation is uncertain. That there was a serious ruckus over teaching assistants, and that the TAA had something to do with it, is undeniable. Despite the earlier reduction of the Freshman English program from two semesters to one and the admission of some teaching assistants to the policy-making committee for the course, their morale had continued to sink. The problem was still regimentation: many assistants balked at being required to use a textbook chosen by somebody else, according to a schedule set by somebody else, in order to achieve goals established by somebody else. For several years many teaching assistants, especially the more experienced, had been silently ignoring the prescription, teaching their own courses in their own ways. Department authorities knew this, of course, but were content to ignore it as long as no students complained. But in October 1969, a conscientious, politically aggressive teaching assistant publicly informed the director of Freshman English that he could no longer teach the course in the prescribed manner. The director told the chairman, who in turn relieved the assistant of his teaching duties on the grounds that he had known about the way the course was run when he accepted his appointment the previous spring. His refusal to follow directions therefore constituted a violation of his implicit contract with the department.

Within a few days, the chairman received overtures from the departmental contingent of the TAA, which at that point had been recognized as the official bargaining agent for Wisconsin teaching assistants and was bargaining with the administration, but not yet (by a matter of some months) fully planted in the university by contract. The TAA wanted to represent the suspended teaching assistant in a grievance procedure of some not very clearly specified sort. The chairman refused. As it happened, a meeting of the Freshman English staff had been called for that week, for the purpose of nominating teaching assistant members of the Freshman English policy committee. When the chairman arrived, he was met with hostility and the now-customary set of demands—complete control of the course by teaching assistants, relief from arbitrary firing and suspension, open personnel files, and so on. A stormy session ensued, and all knew that a department crisis was brewing. In an effort to forestall open war, the chairman convened an emergency meeting of the whole department—faculty and students—on the town hall model, a procedure he had used to rather good purpose in two or three earlier all-university crises. But it failed here when it became an occasion for articulating the students' multiple grievances—Vietnam, ROTC, suppression of the Black Panthers, and so on—and for pushing the claims of the TAA, actions which infuriated the more conservative faculty members and distressed many moderates, so that the forum was in the end counterproductive, leaving the department atmosphere very tense.

Even so, it came as a great surprise to most members of the department when at the next regular session of the departmental committee the director of Freshman English proposed that the course be abolished.

(See Chapter Twelve.) The basis for his case was that accumulated evidence had come conclusively to demonstrate that the ordinary freshman rhetoric course did not do what it claimed to do—improve student writing—and that anyhow Wisconsin students now arrived well enough prepared that few of them needed additional instruction in rhetoric. These things had been said before. But three aspects of this announcement were surprising. First, the source: The director of the program, whose commitment to it had previously seemed firm, was in effect putting himself out of a job (although as a tenured member of the department he was pretty well guaranteed some other employment). Second, the conditions: The proposal made no effort to suggest alternative uses for the teaching resources that would be released by the abolition of Freshman English, or, to put it another way, the proposal wrote off close to a quarter of a million dollars a year of graduate student support. Third, the timing: Despite demurrers by both the chairman and the director of Freshman English, the proposal looked suspiciously vengeful and reflexive and was therefore likely to lose support within the department that might be forthcoming under less convulsive circumstances.

Action on this proposal was summary in quality though somewhat prolonged in time because of a legal confusion that also provoked the most flagrant evidence yet of the rift within the department. Within two weeks of the first appearance of the proposition, and without the prolonged committee work that usually accompanied such major modifications of department policy, the departmental committee was convened to vote. When members arrived in the meeting room at the appointed hour, they found it already occupied by a number of teaching assistants, who announced that they wished to be heard, since their course and their jobs were on the line. The chairman responded by summoning several persons from the university's security force, who stationed themselves at the door of another room from which they barred all who were not members of the department. But a number of younger faculty members refused to cross the line. It was, therefore, a diminished committee that rejected by fairly close votes several attempts to postpone the decision until further study could be carried out and then passed the abolition motion by a comfortable majority. As it turned out, the meeting was declared illegal when the Wisconsin attorney general ruled that the department was covered by a provision of state law admitting the public to all meetings of state agencies in which individual personnel decisions were not being made. The process had to be repeated at a later date. But most of the people who left the first meeting refused to come to any subsequent session, and Freshman English was duly abolished.

The long-range effects of this decision remain to be seen. In the short run, it contributed to the increasingly acrimonious and uncertain temper of the department. During the winter of 1969–1970, virtually all of the younger members of the faculty, including some with tenure, talked openly of leaving the university at the first opportunity. A few actually did depart; no doubt more would have left had jobs been more readily available elsewhere. All-university convulsions continued, but in particular the prolonged TAA strike, which seriously impaired academic activities throughout the College of Letters and Science early in the second semester. A few members of the department openly honored the strike by cancelling their classes; many more gave tacit encouragement by moving classes off-campus. The department's official response was, in effect, to ignore the whole thing. But the disruption of courses on whatever grounds so early in the term turned out to be deeply disturbing to faculty on both sides of the fence, and the strain thus placed on nerves already frayed by three years of repeated shocks contributed to the last three dramatic episodes in the affairs of the English department.

The first of these commenced in February 1970 when, contrary to recent department custom (though not to its official stated policies), the department's most visibly and vocally radical assistant professor was told that his services would no longer be needed after the statutory year's period of grace in which to find another job. The public explanation alleged shortcomings of teaching and research, but given his reputation, it was being said within a few hours of the announcement that he was being discharged because of his political activities. Later in the spring, he entered a suit in United States District Court charging the executive committee, the chairman, the university chancellor, and the Regents with violation of First and Fourteenth Amendment civil liberties. The case has not yet come to trial. But more than any other event, this one served as a focus for accumulated resentments and suspicions. In March, the chairman, exhausted by two years of unceasing department strife and eager to return to scholarship, let it be known that he did not intend to serve the usual third term. During the feeling-out period, two candidates emerged, neither one an extremist, one of them clearly the choice of the majority of members of the executive committee and ultimately named by the dean to chair the department. Neither of them took the fancy of the junior faculty caucus, who, after straw ballots in which they sought to mock the entire process by nominating the likes of Mickey Mouse and Robespierre, cast their bloc vote for their fired junior colleague.

It was an ugly way to end an ugly year; it is perhaps just as well that the action was soon smothered by the total chaos that descended upon the whole university following the Cambodian adventure and the shootings at Kent State. Several members of the department were included among signatories of an open letter declaring that they were leaving their classrooms to teach in the wider community outside. In effect, this action supported the student strike. The department as a whole took no action. Many professors were antagonistic to the war and largely sympathetic to the student cause, yet could not bring themselves to renounce the work they were trained and hired to do. There were two meetings of faculty and students together, called at the request of the chancellor, which considered and voted on various sense-of-the-body resolutions condemning the war, urging the abolition of ROTC, and so on. From one of these some senior faculty staged their own walkout, terming the entire proceeding a perversion of the university's proper function and a waste of time to boot.

I have dwelt on these incidents chiefly in order to provide specific illustrations for the analytical generalizations that follow. Let me begin by noting one or two universal factors that nevertheless gain a peculiar significance, it seems to me, when they operate in the university situation. Bureaucratic inertia, of the kind endemic to all large settled institutions, clearly contributed to the brawl over Freshman English. Some were motivated to resist radical innovation in that course by principle and some by a sense of threatened privilege, but these were undergirded by a dislike of the administrative inconvenience that would have accompanied any major change. Or, consider the matter of self-interest. When the ad hoc committee to study the undergraduate course offerings took its first proposal to the departmental committee, some people were initially surprised by the harsh reception it got from the junior faculty. In the nature of things, they would have done most of the teaching of the proposed super surveys, since the efforts of the senior staff are so largely claimed by the graduate program. As a group, the younger people had been the most vocal adherents of the kinds of pedagogic innovation the new course claimed to promote—freedom for independent study, for instance. As a group, they had been actively seeking the kind of control over undergraduate work that their de facto control of this course would have given them (some senior staff members opposed the proposal on these very grounds). Finally, it seemed to embody in a real way the concept of radical change which many young professors appeared to endorse as a value in and of itself. Yet the young people would not buy it. The fact was that the department practiced academic natural selection (publish or perish, that is) and that teaching survey courses interferes with research, while specialized upper-level courses enable the professor to combine research time and course preparation time and thereby earn writing time. The new proposal was simply not in the junior faculty interest.

However, many assistant professors objected to the course not on the grounds of interest but of principle. Again, this is scarcely surprising. Academics, at least the academics who profess the liberal arts, are principle-mongers. We brandish principles the way businessmen brandish contracts; principles are our most important product. But we are not much, if any, better than other people at self-sacrifice; we tend to choose principles that, if institutionalized, further our interests. Since we are not always clear about this—often we see no conflict—we can sometimes be accused of hypocrisy. I wish to make this point because I think it very relevant to the continuing, and worsening, crisis of faith that afflicted relations between faculty and students, and between older and younger faculty members, during the period of which I write. It is currently a commonplace that the ubiquitous revolt of the young at the end of the sixties is partly predicated on American society's failure to enact the promises made at the beginning of the decade. Similarly, English literature is offered to students as an exciting and revealing discipline, and its professors often portray themselves as relatively altruistic. But when English literature seems about to dead-end in sterile pedantry, and some professors turn out to be motivated by ambition as well as by ideals, the resulting disappointment can fuel many a protest and help set the intemperate tone of many a list of demands. Yet in fairness I will insist that the disillusionment can cut both ways, and that faculty members can be equally disgusted when a cry for freedom from the tyranny of grades, for instance, turns out to be in some mouths a cry for licensed sloth. In either case, it is the confusion between principle and interest that causes most of the trouble. And again, that confusion is both more likely and more destructive in the university situation, in which the appeal to ideals is so incessant.

The next factor to consider is the factor of size, both absolute and relative. Most of the institutions and policies governing the operations of the university were established before the Second World War, at a time when both the university and the department were much smaller. The department had perhaps fifteen tenured members, who taught the specialized courses, made the policy, and rotated the chairmanship among themselves, plus four or five transitory instructors and assistant professors who helped to teach the service courses. The permanent group was small enough so that communication was free and consensus relatively easy to achieve; most decisions were actually made outside formal meetings of executive committee or departmental committee, though those bodies might assemble to ratify them. After the war, of course, the department grew cataclysmically. In the peak year, 1969, there were about seventy full-time faculty members, nearly six hundred graduate students, including about two hundred teaching assistants, and about eight hundred undergraduate majors. Such enormously increased numbers increase the possibilities for disagreement, dispute, and dissension. The number of faculty seems to me especially significant, for where a group of fifteen can sustain mutual intimacy and a sense of corporate unity, a group of seventy persons, widely disparate in age, background, temperament, and interests, will tend to break down into subgroups of more homogeneous character, between which differences of a political sort may very well arise—certainly they did at Wisconsin. There, however, not only the gross number of faculty members but their distribution became important. Specifically, the proportion of younger to older faculty increased very greatly. During the years 1965–1967 alone, more than twenty new-minted Ph.D.s joined the department. In numbers there is strength, especially where there is also some organization (of the kind provided by the junior faculty caucus). It therefore became psychologically easier for the junior people to speak out. Furthermore, they were on surer ground than their predecessors in other ways. As beneficiaries of the intensely competitive seller's market of the mid-sixties, they arrived assured of their professional value. They came as assistant professors rather than instructors, at good salaries, able to request and receive attractive teaching assignments (no composition) and decent schedules and offices from the beginning of their careers. These factors certainly encouraged a degree of confidence—not to say cockiness—in this generation of young scholars which appears to have been lacking in earlier ones, whose first years of service had been spent in probationary drudgery. During this period the junior staff offered a whole string of challenges—in the areas of curriculum, teaching methods, hiring procedures, promotion procedures, department organization and government—almost all of which contained provisions giving the lower echelons more power. Most of these challenges were ostensibly or actually beaten back. But the struggle demanded time and energy—most notably, the departmental committee increasingly became the arena for department decision making. And in the end the process habituated the members of the department to the politics of confrontation within, while the university as a whole was being assaulted from without.

For, of course, all the conflicts within the department were related, directly or indirectly, to the general turmoil. I doubt that there is at any university a pure faculty problem. Even matters like office assignments affect morale, which affects teaching and hence students. In turn, the in loco parentis issue, for example, can affect student morale and receptivity and hence impinge on teaching and faculty. Even as an undergraduate in the amniotic isolation of a small college during the placid fifties, I was conscious of a certain tidal activity of student sentiment and faculty-administration response. But our demands were exclusively local. Things changed, of course, with Selma, Kennedy, and the emergence of the student activist. By 1968, it was quite impossible for the department to discuss its position on a black studies resolution without raising the issue of racism on one side and student power on the other. Many of the problems here were actually rhetorical, but the truly destructive issues were only too real. In those five years of department debate, no question came up more often, or aroused more passion when it did, than the question of whether and when and how far the university or any of its organs, such as the department, should actively tangle in political affairs. The pressure on the department from the student left (and later from the junior faculty left) to make corporate public statements about Vietnam and ROTC and the other pressing questions of these times mounted year by year and crisis by crisis. But so did counterpressure to keep the department clear of all matters not overtly involved with the teaching of English and American literature and language. And, distressingly, the resistance to the radicals was based less and less on principles of educational philosophy and definitions of the liberal university and more and more on fear of retaliation by the Regents and the state legislature, usually expressed by older members of the department and usually prefaced by remarks about the days of Joe McCarthy. Inevitably, the results were still more acerbity and animosity and still less hope of a return to department unanimity.

In all this turbulence, one further factor or set of factors deserves mention. Here again the fate of the ad hoc committee's major proposal is illustrative. After the rebuff so vigorously administered to the super-survey plan, the committee, realizing that it had perhaps gathered fewer data than it should have, distributed to department members a lengthy questionnaire. When the questionnaires came back, their import was clear: it was not going to be possible to devise *any* program able to attract more than the grudging support of a majority of the members of the department.

In retrospect, a number of things now seem clear. On the very first day of the committee's deliberations, its two hairiest members had proposed that the major be defined solely in terms of credit-hours of English, to be accumulated in whatever assortment of upper-level courses the individual student wished. All requirements, all patterns, all configurations were to be abandoned. And to be abandoned with them were the a priori definitions of the discipline implied by the requirements and configurations. The existing major, for example, by its insistence that each student spot his courses along a chronological continuum, clearly implied a definition of the study of English literature as a species of history, its subject matter a body of historical data, to be examined in terms of at least generally fixed relationships of priority and influence. Other axes of interest—esthetic, for example, or political—may be accommodated to the historical frame of reference, but they tend to remain at best peripheral, at worst positively digressive elements because they introduce occasions for uncertainty and disagreement of a different logical order than the historical uncertainties created by inadequate information. Moreover, the discipline was clearly differentiated from others, as the very concept of "department" implies. Plays are taught, but not theatre; language, but not linguistics. And furthermore, by fixing the course requirements and descriptions (and hence to a large extent their structure and syllabuses) in a rigid form quite independent of the individuals doing the teaching, the old program tacitly postulated a homogeneous or monistic view not only of the discipline but of higher education generally.

I take that view to be characteristic of most departments in most colleges, even quite recently. In part this unanimity had arisen because everybody did largely share the same assumptions about the nature and purpose of higher education—assumptions easily inculcated into a socially homogeneous student body and handily indicated by the term "liberal." Education was designed to help a man free himself from the particularities of his own situation, from the bonds of his private experience, by exposing him to a fixed body of accumulated human knowledge (The Classics) organized in terms of a relatively fixed and limited body of categories (The Liberal Tradition). A further assumption, the master assumption, was that despite one's obligation to exercise a constant benign scepticism toward all phenomena—but most particularly those peculiarly thrown up by the historical present—that scepticism, and the detachment it fed, would in the end lead everybody to much the same understanding, the same insight, the same truths. In practice, then, the effect of the liberal tradition is to insure a substantial measure of intellectual uniformity. And yet the rhetoric of the tradition, and hence the image graven in the minds of its followers, is ruggedly individualistic.

Such an authoritarian and monistic set of assumptions did, I judge, govern American higher education from, say, 1890 until very recently, and there were a great many members of the department of English at the University of Wisconsin during the years 1965–1970 who shared those assumptions. But there were a substantial number of others (mostly younger) who felt alien and uncomfortable, who organized life and knowledge according to many competing truths, each possessing at best a provisional and situational validity, and who therefore felt that all one could work for in a university program is the inculcation of certain intellectual habits (a constant suspicious scepticism?), mastery of some academic tools (the library, the computer, a language or two, rhetoric and logic), and familiarity with a common terminology in which initiates could communicate. This view, of course, encourages precisely that kind of active individualism—the application rather than the suppression of the peculiarities of one's own past—which the other view discourages. Paradoxically, it encourages communal effort, like the TAA, because if no one man has more than a partial grasp of a partial truth, only the combined insights of many men will offer a hope of getting a whole grasp on a whole set of truths. It also encourages precisely that constant concern with the here and now that the absolutist and idealistic view resists. It thereby encourages meddling in politics. And it was to a considerable extent on these grounds that the adherents of the other view, mostly older, fought against such encroachments of the new pluralism as the TAA or the proposition that a patterned major be replaced by a mere calculation of credits.

The struggle was all the keener because it had immediate practical as well as philosophical implications. The relativistic new idea, needless to say, now governs most English majors and even graduate students at Wisconsin. They are convinced that the function of their education is not to help them *know* themselves but to *find* themselves—*make* themselves, in order that they can then help make their society. This means that they naturally seek out those areas of study which speak most immediately and directly to them—in English, contemporary literature, especially contemporary American literature. Practically, this means that unless requirements dictate otherwise, five hundred students line up for the course in modern fiction and perhaps only five for the course in medieval narrative—a fact that entrains devastated faculty morale, endless budget and personnel problems (given the nature of the existing faculty and especially given the fact that these questions are to be decided largely by the men being affronted by contemporaneity in its various aspects), scheduling difficulties (since student enthusiasms, as we know to our sorrow, shift very rapidly these days), advising problems (since the graduate schools are even more conservative than the undergraduate schools). Most American universities, I suspect, have not yet worked out the executive apparatus necessary for a truly open intellectual marketplace. And yet the very concept of the multiversity—something for everybody, everybody for something—seems ultimately to drive in that direction, assisted by those social and economic factors which have since World War II admitted to academia people much more various in their backgrounds, much less purely white upper-middle-class professional than was the case before 1940. It may well be that much of the present turmoil in the universities only reflects their final effort to attain their distinctive shape.

If that is the case, though, the introduction of some further uncertainties opens up some rather startling possibilities. First, just at the moment when the intramural tensions in the University of Wisconsin English department were approaching their peak, higher education as a whole, but graduate education in particular, went over its celebrated cliff. In 1969, the academic market suddenly collapsed, and during the debate over the abolition of Freshman English, there was some public talk to the effect that by cutting back on funds for graduate support the department was only doing a kindness to unrecruited generations of students by encouraging them to avoid an overstocked field. There was also a certain amount of private muttering, especially among the young untenured professors, that the cutback in graduate enrollment thus being engineered was in fact a way to get rid of undesirable young faculty on the grounds that there was no longer anybody for them to teach. It was certainly my own feeling that the rancorous protest entered during the election for chairman of April 1970 owed some of its venom to the fears induced by a collapsing market, as the younger men faced the possibility of being turned out the following year or the year after into a system that could no longer use them—feelings all the more passionate in view of the way these same people had been courted only a few years earlier.

Worse yet, there were and are signs that the whole profession is in some danger of withering away. The visible causes here are legion— TV, drugs, rock music, freer love, the Whole Earth notion, radical politics. Whatever the specific causes, the fact is that, as one advocate of the counter-culture observed, "We don't read much anymore." Of course, that attitude threatens the whole university establishment. But even the students who do still read are threatening to leave English (and the traditional humanities generally) for what they call "the media" on the one hand (TV, film, drama) and the social sciences on the other—each proposing its own kind of engagement or commitment in place of the liberal detachment I have already asserted as the characteristic stance of English professors (and their colleagues in philosophy, foreign languages, cultural history, and so on). And teachers are attempting to follow. Within my discipline, the movement away from the traditional specialties is not yet a stampede, but a growing number of my associates are developing interdepartmental interests which no doubt reflect both genuine interest in escaping the apparently outmoded confines of the traditional approach and the desire to divide eggs among baskets. Three of these connections strike me as particularly interesting and revealing. One is to black studies, involving both the urge toward social relevance and perhaps also some expiatory compulsion. The other two are toward disciplines deeply enmeshed in technology—film-making and criticism, and linguistics—one adapting the traditional approaches to traditional esthetic and historical questions from the verbal to the cinematic medium, the other attempting to substitute for the uncertain probings of those traditional approaches a new quantitative assurance. But almost more interesting is the movement toward interdisciplinary approaches to knowledge in the humanities *in an institutional way* (the italics called for because scholars have been developing and using secondary competences in other fields on their own at least since Aristotle).

What is challenged here is the very idea of *department*, of a subsection of the university community—students, teachers, researchers—bound together by a common subject, a common heritage, a small number of common methodologies, a common technical language, a fairly limited and fairly well-defined set of common goals. It may be that the university as a whole, or at least the humanities section of it, will melt away because its present clientele wants some other kind of experience or is kept away by prolonged economic tribulation or because the funds from the legislature are withheld in order to punish dissent. But assuming that these catastrophes do not occur, I still must wonder how long the idea of the department can survive (knowing full well the tenacity with which even outmoded institutions can hang on to life). I am convinced that the concept fosters a great variety of intellectual sins—incest, simony, tyranny, redundancy, inefficiency, in some places a mindless reverence for the past, in others an equally mindless acceptance of the present. But weaknesses like these are apparently inherent in all institutions once they pass a certain point and it is other questions that lead me to wonder whether there will actually still be an English department at the University of Wisconsin in 1980. Or a history department, or a French department. (I have fewer doubts about the department of meat and animal science.) If they have disappeared, will their demise have been caused by internecine strife, or dried up funds, or desertion by students? Or will it have been because the multiversity has realized itself, has located the action on the frontiers between departments and disciplines in a more completely ad hoc, systems-oriented approach to teaching and learning, employing in a sustained and effective way the resources of technology for information-retrieval and communication? Or will the departments thrive, having rejected the turbulence of a thorough-paced commitment to relativism and pluralism, having recovered and reaffirmed the gracefulness and dignity of the older view with its idea of the university as a curatorial institution whose main function is to keep us in touch with our past? Will the convulsions that afflicted the Wisconsin English department from 1965 to 1970 prove to have been exemplary of a general convulsion in American society and American higher education or only the local anguish of a locally afflicted institutional organism? I do not pretend to prophesy, but I await further developments—from a distance —with some interest.

Notes

[1] My friend and colleague, Barton Friedman, has read the manuscript with an eye for positive errors. But any that remain are mine, not his, and any and all biases and tonal distortions are, of course, altogether my responsibility.

[2] Politically cynical colleagues insist that the committee was put together in such a way as to insure that no truly radical proposal would be offered.

PART THREE

TEACHING ASSISTANTS
AND STUDENTS

Students are responsible for a large portion of the attention given to academic governance, curriculum reform, and other aspects of the university crisis. Without the dramatic growth of student activism in the early sixties, many universities would have remained silent and would clearly not have begun to think seriously of academic reform. This is not to say that the student move-

271

ment has taken an active role in academic reform because for the most part political goals or a wide-ranging dissatisfaction with the "system" has been at the root of the movement. Nevertheless, students have caused a growth in the trend toward academic reform and have stimulated no small part of the over-all academic crisis. Wisconsin, as Shlomo Swirsky points out in his chapter, has a long tradition of student activism and has been one of the most militant campuses. As a barometer of student activism, it is an especially good example of a widespread phenomenon.

Chapters in this part deal with a number of aspects of student activism which have received only limited attention elsewhere. Problems of graduate students are considered in the chapter by Philip Altbach. Steven Zorn discusses the history and development of the Teaching Assistants Association, one of the first unions of graduate teaching assistants. The activism of graduate students at Wisconsin is an important aspect of what may well be a growing development. Judith Lyons and Morgan Lyons discuss the response of students to crisis and point out that substantial polarization often takes place during confrontations on campus. Moderate students, they point out, often side with militants when the university overtly represses demonstrations or other protest activities. Again, Wisconsin provides a particularly good example of the response to confrontation politics since it has been subjected both to militant tactics by student activists and to the presence of national guard troops in large numbers on a number of occasions. Finally, Robert Laufer and Sheila McVey discuss the question of generational conflict and the differences among student generations on campus. Their analysis points out that campus events have very substantially shaped the outlooks and socialization of the students involved in them. In this sense, campus violence has tended to radicalize students in conjunction with national and international events.

CHAPTER 14

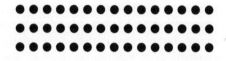

GRADUATE STUDENTS

Philip G. Altbach

Among the many forces involved in the changing situation of American higher education, the graduate student has been one of the least considered. Yet graduate students are deeply involved in the academic enterprise—traditionally as teachers of undergraduates (in the larger universities at least), as apprentice scholars, and as the source of prestige for many universities. They have also played an active role in recent changes. Graduate student unions have been organized on a number of campuses, and graduate students have at times been involved in political agitation.

This chapter describes the situation of graduate students in large American universities. The University of Wisconsin's Madison campus is the touchstone for this commentary both because of my personal knowledge of it and because this institution is rather typical of the twenty or so universities which produce a large proportion of doctorates. It is my purpose also to place the graduate student's situation in the context of American higher education, to stimulate thought on means of improving the lot of these students, and to focus attention on an increasingly important and volatile element of the American university.

If the demonstrably unenviable situations of many graduate students did not necessitate this chapter, then the new militancy and articulateness of graduate students and their centrality to the crisis of the university would demand it. For one thing, the graduate students on the Madison campus constitute an important element of the student community. The Teaching Assistants Association (TAA), now functioning for more than two years, has focused attention on graduate students and has in many respects made changes in their traditional role on the campus. Graduate students have also been organizing at the department level and have been seeking a role in academic policy making. Some academic departments at Wisconsin and other universities have included them in the decision-making processes. An even larger number of departments have recognized their associations on an advisory basis.

Graduate students are important to the university for a number of reasons. From their ranks come virtually all academic staff members, a large proportion of research workers in industry, government, and the universities, and many secondary school administrators and teachers. In many large universities—particularly state-run institutions—graduate students do a substantial share of the undergraduate teaching. At Wisconsin, for example, teaching assistants perform 56 per cent of all undergraduate instruction and, in the College of Letters and Sciences, probably a higher proportion. Teaching assistants provide 68 per cent of freshman and sophomore instruction. Graduate students also provide the research manpower without which many university projects could not function.

American universities are marked by their inability or unwillingness to deal with key problems until they are of crisis proportions, and the University of Wisconsin is no exception to this rule. In response to the crisis generated by student protest, countless studies of undergraduate attitudes were published, libraries of books appeared on reform of the curriculum, and a score of experimental colleges were begun at the undergraduate level. As long as no one was concerned about defense-related research projects on campus, they were allowed to continue without question. Students were not added to various academic committees until the 1964 Berkeley student revolt. At Wisconsin, it took the Dow crises and the Wisconsin Student Association's "student power" bill to push the institution toward granting student participation in academic governance. It seems that graduate students, too, will no longer remain silent, and that therefore they will be of growing importance to university policy makers.

While graduate students are part of what has been called the crisis of the American university, their situation also reflects broader academic problems. The golden age of American higher education, in terms of funds and promising job opportunities, seems to be at an end. The employment situation for new Ph.D.s is indeed serious and places great

stress on graduate students. This crisis may in the long run have implications for political activism and general discontent. At the same time,
financial conditions on the campus are growing more difficult. Student
financial aids have been cut—at Wisconsin the federally supported work-
study program was cut by 45 per cent in 1969–1970—and at the same
time tuition costs continue to rise. There are fewer fellowships and it is
more difficult to obtain funds for doctoral research. The university is
caught in a serious financial squeeze which affects students directly and
immediately. It is painful enough for a professor to have his research
budget cut or to receive a lower than expected salary increase. It is quite
another matter for a graduate student to lose his sole means of livelihood.

The national economic situation is of critical importance, but there
are many stresses inherent in the academic setting itself. For the sake of
dramatic impact, a short listing of those conditions of graduate student
life which cause friction, disaffection, and general unhappiness is included here. The list is by no means exhaustive, nor is it based on any
scientific sampling of student opinion. (1) Graduate students are adults
in every sense of the term but are often treated like children by their
universities. (2) Graduate students are often woefully exploited by individual professors, departments, or universities in terms of inadequate
remuneration for work performed, work loads which almost preclude
prompt completion of academic work, or occasional plagiarism of original
work by senior professors. (3) Graduate students are the subjects of
often arbitrary treatment by professors, departments, or institutions and
have few means of resisting such treatment. (4) Graduate students are
often almost totally dependent on their professors or departments for
livelihood, for certification as scholars, and possibly for future academic
positions. (5) The role of a graduate student as a teaching or research
colleague with a senior professor is often ambivalent.

This situation of substantial powerlessness should not obscure a
number of positive factors associated with graduate student life. A strong
subculture often provides support. Many graduate students do have the
leisure to pursue their studies or their intellectual interests without much
interference. And for some, graduate student existence forestalls entry
into the hard, cruel worlds of academe or industry. Conditions differ
greatly from institution to institution as well, and in some universities
graduate students are substantially better off than in others.

Graduate students are in the university to earn advanced degrees;
their other roles are, or should be, subsidiary to this primary task. Yet,
a great deal of time and attention is taken up with such activities as part-
time work and department politics. The graduate student is involved in
taking courses and seminars, sitting for examinations, writing research

papers, and fulfilling the other obligations of his department. He is, after passing required preliminary examinations, finally involved in writing a doctoral dissertation. The choice of a dissertation advisor and topic is a particularly important one for arts and sciences students, many of whom will be heading for academic careers. The advisor is often crucial in securing a first academic job and of course in seeing the student through the completion of his doctorate.

There is a curious dichotomy in graduate student academic life. Grades count for fellowships and prizes as well as for the completion of the academic program. Letters of recommendation are important, too, and it is often crucial to impress particular professors for one reason or another. At the same time, professors often insist that they want to be friendly and low-pressured with their students. There is an effort to separate undergraduate from graduate study by insisting on closer and more informal relations with graduate students, although in many large graduate departments this is more myth than reality. But even this familiarity, where it exists, is often difficult for the student, since evaluation is taking place all the time in the American academic system, and the student is pitted against his peers in his department and ultimately in the job market.

The feeling of powerlessness, a constant in the graduate student syndrome, is especially keen in his relationships with senior faculty. Their constant judgments of his course work, particularly in seminar or research situations, and their decisions about his doctoral dissertation serve to remind him daily of his dependence on their opinions, goodwill, and so forth. Even when there is confidence in the criteria of judgment and in the responsibility felt by the professors involved, the student still feels great anxiety as he enters these academic relationships. Students often spend as much time debating the political or methodological biases of the professors as they do in more intellectual tasks.

Academic politics, too, may enter into the evaluation process. The views of a student toward, for example, survey methods versus historical orientations in a field like sociology might make a difference in his acceptance by the dominant forces in his department, in his chances for success, and ultimately in his prospects for a job. While most academic decisions are made on the basis of merit, the vagaries of the decision-making process and other variables in the situation cause substantial frustration and strain. And it is not unknown for a graduate student to quit or be forced out of academic programs because of disagreements with professors or general nonconformity unrelated to his intellectual merit.

One of the major complaints of undergraduates has been the

growing bureaucracy and depersonalization of the universities. They complain that they have little contact with faculty members and feel they are only numbers in a computer. Graduate students encounter many of the same conditions, but at the same time they are more directly involved with faculty members. In large graduate departments—some departments at Wisconsin, such as history, English, and mathematics, have five hundred or more students working on advanced degrees—there is little direct contact with senior staff before passing preliminary examinations and sometimes afterward as well. Graduate students must wait in the same interminable lines as undergraduates at registration and they must, at least in the larger departments, meet set requirements in terms of courses and examinations. As a result, many graduate students feel that their academic program is beyond their control and may not be suited to their interests. If bureaucratically set academic requirements are justified at any level in higher education, they are certainly not justified in the case of advanced students.

It is very difficult to separate the roles of graduate student as student and graduate student as employee. This ambiguity and conflict has led to a dramatic mobilization of graduate students in the seventies. At Wisconsin, 59 per cent of the 8,900 graduate students on campus receive some sort of financial aid from the university, and 30 per cent (or almost 3,000 students) are teaching, research, or project assistants; 1,440 have teaching assistant appointments. The problem of student as employe is therefore of critical importance to a large number of graduate students.

The spring, 1970, TAA strike at the University of Wisconsin improved the situation of the teaching assistant, and conditions at Wisconsin are now somewhat better in terms of work hours, evaluation, and other aspects than those at comparable universities. Nevertheless, the basic ambiguity of the teaching assistant's position remains, and it is this situation with which I am concerned here. The student/employee often works for and studies under the same professor, and even with a TAA contract which specifies to some extent working conditions and other matters, the individual teaching assistant must function in this potentially difficult situation. Many teaching assistants have substantial teaching responsibilities and may in fact have more day-to-day contact with undergraduate students than senior professors. They are often highly committed to the university and to academic life (this is particularly true in the traditional arts and sciences departments), but at the same time they are exploited by the university (at Wisconsin, teaching assistants are paid about $3,600 per academic year for an average twenty-hour work week). They feel a strong conflict between their roles as teachers of and sometimes advisors to undergraduate students and their responsibilities to their academic programs. As a result, many teaching assistants often take longer than the average amount of time to finish their degrees. Teaching assistants are at a particular disadvantage under such new programs as the Ford Foundation's assistance to graduate departments, which stipulates that students must finish their degrees in a set period of time. In addition to receiving fairly low wages for teaching, the teaching assistant often has very little control over what he teaches, the grades given out in his course, and his general working conditions. Yet, it is fairly clear that many large state universities would find it difficult to function without their teaching assistants.

The natural sciences and, to an extent, the social sciences make use of research assistants, almost always graduate students, whose position is also difficult. The student typically works on a research project directed by a professor; his work, however brilliant, is often unrewarded. He is often pressed to write his doctoral dissertation on the basis of his research assistantship and, regardless of whether he is seriously interested in the project, he must often accept. In many departments, research positions are used mainly as a means of financing graduate education, and the work required is minimal or directly related to the interests of the graduate student. However, there are many complaints about the exploitation of research assistants by both professors and departments, and despite the fact that many of the stories are probably exaggerated, there is no doubt a grain of truth in a number of them. The most blatant stories concern "stealing" of research by the senior professors. Some research assistants are overworked by professors or departments. Regardless of the reality of specific instances, students are convinced that they are in a very vulnerable position and that they are likely to be misused by senior academic staff. Reaction to exploitation ranges from resignation ("it's only a temporary situation"), in most cases, to active revolt against the individuals and the academic system that permit these excesses.

Many graduate students have largely good experiences during their careers. Many, particularly at the most prestigious universities, are supported by fellowship funds from the university, the government, or private foundations. Those who have selected a sympathetic professor or a congenial department are not exploited and are able to finish their academic programs with minimum delay and frustration. But the fact remains that there is a great deal of ambiguity, arbitrariness, and injustice in American graduate education. That the system has functioned reasonably well so far is more a tribute to the adaptability of the individuals involved in it, both professors and students, than to its inherent merits.

Graduate students exist not only in an academic milieu but also in the more informal aspects of the university and its community. This is perhaps especially true at universities like Wisconsin, where nine thousand graduate students constitute a large community and subculture of their own, linked to the broader student culture but in many ways separate from it. The graduate student community is extremely difficult to describe since it is so diverse, encompassing both the most avant-garde political and cultural activists and doctoral candidates in educational administration or agriculture with solidly middle-class aspirations. Nevertheless, it is important to devote some attention to this subculture and its patterns of life within the community.

Just as graduate students are often in a difficult, perhaps somewhat unnatural position with regard to their academic status, their situation in society is also somewhat abnormal. Although most graduate students come from middle-class backgrounds, their standard of living is often low, and many fall below the official poverty level. Yet, graduate students are only temporarily poor. They look at the world through the eyes of the middle class, although they have neither its financial resources nor its responsibilities. It may be that graduate students are among the last Americans to observe the Protestant ethic in that they forego income and status now with the expectation that they will earn them later. Without the usual accoutrements of the middle class—home mortgages, car payments, and the like—graduate students are perhaps freer and also more alienated from the American consumer society than are their nonstudent peers.

A large proportion of their social interactions probably involve other graduate students, especially for those in student housing complexes. Yet, despite the common experiences of graduate students in a large university, they generally have no strong sense of community. Differences in discipline, professional orientation, or background often prevent the emergence of a pervasive subculture. The differences among the kinds of students attracted to such diverse fields as sociology, English, business, or physics are great enough to prevent the emergence of a community.

However, an articulate and highly visible minority of graduate students (largely in the humanities and social sciences) has joined the underground student subculture in the sense that there is an increasing amount of social experimentation, particularly among unmarried students or couples without children. This experimentation, which includes communes and other living arrangements, may have some effect on later social patterns, although this is by no means clear. Graduate students are, in a sense, part of the youth culture, and there is certainly widespread use of marijuana and similar drugs. Nevertheless, many graduate students are too professionally committed, too much a part of an earlier period of campus culture, or too involved with family life to participate fully.

Apparently, however, the differences between graduate and undergraduate students in terms of aspirations, age, and educational situation have been partially overcome in pursuit of common cultural and political goals. The general impact of the counter-culture has probably decreased the professional commitment and goal orientation of many of these graduate students. In part, this group is composed of young men who would not have gone on for advanced degrees if selective service policies had been different. Changes in these policies, combined with a contraction of graduate enrollments in many universities including Wisconsin, changed this situation somewhat. In addition, the popularity of careers in private business has declined, and many young people have gone on for advanced degrees in social work, teaching, or similar service areas. Thus, the graduate student population in Madison has grown substantially (from 4,108 in 1960 to 8,777 in 1970), and its orientation has changed as well. While statistics are unavailable, it is likely that the graduate student population became younger and considerably more radical in the 1960s.

Militant political activism among graduate students is a relatively recent phenomenon. Historically, graduate students have provided much of the intellectual sustenance to activist politics and to radical social thought in the United States. Graduate students, largely in the social sciences and history, were crucial to many of the radical intellectual journals which appeared in the post–World War II period. They were also active in the various intellectually oriented radical sects which survived, although in attenuated form, the McCarthy period of the 1950s. Without ideologically sophisticated graduate students, mostly in the social sciences, it is possible that the radical movement would have ceased to exist at that time.

Radical graduate students also played a key role in laying the foundations for the New Left of the 1960s. They have been especially active in radical journalism: *New University Thought,* founded by graduate students at Chicago, *Studies on the Left,* from Wisconsin, and *Root and Branch,* from Berkeley, emerged at the end of the apathetic fifties and raised many of the issues which became important to the New Left. Perhaps most important, their shift away from the sectarian politics of the earlier period of American radicalism brought many of the accepted notions of radical politics into question. The hold of the Communist Party on the radical movement was broken in part because of the continuing criticism of the leftist journals. Questions concerning the nature of the cold war, the racial crisis, and other issues were also raised. More recently, *Radical America, Viet Report* and its successor *Leviathan,* and a new quarterly, *Socialist Revolution,* reflect the radical but intellectually oriented politics of graduate students and some young faculty.

Radical graduate students helped to make the work of men like C. Wright Mills popular on American campuses in the late 1950s and provided a market for radical social analyses. Through their work as teaching assistants in the social sciences as well as through their political writing, radical graduate students involved themselves in popularizing social protest literature on the campuses. In many cases, older graduate students provided a link between the old left and the new trends in campus activism. A number of the founders of Students for a Democratic Society were graduate students who reflected a synthesis between the radical critiques of the old left and newer styles of social protest and analysis. Significantly, as the student movement has become more militant and disenchanted with more intellectual styles of social protest, fewer graduate students have been involved in it, and the movement's ties to older radicals have weakened.

Wisconsin provides an interesting case study in the relationship of graduate students to the movement at large. During the dark days of the 1950s, the Madison campus was one of few places where a viable radical movement continued to exist. In part due to the civil libertarian stand of the university administration but also because of a small group of radical professors who provided intellectual sustenance to their graduate students, Madison maintained a radical community throughout this period. The last chapter of the Communist Labor Youth League in the mid-1950s, for example, was at the University of Wisconsin. *Studies on the Left,* a key radical intellectual journal, was founded in 1959 by Wisconsin graduate students, mainly disciples of William Appleman Williams in the history department. *Sanity,* a student-run magazine associated with the left wing of the peace movement, operated from Madison in the early 1960s. During this period, political activism was limited to a few hundred on a campus of at least twenty thousand students. And the activism itself was almost exclusively of a moderate sort, focusing on the publication of journals and other educational efforts.

The more recent period has seen a change in the nature of student activism at the University of Wisconsin, as on other campuses. Yet, with some exceptions, graduate students have not been active in large numbers in the more militant activist groups. Some key student leaders have been graduate students, however, and there has been some shift toward more militant politics. The more intellectual strain in Wisconsin radicalism continues, however, in journals like *Radical America,* edited by Madison graduate students in history, and in various literary and dramatic efforts. The local underground press also flourishes in part with the assistance of graduate students.

The role played by graduate students in campus unrest has been curious and reflects the orientations mentioned earlier. Graduate students, particularly the radical minority among them, are alienated from the social and economic system, and many are well versed in radical theory. They are, however, often hooked into the academic system and many graduate students are unwilling to risk arrest by police or expulsion from the university for their political activities. They often play key tactical and ideological roles in campus crises (although this is probably decreasingly true as protests become more militant and, in the eyes of many older radicals, more irresponsible). Many of the members of the Berkeley Free Speech Movement were graduate students. Similarly, graduate students were active at Columbia, at Harvard in 1969, and in the various Wisconsin struggles of the past few years. In a number of these events, graduate students helped to turn at least some of the attention of the activists to university-related issues.

The organization of the TAA and similar unions is clearly the most important and, to academic administrators, threatening aspect of the new graduate student militancy. At Wisconsin the TAA has been most successful in those departments where conditions are the worst and which, at the same time, enroll the most liberal and radical students. Such departments as English, sociology, and history are among the strongest supporters of the TAA. These departments use large numbers of teaching assistants in their beginning undergraduate courses. They have a rather highly bureaucratized graduate program, and there is relatively little teacher-student contact. It is significant that the TAA has emphasized both its demands for better conditions and more job security for its members and its commitment to student involvement in academic planning and broader reforms. On the basis of this reform program, substantial undergraduate student support was available during the TAA strike in 1970.

The Wisconsin TAA, after a year of rather intensive organization, asked the university administration for recognition as the sole bargaining agent for teaching assistants on campus. Somewhat to the surprise of many observers—and most faculty members—the university agreed to hold a collective bargaining election which the TAA won. During negotiations the TAA presented a series of demands covering such issues as job security, working conditions, academic planning, and some restructuring of decision-making on the department level. After the university and the TAA bargained without result for almost six months, the TAA called a strike during the 1970 spring semester. The strike lasted almost three weeks and was fairly successful during its initial phases in shutting down classes in the College of Letters and Science. Other parts of the university, such as the schools of engineering and agriculture, were basically unaffected. During the early stages of the strike, which was marked throughout by nonviolence and an impressive amount of self-discipline by the TAA and its undergraduate supporters, the university offered a compromise proposal which made some concessions to TAA demands without accepting most of them. Because the TAA began to lose support for the strike, due to vacations and impending mid-term examinations, it accepted this compromise in the third week of the strike, and this formed the basis of a subsequent contract which was approved by both the TAA and the university. Although both sides only reluctantly agreed to the contract, it marked a dramatic departure from the traditional graduate student-university relationship.

The provisions of the contract include: a three-year guarantee of support for a teaching assistant after his initial appointment; agreement concerning such aspects of working conditions as hours of class time, number of students in sections, and office facilities; and a delineation of those issues open to bargaining, such as disputes over working conditions. The reaction of most university departments has been negative, and it is clear that most faculty members oppose both the contract and the TAA. Nevertheless, the contract is in force and has caused some changes in the tenor of department-student relationships. Many departments have become substantially more bureaucratic in their relations with students and a few have involved students in some levels of decision making. On the surface, the gain for those graduate students holding teaching assistantships has been substantial, although the long-term results are unclear as faculty members solidify their anti-TAA attitudes. Some departments plan to eliminate the teaching assistant system altogether.

The TAA finds itself in a difficult situation. A new contract has not been signed, and many teaching assistants are sceptical of the TAA's power. Some of its support among its own constituency has weakened— and it should be noted that only a little more than half of the teaching assistants held TAA membership when the group was most powerful. The faculty has grown more intransigent as TAA grievance procedures, sometimes concerning small matters, have been used against faculty members. Despite the TAA's problems, the implications of the contract and the existence of a viable, reasonably sophisticated, and successful union of graduate students are not yet fully apparent. The whole concept of unionism in academic relationships is a new one and may well have wider implications when other segments of the university community, notably the faculty, begin to organize. In addition, TAA action cannot but cause repercussions in the academic relations between the faculty and graduate students. Relationships may become more bureaucratized and formal but this change might be an improvement over the arbitrariness described earlier. It is also likely that graduate students will become more politically conscious on other levels as well. The success of the TAA at the University of Wisconsin is by no means assured, although an important step has been taken. It seems almost inevitable that such organizational efforts will be repeated in other American universities soon and that a major national movement is developing.

The growth of departmental associations at Wisconsin and other institutions is also an important new development on the American campus. Less successful than the TAA, these efforts have produced serious conflicts in some departments, have politicized some graduate students, and have on occasion changed conditions. Most efforts at organizing student groups in academic departments at Wisconsin failed after a short period of initial success in 1969. Divisions in opinion among the students in the departments, unwillingness to take substantial risks, apathy, and tremendous pressure from faculty members proved too much for most. The organizing was confined largely to those departments in which students were most vocal about their dissatisfaction with the state of academic affairs—English, history, sociology, political science were most affected, although others were involved as well.

These efforts at departmental organizing involved some undergraduates but were mainly initiated by graduate students. Despite their lack of any notable long-term success, these attempts indicate that at least some graduate students are willing to involve themselves in department affairs in an effort to obtain a role in decision making and a sense of participation. Although the leadership for some of these associations was in the hands of radical graduate students, most of the demands were related largely to department affairs and had little direct political content. Many departments responded to these pressures not by permitting students a direct role in decision making but by undertaking some reforms in various aspects of academic life. For example, some departments now allow student representatives to attend and speak at departmental faculty meetings. Some have modified preliminary examinations or relaxed foreign language requirements.

While most of the attention of these new organizations has been directed toward the departmental level or in the direction of specific improvements in working conditions for graduate students, there has been some broader activism by graduate students. Student concern for the general role of the university in American society has become vocal in recent years. The campaigns against ROTC, against the existence of various military-related research facilities, and other links between the universities and the Establishment are examples of this concern. Radical graduate students have provided much of the research which has formed the basis of these campaigns. The role of the university in its immediate community has also become an issue, and this concern has brought about demands for open enrollments, university participation in day care facilities, medical programs, and other community services.

The growing diversity of graduate student political interests is reflected in another recently formed organization, the New University Conference. Founded in 1968 largely by graduate students and younger faculty members associated with the New Left, the NUC has chapters in most major universities and reflects a sophisticated version of New Left politics. The NUC sees the university as an agent of the American "ruling class" and as a basically counterrevolutionary institution. Attacks on the university, by students or militant faculty members, are therefore justified. The NUC's major demands involve the disengagement of the university from the power structures of American society, although support has been given to various programs for academic reform as well. The basic thrust of the NUC, which calls itself an organization of socialist graduate students and younger faculty, has been primarily political. It has tried, usually without success, to defend younger faculty members fired from academic posts for political reasons.

The NUC at Wisconsin has been notably unsuccessful in organizing a viable group. In part because of its super-militant rhetoric and its aloofness from "reformist" campus issues, the NUC has been able to attract only highly committed radicals who are alienated from the academic system. It has had almost no success among younger faculty members. The NUC has been more successful in other universities, where it has been able to build an organization concerned with broader issues while retaining its radical perspective. The NUC indicates another trend on the campus, and it has served as a kind of alumni organization for ex-SDS members. Given effective organization and a somewhat broader approach, the NUC might become a more important force on campus.

The politics of graduate students have developed in both scope and militancy in the past several years. Although there are still some important distinctions between the movement and the political activism characteristic of graduate students, the expansion of the student movement has substantially affected the graduate schools.

Successful graduate students become young faculty members, and although their salaries jump, young faculty retain many of the values and opinions and work under some of the same pressures they had as graduate students. At many universities there is also a fairly close relationship between at least some advanced graduate students and some younger faculty members. Thus, it is important to consider the junior faculty in any discussion of graduate students. The new militancy of graduate students and their skills in political organization will probably have an effect on faculty members in the near future in terms of opposition to academic administrations, organization of faculty unions, and general anti-Establishment activity.

It has been said that today's younger faculty are a new breed. In the more prestigious universities, there is a grain of truth to that statement, although the small amount of research available indicates that while younger faculty may be somewhat more liberal than their older colleagues, they generally accept the norms and values of the universities. A small group, however, does constitute a new breed, and these individuals are often important in the academic equation. Many were involved in activism as students and are profoundly critical of many aspects of the multiversity. Many consciously reject the traditional academic norms of research and publication and thus have very little in common with their senior colleagues. They are, indeed, a threat to the entrenched values of academe.

Young faculty members in major universities are not in an enviable position. Their salaries, while better than in years past, are not high, and they are under tremendous pressure to publish while at the same time preparing courses and seminars. Expecting after the completion of the Ph.D. to enter the community of scholars and be relieved of some of the pressures they felt as graduate students, the younger faculty must instead submit to great pressure to "make it" in the academic system of the large universities. They are encouraged to be loyal to their departments but at the same time do not usually have much power in academic decision making.

It is not surprising that many younger faculty members are critical of various aspects of the university and do not feel themselves truly a part of the institutions in which they teach. This state of affairs, of course, greatly increases the likelihood that young, nontenured faculty members will play some dissident role on the campus. The fact that a number of younger faculty members, particularly in the social sciences, are radical in their political views is also important. This means that students, particularly graduate students, will be exposed to radical positions on various issues by their professors. Even when radicals on the faculty do not approve of a particular demonstration or sit-in, they generally take a radical position and in this sense legitimate the viewpoint.

It is also true that younger faculty members are often able to communicate effectively with students, generally tend to be more aware of trends among students, and are therefore a crucial element in any crisis situation.

It is difficult to predict the future for Wisconsin or other universities. The fiscal crisis in education has most dramatically affected the graduate schools. And while many graduate students are alienated from middle-class society and from academe in a period of cutbacks, it is by no means clear in what direction alienation will move them. For the first time, however, they have organized an articulate organization and have taken a major interest in academic affairs. Faculty members, under pressure from many sides, have often listened and in a few instances have responded constructively. Within a generally pessimistic situation lies the possibility of change.

CHAPTER 15

●●●●●●●●●●●●●●
●●●●●●●●●●●●●●●
●●●●●●●●●●●●●●

UNIONS ON CAMPUS

Steven Zorn

●●●●●●●●●●●●●●
●●●●●●●●●●●●●●
●●●●●●●●●●●●●●

There are at least two ways to look at a university. One is to see it as an intellectually oriented institution, a place where knowledge is pursued for its own sake and where the best of culture is transmitted from one generation to another. The other is to see it as an institution performing a set of functions that contribute to the maintenance of the overall stability of society—functions like the advancement of technology through research, the supplying of trained personnel for the economy, and the provision of extended child-care facilities to avoid overcrowding in the labor market. Along with the first of these two views goes a set of attitudes generally recognized as "professionalism," or academic freedom, the idea that university staff members are in fact functioning as free, independent professionals, limited only by their own concepts of service to their clients (students) and by the collective judgment of their peers (colleagues in their discipline). Along with the second goes a set of attitudes that would be equally appropriate in any other large institutional or industrial setting—the idea of a distinction between workers and managers, the acceptance on the part of workers of collective action as a valid means of dealing with problems.

There can be little doubt that the situation at most large American universities conforms more closely to the second model. Leading college administrators have described the multiversity as essentially a service institution, providing certain functions that the society needs.[1] The real customers of the university are not the students who pass through the classrooms, but rather the industries and government agencies for whom the university produces both research findings and trained, certified, skilled personnel. In this sense, the university is a basic industry, part of the infrastructure of the American economy, as basic and necessary as a transportation network or a dependable supply of energy.

If one accepts the view of the university as industry, it is not difficult to understand why, in the past few years, many of those within the industry have begun to question the traditional view of the university as a place for disinterested scholarly inquiry. Both workers and students have questioned the adequacy of the professionalist, academic ethic. One result of this questioning has been the emergence, at Wisconsin and elsewhere, of new labor unions, involving teaching assistants and, in some cases, untenured faculty. Some of these unions have restricted their activities to seeking redistribution of some of the material benefits available within the higher education industry; others have raised more basic questions about the nature of the university itself, and have sought not only to gain more benefits for their members, but also to limit the degree to which the customers—government and industry—can control the production process. The following essay attempts to describe briefly the condition of one of those groups of campus workers—teaching assistants— and to discuss the process by which collective action by those workers, in the form of labor-union activity, came about.

Problems Faced by Teaching Assistants

As college enrollments increased rapidly in the 1950s and 1960s, an increasing share of the teaching that was required came to be done by teaching assistants. For example, between 1953 and 1965, total U.S. undergraduate enrollment increased by 154 per cent.[2] During the same period, the number of faculty members with the rank of instructor or above increased by 102 per cent, while the number of junior staff, primarily teaching assistants, increased by 145 per cent, from 27,000 to 65,000. Teaching assistants have been concentrated at relatively few institutions—the same institutions that most clearly demonstrate the industry-like aspects of higher education. In 1963, for example, 87 per cent of all teaching assistants were in large universities[3] employing 100 or more TAs. In that same year, the number of TAs in large publicly-supported institutions averaged nearly 450.

In the early 1950s, assistantships represented almost half of all graduate student support; by the mid-sixties the influx of scientific research funds into the universities had made teaching-assistant appointments considerably less prized. In natural sciences, appointments declined from 40 to 32 per cent of the total graduate stipends between 1953 and 1965. Similar declines occurred in other academic areas—even in the humanities.[4] While the dollar value of teaching assistantships often matched or even exceeded research and fellowship stipends, the work required for the money was considerably more taxing and often produced a major delay in academic progress. The median work load, according to a U.S. Office of Education survey in 1965, was more than twenty hours per week, with over 20 per cent of all TAs working more than thirty hours per week.[5] The assistant's work on his own studies is not included in these figures. Work as a teaching assistant (particularly if the graduate student is at all concerned with doing something more than showing up in the classroom on time and merely running through the syllabus material) has been shown to have a direct impact on the length of time needed to earn the Ph.D.[6] Given these problems and the widespread recognition of the modern university's industrial nature, it is not surprising that at least some teaching assistants have begun to meet the inadequacies of their job situation through collective action. The direction in which that collective action leads can perhaps best be seen by looking in some detail at the situation of the teaching assistants at Wisconsin, as their condition is roughly comparable to that of assistants at other large public universities.

The teaching-assistant work force at Wisconsin grew from 624 in 1955 to 1170 in 1965 and to 1650 by 1969. Although the university administration repeatedly cited statistics showing Wisconsin assistants to be among the highest paid in the Big Ten, these statistics were misleading. Much of the "salary" included by the university in its widely publicized $5500 figure consisted of the out-of-state tuition remission granted to all teaching assistants; and, in fact, to most graduate students. Admittedly a fringe benefit of sorts to students from out of state, the remission certainly could not be considered part of the earnings of a teaching assistant who was a Wisconsin resident. Also, the $5500 publicity figure was based on an assumed work load of one-half time. In fact, the average assistant worked one-third time or less and so received a gross salary of approximately $2500 per year, out of which he still had to return the five-hundred-dollar in-state tuition charge.

Working conditions were little better. In many departments, teaching assistants were forced to share desk and office space with far more of their fellows than the facilities could comfortably accommodate;

in the speech department, for example, sixty assistants were assigned to an office with desk space for fifteen. While some science departments provided substantial desk space and office supplies not only for their teaching assistants, but for all sponsored graduate students, other departments, particularly in the humanities, offered only the most minimal and inconvenient working conditions. Office supplies (for example, stencils and paper for preparing course materials) were often unavailable; there were few facilities for private consultation with students. In general, assistants recognized a vast disparity between the conditions under which they worked and those enjoyed by the full-time faculty.

The lack of any fair, available, and impartial grievance procedures was another major element in the dissatisfaction of Wisconsin teaching assistants. Prior to 1968, an assistant with any sort of complaint about overwork, unfair treatment of himself or of undergraduates by the faculty member in charge of his course, or dismissal (or "failure to renew" his appointment) had only informal, random access to departmental administrators, with no authoritative channels for resolving his grievance. With the adoption of Faculty Document 10D in 1968, the administration attempted to provide the appearance, if not the substance, of a grievance procedure by setting up a system for hearing complaints, leading ultimately to decision by a faculty tribunal. Predictably, teaching assistants saw this as little improvement over the existing informal procedures, since in either event the final judge remained the faculty.

Although administration and faculty discussion (as, for example, in the catalogue descriptions of teaching assistantships) stressed the role of the assistant as an apprentice teacher, in fact TAs were given relatively little guidance in conducting their classes or in general questions of how to teach. The faculty's own committee to study the teaching assistant system in 1967–1968 found that at least 40 per cent received no help at all from their departments in preparing for teaching. In many other departments, the help that was provided consisted of no more than one afternoon of discussion at the beginning of the fall term. This lack was seen as a particularly severe handicap by assistants in departments such as mathematics or English where the teaching assistant was the sole instructor for a class, not merely a discussion leader in a lecture course.

Finally, many assistants resented their lack of voice in educational policy decisions at the course and department levels. In many courses, the syllabus was determined by committees of senior faculty, few of whom had any contact with students actually enrolled in the course. Even in areas like English composition, where there was little reason for a rigid syllabus, since one course does not lead into another in the same way, perhaps, that introductory language or math courses do, the assistants who actually taught the sections had no freedom. And the broader concept that became the Teaching Assistants Association "educational planning" proposal—namely, that course planning should be a cooperative effort, involving both students and teachers in the decision-making process—was unheard of.

One possible response to these conditions is for the individual assistant, or perhaps a small group of teaching assistants, to take ad hoc action responding to a particular situation rather than working for structural changes in the system as a whole. For example, an assistant might protest to the faculty member responsible for the course and that may end the issue. Another tactic that appeared at Wisconsin and at numerous other schools in the early and mid-sixties was the emergence of departmental graduate student groups to act on particular problems, like mobilizing support for demonstrations against Dow Chemical recruiters in 1967 or supporting the demands made by black students in 1969. These department organizations also acted on matters of concern only to their own members—for example, the reform of preliminary exam requirements for Ph.D. candidates, department financial aid policies, and so on. In only one or two cases, however, were the organizations able to survive in any meaningful sense between periods of crisit; at the university-wide level, and in almost all departments, there was no continuing presence, no counterforce to that of the administration.

Much of the general dissatisfaction over educational issues has been channeled into educational reform movements. At virtually every large university in the country there has been, in the past decade, a profusion of student-faculty committees to deal with virtually every aspect of higher education. By this time, it should be unnecessary to document in detail the relative lack of success achieved by these efforts—that is, success measured as substantive changes in curriculum content, or in a shift of decision-making power.[7] Certainly at Wisconsin, despite many student-assistant-faculty committees, there has been only a very slow change in the most irksome aspects of the educational program—the heavy load of degree requirements for undergraduates and the relatively rigid and inflexible course syllabuses. Beyond the lack of substantive change, there has been, as the sharp faculty response to the possibility of student and teaching assistant involvement in course planning has shown, no fundamental change in the desire of those who presently control those aspects of the industry to share that control. While educational reform efforts are likely to continue, the Wisconsin experience certainly indicates that, to date, they have been more a device for cooptation of students and teaching assistants and for providing the appearance of change than for securing its reality.

A third possible response to unsatisfactory conditions has been the formation of unions devoted primarily to bread and butter issues. This pattern was followed at Berkeley, where the teaching assistants' union that arose from the Free Speech Movement demonstrations of 1964–1965 rapidly became very like a traditional labor union, concerned primarily with wages, hours, and working conditions (the last taken in the narrow sense of physical work surroundings, grievance procedures, and so on). Since its formation, the Berkeley union has limited its activities largely to such matters as criteria for appointment of assistants, standardization of work loads among departments, and installation of such amenities as telephones and typewriters in teaching assistant offices. One analysis of the Berkeley situation has concluded that the continued control of the union by the bread and butter faction demonstrates the essentially professional orientation of a majority of assistants, or the concern for acquiring what they see to be the proper perquisites of their quasifaculty status within the existing educational system, rather than producing major changes in the overall nature of that system.[8]

From the point of view of those who have been active in the Wisconsin TAA, this concern for economic and status issues is likely, as in the case of Berkeley and similarly oriented unions at City University of New York and elsewhere, to make the initial organizing task relatively easy because large numbers of assistants will probably willingly act collectively for economic benefits without engaging in the long and often agonizing process of working out a position on more political issues. However, in the end, bread and butter issues may fail to produce significant changes in the allocation of power within the multiversity.

The fourth potential model for response to the unsatisfactory situation of teaching assistants at the large universities is the one taken by the TAA. This model involves at least four distinct elements: a concern for economic issues; a focus on questions of control, or the allocation of decision-making authority; a concern for the interrelation between specific teaching-assistant issues and broader political issues within the higher education industry; and, finally, a concentration on questions of internal union democracy and power-sharing.

The TAA approach to bread and butter issues is that economic benefits are something to be won from the employer, simply because the employer has the funds available to pay for them and because the benefits are those any worker feels entitled to. For example, the union's economic demands concentrated on such areas of major expense as health insurance, job security, and higher work loads (with corresponding pay increases). Although the union has made extensive analyses of the inadequacies of physical work surroundings, these issues were, for the most part, less important to the TAA membership than the large economic package. The status conferred by more office space and more telephones, while an issue for some assistants in bargaining at the department level, has not been the focus of attention. A possible exception was the insistence of TAA departmental units on the elimination of some faculty perquisites (for example, elevator keys), but this demand was in the context of a concerted attack on faculty power per se; they were not trying to gain faculty status for teaching assistants. (In the case of the elevator keys, the TAA affiliate demanded that all elevators be open to the public—students as well as assistants and faculty.)

The second focus of TAA action has been on a sharing of power within the university. Much of the membership support for the educational planning proposal, for instance, has been phrased as a desire to win a more democratic means of making decisions, of determining course and curriculum content with the participation of students and teaching assistants as well as faculty. Power sharing, a central theme in TAA propaganda, has raised the possibility of community/worker control of the industry as a serious long-range program and has posited a number of models of how such control might work. For example, a TAA leaflet on possibilities of unionism for research workers includes the following proposal:

The university should establish a committee to review research grants. The committee would represent faculty, research assistants, specialists, and community groups such as labor unions and conservation groups. Business interests would not be included, since industry is already well represented through its grants and its influence in government. The committee would require reports from all researchers concerning the possible social impact of their work; these reports would be open to public inspection and rebuttal.

Similarly, a TAA leaflet proposing new contract demands in the educational planning area states: "Until we come to terms with the power structure of the university and challenge its definition of community control—that is, control by the departmental administrators, by the tenured faculty, by the state education bureaucrats—the community of teachers and students will not be able to exercise any meaningful control over education."

Control, or power, then, is recognized as the real issue. Among a substantial proportion of the union membership at least, this ultimate goal is, in fact, the chief focus of union activity, and some short-term gains (like telephones and office space) may be, and have in fact been, sacrificed in order to pursue the establishment of the union as a visible alternative center of power and a reminder that other arrangements for the allocation of decision-making authority are possible.

The union's third broad area of concern has been to make both union members and others in the industry aware of the more general political lessons that can be drawn from the particular situation of teaching assistants. The union has, for example, repeatedly raised questions about university discrimination against women, not only against women as assistants, but also in admissions policies and in faculty hiring and tenure decisions. Similarly, the union has been willing to cooperate with groups seeking open admissions policies, even though such policies might bear only a tangential relation to the day-to-day teaching situation of the average assistant. Finally, union members have been among the more active on campus in explicitly political activity—in protests against the war and against the use of police and troops on campus, for example. In contrast to the distinction that may exist at Berkeley between economic and political issues, much of the active TAA membership tends to see key issues as containing both components and to make links between the particular economic difficulties that the industry imposes on teaching assistants and the broader political questions of how power is wielded within the industry and how that power is related to other basic political issues in the society as a whole.

The TAA's fourth focus has been on questions of internal union structure and democracy. Large portions of membership meetings have been spent in criticism of actions that the TAA executive board took without specific membership approval and in discussions of the potential dangers of the charismatic leadership that has seemed at times to be emerging within the union. The TAA constitution, requiring advance notice to all members of matters to be acted on at membership meetings and giving the executive board no independence in policy matters, is among the most democratic of any American union. In addition, the by now well-established membership distrust of the leadership, while at times creating delays, has the advantage of making it more likely that, when the union does act, most members will understand the bases of that action, since they will have debated it themselves at membership meetings and in departmental discussions. For a large proportion of union activists, the democratic union is seen as a first step toward a more democratic society at large.

Brief History of the TAA

The TAA has not come to these positions quickly or easily. In fact, the history of the union shows a number of swings from political to educational to industrial-economic emphases, leading up to the present transient synthesis. The TAA first arose from a series of meetings held by Wisconsin teaching assistants in May 1966; assistants were concerned with campus protests against the draft and, in particular, with their desire not to be put in the position of sending students into the army by giving them poor grades. Following these meetings, which were primarily forums for airing complaints, essentially the same group of somewhat less than fifty assistants began meeting to discuss such issues as pay differentials between departments and hiring and firing practices. Despite the group's relatively small membership, the university administration quickly moved to coopt its leadership, requesting the group to elect a member to a faculty committee then studying the teaching assistant situation and seeking its advice—though not giving it a decision-making role—in some matters affecting assistants.

A new kind of action began in February 1967 when the TAA took up the case of an assistant who had not been rehired, despite promises by her department. The success of the TAA in winning her job back led to further grievance actions and to the development of a demand for a standard university-wide contract, involving the individual assistant, the union, and the university as parties. The proposed contract would have replaced the largely informal and arbitrary hiring and firing practices then in effect. When it became apparent, however, that the university administration was not ready to grant the formal recognition that such a contractual arrangement implied and that the TAA was not yet in a position to demonstrate the support of a large enough number of teaching assistants to compel recognition from the university, the organization decided to concentrate its efforts on handling grievance cases and publicizing the unfair and arbitrary nature of university action in each case in order to create awareness of the job situation. At this same time, in the fall of 1967, the TAA also rejected the advisory role that had been offered by the administration, instructing its representative on the faculty committee to resign because he was not allowed by the committee to make public the information he received as a member.

In October 1967 more than four hundred teaching assistants met to respond to the university's calling out of club-wielding police to disperse an anti-Dow demonstration on campus. Most of the assistants, acting through the TAA, supported a student-led strike and called off their classes until the students ended their own action. But the incident did not immediately generate a large, continuing organization. The Dow demonstration did create the opportunity, however, for further use of the TAA's grievance procedure. In pursuing the cases of assistants fired or not rehired because of political activity, the TAA was able to make arbitrary action by management a real issue for more campus workers.

Despite this growing awareness, most assistants still saw themselves as preprofessionals, or junior faculty. What agitation existed at the department level through 1968 was concerned primarily with educational issues—reform of course syllabuses, participation in department curriculum committees, and so on. In early 1969, however, the TAA began to transform itself from a minority faction, concerned primarily with educational reform issues, to a majority labor union, concerned with economic, educational, and control, or power, issues. The immediate impetus for this change was a legislative proposal to cut the out-of-state tuition remission for teaching assistants. The union leadership publicly announced a strike vote of all assistants—a tactic designed to put pressure directly on the legislature.

The running of a strike vote led to planning not just for a one-shot strike but for a full-scale organizational drive designed to secure recognition for the TAA as exclusive bargaining agent for all teaching assistants on campus. Within a month, more than half of all assistants on campus had signed cards authorizing the TAA to act as their exclusive collective bargaining agent. At this point, the union publicly sought recognition from the administration. After six weeks of negotiations, the administration agreed to a set of ground rules by which the TAA could be recognized as bargaining agent following a state-supervised representation election.

At the time of the election—won by the TAA, with more than 77 per cent of the vote—many teaching assistants assumed that the university was interested in good-faith bargaining and that there would soon be a signed UW-TAA contract. In fact, the bargaining process was considerably more drawn out. First, the union itself went through a long period—virtually the entire summer—during which it developed contract demands based on a series of discussions in the departments and then among department representatives. While many of the bread and butter issues were relatively easy for the union to deal with (few assistants had any reservations about asking for long-term job security, better health care, or adequate working conditions) much time was needed to work out the union's position on the control issues, such as educational planning. Not until late in the summer was there substantial agreement within the union on this clause and then only on a formula that left the details of sharing power over courses and curriculum to be worked out at the department level. Second, the administration bargaining team quickly showed that it was not interested in serious, productive negotiations. The early bargaining sessions repeatedly bogged down over minor issues. For example, one entire day of bargaining was spent considering the university's objections to a union proposal that only union members be allowed to remove material from union bulletin boards. Similar episodes continued throughout the fall. Because of the administration's use of stalling tactics, the union membership voted on January 8, 1970, to suspend its participation in campuswide talks until the university responded with positive new proposals. The suspension lasted for two months and ended with the strike vote.

At this point there were seven key issues still unresolved. Most important to the TAA membership was the question of educational planning—the sharing of control over grades, course content, and requirements among students, teaching assistants, and faculty. In addition, the university and the TAA were far apart on the issues of minimum stipends, class-size maximums, health care coverage for assistants and their families, the structure of a grievance procedure, the length of time for which an assistant would have job security, and the question of whether the university could continue to maintain and act on secret files relating to teaching assistants.

On March 8, more than two-thirds of the union's total membership voted to strike; in addition, most undergraduates honored the union's picket lines. Class attendance in the College of Letters and Science dropped to 20 per cent of enrollment. Local teamster members also honored the picket lines; campus bus service was halted, and deliveries of supplies were interrupted. These successes, though, were at least partially matched by increased pressure from the university. Mass firing of the strikers was threatened, and the administration secured an injunction against the strike. In addition, although the administration had earlier offered an educational planning clause granting some power to teaching assistants but not to students, the interest of the faculty in preserving its power in this area became apparent. Numerous faculty members made public statements threatening to resign if the university gave in at all on educational planning (one departmental faculty sent its statement to the chancellor written on asbestos, to show the strength of their determination to keep control).

While these counterpressures did not convince many assistants to return to work, it gradually became evident that the strike had reached a stalemate; the union's effect on normal operations—especially ongoing research activities—was not severe enough to cause the university to agree to the TAA demands, but the university was disrupted enough so that some concessions were made to effect a settlement. The resulting contract, accepted by the TAA membership April 8, made virtually no concessions on the educational planning issue. It did, however, set up an impartial grievance procedure, give teaching assistants a guarantee of long-term appointments, and improve working conditions to some degree. While the failures of the contract were well recognized within the TAA, most members believed that the strike had at least established the union as a more or less permanent alternative source of power on the campus.

Developments since the strike have, however, raised questions about that belief. The university attempted to fire more than forty assistants who had participated in the strike, despite a no reprisal clause in the contract. Almost immediately after signing the contract, the administration attempted to renege on the health-care provisions. The same stalling tactics that had been used in the campus-wide bargaining appeared in departmental negotiations over local issues. Finally, the university revealed plans for an attempt to decertify the TAA as bargaining agent. Although the fall 1970 membership drive showed that the union had sufficient strength to withstand these challenges, and although the grievance procedure was successful in rebuffing most administration attempts to avoid contractual responsibilities, the evidence was clear that the union had not been accepted as a permanent center of power within the university community.

Analysis and Prediction

There are several lessons to be drawn from the TAA experience. First, organizational strength is increased by a linking of economic and political goals. Second, even relatively strong organizations, like the TAA, need some breaks, some missteps by management, if they are to succeed. And third, there is evidence that, even among such a relatively elite group as teaching assistants, a spirit of antiprofessionalism is increasing.

The overall strength of the TAA was built on both the economic goals that ended up as the bread and butter demands in the union's contract proposal and on the political goals of decentralized power, manifested in the educational planning proposal. Although, in the course of the bargaining and the strike, many TAA members began to identify with both issues, it was the presence of both issues within the union that made it possible in the first place to attract a large membership.

As is the case with most successful campus activist movements, the TAA was aided considerably by the mistakes of its opponents. The initial spur to a mass organizing campaign, for example, came from the legislative proposal to cut teaching assistant salaries. Organizing also was helped by numerous documented instances of disciplinary action or firings for obviously political reasons. Comparison of the relative ineffectiveness of the TAA while Robben Fleming, a skilled labor mediator, was chancellor with its growth during the recent regimes of less adept administrators gives some indication of the degree to which administrative blunders can at least speed the pace of activity for groups like the TAA.

Finally, the strike showed that many assistants had crossed a kind of attitudinal threshold and were no longer willing to see themselves solely as apprentices in a professional caste system. Even during the strike there was development in this direction; in the first days, picketing assistants rarely said anything to faculty crossing the picket lines but by the last week of the strike, few faculty members crossed without being the target of verbal abuse, even from their own graduate students. While this developing antiprofessionalism is by no means the dominant attitude, even among Wisconsin assistants, it presages a growing alienation and militance even among the most faculty-like portions of the student community.

If the above trends are real—and the Wisconsin experience, at least, suggests that they are—where will organizations like the TAA move in the future? At this point, one can identify at least three possible developments: first, an expansion of the scope of demands being made by unions representing teaching assistants and other campus workers; second, a broadening of union activity to include other kinds of workers; and third, the attempt to build links between campus unions and other segments of organized labor.

The TAA's own experience indicates that initial contracts are only a first step; in subsequent negotiations, the demands made by union members will be greater. In the case of the TAA, demands are being increased on both the economic and political fronts. Economically, the next set of contract proposals will call for vastly expanded health-care provisions, greater minimum stipends, and better physical facilities in which to work. Combining both the political and economic aspects of the union will be a proposal for university-sponsored day care for the children of assistants; this is aimed both at easing a real financial hardship and at raising the possibility that women will be considered as equals when hiring decisions are made. The political demands will probably center on new versions of educational planning and on some kind of open-enrollment program.

At the same time that the union is expanding the scope of its demands for assistants it is also taking some initiatives in organizing other campus workers, particularly those falling outside the blue-collar civil-service categories that are represented at Wisconsin and at many other large public universities by AFL-CIO unions. For example, research workers, non-civil-service technicians, and undergraduate workers in the cafeterias and libraries have all been involved in discussions about forming unions or joining with the TAA.

The increased union activity on campus has already produced new interest in university organizing on the part of several established unions. The AFL-CIO American Federation of Teachers has expanded its college organizing staff and has attempted to induce teaching assistants' unions at several Big Ten schools to join it. The teamsters are organizing faculty at some state colleges. And the recent National Labor Relations Board decision extending bargaining rights at private colleges and universities has made the field even more attractive to established labor. To date, most of the new unions on campus have not joined any established unions. This is not to say that some links do not exist; the Wisconsin strike depended heavily on teamster support, for example. Pressure from the larger unions for affiliation will increase as campus unionism becomes more widespread. From the point of view of university administrators, the established national unions may be easier to deal with; it is unlikely, for example, that an AFT local would place the same emphasis on political demands that the TAA or similar new unions at other schools do. The fact that many TAA members see the university as an industry does not mean that they view traditional American unionism as an adequate means for effecting change. On the contrary, TAA activists contend that both political and economic demands must be raised to challenge the power of *any* industry. If the new campus unions maintain their political emphasis, they may be unlikely to affiliate with well-established, large national unions.

In summary, then, the experience of the TAA at Wisconsin reflects the increasingly industrialized setting in which members of the university community find themselves and the political consciousness common to many activist movements on campuses in the past decade. If the new unionism on campus is to have any lasting impact, it will be because unions like the TAA are able—and at this point it is impossible to say if they will continue to be able—to maintain the connection between the political and the economic in the minds of their memberships, and so create a larger force for change than either a bread and butter union or a campus political action group could create alone.

Notes

[1] C. Kerr, *The Uses of the University* (Cambridge: Harvard University Press, 1964).

[2] U.S. Office of Education, *Graduate Teaching Assistants in American Universities* (Washington, D.C.: Government Printing Office, 1970), p. 16.

[3] U.S. Office of Education, p. 17.

4 U.S. Office of Education, p. 24.

5 U.S. Office of Education, p. 27.

6 K. W. Wilson, *Of Time and the Doctorate: Report of an Inquiry into the Duration of Doctoral Study* (Atlanta: Southern Regional Education Board, 1965), p. 47.

7 C. Muscatine, *Education at Berkeley* (Berkeley: University of California, 1966), p. 184.

8 R. Dubin and F. Beisse, "The Assistant: Academic Subaltern," *Administrative Science Quarterly*, 1969, *11*, 544.

CHAPTER 16

●●●●●●●●●●●●●●●
●●●●●●●●●●●●●●●●
●●●●●●●●●●●●●●●●

BLACK STUDENT POWER

Judith Lyons, Morgan Lyons

●●●●●●●●●●●●●●●
●●●●●●●●●●●●●●●●
●●●●●●●●●●●●●●●●

The University of Wisconsin has long played a leading role in the ongoing drama of student protests. Kenneth Keniston mentions Wisconsin as one of three major state universities which, by combining a reputation for academic excellence and freedom with highly selective admission policies, tends to congregate large numbers of potentially protesting students.[1] In Feburary 1969, this potential erupted, and national attention was focused on the Madison campus when a massive student strike followed the presentation of thirteen Black Demands to the university administration by black students and their white allies. This chapter is a descriptive case study of the strike and demonstrations mounted in support of those demands, and concentrates on campus reactions to both specific incidents of student activism and the general issues behind them.[2]

At the most elementary level, we are concerned with obtaining accurate information as to the magnitude of student protest in order to assess its impact on colleges and on the nation. For example, the difference between estimates of a tiny and a substantial minority of dissenters represents an important indicator of the power potential of activists. Similarly, data on the proportion of students that easily can be, or has been, mobilized on a given issue suggests recruitment potential that may be altogether as crucial as information on the proportion of students affiliated with activist campus organizations. Perhaps equally vital for accurate diagnosis of portending conflict and potential change is a focus on the other side of the activist coin—delineation of the proportion of nonprotesting students who defend the Establishment and those who are simply apathetic.

The data reported here consist of questionnaire responses gathered from a 2 per cent sample of the entire University of Wisconsin student body, when memories of the strike were less than a month old.[3] Six hundred and fifty questionnaires were originally mailed, and comparison of the sample finally attained (547 respondents, an 84 per cent return) with university statistics indicated that this sample comprised a fair representation of the Wisconsin student population. The possibility that certain groups, such as student radicals, were underrepresented must of course be acknowledged, though misrepresentation of relatively small groups would change the emerging general picture relatively little.

As a backdrop for the presentation of data on Wisconsin student reactions, a brief description of some of the crucial strike events follows. The major source for this account is *The Daily Cardinal* (the university's student newspaper). The 1969 spring semester opened in the first week of February with capacity audiences attending speeches at a week-long all-university conference on the topic "The Black Revolution—To What Ends." On Friday, February 7, the last day of the conference, black students presented their thirteen demands to the university administration; following a brief rally, students, both black and white, disrupted classes. Over the weekend a list of the demands was distributed and open conferences were set up all over campus with black leaders discussing the demands, answering questions, and urging support of the upcoming strike. The focal point of five of the demands was the creation of a degree-granting black studies department, with approval of black students being required for all decisions relevant to the establishment, staffing (hiring and firing), and running of that department. Additional demands related to: admission of (five hundred) more blacks by the fall of 1969; hiring of black financial aid counselors; scholarship support for all athletes until they receive their degrees; black student control of the Black Cultural Center; immediate admission of all students recently expelled from Oshkosh University (another state school) for a black protest; amnesty to all students participating in any actions related to the demands; and proof that the above demands had been met.

According to *Daily Cardinal* reports, "At first these demands were met with much hostility and disbelief by a majority of the student body. They agreed with some of the demands in spirit, but the constant reiteration that everything had to be approved by black students had many people up in arms. The weekend conferences helped to quell many students' feelings of uneasiness." The strike got underway on Monday, February 10, with picketing and many scheduled classes being turned over to strike-sympathetic students for discussion. As requested by black leaders, there were no physical confrontations; the day climaxed with a peaceful march by fifteen hundred students from the campus to the state capitol building some ten blocks away.

On the second day tactics were escalated to the use of impenetrable picket lines and noisy disruptions in which classrooms were "liberated"; dispersal rather than confrontation occurred when police arrived. Another march occurred that evening. The third day was the most violent and had the greatest impact on the strike and the campus. The hit-and-run harassment tactics continued, with crowds of demonstrators ebbing before the police only to re-form later or elsewhere. Several violent minor confrontations occurred when counterdemonstrating students, trying to force their way through the crowds and pickets, sparked some fights and also, by their charge, pushed some picketers into policemen who responded with clubs. There were several injuries during the day and five arrests. Sporadic traffic obstruction and picketing on streets bordering the campus were also part of the day's activity. Various departmental faculty and student meetings voiced support for the strike, and the Teaching Assistants Association voted a walkout for the following Thursday, Friday, and Monday with teach-ins planned throughout the campus to discuss strike issues. Stating that the police were becoming over-tired from long, tense hours Governor Knowles, with the endorsement of university and city officials, called up nine hundred National Guardsmen.

Thursday, the on-campus presence of soldiers with fixed bayonets produced a strong reaction, and the previously small numbers of strikers swelled to seven thousand. Their mobile groups maintained pickets and continued to obstruct traffic. For the most part, violent confrontation was avoided, though Guardsmen once fired tear gas into a street crowd. This fourth day of the strike was climaxed by a torchlight march estimated at ten thousand students—nearly a third of the student body— from the university to the capitol.

The harassment tactics and traffic obstruction continued on Friday. An evening march of more than one thousand students was marred by police clubbings as marchers returned from the capitol. It was announced that the Guard would be removed from the campus for the weekend and stationed nearby until needed. Because militant strikers dwindled to six hundred to seven hundred over the weekend, new tactics were announced on Monday, February 17; strikers were to go back to classes and urge discussions. There was hope that a statement of faculty support for the demands would come out of a general faculty meeting scheduled for Wednesday afternoon, and thus provide bargaining strength for the strikers. This hope proved ill-founded. Fifty faculty members walked out angrily after a narrow vote which refused admission to the expelled Oshkosh dissidents, and no concrete action was taken on the various committee reports dealing with minority issues.

The strike nominally resumed Thursday, but students were apparently tiring of the offensive and discouraged by lack of progress. The number of pickets was quite small and action diminished. One final desperate tactic was employed; on Friday, February 27, about one hundred black and white demonstrators entered academic buildings and disrupted classes, breaking doors and tossing chairs through lights and windows, setting off stink bombs and fire alarms, and smashing vending machines. Moving rapidly, they hit half a dozen buildings with their guerilla attack before police arrived and five arrests were made. That evening three hundred persons participated in a march, with nearly equal numbers of police trailing and observing every move. The Guard was sent home and the strike was thoroughly abandoned that weekend (March 1–2), although its effectiveness as a class boycott had ended the previous weekend.

Campus Political Climate

A portion of the questionnaire was designed to tap the general political climate of the campus at the time of the disruption in order to provide a context for interpreting statements of student reactions. Although several incidents had focused attention on black student unrest prior to the issuance of the thirteen Black Demands—a black revolution conference and an earlier set of demands—nearly one-half the students in our sample were unaware of a great deal of discontent among black students. These students report that before the strike brought the issues to prominence they were either largely unaware (12 per cent) or only somewhat aware (35 per cent) of grievances felt by black students.

Nevertheless, the magnitude of sympathy and involvement elicited by the strike was fairly substantial. To ascertain the potential for political activity we attempted to get students to pin some general labels on themselves. First we asked for standard partisan identification, but found students to be remarkably label-shy. The categories of "independent—lean toward Democrat/Republican" and write-ins of "independent" with no qualification accounted for 40 per cent; the partisan "liberal/conservative–Democrat/Republican" tags were decidedly shunned, and 10 per cent of the respondents did not answer the question at all. Somewhat surprisingly, this question did pick up a combined total of 13 per cent in the categories "revolutionary left," "radical–New Left," and "socialist."[4]

Another question asked the respondent to locate his views relative to those of other students on campus. Just under one-half opted for the middle ("moderate") position. Thirty-three per cent chose "left" positions (including 6 per cent "radical left"), while 18 per cent chose "right" positions (including 4 per cent "very conservative"). Thus, the left of center students outnumber the right of center by almost two to one (27 per cent to 14 per cent). The answers to this question, then, suggest the existence of a substantial recruitment pool for campus activities of a left political nature.

The Black Demands strike, though its central purpose and other of its characteristics were specific to black protest, is here viewed as an example of the student power genre of demonstrations—as distinct, for example, from war protest demonstrations. Student power types of demonstrations and black student protests increased significantly on American college campuses between 1965 and 1968.[5] Black student protest is characterized as "instrumental" and "directed toward realistic achievable goals"[6] and, in fact, at the University of Wisconsin in February 1969 was directed toward the attainment of very specific and institutional power.

Information as to campus feelings about the issue of student power, then, is pertinent to our assessment of the prevailing campus political climate. How did the student body relate to the general abstract cause of student power? Our survey indicates general moderate endorsement. Asked to personalize—"How important is the cause of enhancing 'student power' to you?"—two-thirds checked either "important" (28 per cent) or "somewhat important" (38 per cent). Twelve per cent feel it is "very important"; less than a quarter of the sample responded that it was "unimportant" to them. There were distinct graduate-undergraduate differences in extreme responses even though moderate endorsements are nearly identical for the two groups. Graduates are represented proportionately less in the strongest endorsement of student power (8 per cent versus 13 per cent for undergraduates) and are represented proportionately more in lack of endorsement (28 per cent versus 19 per cent).

Another question directed toward student power asked the respondents to indicate the ideal power arrangements in the university as well as their perceptions of the existing power structure. The power groupings were as follows: students, faculty, administration, Regents, and legislature. The student ideal appears to call for a diminution of overall power and also for its relative homogenization across groups: the legislature and the Regents would lose power, and the students and faculty would gain. The administration, toward which the thrust of the strike was directed, neither gains nor loses in absolute power rating, and it actually gains a considerable amount in relative power standing, simply because the Regents and the legislature lose considerably. In other words, the perceived power clustering of Regents-legislature-administration, situated above faculty and particularly students, would ideally be replaced by somewhat distinct power levels: administration-faculty, then Regents-students, and, on the bottom, the legislature. Thus, the administration emerges as a university power of a relatively high degree of legitimacy in the eyes of the average student. This legitimacy is seen as both relative to other power groups and even moderately high in absolute value. To the extent that such legitimacy exists, it is based on students' general trust that the administration will use its power with their interest in mind.

However, trust must be viewed not as an absolute but as a variable upon which the campus as a whole (and individual groups and students) may be located relative to extreme poles of total trust-mistrust. Discovering the approximate position and distribution of the student body on the trust-mistrust continuum is crucial for understanding the potential for mobilization of forces for change and, hence, of conflict.

Two questions bearing directly on the trustworthiness of the administration were posed by our survey, one of them quite general and the other specific to the strike. The first asks whether the administration could be counted on to "give sufficient consideration to the rights and needs of students in setting university policy." With responses of "hardly ever" (17 per cent), "sometimes" (36 per cent), "usually" (33 per cent), and "almost always" (12 per cent), there is a slight lean toward negative evaluation. There is good evidence that trust—or its lack—is an important link in the explanation of mobilization for change. Among those whose trust in the powers-that-be is high ("usually" and "almost always"), 14 per cent are stirred to some participation in defense of the status quo by joining anti-strike activities, while nearly half remain neutral. When trust in the administration is low ("sometimes" and "hardly ever"), more than two-thirds join the protest, and only a quarter remain neutral, leaving a paltry 5 per cent who are actively willing to defend the system in which they have so little confidence.

The broader implications of the fact that so few persons actively take up the antistrike cause to defend the present structures will be discussed later. The main interest here is in beginning to establish the existence of a general context of support for change on the campus. An earlier point suggested that the leftish political distribution in itself set the stage for change. The question posed now is whether the trust dimension adds significantly to the explanation of mobilization or whether it is simply that the left is the sole source of both distrust and active protest potential. Table 6 allows us to address that query with data.

Clearly, leftist students are more likely to have a low degree of trust in the administration and those on the right are more likely to see it as benevolent, and the evidence that protest recruitment is by far strongest from the left while those on the right are more likely to be among the antistrike forces is hardly surprising. The most interesting information added by consideration of the trust dimension, however, is evident in the large "moderate" column (political moderates are strongly represented in both high- and low-trust categories—the figures are 149 and 105, respectively). Regardless of their level of trust, a high proportion of moderates are neutral with regard to participation. When moderates are mobilized, however, knowing their degree of trust gives a great predictive advantage; with high trust identical numbers join the antistrike and the protest, but when trust is low the recruitment is seven to one in favor of the protest. If mistrust is in fact such an effective mobilizing condition for moderates, the very size of this group makes the potential for large-scale protest seem very real indeed should their trust be further reduced.

The finding that a majority of students show a low trust of the administration must be reconciled with the previous interpretation that students seem to afford the administration a certain legitimacy of power in running the university. Given the essential validity of both conclusions, it may be that students have awarded the administration a kind of provisional legitimacy—hoping a poorly trusted administration might begin to exercise power appropriately—or that students have simply begrudged the administration legitimacy out of a feeling that that particular power arrangement is the best they can hope for.

We have treated degree of trust as a precondition for strike mobilization. However, responses to the general question about trusting the administration almost surely were affected by reactions to the administration's handling of the strike. The similarly negative distributions of answers to our two trust items probably reflect some erosion in general trust due to student feelings that their confidence in the administration had proven to be misplaced during the crisis.

Our second trust question asked specifically for an evaluation of the administration's response to the strike. The most salient aspects of the administration's role in the strike include both its partial accountability for the summoning of the National Guard to the campus[7] and

Table 6.   TRUST AND STRIKE PARTICIPATION

HIGH TRUST (ALWAYS AND USUALLY)

| | *Political Position* | | |
Participation	Radical Left and Left-of-Center	Moderate	Right-of-Center and Very Conservative
	Per Cent	Per Cent	Per Cent
Protest[a]	18.2	12.1	9.5
Neutral[b]	69.7	75.1	76.2
Antistrike[c]	12.1	12.8	14.3
	100.0	100.0	100.0
	(33)	(149)	(63)

LOW TRUST (SOMETIMES AND HARDLY EVER)

Participation	Radical Left and Left-of-Center	Moderate	Right-of-Center and Very Conservative
	Per Cent	Per Cent	Per Cent
Protest[a]	68.0	28.6	12.9
Neutral[b]	30.0	67.6	61.3
Antistrike[c]	2.0	3.8	25.8
	100.0	100.0	100.0
	(147)	(105)	(31)

[a] Protest participation is defined as having joined marches or picket lines or having obstructed classroom buildings.
[b] Neutral includes both inactive students and students whose only participation was attendance at rallies or meetings, since such presence does not necessarily imply sympathy with the proceedings.
[c] Anti-strike participation is defined by a "yes" response to the question "Did you take any active part in antidemonstration activities?"

its reaction to the Black Demands themselves, which were at first attacked, then selectively dismissed or coopted. Just over a third of the students felt the administration's response was "somewhat closed-minded" (35 per cent). Combined with the 17 per cent who responded "repressive," this means that slightly more than half the sample was fairly critical. The most frequently endorsed response alternative was that the administration had been "reasonable" (41 per cent). Only 4 per cent endorsed the fourth alternative characterizing the handling of the strike as "too lenient."

Reviewing these measures of trust in light of both the theoretical statements and the ideal university power structure sketched above, we must again emphasize the more-or-less nature of both trust and mobilization. Distrust of the administration is far from total, and, especially relative to feelings toward the Regents and the state legislature, many students seem willing to accept the administration's considerable authority over them. Nonetheless, neither is trust absolute; trust was sufficiently low that a significant portion of the student body was mobilized to push for changes and reforms, and the indication is that if the administration acts in such a way as to further lower that trust, even more mobilization could be expected.

As our focus now shifts to questions of the size of the "minority" of dissenters, it will be well to keep in mind that the concept of minority is also a variable and that sizes and size distinctions may be crucial even when they do not refer to majorities.

Mobilization

Many stereotyped, sometimes preposterous, and often widely shared explanations exist as to "who's responsible" and the "whys" of student activism. Numbers play a very important role in these conjectures. One of the most standard reactions to any eruption, one frequently emphasized by government officials and the news media as well as local conservatives, is the "small minority" assessment of who is responsible for all the trouble on campuses. The mass media play heavily on numbers and proportions in their coverage of student demonstrations. "The majority" (51 per cent?) often becomes an almost sacred proportion although concern and disapprobation also vary with the absolute number of persons involved in protest.

Throughout the University of Wisconsin Black Demands strike the frequent reports of the local newspapers and broadcast media usually presented two standard breakdowns: the number of active demonstrators and this number as a proportion of the total student body; and the number and proportion that was black. The numbers of student demonstrators went from "about 250 demonstrators" including "fifty blacks" on February 7 to the "eight thousand or more" who participated in the mass march to the capitol on February 14. The number of visibly active supporters mobilized is of course of tremendous concern to activist leaders as well as to the university administration, government officials, the police, the mass media, and others. The extent to which activist students are "isolated lunatics" as opposed to "only the top of an iceberg of unrest" bears important implications for their role in the future of higher education in America. To answer this question, some empirical questions must be posed: Are the disrupters a tiny leftist minority? What is the reaction of the rest of the student body to the protestors? How many students can be activated as defenders of the present system against protestors?

Lipset has referred to campus radical activists as "the powerful 2 per cent,"[8] and Keniston assessed the number of active dissenters among students in 1967 as generally well under 5 per cent.[9] Peterson set "members" of the left at about 2 per cent, with another 8 to 10 per cent strongly sympathetic and capable of "temporary activation depending on the issues."[10] These figures perhaps underestimate current activism; however, Peterson found evidence that although the absolute number of student activists increased from 1965 to 1968, their proportions on the nation's college campuses may have been stable.

In comparing these figures to our data on activism related to the Wisconsin Black Demands strike, we must begin by noting possible differences in referent. Some of the aforementioned authors base their figures of campus activists on membership in leftist organizations—a definition that focuses exclusively on students with organizational commitments to activism. Our usage is concerned instead with degree of participation in a specific protest, a difference which at least partly explains the generally higher incidence of activism found at the University of Wisconsin in February 1969. Too, the popular black-civil-rights nature of the issue might be credited with inflating the figures, although the radical tone of the Demands statements and the presentation style probably offset easy bandwagon recruitment. Also, mobilization for a specific type of action may be indicative of a more general readiness to support change; if so, analysis of the extent of disinterested noninvolvement versus countermobilization in defense of the system should hold clues as to how effective insurgent moves might be.

Our lowest figure for militant protest behavior is 3 per cent of the sample who indicated they actively disrupted classes, "not to lead discussion, but to end the class." Approximately 7 per cent admit obstructing entrances to classroom buildings—which compares with the 6 per cent antistrike activists who admit to purposefully forcing their way through strike lines or into buildings, or the 8 per cent who said they were active against the strike in any way (including discussions).

Less militant forms of strike behavior count increasing numbers of participants: 20 per cent say they joined picket lines at least once;

27 per cent deliberately missed class at some time out of sympathy to the strike. Behaviors not necessarily requiring commitment to the strike show the highest number of participants: 37 per cent of the sample report attending meetings to discuss issues or tactics, and 45 per cent attended at least one prostrike rally.

A second approach to this same type of information was employed in another section of the survey questionnaire. Rather than asking students about specific involvement, the inquiry was whether they felt certain tactics were "ever justifiable means for expression of student grievances." Here we find 11 per cent who justify preventing other students from attending classes (against 7 per cent who actually attempted this), and 14 per cent justifying the disruption of classes for student protest (compared with 3 per cent actually doing this). In reference to other tactics actually employed, 84 per cent endorse picketing, 76 per cent boycotting classes, 81 per cent pressuring teachers to discuss issues, and 5 per cent could justify the destruction of university property or facilities.

The proportion of students actually disrupting the education of others is, by some standards, very small—if we are talking about the number of students who entered classrooms and attempted to halt instruction by physical means. The 7 per cent blocking class buildings is no longer a tiny number (it represents 2,500 students), but is still a small minority. If "disrupting education" designates any attempt to bring it to a temporary halt, the minority involved is quite a substantial one (for example, more than a quarter opted to boycott classes), and we are talking about sizable majorities when we refer to students who might endorse such tactics given the proper circumstances. Applied to the University of Wisconsin Black Demands strike, theories that refer to a "tiny minority" of students with proclivities toward the disruption of the educational process are inadequate. Nor does there appear to be any vast majority that is "fed up" with disrupters.

Our most general items assessing campus sentiment for and against the Black Demands strike asked students whether they felt a "general identification" with either the protestors and/or the antistrike. Identification with the strikers (41.9 per cent) is clearly more prevalent than identification with those involved against the strike (23.8 per cent).[11] Considering only undergraduates, the difference is two to one in favor of strike-identifiers (46 per cent versus 23 per cent). Graduates reveal closer percentages for the two sentiments (33 per cent versus 25 per cent), but even here we are comparing a third of the students with a quarter.

The fact that 38 per cent of our respondents identified with neither side throughout this crisis situation is worthy of note. Feelings ran high during the two weeks of the strike and "occupation"; the media as well as casual conversation had one major focus; campus activities were sufficiently disrupted that none could ignore what was occurring, and pressure to align one's sympathies with one side or the other would seem to have been very strong. That as many as 38 per cent of the student body avoided even the involvement of emotional or verbal identfication indicates significant disaffection or apathy.

With over a third of the student community opting out through apparent disinterest, the implications for change would seem to be great. The size of the minority which is active against the status quo takes on new proportional importance if we consider it as opposed only by those sufficiently interested and involved to at least identify with, and perhaps defend, the system. With 38 per cent of the students serving simply as an acquiescent backdrop, the battle lines are drawn differently; of the remaining effective population of students who are at least minimally involved, identifiers with the protest constitute nearly two-thirds; antistrike sympathizers, only one-third. Advocacy of the antistrike position in discussions was admitted by only forty respondents—7.3 per cent of the total sample (or 12 per cent of the number in the effective population). This indicates a very small contingent willing to defend the status quo against movements for change.

These figures are not intended to imply that the protesting forces on the University of Wisconsin campus need only to recognize their strength and make their move in order to effect revolutionary change. The point is simply that there is considerable support for change and a reordering of power. In order to translate this attitudinal support into predictors of action one would need to deal in terms of a theory of the role of minorities in social change. Such a venture is somewhat beyond the scope of this chapter.

Somers' analysis found that consideration of endorsement of activists' goals versus endorsement of their tactics provided a meaningful distinction within the general student population.[12] Agreement with goals-only represents the least radical commitment, since verbal agreement, particularly in the anonymity of a mailed questionnaire, is abstract and easy. Tactics, insofar as they represent a more concrete and explicit statement of the goals, require of the endorser a specific condonement of behaviors and perhaps, therefore, a more militant stance. Nevertheless, when dramatic changes in entrenched institutions are called for by the official goal statements, the extent of verbalized sympathy itself may be fairly informative.

In the survey, six demands were drawn from the original list of thirteen so as to represent a broad range from moderate to more radical. Respondents were given six response alternatives from "necessary; should be effected without delay" to "absurd; the antithesis of reason and fairness." A seventh item asking for a general response to the demands was included as well. Responses are shown in Table 7.

One clear finding is that students make definite discriminations among the indivadual demands, from general acceptance of most of them (summing the first three response categories as indicating some degree of acceptance, the first four demands listed got from 68 to 80 per cent endorsement) to a strong rejection of one or two (demand ten got only 14 per cent acceptance; demand twelve, 33 per cent). The last item indicates that, overall, the demands were fairly well received—63 per cent acceptance. The most popular response category for most demand statements, including the question about reactions to the full set of demands, reads "a just demand—with reasoned interpretation."

As noted previously, students also responded quite differentially to the tactics of the strike, with endorsements ranging from 84 per cent for picketing down to relatively meager endorsements for highly militant tactics. In another attempt to assess student endorsement of tactics, a set of items mentioned some of the more radical tactics used by strikers, then asked respondents to consider a list of arguments and indicate which if any of them they felt would justify such tactics. Table 8 presents the distribution of responses to the arguments which explicitly referred to the tactics. The average support for these arguments is 37 per cent; the average nonsupport, 63 per cent. If one considers "probably not supportable" as not really a rejection response, the percentages reverse themselves: 64 per cent in categories 1 through 3, and 36 per cent "definitely not supportable."

In order to construct a typology of agreement with goals and/or tactics, we can cross-classify the General Demands item from Table 7 with support (responses 1 and 2) on item b from Table 8, with the resulting percentages: accepts both goals and tactics (37), accepts goals but not tactics (28), rejects both goals and tactics (28), accepts only tactics (or no response) (7). Somers labeled the first three categories "militants," "moderates," and "conservatives," respectively, and then observed differences in characteristics among the three groupings.[13]

This typology yields yet another index for assessing the proportional representation of strike proponents among students. A majority of students do not feel they can support the strikers' tactics, though this majority does not seem vast, nor especially fed up when one recognizes that these numbers include slightly more "probably not" than "definitely not" responses.[14] The 37 per cent accepting both goals and tactics—again in varying degrees, but even so this represents a fairly militant stance— is, to be sure, a minority, but hardly a tiny one.

Table 7. STUDENT ENDORSEMENT OF SELECTED BLACK DEMANDS

Demands	Per Cent Answering						
	Necessary	Reasonable	A Just Demand	Overly Strong	Not Acceptable	Absurd	Total
ONE. "Autonomous Black Studies Department controlled and organized by black students and faculty, which would enable students to receive a B.A. in Black Studies."	19.0	20.3	28.7	19.6	6.0	5.5	99.1
TWO. "A black chairman of the Black Studies Department, who would be approved by a committee of black students and faculty."	18.8	27.1	26.9	14.6	7.3	4.0	98.7
THREE. "That at least 500 black students be admitted to UW for the semester of September, 1969."	20.5	22.7	36.7	16.3	5.9	7.0	99.1
SEVEN. "That black counselors be hired by the Student Financial Aids Office with the approval of black students."	19.0	22.1	27.2	19.2	6.2	5.3	99.0
TEN. "That it be established that black students have the power to hire and fire all administrators and teachers who are involved in anything relating to black students."	2.2	1.5	10.2	22.1	19.2	43.9	99.1
TWELVE. "That all expelled Oshkosh[a] students who wish to attend UW be admitted immediately."	10.2	8.0	14.3	21.0	20.5	24.5	98.5
In general, how do you feel about these demands?	11.7	20.7	30.4	21.0	7.0	4.0	94.9

[a] Wisconsin State University at Oshkosh, where ninety-four black students had been suspended following a campus distur-

Table 8. STUDENT ENDORSEMENT OF STRIKE TACTICS

"A number of arguments have been advanced to justify actions such as the disruption of classes and blocking of entrances to class buildings. How valid or supportable do you consider the following arguments?"

	Definitely Supportable	Probably Supportable	Probably not Supportable	Definitely not Supportable	Total
a) The experience of black men and women in America justifies violations of normal rules of conduct when blacks really feel deeply about an issue.	12.4% (68)	25.2% (138)	30.2% (165)	31.3% (174)	99.6% (545)
b) Black students at the UW really had no recourse but this in order to gain redress for legitimate grievances with university policy.	14.6% (80)	26.1% (143)	31.8% (174)	26.9% (147)	99.4% (544)
c) Black demands were just, and nearly any tactic that black students would have thought would work was appropriate.	4.6% (25)	9.7% (53)	28.0% (153)	57.2% (313)	99.5% (544)
d) Disrupting classes, striking, and blocking class buildings were actually "moderate" tactics. Demonstrating students showed self-restraint in not initially protesting their grievances in more dramatic or even violent ways.	24.3% (133)	29.8% (163)	17.0% (93)	27.6% (151)	98.7% (540)

Lipset feels that the real power of the active 2 per cent is not in its numbers (which are considerable on large campuses) but in its capacity to mobilize a sympathetic community.[15] One might expect certain kinds of student demonstrations to effect a polarization of student allegiances, radicalizing the susceptible and disgusting those with an initial propensity to oppose such demonstrations. If such a polarization occurred, it would logically follow that a comparatively smaller proportion of students would remain uninvolved, with larger proportions recruited into opposing camps.

Somewhat in opposition to this expectation, our questions on general strike identification reveal that many students remained uninvolved (38 per cent identified with neither side). Of those who were involved to the extent of identification, 42 per cent aligned themselves with the pro-strike movement; approximately half that number (24 per cent) identified with the antistrike.

Remembering that 47 per cent say they are "moderates," 33 per cent "left of center" or "radical," and 18 per cent "right of center" or "very conservative," we can inquire about the recruitment from these categories into strike and antistrike identification as the result of political events.

As Table 9 shows, the strike was able to recruit 16 per cent of those students seeing themselves as "right of center," and even 5 per cent of the "very conservative." In contrast, none of the "radicals" and only 9 per cent of the "left-of-center" students identified with the antistrike. The most sizable portion of "moderates" identified with neither (42 per cent), and the remainder divided fairly evenly between the two camps, with the pro-protest having a slight edge.

These findings indicate that moderates, the largest single political category and the supposed bastion of the status quo, are largely uninvolved. The substantial number of nonidentifying moderate students appear to be merely bystanders as the active pro- and anti-change forces act out their dispute. Although status quo supporters would like to—and often do—read this lack of involvement as lending support to their position, a more realistic assessment would seem to be one that recognizes that since these students have overtly avoided alignment with either side, they can hence not really be claimed by either camp. Moreover, were they to become more open to being mobilized, the best prediction of their partisan choices might be simply a projection of the nearly even division into the two identifications found in the present study.

Generally, this study has revealed that activists are not "a tiny minority" opposed by a polarized "fed up" majority of students. The ac-

Table 9. RECRUITMENT FROM POLITICAL POSITIONS INTO STRIKE AND ANTISTRIKE IDENTIFICATIONS

Self-Located Campus Political Position	N		Identification with Protestors	Identification with Antistrike	No Identification or No Response	Total
			Per Cent	Per Cent	Per Cent	Per Cent
1. Radical Left	(32)		90.6	0.0	9.4	100.0
2. Left of Center	(149)		67.8	8.7	23.5[a]	100.0
3. Moderate	(257)		30.7	27.6	41.7[a]	100.0
4. Right of Center	(74)		16.2	40.5	43.3[a]	100.0
5. Very Conservative	(20)		5.0	70.0	25.0	100.0

[a] Slightly underestimated due to "both" identifiers (twenty total), fourteen of whom consider themselves "moderate."

tivists (depending on what assessments are made) may include more than one-third of the student population and the "majority" includes sympathizers and many who are unconcerned as well as the small number of anti-activists.

More importantly, the protest was found to "recruit" both more widely and more successfully than the antidemonstrator cause. A projection of this finding for other campuses is not unreasonable. If this is indeed the case, then questions of absolute majorities become irrelevant, since a large and unopposed minority can successfully dominate a campus. At any rate, documentation of the facts of student protest provides a sound first step toward sorting out which ideas and theories can reasonably explain what has transpired, as well as lead toward prediction.

Notes

[1] K. Keniston, "Sources of Student Dissent," in E. E. Sampson and H. A. Korn, *Student Activism and Protest* (San Francisco: Jossey-Bass, 1970).

[2] This research was supported by funds from NIMH grant MH16661, the Wisconsin Survey Research Laboratory, and the University of Wisconsin Computing Center.

[3] We wish to thank Harry C. Sharp and the Wisconsin Survey Research Laboratory for their consultation and for funding the sampling operation for this project.

[4] Part of the surprise stemmed from our expectation that leftists were precisely those likely to be most offended by labels, and therefore would disproportionately refuse to answer such an item.

[5] R. E. Peterson, *The Scope of Organized Student Protest in 1967–68* (Princeton, N.J.: Educational Testing Service, 1968).

[6] See S. M. Lipset, "The Activists: A Profile," *The Public Interest*, 1968, *13*, 39–51, and J. H. Skolnick, *The Politics of Protest* (New York: Ballantine, 1969), p. 110.

[7] Bringing in the National Guard met with mixed emotional reactions from students (66 per cent found the sight of the Guard on campus "disturbing"; another item yielded 36 per cent feeling they would rather see the Guard there than overtired police), and it brought nationwide attention to the strike. Twenty-two per cent of the students sampled indicated they became more active in the strike because of this action.

[8] Lipset, p. 45.

[9] Keniston, p. 109.

[10] Peterson, p. 39.

[11] An overlap in identifications was produced by twenty students (3.7 per cent) checking *both* pro- and anti-strike identification.

[12] R. H. Somers, "The Mainsprings of the Rebellion: A Survey of Berkeley Students in November 1964," in S. M. Lipset and S. Wolin (eds.), *The Berkeley Student Revolt: Facts and Interpretations* (Garden City, N.Y.: Doubleday-Anchor, 1965), pp. 530–557.

[13] We should note that the items on which Somers based his division were more straightforward for this purpose: "Were you for or against the goals (tactics) of the demonstrators?" In our survey, using a questionnaire rather than a personal interview, these items seemed too nonspecific and ambiguous to elicit interpretable responses.

14 Our previous look at self-identified political "moderates" adds support to this point when we recall that over 50 per cent were uninvolved throughout the strike period and a third of those who had low trust of the establishment (therefore probably tending to accept the general goal of change) actually joined the protest. Indeed, nearly a fifth of even the high-trust moderates protested.

15 Lipset, *op. cit.*

CHAPTER 17

●●●●●●●●●●●●●●●
●●●●●●●●●●●●●●●
●●●●●●●●●●●●●●●

FOUR DECADES
OF ACTIVISM

Shlomo Swirsky

●●●●●●●●●●●●●●●
●●●●●●●●●●●●●●●
●●●●●●●●●●●●●●●

The University of Wisconsin has a national reputation for the radicalism and militancy of its students and the generally open atmosphere of the campus. Student activism at Wisconsin is by no means a new development; in fact, students at Madison have been involved in social and political activism for many years. Knowledge of this historical context will, perhaps, make some of the activism of the 1960s more understandable. At the very least, it will provide a background for both the student militancy of the recent period and the institutional response.

This analysis stresses changes in American college students' perceptions of their role in society between 1930 and 1968 as well as specific incidents of conflict involving students. The data were gathered from *The Daily Cardinal*, the student newspaper, for every other year beginning with 1930. The unit of analysis is a conflict between students and one or more other groups. A conflict is defined as any situation in which an organized group of students—student government, dormitory council, fraternal organization, ad hoc group organized around a specific issue, political organization—engaged in activities (strikes, demonstrations, oral or written public statements, and so forth) designed to affect existing or projected policies in areas of concern to them either on or off campus. An "organized group" is considered one in which a recognizable leadership exists.[1]

The results of this study of students at the University of Wisconsin over the last forty years revealed in their pattern of political activity changes in the way they perceive their roles as a group in the university and outside of it. Notable changes occurred in the frequency of conflicts between students and others with whom they interacted, in issues over which conflicts arose, in the student organizations which initiated most of the conflicts, and in the means used by students to achieve their ends.

One hundred and thirty-nine conflicts were identified in the sampling of the years 1930–1968. It should be emphasized that this is not a correct historical figure, since the study included only every other year. Of the 139 conflicts, 32 (23 per cent) took place in the thirties, 22 (16 per cent) in the forties, 17 (12 per cent) in the fifties, and 68 (49 per cent) in the sixties (see Figure 6). The figure for the thirties includes 1940, since that year resembles the years of the thirties with regard to issues over which conflicts arose and the organizations that participated in the conflicts. (Throughout this chapter, 1940 will be considered part of the thirties.)

Generally speaking, we can see three peaks of activity during the forty-year period. The thirties show a consistent pattern of five to seven conflicts every year from 1932 to 1940. The second peak comes during the late forties, the postwar period. The third peak comes in the middle and late sixties. Each peak is higher than its predecessor. Of the three peaks, the only surprising one is that of the late forties, since that period is not usually thought of as a period of student activism. There are also three periods in which student activism was very low; the first one is in 1930—we have no evidence as to the pattern before that. The second low comes during the period of the Second World War, and the third occurs in the early and middle fifties.

The 139 conflicts arose over a variety of issues. Two broad types of issues were most frequent—those involving war and the military and those involving racial or religious discrimination. War and military issues were involved in 38 conflicts during the forty-year period (27 per cent of all conflicts); race relations figured in 22 conflicts (16 per cent). The single most frequent type of issue in both the thirties and the sixties concerned war or the military. However, in the thirties war and military issues were numerically more important than in the sixties (they constituted 41 per cent of all conflicts in the thirties and 30 per cent of all

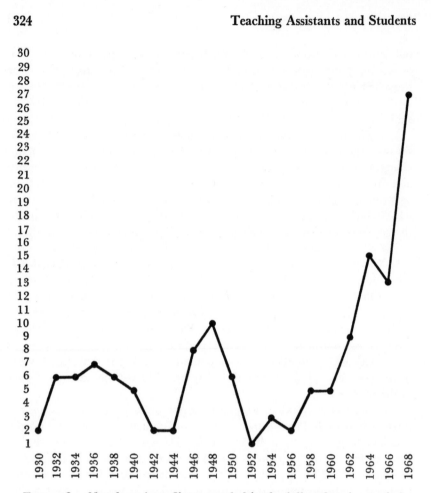

FIGURE 6.   *Number of conflicts recorded in the fall and spring periods
of every second year from 1930 to 1968.*

conflicts in the sixties). In the late forties and throughout the fifties only
four war and military issues were found. Within this broad category three
subgroups stand out: ROTC-related conflicts—eleven conflicts distributed
almost evenly among the different decades; antiwar activities of the
thirties—8 conflicts; and specifically anti-Vietnam conflicts—twelve conflicts. Other issues included in this grouping—draft resistance, intervention in Cuba and the Dominican Republic—are less frequent and are
concentrated mainly in the sixties.

The second largest group of issues concerns racial or religious discrimination. This issue came up throughout the forty-year period, with

no significant concentration in any particular decade. It should be noted, though, that in the thirties the issue was not very important. Besides protests against anti-Semitism in Germany, there were only two conflicts in the thirties over racial discrimination, while in both the forties and fifties there were five such conflicts, and in the sixties there were eight.

The next two most frequent sources of dispute are economic issues and school facilities (dormitory conditions, food, class facilities, and so on). Economic issues are concentrated in the thirties (six out of thirteen such conflicts), while in the sixties they are not prominent at all. Conflicts involving school facilities are found throughout the decades, without any significant pattern. Some of the other types of issues appear to be concentrated mainly in the sixties—campaigns against legislative investigations of radicals on campus, including anti-HUAC campaigns; aid to labor groups; expressions of support for students at Wisconsin or other campuses who are harassed by authorities on and off campus; and issues specifically involving student participation in decision making.

A salient characteristic of the sixties is the variety of issues that are involved in conflicts. Though war and military problems compose the single most common type, we find a significant number of conflicts over other issues. If we sum the most frequent sources—war and military, racial discrimination, school facilities, and economic issues—for each decade, we see that they were the subjects of 81 per cent of the conflicts in the thirties, 64 per cent in the forties, 71 per cent in the fifties, and only 53 per cent in the sixties. We find a greater variety of issues in the sixties than in the thirties, the decade to which they are most often compared.

When we divide all the conflicts into two broad categories, one involving internal university policies and decisions and the other non-university issues, we see that across the years there were as many on-campus issues as off-campus ones. However, when we look at the decades, the differences are notable: in the thirties the distribution was about equal, in the fifties and forties the majority of the conflicts were related to internal university affairs, and in the sixties the majority of the conflicts centered around off-campus issues.

Information was gathered on the student group or groups which started or first entered each conflict. *Initiator* denotes a group from which the initiative for the action came, an *ally* is a group that later joined in the action or expressed support for the initiator. Here we will deal only with the initiator (see Table 10). Left and peace organizations were involved in the initiation of the most disputes throughout the years: 47 of 139 conflicts (34 per cent). The second most frequent initiator is the student government, which initiated 29 conflicts (21 per cent). Third is

The Daily Cardinal, initiating 25 conflicts (18 per cent). Dormitory associations, class organizations, and departmental organizations started 15
conflicts.

When we compare the various groups across the decades, we see
some interesting differences: the left and peace organizations started 22
conflicts in the thirties and 26 in the sixties; however, in the thirties that
meant 69 per cent of all conflicts, while in the sixties it was only 38 per
cent. Thus, while we hear all the time about Students for a Democratic
Society (SDS) and other New Left organizations, we see that student
activity in the sixties was not confined to them alone. In the thirties, however, the student movement can be attributed almost entirely to the left.
Had there been no left, the thirties might have been very similar to the
forties and fifties.[2]

The student government was in the center of affairs in the forties
and fifties. In each of these decades, the student government was the
most frequent initiator. In the thirties and sixties, the student government
began only a minority of conflicts. *The Daily Cardinal* was most active in
the thirties, forties, and fifties; in these decades it was the second most
frequent initiator. Religious groups were quite active in the thirties but
have not been very active since that time, judging from the number of
conflicts they initiated or helped initiate. The partisan organizations were
among the initiators of nine conflicts; two in the late forties, one in the
fifties, and six in the sixties, most of them in the early sixties. The most
active organization was the Young Democrats.

Finally, it is interesting to note that ad hoc organizations were
among the starters of ten disputes in the sixties—the second most frequent initiators in this decade. Five other conflicts initiated by ad hoc
groups are distributed among the other three decades. This distribution
is a good indication of the stronger general mood of activism in the
sixties.

The greatest single change in the means used by students during
their conflicts with other groups in the forty years under study is the
shift toward increased use of mass tactics—demonstrations, mass meetings, sit-ins. All the means employed in a particular conflict were recorded. The techniques most frequently used could be grouped into three
major categories: representational means, petitions, and mass tactics.
Representational means include those that involve mainly the action of
elected representatives of the student body or of student organizations.
They include resolutions by any of these bodies; representatives sent to
the faculty, administration, or public official; and delegations to off-
campus events. Representational means were used most frequently in the
fifties, in 76 per cent of all conflicts. They were used least in the sixties,

Table 10. STUDENT GROUPS THAT INITIATED AT LEAST
FIVE CONFLICTS, BY DECADES

	1930s[a]	1940s	1950s	1960s
1. *Daily Cardinal*	7	6	6	6
2. Student Government	6	10	7	5
3. Dorm, Class, Departmental Organizations	6	3	2	6
4. University Religious Groups	6	—	—	1
5. Black and Civil Rights Organizations[b]	1	3	1	8
6. Left and Peace Organizations[e]	22	5	2	26
7. Partisan Organizations[d]	—	2	1	6
8. Ad-hoc Student Organizations	1	4	1	10
Total	32	22	17	68

[a] The year 1940 is included in the 1930s.

[b] Includes the Negro Culture Foundation, Concerned Black Students, Black People's Alliance, FSNCC, Student Council on Civil Rights.

[e] Includes, in the thirties: Young Communist League, Student League for Industrial Democracy, National Student League, Wisconsin Student Alliance, Progressive Club, University League for Liberal Action, Youth Committee Against the War, Anti-War Committee, Peace Federation. In the forties: American Youth for Democracy, Socialist Club, Progressive Club. In the fifties: Progressive Club, Student Peace Center. In the sixties: Socialist Club, Young Socialist Alliance, W.E.B. Du Bois Club, Students for a Democratic Society, Committee for Direct Action, Wisconsin Draft Resistance Union, Madison Resistance, Committee to End the War in Vietnam, Student Mobilization Committee, Student Peace Center, Students for Peace and Disarmament.

[d] Includes the Young Republicans, the Young Democrats, and the Students for Democratic Action.

NOTE: The table includes only those student organizations that were involved in the initiation of the conflicts recorded. It does not include all student organizations that existed on campus throughout the last forty years.

in 44 per cent of all conflicts. In the thirties and forties the proportion of conflicts in which representational means were used was about the same: 59 per cent and 52 per cent, respectively.

Petitions include both petitions and letters directed to public and university officials. Again, as with representational means, the fifties saw the greatest use of these tactics—in 71 per cent of all conflicts. In the thirties, petitions were used in 56 per cent of all disputes, while in the forties and sixties the proportions were 33 and 34 per cent, respectively. Mass tactics include all means that involve the participation of large numbers of people: demonstrations, mass meetings, occupation of buildings, sit-ins. Mass means, expectedly, are used most frequently in the sixties: in 54 per cent of all conflicts. In this decade they are the single most frequently used means. In the thirties, mass means were utilized in 37 per cent of all conflicts. In the forties, such tactics were used in only 15 per cent of the conflicts, and in the fifties no use of mass means was recorded.

Findings concerning changing student perceptions of their position as a group in the university and outside of it were somewhat hard to obtain. Attitudinal statements are not found in abundance throughout the years. There are several reasons for this scarcity. First, the newspaper reports action more than attitudes. It reports what each group did, or plans to do, more than what members of each group involved in the conflict say. Secondly, what student leaders or other group members involved in the conflict do say will more often refer to the substantive issue at hand than to the general consideration of their role as students. The frequency of appearance of the attitudes studied here is thus relatively low, but the trends are clear. Furthermore, changes in the attitudinal variables are corroborated by trends in the other variables recorded for the conflicts studied: number of conflicts, types of issues, initiating groups, and means employed by the students.

The attitudes here reported are grouped into four dimensions: desire for freedom from control by other groups; demand for greater decision-making rights; rejection of the image of students as immature citizens; and the presence of class consciousness on the part of students.

The dimension of freedom from control was measured by assertions questioning the right of other groups to make the given decision involved in the conflict or the right of those groups to make decisions affecting students in general. Examples of the first type of assertion include: "That is a decision that they [SLIC] have no right to make"; "How dare they dictate what we shall or shall not hear or read?" "But the university does not have any right to forbid a student from living where, and with whom, and among whom, he wants to." Examples of the second type include: "We reject the implication that such direction and control [by the university] applies to spheres of activity outside the academic world" and "The question is, should we always have to depend on their good graces when they are not even a legitimate representative of our wishes?"

The first type of assertion, questioning the right of other groups involved in the conflict to make the specific decision under dispute, was found in eight conflicts. Of these, six took place in the sixties, one in the thirties, and one in the fifties. The second type of assertion, that questioning the right of other groups involved in the conflict to make decisions concerning students in general, was found in only one conflict, in 1966, when the Wisconsin Student Association passed a bill giving it all the powers to regulate students' social and group life, while taking those powers away from the faculty and administration. Throughout the years, most of the groups whose rights were questioned were within the university—the faculty, the administration, or the Regents. Most of the questioning of the rights of others to make decisions affecting students was done in the sixties.

The dimension of students' rights to participate in decision making involves two main types of assertions. The first type refers to the rights of students to make decisions on the specific matter under dispute, such as housing regulations or women's hours. The second refers to the right of students to participate in decision making in general, not just in the conflict area. Within each of the two types of assertions, three degrees were recorded. Students were seen as asserting their right first to be consulted (including such expressions as "have a voice," or "be heard," "have something to say," "right to question"); second to be represented (including such expressions as "participate," "help formulate," "share authority,") and third to make the decision themselves.

Students asserted that they were entitled to a role in decision making mostly in the sixties; more than sixty per cent of the assertions regarding specific decisions were found in this decade. Demand for participation in decision making in general areas of student concern, not just in the ones directly involved in the conflict, was made only in the sixties. Furthermore, when we look at the degree of decision-making power requested, we find that in the previous decades the assertions concerned mostly consultatory and representational rights, while in the sixties both representational and exclusive student decision-making rights are demanded—in areas under conflict as well as in other areas. It should also be noted that in the sixties the areas in which students asserted their rights to decision making went beyond the limits of the campus to include local as well as national issues.

The third dimension taps the acceptance or rejection by students of their image as citizens-to-be, as not yet adults, not yet responsible and capable of making their own decisions. Examples of expressions which belong here are: "It is the cry of students who believe they are mature enough to accept the freedom . . . and the responsibility of regulating their own lives"; "If students are old enough to be sent to Laos and fight for American ideals they are discriminating enough not to be swayed by the raving of an extremist"; "University students have the ability to discern fallacious propaganda." Statements to the effect that students are mature, responsible, and able to make decisions appeared mostly in the sixties—ten of the twelve conflicts where these attitudes were expressed took place in the sixties. The assertions appeared in issues of direct concern to students within the university, such as housing and women's hours, but also in conflicts where the students acted in areas not traditionally seen as their concern. In such cases students defended their right to speak or act on the basis of their maturity.

Attitudes toward the concept of in loco parentis, although related to the issues already discussed, were recorded separately when it was mentioned specifically. All expressions concerning in loco parentis were negative, and such rejection appeared only in the sixties. The actual breakdown of the concept came in the fifties, when students demanded changes in hours and other regulations. Many of these demands were met with positive response from the administration and the faculty and thus do not appear here since they never developed into conflicts. Liberalization was slow, to be sure, but steady. It appears that the period of the Free Speech Movement and the increase in student activity in the sixties brought about a reactionary move within the administration in the area of in loco parentis policies—retraction of certain liberalizations or, in any case, opposition to new ones. So, while many regulations were lifted in the fifties without conflict and thus without the opportunity to express the type of attitudes we are studying here, the statements we do find come later, after the concept of in loco parentis had begun to erode.

The fourth grouping of attitudinal change relates to class consciousness. This dimension includes statements asserting that students have common problems, interests, and enemies, as well as statements that students are a powerful or relatively powerful group that can change or influence policies. Examples are: "This is a problem that belongs to every student in the university"; "It is we who receive the benefits of education, and it is we who lose if there are flaws in the educational process"; "We can't make our country's policies, but we can make our voices heard"; "In union there is strength." Expressions of class consciousness appeared in the thirties and the sixties, but not in the third period of high activism, the forties. In the thirties, the most frequent assertion was that students are a group with potential power to influence decisions; common problems were less frequently mentioned. In the sixties, statements that students have common problems were as frequent as assertions that they are a powerful group.

In general, it should be noted that while in the thirties class-consciousness expressions appeared mostly in relation to off-campus issues, in the sixties they appeared mostly regarding on-campus issues; this division may be related, of course, to the questioning of the distribution of decision-making power which took place in the sixties and which was most prominent in the on-campus issues. As for the absence of assertions of class consciousness in the late forties, the explanation might lie in the nature of the conflicts of that period—they were fought mostly by the student establishment, without mass involvement and without questioning present relationships between students and other groups. Furthermore, a large proportion of students were veterans, many with families, and they identified as veterans rather than as students.

Drawing together the findings regarding patterns of student political activity and students' perceptions of their role in and outside the university, the dominant themes in each decade can be characterized. Much student political activity in the thirties was devoted to antiwar efforts and economic issues. Other issues which made their appearance periodically during this decade revolved around attacks on radicals and "reds" in the university on the part of conservative elements throughout the state, most notably in the state legislature, and attempts by the same body to reinstate compulsory military training (ROTC had been voluntary at the University of Wisconsin since 1923) so that university radicals, who "come to it from the East because they dislike military training," would no longer enjoy their refuge.

Antiwar activity took the form of Armistice Day demonstrations against participation in future wars (even before World War II was imminent), conferences against war, and annual antiwar strikes, beginning in the spring of 1934. These were generally national in scope and sponsored by student communist, socialist, and religious organizations. The antiwar strike of April 1935 was attended by 830 Wisconsin students. Efforts on the part of the university administration to take the "radicalism" out of the strikes by declaring solidarity with the students and offering sponsorship of "peace convocations" instead of antiwar strikes made the fight against war (or for peace) a respectable, very American activity by the spring of 1937. The antiwar strike at the University of Wisconsin that year was marked by an absence of controversy, which its sponsors blamed for the small turnout of 500 students. Two years later, when a

European war was imminent, an antiwar strike could no longer draw large audiences. While 2,200 students attended a "peace convocation" at which Harold Laski argued for collective security, fewer than 100 students attended the strike organized by the local chapter of the Youth Committee Against the War (YCAW).

The peculiarity of the campus peace movement in the thirties which distinguished it from the adult organizations was its argument that the ones to die in the battlefields would be the young, and thus the special stake of the young, the students, in the movement. It is important to note that the movement was referred to at the time as a youth movement as often as a student movement. (See, for example, *Daily Cardinal,* December 16, 1934.) It was not conceived as a movement of students, as such, trying to play a part in national politics, but as young people—most of them in colleges—sharing in the efforts of their elders to improve the world, or, if you will, to change it. There was no rejection of adult solutions as such—only a preference for some adults' solutions over those of others.

What we now call student power issues were nonexistent; student government was an idea more or less imposed on the students from above so that the administration of student affairs would be easier for faculty and administrators alike. There was no questioning of the relations between students and faculty and administrators. Disciplinary powers of the faculty were taken for granted, and the *Cardinal* apologized for discussing them in an editorial (*Daily Cardinal,* May 14, 1931). It was the faculty that proposed student representation on their committees dealing with student interests (in 1936); faculty initiated curriculum changes and had to campaign to get students' opinions on the issue (in spring 1939).

Campus issues were largely an adjunct to off-campus political questions. They arose, in part, from an effort by the radical groups to legitimize themselves before the student body as well as in the eyes of campus authorities. Otherwise, it could probably be stated that student political activity in the thirties was a reflection of political activities in the larger American political scene; the National Student League (NSL) and the Student League for Industrial Democracy (SLID), later united in the Wisconsin Student Alliance (the name for the local chapter of the American Student Union), were organizationally related to adult socialist and communist political organizations; successes of student chapters depended largely on developments in the adult political scene.

It should be noted here again that these organizations initiated or were among the initiators of twenty-two out of thirty-two conflicts recorded for that period. The student movement of the thirties was largely due to the work of the NSL and SLID and the various other organizations which grew out of them, were formed by them, or were dominated by them.

Very important in those years were the various religious organizations on campus and in the local community. Besides being initiators of six conflicts during these years, religious leaders and organizations were usually more ready than other organized groups to publicly support the leftist activities and join them in their causes. Other nonpolitical student organizations were rather inactive in conflicts; we refer here to dormitory associations, class organizations, student governmental units, and so on. Fraternities and other social organizations sometimes joined the action but were rarely among the initiators.

During the first half of the thirties the university administration was rather tolerant of and cooperative with the student activists. Above all, it defended the right of the radical groups to carry out their activities and came out strongly against attacks on academic freedom from outside the university. The administration cooperated with students in opposing reinstatement of compulsory ROTC and in protesting against budget cuts by the legislature; it endorsed the first antiwar activities, as well as the peace convocations of later years. Toward the end of the decade, the mood changed; in the spring of 1939, when students supporting a peace strike—not the officially-sanctioned peace convocation—distributed handbills on campus, they were rebuked by a Regents' resolution prohibiting such action.

The appointment of President Dykstra to the directorship of the draft in 1940 was accompanied by an increasing antiradical, patriotic mood. There was some resistance to the draft on the part of the YCAW and the University League for Liberal Action (a local organization affiliated with the American Student Union), but these activities did not get much coverage in the student newspaper. The *Cardinal* discussed radicalism at the university under the heading "The Myth of Wisconsin Radicalism" and concluded that actually the campus had never been receptive to radical ideas and activities, or, as they put it, "In every bushel, only one bad apple" (*Daily Cardinal,* April 29, 1941). And in the winter of 1941, Dean Goodnight requested that all student organizations submit complete membership lists to the university. The Youth Committee Against the War could not find room in the university to hold its national convention (in spite of the fact that the university had hosted the American Student Union convention the year before). A new era of student inactivity was heralded by a football pep rally attended by 12,000 fans who had been urged by the *Cardinal* to cheer loudly at the game because football represented a part of the American way of life.

The decade of the forties contains two distinct periods of student political activity. The earlier forties, when the ranks of students were depleted by the war effort, saw, as might be expected, very little student activism. Only two conflicts, one in 1942 and one in 1944, deserve mention here; both were over the issue of religious and/or racial discrimination in housing. The 1942 issue was initiated by the *Cardinal* in the wake of rumors that black, Jewish, and Chinese students were having difficulty finding rooms. The 1944 issue arose over the University Club's ouster of a black English instructor who had evidently been accepted by mail (the Club is a social organization for faculty members, some of whom live there). Great pressure was brought to bear on the faculty club members, until the instructor was finally offered membership and residence in the Club.

The postwar years are not generally regarded as a period of student activism, yet in 1946 and in 1948 we found eight and ten conflicts, respectively—each year having more conflicts than any single year studied in the thirties. What was behind this activity? It certainly was not a manifestation of a student movement like that of the thirties and the sixties. Rather, it reflected active defense of a variety of student interests and some broader social issues by several student groups, most prominently student government bodies, the American Veteran's Committee (a liberal veteran's organization formed nationally by veterans who rejected the more conservative, flag-waving organizations of former soldiers), and a few leftist groups. The single most important organized factor was the AVC—they participated, as initiators or supporters, in at least twelve out of the eighteen conflicts recorded for 1946 and 1948. Outside of the AVC, veterans were probably active in other organizations as well. The position of veterans was different from that of traditional political activists on campus; they came to college late and wanted to get an education which would enable them to enter the job market. Moreover, the veterans would not accept the argument that they were not yet mature or responsible enough to make decisions. After fighting in Europe and in Asia, they would become indignant when told that anything was none of their business.

A variety of issues were involved in the conflicts of those years. There were the direct student-interest issues—increase in veteran's allowances, demands for more basketball tickets for students, as well as two celebrated attempts to get football coach Harry Strudreher fired. There were antidiscrimination activities—participation in a drive to unseat a racist senator from Mississippi, as well as a drive to eliminate discrimination from university housing. There were civil liberties issues—opposition to legislative attempts to get rid of communists on campus, as well as opposition to the administrative attempt to have all organizations submit complete membership lists. Finally, there were drives to return voluntary ROTC to the campus.

The politics of the period—as exemplified by the conflict over discrimination in housing—were establishmentarian. The main actors worked through established channels; there were few demonstrations, mass rallies, or strikes. The primary means utilized were resolutions, petitions, and delegations to the relevant authorities. There was no question of the superior role of the other groups in the university or outside of it. Students played the game of politics in a trade-unionist fashion. Results of student actions were not always positive, yet they did not give up the channels used or question their utility.

In general, the administration was not as involved in student activities in the forties as it had been in the thirties. On such issues as ROTC and legislative investigations of campus radicals, it remained aloof, probably due to the general mood in the country at the time. On other issues, such as discrimination in housing and a student request to remove a Lake Mendota boathouse concession run by a reputed anti-Semite, the university administration kept postponing its decision and in the final analysis, did not give in to student demands. The administration attempted to clamp down on radical groups—especially the American Youth for Democracy—through the application of a wartime ruling requiring all student organizations to file complete membership lists. The ruling was shelved only in the face of a strong united protest from the leaders of several student organizations.

With the graduation of the veterans, and under the influence of the Cold War and an internal drive against anything that could be called "red," activism on the campus slowly disappeared. Compared to the other periods—with the sole exception of World War II—the fifties present the quietest campus scene. Radical groups were few and inactive. The conflicts in this period usually dragged on for long periods of time and were almost never accompanied by the excitement of mass participation or the tension of sharp confrontation. Most of the conflicts were fought by the official organs of the student body, the *Cardinal* or the governmental organizations. The *Cardinal* was clearly the most active student institution, and it kept calling throughout the period for more student interest and involvement in political or social issues. The *Cardinal* also kept analyzing the "silent generation" or the "jellyfish generation" in attempts to explain student inactivity and also to find a way out of it. The paper openly attached the one cause it mentioned most frequently—Senator McCarthy.

The most frequent issues in the fifties were protests against compulsory ROTC and budget cuts by the state legislature. The fights against proposed budget cuts were usually fought by the university as a whole, not just the students; it was relatively easy to get student signatures on a subject on which faculty and administration openly agreed with the students and had initiated the action. The fight against ROTC should be seen in light of the fact that ROTC had been voluntary at Wisconsin since 1923 and was made compulsory again during the war, so the drive was to restore something that had already existed, not to offer a completely new policy. Even so, the protests against compulsory ROTC were mild. In 1950, as well as in 1956, a small group of silent, walking protestors carried signs at an ROTC function. In 1954, the immediate issue was a new loyalty oath for ROTC men; the strongest protest against the oath came from the faculty, the students (except the *Cardinal*) being too timid to use the issue for a general attack on compulsory ROTC. In 1958 the ROTC issue was in the hands of the student government, which approached it by way of a detailed study and several resolutions. This time, however, the student government succeeded in getting a voluntary ROTC bill to the legislature.

There was also activity in the field of racial discrimination, starting with the defeat of a student proposal for the elimination of discrimination in housing in 1950, after a two-year effort, and including a protracted effort—which lasted into the sixties—to have the fraternities eliminate discriminatory clauses from their charters.

Another theme in several of the conflicts was the defense of free speech. In 1950–1951 student organizations made some stir over the refusal of the Kemper-Knapp Fund, which usually supported guest speakers, to finance the appearance of Max Lerner. The students succeeded in bringing him the same day Senator McCarthy appeared on campus for a speech to the Young Republicans. McCarthy was laughed at by part of the audience, while Lerner was applauded, which led the latter to declare that students at Wisconsin were not part of the "marshmallow generation." In 1954, Students for Democratic Action led a drive against McCarthy, and in 1956 the campus organizations put up a united front against a ruling by SLIC that would require them to submit their complete membership lists. This conflict, which resulted in a partial victory for the students, drew together the largest number of organizations of any of the conflicts recorded during the decade.

The issue of membership lists had started out of a dispute between the Labor Youth League and SLIC, a dispute which led eventually to the disbandment of LYL. *The Daily Cardinal* (October 2, 1956), commenting on the case, said:

The spirit of radicalism is dying. This became painfully evident . . . with the announcement that the Labor Youth League has finally succumbed to the combined pressures of the American Legion, the university refusal to accept officers, and lack of membership. It seems likely that the third reason is the strongest.

Which is a good commentary on the status of radical groups on campus in the fifties. But radical groups were not the only ones that failed to recruit an active membership. Student interest in student government activities was not abundant either. In April 1953, for example, a laborious effort on the part of members of the student government to restructure their organization was shelved after it failed to be approved in a campus referendum because not enough students showed up to vote.

Throughout the fifties, the administration's behavior toward student activism could best be described as midway between traditional liberalism and harassment of radical groups. Thus, the administration joined other university administrations in protesting a ROTC loyalty oath introduced in 1954 by the Defense Department, but it also did everything possible to make life difficult for the Labor Youth League. Since the radical groups were very small and generally rejected by the student body, the administration rarely met opposition to these actions, and its liberal reputation was rarely challenged by students. It should be noted here again that throughout the decade the administration liberalized regulations concerning student life. The impetus for such changes came from student organizations, with whom the Administration cooperated—albeit without enthusiasm—in liberalizing in loco parentis rules.

The development of the student movement in the sixties was characterized by a variety of issues, tactics, groups, and patterns of participation; the picture is one of a growing general fermentation rather than that of one or few organizations striving cohesively and in unison for the achievement of a number of goals. In 1960, we find small-scale action lacking any noticeable following on the campus at large—by the Socialist Club (against U.S. intervention in Cuba), by the Student Peace Union and other small peace groups against massive spending for civil defense and for disarmament, as well as anti-HUAC activity, a reaction to the San Francsico anti-HUAC demonstrations and the infamous "Operation Abolition" film. Student government started to show interest in off-campus issues, although limiting itself to the passage of resolutions such as one expressing sympathy for Algeria. This action—not to mention the activity of the socialist and peace groups—drew strong criticism from the *Cardinal*, which argued that students should not concern themselves with affairs which are "neither of our [student] making nor within our power to resolve" and are "completely outside the area of student responsibility" (*Daily Cardinal*, April 25, 1961).

The 1962–1963 school year is similar to that of 1960–1961. The Socialist Club and peace groups such as the Student Peace Union and SPAD (Students for Peace and Disarmament), as well as the Young Socialist Alliance, were the groups that showed concern with off-campus actions (Cuba, HUAC, help to Kentucky miners). The biggest conflict, however, was a protest by fraternity and sorority members against a faculty rule that required campus fraternal organizations to be autonomous from their national organizations with regard to membership regulations, so as to be able to accept members without racial or religious discrimination. Failure to comply with the rule brought a threat of expulsion to one sorority, and this, in turn, ignited a strong controversy about how much the faculty and administration could regulate student organizations, as well as a demonstration by twelve hundred Greeks on Bascom Hill.

The year 1964–1965 was different. In the spring of 1965, the campus had already seen an anti-Vietnam demonstration, and now the Student Faculty Committee to End the War in Vietnam organized a teach-in on the war, similar to the first one held at the university of Michigan, attended by around five thousand students. The event aroused bitter opposition from an anti-left, pro-Vietnam group, which organized a Committee to Support the People of South Vietnam and gathered six thousand signatures supporting the government's policies on the war. The same spring also saw strong civil rights activity, focused around the drive to help civil rights workers in the South, with relatively large delegations sent to Selma, Alabama, and Washington, D.C., as well as local rallies in support of these struggles. In the same year, as if to exemplify the rather absurd position of the student in the university—at the same time that thousands of students were participating in activities concerning the war in Vietnam and hundreds were getting involved in the struggle for civil rights—residents of the dormitories were arguing with administrators over how they were to dress for dinner.

The 1966–1967 school year saw war protest as its major issue; there were silent vigils against the war and Edward Kennedy was heckled for his refusal to address himself to the questions of the war. Pickets at election booths protested the lack of discussion of the war in election campaigns. Other protests centered around the Spring Mobilization Against the War—two nationally-coordinated peace rallies, one in New York and the other in San Francisco. At the same time, though, we see the appearance of labor-union type organizations for the protection of student interests, the most prominent in that year being the Student Tenant Union. There were also protests over failure to consult residents of the dormitories on the hiring and firing of housefellows, as well as a huge protest over the city's refusal to remove a hazardous bus lane from a campus street.

The year also saw a big student power conflict. Arising out of an SDS anti-Dow sit-in and an attempt to revoke the status of SDS as a student organization, a dispute developed as to who had the final say regarding the status of a student organizaion, SLIC or the Student Court. Two campus parties, one of them the University Campus Action, which had been formed earlier that year by members of radical groups on the assumption that the best way to achieve their goals would be to form themselves into a regular student party, introduced a bill to the Student Senate that would put final responsibility for student group and social life in the hands of the student government. The bill was passed, over the opposition of conservative student delegates. A long discussion of the constitutionality of the bill ensued, including a campus-wide referendum in which 6,146 out of 10,052 students approved the bill. The issue was not resolved during that school year, but the conflict represented the culmination of the issue of student independence from faculty and administrative tutelage.

The year 1968 was characterized by student attempts to participate in several aspects of university life—admissions (of black students), curriculum, teaching-assistant salaries, and student discipline. The biggest conflict occurred over demands of the Black People's Alliance (see Chapter Sixteen). Students, the "unconsulted consumer" (*Daily Cardinal,* November 20, 1968), tried to achieve participation in making educational policy by working through the system; students in departments of history, psychology, political science, English, and engineering and science formed departmental associations concerned with "creating a community of scholars in which professors and students treat each other as equals and, as groups, have an equal voice in determining the policies which affect them" (*Daily Cardinal,* November 5, 1968). When communications between departmental associations and faculty broke down, students protested, as when the history faculty passed a resolution excluding students from department meetings a month after they had unanimously agreed to open these meetings to students.

The same year, the Teaching Assistants Association demanded "participation in and negotiation of the decisions that affect the terms and conditions of the employment of teaching assistants at the university," that is, recognition of the TAA as the exclusive bargaining agent of the teaching assistants at Wisconsin. Their demand was at first refused, but in May, following a referendum in which the overwhelming majority of assistants voted for the TAA, the organization was certified as the official union.

The year also saw students viewing their community as apart from the rest of the city, a community over which they alone had the right to exercise control. Attempts on the part of the district attorney and chief of police to censor a rather risque version of the play *Peter Pan* were met with defiance on the part of the director and cast and a barrage of letters to the *Cardinal* from outraged students. When the Board of Regents attacked the *Cardinal* for its use of obscene language, the traditionally independent paper's reaction was, "Up against the Wall, Re . . . ts," a denouncement of the "outright effort to exert Regent authority on students' life and interests as well as a violation of the freedom of the press and free speech [sic]" (*Daily Cardinal,* November 5, 1968). In May a block party held in the Mifflin Street area turned into a riot when police came to break it up. It was followed by several days of protests and battles between students and police. The incident aroused general demands for "the right to control the business of life in our own community" (*Daily Cardinal,* May 6, 1969).

During the 1968–1969 school year, SDS and WDRU (the Wisconsin Draft Resistance Union) worked together on labor issues; they joined picket lines with striking teamsters and city employees and picketed local supermarkets carrying California grapes during the grape boycott. This year was also characterized by the sheer numbers of students that participated in protests or demonstrations. In addition to the protests already mentioned, three thousand students participated in a march designed to express support for GIs in California who were opposed to the war, and two thousand participated in a march whose dual purpose was to protest the U.S. election system and the return of Dow Chemical Company recruiters to campus.

Finally, students did not limit their protests to university authorities but brought their grievances to the Madison city council and the Dane County board of supervisors, probably because of the presence of student members on these bodies: draft cards were burned before the eyes of members of the board of supervisors, and draft resisters turned in their draft cards to the mayor at a meeting of the city council. Students also attended hearings on rezoning proposals and attempted to prevent high-rise buildings from being built in low-rent residential areas.

The sixties saw a student movement on the campus which was quite different from anything seen before. In sheer numbers of participants, variety of activities, and scope of issues, this movement was un-

precedented. But there are other characteristics which are more important. In the sixties students as a group questioned the relationship between themselves and the traditional groups with whom they interact—
the administration and the faculty, as well as a variety of local authorities; they also went beyond the campus to declare their views on matters
of national concern to a larger degree than ever before. For the first
time, student groups rejected the rights of other groups to make a variety
of decisions concerning them, and they asserted their own right to participate with other groups in the making of certain decisions. In a number of areas, students stated that they were the only ones who could
make decisions. There was a repudiation of the image of students as
immature, irresponsible young people not yet able to make or participate
in the making of decisions of the adult world. Expressions of class consciousness were heard in both on-campus and off-campus conflicts, and
concern extended to students in other universities. Rejection of the traditional concept of in loco parentis was also found.

Furthermore, we see a very large number of conflicts—larger than
in any other period—and a greater variety of issues around which conflicts arose. Student groups utilized a variety of tactics when they were
involved in conflicts. The traditional resolutions, representations to authorities, and petitions were still in use, but the methods most frequently
used were mass means—demonstrations, sit-ins, mass meetings, and
strikes. Large numbers of students were visibly and sometimes violently
involved in the conflicts. And when student demands were not met, students insisted on their rights rather than backing down, even when university authorities sought help from local and state forces.

In the sixties, students were in the center of politics; they did not
—like their predecessors of the thirties—follow the policies of adult organizations. Rather, they initiated issues, and they were among the most
active supporters of those issues, if not the most active ones. The faculty
that in prior periods had had to campaign to recruit student support in
political action now found themselves playing second fiddle, when not
playing a different tune altogether. The same holds true for many of the
traditional adult organizations that in earlier periods had declared some
of the issues student groups raised in the sixties. Students were not merely
in the position of supporting other groups in the process of change but
were among the central actors, if not, as some members of the New Left
have suggested, *the* central actors.

Notes

1 The actual procedure for the content analysis was as follows. All the issues
of the newspaper, from the registration issues to Christmas break, and from March
1st to the end of the regular school year, were read. Once a conflict was identified,

all the information about it—from the first reported activity to the last one—was recorded on two different types of coding sheets: attitude sheets and summary sheets. One attitude sheet was used for every unit of recording (A unit of recording is the smallest section of a text in which a reference is recorded.) The unit of recording was a letter to the editor, an editorial, or a speech reported in a news story—in other words, a piece of writing containing the opinion of one person. The attitudes that were recorded on the attitude sheets were those concerning the position of students as a group in the university or in society. We are not interested, for example, in substantive arguments for or against ROTC, the war in Vietnam, or the quality of food in a given dormitory. Rather, we were interested in what students involved in the conflict thought their role—as a group—should be; for example whether students thought they had the right to participate in the making of a given decision or whether they accepted the authority of other groups when decisions concerning them were made. One summary sheet was used for each conflict. On it was recorded the chronological development of the conflict, the student groups that initiated the action or were the first to enter it, the means that students used in order to achieve their aims, the types of issues over which the conflict arose, as well as other factual information about the conflict.

    [2] It could be said, of course, that members of leftist groups activate other student organizations; we had no way to check that systematically, although some examples of participation of members of leftist groups in other campus organizations could be found in the newspaper.

CHAPTER 18

GENERATIONAL CONFLICT

Robert S. Laufer, Sheila McVey

The consciousness of generations is formed by the common historical experiences that shape the perceptions of man and society held by individuals who share the same generational location. Conflict between generations arises when the historical experience of two generations is so disparate that each views the social world from a radically different perspective. Thus, knowledge of the differing images of the world held by young and old is essential to an understanding of the process of generational conflict.[1]

In winter 1970, we began a study aimed at exploring the consciousness of contending generations. This chapter is a report of that research. We attempted to investigate the sources of generational conflict through open-ended interviews which focused primarily on the respondent's personal reaction to or experience of a series of significant historical events that began in the early 1960s, or in the time period which we thought critical to the formation of consciousness in our respondents, who ranged in age between eighteen and twenty-four. Because we wanted to explore the formation of consciousness in that segment of the younger generation which is engaged in conflict with the older generation, yet not necessarily defined by membership in a radical group, we selected our respondents from a pool of 150 students who, through their enrollment in an experimental, student-run course in the department of education policies studies at the University of Wisconsin, showed some dissatisfaction with the educational system.[2]

Indeed, the responses provided by the students interviewed confirmed our expectations; generally, they represented a group extremely critical of and deeply alienated from American society, yet, at the same time, they were not hard-core radicals totally engaged in movement work. In other words, these students are not part of the vanguard of the revolution (only two of the students claimed membership in any radical campus organization) and are probably more typical of that fairly large segment of the student body which is mobilized by demonstrations, but who are not leaders or organizers of protest. Our specific purpose in this chapter, then, is to present the values held by these young people, examine their criticisms of society, and try to come to an understanding of their generational consciousness.

Initially, we had hoped to interview 50 of the 150 students enrolled in the experimental course, but the 1970 spring semester at Wisconsin was interrupted by a teaching assistants' strike and a series of demonstrations in response to the Kent State–Cambodia crisis. These events reduced the normal sixteen-week semester to nine weeks and cut the number of our projected interviews almost in half. Therefore, this study, given the size of the sample (24), must be treated as a case study. However, our experience at Madison suggests the attitudes represented by our respondents are fairly widespread.

Those who participated represent a specific type of community— white, urban and suburban middle- and upper-middle-class youth from the Middlewest and East. The family income of these students is extraordinarily high for a public university—the median is in the twenty to twenty-five thousand dollar range. Furthermore, the educational attainment of both parents is also quite high; a majority of the fathers (nineteen) and mothers (fifteen) have attended college for at least some time, while a significant minority of fathers (eight) and mothers (seven) have spent time in graduate school or have a graduate degree.[3] Parental religious affiliation was varied both between and among families.[4] With regard to political affiliation, twelve mothers and twelve fathers are listed by their children as Democrats, three mothers and three fathers as independents, and eight fathers and six mothers as Republicans. No answer was given for one father and three mothers.

The median age of the students interviewed was twenty-one. Thirteen were males and eleven females; all except two were single. The majority of the group were in the social sciences (eleven), while humanities (six), pre-professionals (four), and those undecided about a major (three) accounted for the remainder. When asked to indicate religious preference, ten said they had none, seven indicated Judaism, two Protestantism, two Zen, one Catholicism, and two made no response. In other words, the dominant response to religion is rejection.[5] With regard to political party preference, nine chose the label radical and nine felt none of the categories offered (radical, liberal Democrat, conservative Democrat, liberal Republican, conservative Republican, none of the labels fit) were appropriate; when questioned as to their reluctance to make a choice, these nine indicated they had strong sympathies with a broadly defined radicalism but felt the label implied an organizational relationship they did not have. Four indicated that they were liberal Democrats, and two did not answer. Thus, a clear majority of the students are politically more radical than their parents, although the degree of ideological dissonance varies. Moreover, their definition of politics is not confined to the formal mechanisms of government but extends to almost all social and economic relationships; ideological differences, then, imply basic value differences.

In confirmation of the growing literature on generational conflict, the way in which these young people define success, personal fulfillment, and happiness implies that differences in values held by the young and old in the American middle and upper-middle class are the basis of much conflict. However, conflict between generations in relation to values is usually not directly between child and parent but between children and the older generation as a collectivity—the Establishment. In other words, the students are not alienated from or rebelling against their parents as individuals but against the structural position held by their parents in society. In fact, most of the students have warm family relationships often characterized by discussion of contemporary problems in which students try to maintain contact with and "reeducate" their parents. "I disagree with him [father] a lot; he's a Republican, and my mother has no political views at all. She doesn't vote, never has. I'm sure he'd be shocked at my ideas. I do discuss things with them, but I water things down one hell of a lot to try to communicate with them."

Students and parents are often able to reach agreement on or at least an understanding of abstract ideological positions, but the students are quite aware that private verbal support or understanding does not extend to active public commitment on the part of their parents.

I mean they [parents] . . . agree with a lot of the [radical] analysis I make, but I don't think they would do as much about it as I would.

My parents agree with most of what I do, but they wouldn't give up the security they have . . . they wouldn't change their lives.

Generally, they do not condemn their parents for their inability to act on their convictions, but instead more accurately aim their indignation at the Establishment that so constrains the actions of those who must, because of age and need for security, live within its framework.

Politically I agree with them a lot more than socially. Socially, they say they agree but "for you it is different." They'll admit it is hard for them to see a lot of these social changes because they've grown up in a completely different thing. They can recognize it and accept it, but they . . . can't change and approve it. And I think acceptance is one step . . . before you can approve you have to accept.

They [my parents] see . . . everything I do as a revolt against them, and not their ideas. They take it to heart and they take it personally where they shouldn't. I'm not disagreeing with them, I am disagreeing only with what they stand for.

Although the students realize and in some cases tolerate their parents' inability to act, this remains an area of contention in that one of the primary values they hold is commitment to social action. In fact, their commitment to action seems to stem in part from reaction to their parents preoccupation with sentiment and ideology at the expense of action.

My parents are good liberals, but don't want a colored person living next door . . . I wonder if I have the right to say these things. I [might] be living in the suburbs in fifteen years and not want blacks living next to me, but . . . I think I'll carry through on the things I believe in . . . I want to teach in a high school in a depressed area.

I think to give up is the worst thing to do.

Thus, when we refer to conflict between generations, we are not speaking of direct confrontations within families but rather of conflict between youth and the established social order.

In order to understand the values held by youth, we must also examine their critique of society, since many of the values they hold are a mirror image of that which they regard negatively. For example, our respondents value the needs of people over the sanctity of property.

[America is] . . . the alienation of a person from himself, his society. The emphasis upon capitalism has created a supercompetitive society in which people are . . . used to stepping on each other. The only thing that can save this society is if people begin to care for each other.

Their emphasis on human needs leads them to sharp criticism of what they perceive as an exploitive and materialistic foreign policy.

Imperialistic wealth has to come from somewhere; we're not generating it ourselves . . . we're using other [nations] throughout the world to maintain our economic and political level.

I'm ashamed of this country . . . the way it acts towards other countries, and how others see it . . . I can't be proud [of] America . . . [it] just means materialism and a horrible foreign policy.

However, none perceive foreign policy as an isolated phenomenon; it is usually seen as analogous to elite domination and exploitation in domestic society.

The whole idea of reconciling our economy to how it affects the Third World and the underclass in this society is really a serious problem . . . how to effect a more humanistic society when there is a whole base of materialism, oppression, exploitation.

Accordingly, a shift in national priorities from military and industrial needs to fulfillment of human needs is demanded.

It's exciting . . . the moon [shot]. But I think the whole project is a damn waste of money. Get the hell out of Vietnam and get the hell off the moon and start employing [people] . . . I'd say domestic problems are our major concern —pollution, education, urban renewal, things like that.

However, they realize the formidable obstacles that the dominant American value system places in the way of any major change.

Materialism . . . it encompasses just about everything . . . overdevelopment, the reasons for foreign and domestic policy . . . everything seems to be motivated by material needs.

Thus, the students emphasize the value and dignity of human life and condemn the values of the older generation—all forms of materialism—that deny man's humanity. They also find repugnant the mode of social relations—exploitation and manipulation—imposed by a materialistic orientation. As a result, they attempt to counteract the values and social relationships practiced by the older generation through their own life style. They stress communalism and cooperation rather than individualistic competition.

Communities . . . have to develop . . . places where people's heads are together, thinking in the same way, working for common goals, goals for the betterment of lots of people, not just your [own] personal gain.

The concern with cooperation and communalism does not call for a sacrifice of individualism. Instead, the students emphasize a new kind of individualism that is underpinned by tolerance for the foibles of their fellowman. The individualism they reject is the American frontier brand of "rugged individualism" identified by Alexis de Tocqueville as a narrow economic and social competition produced by an ambivalent reaction to a theoretically open society. Rather than accepting the individualism of the competitive struggle, students emphasize acceptance of the idiosyncratic individual. Thus, the students criticize the intolerance of the older generation.

We are a society made up of different people moving in different ways, yet we must recognize that there is an intolerance of that diversity.

There is intolerance . . . if [youth culture] is a threat to their life style and it poses fear.

A more comprehensive tolerance is called for:

People [should] do what they want as long as they don't hurt others . . . they should have the freedom to do what they want with themselves, to determine their own life styles without being dictated to.

The value of community calls for a development of noncompetitive interdependence as a basis upon which to build a society sensitive to individual needs, respectful of differences, yet capable of sustaining a social ethic which generates community cohesiveness. They realize such social development implies a radical reorientation of the present pattern of social interaction.

People [must be] more open with each other . . . [this] can be a bridge to building a whole new form of personal relationships, not based on the diminution of the other person, [but] more concerned about being free and letting other people be free.

In accordance with their belief in a community of tolerance, our respondents are sympathetic to those who use drugs and are deeply engaged in the counter-culture. Although they have often had extended contact with these communities, they usually do not regard themselves as active participants, probably because their status as students precludes identification with a group essentially defined as separate from dominant social institutions.

I think hippies probably get more out of their lives . . . they don't have to be concerned with the things society considers important, like taxes and schools . . . they don't have to depend on technology . . . they're able to find out what it means to be a human being, not an automaton.

It's [counter-culture] the beginning of a new consciousness . . . it readjusts the balance a bit between man's inner and outer life . . . hippies are more experientially oriented than activity oriented—not as hungry, materialistic.

Most of these students have experimented with drugs, and almost unanimously accept the use of marijuana and hashish, condemn hard drugs such as heroin, and express ambivalence about LSD and other chemical compounds. Generally drugs are valued for their ability to heighten sensual and aesthetic experience, to counteract preoccupation with object-oriented materialism.

It makes it more tolerable. In a society like ours your senses get starved for pretty things . . . everything is so sterile and drab, so useful.

I really think it can be a mind-expanding thing, that you can become aware . . that sounds sort of silly, but it's true—it does heighten your senses.

However, use of drugs is consistently viewed as an individual decision rather than a matter for public legislation. Nonetheless, communal living and drugs are usually accepted with a qualification; such activity is valuable as an alternative life style, but it has definite counter-revolutionary tendencies.

They [the hippies] are doing good things with the community. There are a lot of people who want to move out [from society] but . . . it can mean losing reality. You just can't be oblivious to reality.

In a long [term] sense, I think that drugs lead to a creation of your own little dream world. And there is still a necessity for making this a better world, and if it's too easy to escape through drugs . . . the world won't be changed so their kids won't have to escape.

As mentioned earlier, active commitment to change is an integral part of the value system to which these students subscribe. Such a commitment is self-defeating unless they feel it is possible for them to effect change. Generally, the students view America as corrupt but ultimately redeemable. However, their predictions as to America's ability to change vacillate wildly between optimism and pessimism.

America has so much potential . . . [it's] always changing [but] society's not changing, [it's] becoming more repressive.

If America doesn't go fascist, we'll probably develop a pretty good society.

Everything is changing all the time. . . . Young people are becoming more and more aware, and they're going to have more of a voice and they're not going to let older, stupider, pedantic, ridiculous people run the country.

Much of their optimism is curtailed by their perception of the society's reliance upon violence and repression as means of solving problems and stifling dissent. They realize that these mechanisms of social control are aimed at preventing the emergence of a socioeconomic and political system responsive to the needs of the people, especially those who lack access to power.

It is very much in keeping for this country to fear and resent anything that is different, anything it doesn't understand, any minority.

They are also aware that their critical stance is a threat to the established social order. They argue that the Establishment attempts to suppress the radical criticisms that would act as a spur to change through media manipulation of public values. For example, concepts of proper public morality are thought to be falsely supported through the fictive image of the silent majority.

Agnew's style . . . what is democracy? . . . anybody that has ever objected to the policies of government is called a name or written off. Name calling—sick degenerates, malcontents, born that way—that's what I really object to.

They also feel that violence is society's natural reaction when other methods of social control fail. This conviction is usually supported by personal experience.

The Mifflin Street riot last spring . . . affected my outlook the most. . . . It reminds me of the movie "Z" . . . people were just having fun at a block dance . . . maybe a few wanted a confrontation, but the police provoked three days of street fighting. . . . The fact that the police wanted to start a confrontation revealed American society for what it is.

The reaction to violence is ambivalent. Some grow to feel that in a society characterized by violence the dissident is forced to resort to violence to effect change.

I see protests as becoming more and more violent. Peaceful protests seem so ineffective . . . Americans are pigs . . . It's repressive, oppressive society, and violence seems the only way to fight back.

Although many consider violence as a possible and perhaps effective tactic in the struggle for change, most personally reject the use of violence because it contradicts the goals which they wish to attain as well as the values they hold.

I can see intellectually why a revolution is necessary [but] I would like to see change come through peaceful means. I can't be against the war and for a revolution.

Yet, personal rejection of violence does not involve a condemnation of those who feel the use of violence is legitimate.

I can't get involved in the violence . . . [but] the breaking of glass [trashing] doesn't bother me [when] there is so much senseless violence [in society] going on.

Thus, the students seem to be engaged in a cyclic pattern with regard to their attempts to change society. Hope, optimism, and activity are countered by experience of societal repression, reaction, and fear of change. The students respond by striking back with both verbal and physical violence, by dropping out, and by withdrawing into privatistic life, yet the majority keep their commitment to social activism by finally, although often times with greater scepticism, reengaging themselves.

What I'd like to do is leave the intense cycle of consumption and get some place with a group of my friends where we can be self-sufficient and build things with our hands . . . that sounds very idyllic . . . withdrawal from society and the world . . . it's good if it's temporary . . . but it has to end. If one sees things that are clearly wrong one has to move to change them.

Despite their commitment, the students are aware that continued activity is difficult, and are especially worried about what will happen to them after they leave the sustaining environment of the university.

Like I wonder how many from the Mifflin Street [student] community will go back to suburbia? I know a lot who will and a lot who won't . . . I know a lot who consider themselves hip, but it is easy to go back and very hard to re-educate yourself.

Because of the failures they have experienced in their attempts at change, and because of their acknowledgment of the very real pressures they will have to face in the world beyond the university, most of our respondents anticipate a frustrating future in which they will play the role of revolutionary gadfly and part-time social activist.

In summary, the values held by the younger generation reflect a mirror image of the values of the older generation. Their elders are viewed as substituting social criticism for active efforts to change society, ideology is seen as a conscience-salving balm for those who recognize social inequities but are not prepared to jeopardize their structural position in society to remedy them. The older generation is seen as valuing property and material progress more highly than human needs; the students stress the dignity of human life and denigrate all forms of materialism. Competition, exploitation, and rugged individualism are considered as the primary personal manifestations of materialism. Thus, the students value social interaction based on community and cooperation and stress a highly tolerant interdependence. Violence is perceived as the inevitable reaction of such a society when it is subjected to criticism and called upon to change. Although the students are often tempted to meet violence with violence, they more often than not reject revolutionary tactics because they perceive these as inconsistent with their values. However, personal experience of institutional violence has led them to tolerate the use of violence against the established social order.

In the past decade, a series of events set within the context of the Vietnam war form a discernible pattern in the development of a radical student consciousness. As Erik Erikson suggests, "[In] youth, the life history intersects with history"[6] and unless a consonance between personal and political spheres is present, conflict is inevitable. And, as we have seen, there is a great gap between personal ideals and political reality.

The central event is, of course, the Vietnam war. As a respondent said, "Without question, Vietnam is the most radicalizing experience of my generation." However, only two of the students interviewed experienced the war directly;[7] for the rest, the war most often served as a catalyst for the development of radical consciousness. Initially, most students' antiwar sentiment stemmed from principled moral convictions; the killing of civilians and the use of napalm were viewed with abhorrence. More generally, they felt war is insane and not to be condoned by civilized man. Perhaps the pacifistic view is linked with the early civil rights movement. Although the struggle for civil rights occurred before these students were old enough to become actively involved, the events seem to hold significance in that many realized for the first time that gross injustice was present in America. "[It] made me aware that things weren't right in this country. Like the whole civil rights movement at least made me aware of this. . . . I never even thought about it before."

With a precedent for questioning society established, doubt over the validity of the war became easier. And antiwar activity is an educative experience. The student quickly learns that he is "attacking the war for the wrong reasons," that the war is a symptom, not the cause, of the ills that plague society. A respondent gives a succinct summary of the process: "And along with changing my views on the war, I naturally changed my views of American society." Thus, the Vietnam war provides the basis for a radical reassessment.

Reassessment, however, is not an isolated, abstract, intellectual process proceeding smoothly from antiwar sentiment to radical critique. Instead, the development of radical consciousness is spurred by personal experience with political events. A particular pattern dominates student radicalization between 1967–1968. The student, initially uncertain in the university milieu, is a sympathetic witness to local antiwar protests and demonstrations; empathy changes to action as he watches the unequal and often bitter struggle between institution and individual. A stronger and more informed commitment against the war is the corollary of action, and with criticism of the war, a parallel critique of domestic policy is developed. The events on the campus in 1967–1968 make the student a veteran of struggle with social institutions, and because of his personal experience with their inability or unwillingness to respond to legitimate demands for change, he begins to doubt their authority. Protest against the war became national politics with the 1968 presidential campaign. In spite of growing disillusionment with traditional means of change, the students turned out behind McCarthy or Kennedy. The events of that spring and summer—the assassination of Martin Luther King and of Robert Kennedy, the failure of McCarthy, the police riot at the Democratic convention, and the trial of the Chicago Eight—completed the process of disillusionment and loss of faith in existing institutions. In turn, loss of faith pushed the student outside of established society, forced him to define himself in terms other than those provided by the preceding generations.

Thirteen of the twenty-four students interviewed conform to the pattern described above. Because of the dominance of this pattern, we will discuss it in detail, tracing the development of radical consciousness from its origin in the university milieu through the events of the 1968 campaign.

Many students attribute the growth of their radical consciousness to the university experience:

I guess the major change was coming here. Coming here radicalized me . . . getting all these people together and everyone realizing everyone else is just as discontent as they are. That makes it easy for something to start.

I think the biggest thing was coming to Wisconsin mostly.

I was inactive and almost completely unaware before I came to this campus; before, when I was a freshman, I'd gone to this small Catholic girls school in Minnesota, and we hardly knew the war in Vietnam was going on . . . and then I came here and my political views changed from one end of the spectrum to the other.

The university provides an urbane, cosmopolitan setting for students whose previous experience has been almost exclusively suburban.

Prior to the time I transferred here I had been with one particular category of people. . . . When you come to a university this size, you suddenly find that you have all kinds of options open to you. You can find out anything you want.

Interestingly, it is not the university in its role of educational institution that causes radicalization—very few cite courses or professors as having a major impact on their political development—but rather the university as a gathering place for youth. The university experience exposes many students to new ways of life, to people with different backgrounds than their own, to extreme political positions. The student must defend his previously unquestioned and often unarticulated beliefs. He is forced, through interaction with his peers, to think about many issues he may have neglected before. He is unable to avoid the protests, the strikes, the voices of dissent. And in coming to grips with his milieu he is often radicalized.

Although many of the students attribute their radicalization to the university environment, the university more often than not simply serves as the backdrop for a more specific set of events in the development of radical consciousness—institutional betrayal and institutionalized violence. In naming the university as the source of consciousness, the students are correct only in that the university furnishes the stage for the confrontation between youth and institution.

The first event that clearly caused many students to take sides actively was the Dow demonstration in October, 1967 (see Chapter Seven). The Dow protest marked the first instance of the university's use of outside force to deal with disruption of normal activity. The students give eloquent testimony to the role the Dow demonstration played in their radicalization:

I first became aware of protests during the Dow protest when I was a freshman . . . [it] was something I really experienced deeply. I started out as an observer and after witnessing police beatings and that sort of thing, I became a participant . . . it also helped me develop much greater political awareness. I've participated in other protests since then, but that was the really important one in my life.

[I] was here a month and Dow took place . . . October 18, 1967 . . . I saw the riot squad for the first time . . . saw people getting hurt . . . got hurt for the first time . . . it was kind of a shattering experience.

[Dow was] a very educational experience as I think any person who has ever participated in a protest can tell you. Actually being confronted by a cop, or being pushed against a wall, or having a cop throw tear gas at you.

Dow really turned my head around . . . first time in this part of the country where police hit demonstrators at the tail end of a demonstration . . . really polarized my feelings toward political authority by seeing police come in with night sticks and riot equipment and start beating people.

In each case, the student's strongest recollection is his experience of violence at the hands of the police. The direct contact with institutionalized violence is indeed a shattering experience for those who never previously felt the aggression society unleashes against vocal and unruly minority groups or dissidents. Along with the end of their privileged upper-middle-class insulation from violence goes the end of their view of society as rational, or even workable.

When a situation becomes so far deteriorated as to be almost a state of war of some type, everything becomes senseless. Nothing makes sense.

Because students were cast in a socially unacceptable role, they responded by identifying with other outcast groups. Institutionalized violence is the experience of lower-class minority groups, and thus the students try to link their cause with that of the blacks, feeling they have a common oppressor—the police who are the paid instruments of the ultimate enemy, the Establishment. The ferment in the black community is viewed from a new perspective. A student recalls the riots in the black ghetto in the summer of 1966:

Now I see it [the black riots] as kind of like what happened the other Thursday with General Electric on campus. You feel so alienated, so used by every aspect of the system—the university, the merchants—that thrashing out in isolated acts of violence is all you can do to retain some sense of yourself.

Almost all the students glamorize the Black Panthers and feel their struggle and even their tactics are justified; sympathy is further augmented because they believe that the Panthers are victims of a brutal national conspiracy to exterminate them.

In other words, the experience of institutionalized violence causes the student's perspective to coalesce. Of the twenty-four students interviewed, twelve personally experienced violence at one time or another:

During the black strike it was the arbitrary arrest of a guy right next to me. He wasn't doing anything. That radicalized me. That was the first thing I was really in. I was sympathetic to the demands before.

Others comment on the Mifflin Street riot, an off-campus, non-political struggle between police and students over a permit for a block party in a student area. A three-day battle resulted.

I became involved in the Mifflin Street riot simply because I was living on Mifflin Street. . . . I was sitting in my apartment all by myself when five helmeted cops broke down the door, beat me up, hauled me out, handcuffed me, cut my hair, and did lots of other nice things like that, and then let me go . . . so I don't want to become involved in any way whatsoever with the political system or the judicial system; I just want to avoid it entirely; it nauseates me, just the thought of being involved with it in any way.

The fact that the police wanted to start a confrontation revealed American society for what it is; the cops are beyond the law . . . even more disgusting was the whitewash commission that vindicated the police, the mayor, etcetera.

If the student was not a victim of violence, then he was probably a witness; nineteen of the twenty-four students have actively participated in protest, most of which resulted in violence. The experience of violence at the hands of a social institution causes a sharp reevaluation of domestic society, and that new look parallels the evaluation of foreign policy; America is an exploitive, vicious society dominated by the materialistic needs of big business at the expense of the poor, the black, and the helpless.

Deaf ears were turned on cries for justice and redress of grievances after the Dow protest, and the students learned another bitter lesson: the liberal establishment of the university community had too much at stake in the existing order to take any action that would seriously upset it. Definition of both the internal problems of the university and of the university's role in society was avoided; the questions raised by the demonstration were defused by burying them in committees. Of course, the students recognized the committee approach for what it was—a rational, liberal academic evasion of a situation that demanded immediate action. Betrayal by the university as an institution was exacerbated because the students had hoped that liberal sentiment could be transformed into action. Bitterness and distrust were the results of dashed hopes: "The only thing worse than a red-neck conservative is a liberal with a big smile on his face."

The university had revealed its true face, that of a servant to a society the students were turning against. Liberal rhetoric about the intrinsic value of learning could no longer disguise the fact that knowledge was a commodity sold to the highest bidder, and only silence answered the impassioned questions about military research: "How can a university teach its philosophy of life and at the same time teach death and give equal credit for it?"

Despite immediate, visceral experience with institutionalized violence and institutional betrayal, the students did not abandon their attempt to introduce change through legitimate channels. When Eugene

McCarthy joined the presidential campaign on a peace platform, students massed behind him. A political figure of McCarthy's stature lent dignity and promise to the peace movement; he also developed something previously lacking—a strong national organization. Eight of the respondents worked actively for McCarthy; almost all the rest supported him. They worked for McCarthy because he represented "a force for change in the country," because "it was the first time I felt any hope for peace in Vietnam," because "he seemed like an honest type politician."

McCarthy, rather than Kennedy, was the candidate on whom the respondents fastened their hopes, probably because Wisconsin had an early primary which actively involved students. Many of them expended a great deal of time and energy:

I campaigned for him, practically flunked out of school, I was really involved.

I . . . work[ed] around the state, went out to Oregon and worked for McCarthy out there, and then I went on to Chicago.

But in many cases, hope was tempered by distruct: "I was very excited . . . yet I was aware he couldn't win the nomination"; "I glimpsed it as a hope, never really feeling that he would win." In other words, the McCarthy campaign became a test case for the system supported by students already doubting its flexibility. If McCarthy's failure had been an isolated event, perhaps all trust in social institutions would not have been lost, but seen in combination with the war, the death of Robert F. Kennedy, the Democratic convention, and the trial of the Chicago Eight, the presidential campaign of 1968 drove many students to reject the legitimacy of their institutions with finality.

Although few actively supported Kennedy, he too was seen as a positive force for change, and, more practically, as the one who would probably have won the nomination; "he was the one person who could have bridged the gap between blacks, middle-class supporters of McCarthy, and blue-collar workers." He was viewed as a dynamic, youthful figure, a part of the Kennedy legend, and he was deeply mourned, but in a different way from his brother:

It was . . . a depression I couldn't verbalize. I didn't even want to talk about it.

It just reinforced and augmented my feeling that the country . . . was a violent society, neurotic in a mass sense.

It didn't really upset me . . . the shock of it upset me, but it didn't . . . by then I was sour to the whole thing.

I said to myself, you're not going to get into this. When King was shot, it almost did me in.

John F. Kennedy's death was a cathartic tragedy that involved a nation; Robert Kennedy's death was further evidence of a sick society in which violence manifests itself as the primary symptom. The event was coped with privately rather than publicly; it was met with depression rather than disbelief and indignation. Many felt a growing sense of paranoia as they witnessed the deaths of J.F.K., King, R.F.K., many of the Panthers —"a whole line of people who were figures to everyone, of people who meant something . . . who were going somewhere and doing something for change, for social change."

The assassination of Robert F. Kennedy was a harbinger of the coming convention, a foreshadowing of the final lesson on the political process. Of the twenty-four students interviewed, seventeen responded to the Chicago convention in tones of indignation, of outrage, of initial disbelief. Many refer to it as a turning point in their personal loss of faith. Perhaps the following statement is the most concise summary of the general mood:

I remember being very frightened . . . for the first time I was extremely mad, for the first time I was furious . . . I mean really understanding what was going on in this country. It seemed very obvious to me with all the police around a so-called Democratic convention, and all the people getting beat up outside. The idea that the two happened together.

The juxtaposition of events made a mockery of the democratic process, that, coupled with events described earlier, confirmed the student's distrust. The convention has acquired almost a symbolic dimension for them; it represents the rigidity with which attempts for change are met, the cynical maneuverings of politicians, the brutality of the police, the death of hope. The following are a few of the more eloquent comments on the convention:

Well, for a long time I wanted to be in politics. It changed after Chicago.

This had an important effect on me; before I had a vague faith that the people were right . . . give the people the truth and things will be right . . . but now I don't have much faith . . . people live with their myth . . . they felt the protestors were worthless so they didn't care if they were beaten: looked on them like gooks . . . My faith in the legal apparatus effecting social change was destroyed.

It was the first real shock . . . it made me feel the farce of the election process . . . you know that it showed in one instant the whole violence in the country.

I lost my faith in it (the democratic process) that year.

It's [meaning of the convention] gotten deeper in the sense that I'm more firmly convinced of the rightness of the Abbie Hoffmans.

McCarthy was gone . . . students were being clubbed . . . Humphrey was nominated . . . the bottom fell out . . . the country was getting charged up when all the McCarthy kids were going through the proper channels for political and social change. And then we just got slapped in the face. I think if you want to choose a point where forces turned toward the worst as far as violence is concerned, I think that point is the Democratic convention.

It changed my politics more to the left . . . the more I think about it, the more it strengthens my tendencies to the left.

The violence on the streets was indicative of what was happening in the country; the violence on the floor was part of this too.

After the convention, nothing was left to sustain the students. The Nixon-Humphrey campaign was watched with "revulsion," if it was watched at all. "I just felt there was no choice you could make, you were just stuck."

By the time the trial of the Chicago Eight took place, its result was regarded as inevitable.

With the Chicago Eight [the only way] is to totally disregard their [Establishment] concept of justice because it doesn't do you any good anyway.

I was there. It was brutal . . . And Judge Hoffman making a mockery of our whole judicial system—of course, maybe it deserves that any way.

For a few, it was the final betrayal:

Well, it sort of made me lose a lot of my false faith, hope in the judicial system. I thought that sure things are bad, but I thought the court would come through, and it showed me that the courts wouldn't either.

All of the respondents condemned Judge Hoffman, many denigrated the whole court system, but for the most part, indignation and shock were absent. In this country, the trial was to be expected.

The 1968 presidential campaign taught students that legitimate channels for change are blocked. If society is unable or refuses to change, then they want no part of it. Refusal to identify with the system means that traditional mores are no longer regarded seriously. This lack of respect for both the demands and prohibitions of society generally takes two forms: withdrawal or increased militancy. Few of the students have chosen to withdraw, and those that have usually express guilt over their choice. They realize that withdrawal and isolation only postpone problems, rather than solving them. One student tries to justify his plan to start a utopian community:

I think it [community] is an alternative, for you see that is how I rationalize . . . everybody is always working for everybody else, and now I'm going out to be by myself, and they say it isn't fair to the rest of the world . . . But I think it is fair if I can produce a kind of life that is better.

However, the majority prefer increased activity to withdrawal. Because they no longer regard themselves as part of established society, they are not closely bound by its norms. By definition, a democratic society cannot practice violence on its majority: maltreatment of external enemies or minorities is acceptable, perhaps even necessary, but the great middle and upper-middle class must remain unscathed. However, shattered idealism has produced hardheaded political realists who realize that if the sanctity of middle-class property and person is continually threatened, action will result:

At one time I was very pacifistic . . . I've sort of changed from that to a more political person because I saw that peace and love weren't going to get us anywhere.

They are cognizant that the result of provocation may be repression but look upon it as a calculated risk:

more violence . . . not necessarily meaning guns, but there has to be much more friction, it can't be so peaceful and nice because from what I've seen, violence, sadly, has gained a lot of things . . . there've been losses, but many times some of the goals and aims have been achieved. And those losses may have to be incurred to achieve them.

The students know that middle-class Americans abhor violence only if they are personally confronted with it or if they must sully their own hands. Beneath the facade of propriety lies a deep understanding of violence. Perhaps, then, violence provides the most efficient means of communication.

Now we've got seven students killed and he's [Nixon] listening. And it scares me to think we had to go into the streets. We have to fire-bomb, we have to get people killed to get our elected leaders to listen to us. Everybody told us to demonstrate peaceably—so we did—we tried it and everybody just laughs: gee, that's nice . . . fun and games.[8]

When you're in a movement . . . for a long time, for years, and you find out that your method doesn't work, that nobody ever listens to you, your one reaction is that people will understand of you destroy their property, especially in a capitalistic system . . . I don't know if I'll end up that way . . . there's a possibility.

Although they have disassociated themselves from society and look upon it almost as the enemy, the students are nonetheless products of that same society, and there is a reluctance in their espousal of drastic measures. Many realize the efficiency, perhaps even the necessity for escalation of tactics, but most remain conflicted over it. After all, they were protected from violence, taught to shun it, and violence stands in direct contradiction to the desire for peace. In speaking of violence as a tactic, one student says, "Like I understand intellectually why, but emotionally I can't grasp onto it. I just can't." Two other students state their confusion on the issue:

Whatever bias I had against militance has been lessened to the extent right now where . . . I don't condone it, but I can see the problems, I can see why one could become militant to whatever degree.

I can see intellectually why a revolution is necessary . . . [but] I can't be against the war and for a revolution.

Only two of the students interviewed belong to militant political organizations. Almost none of them accept the designation *radical* without qualification. But the majority are dedicated to changing society and refuse to give up even though the democratic process does not respond to their efforts. The situation remains at an uneasy impasse; the students will not give up and the society will not give in.

Thirteen of the twenty-four respondents conform to this dominant pattern through which radical consciousness is acquired. The remaining respondents do not reveal any single pattern but instead represent a variety of trends. Two are Vietnam veterans;[9] four withdrew from active political life into an extremely personalistic milieu before the events of 1967–1968; three were touched by those events and are in the process of radicalization; two are freshmen and therefore did not experience the events as college students.

Of the eleven respondents who did not conform to the dominant pattern, we will consider only that group which withdrew from political commitment because their way of life represents a constant temptation to the majority of active students. The respondents who withdrew were, of course, aware of both the national and local events that took place in 1967–1968. However, they did not experience them in the same way as the other students because their views on society were already crystallized. For example, one student, in speaking of the trial of the Chicago

Eight, says, "I reacted by not finding out about it because I didn't think I would be terribly impressed by either side; I knew what it was about and what my sympathies were." Another says, "I don't read the newspapers or watch television"; another, "I don't pay much attention to the news," yet each is able to give critical and articulate opinions on contemporary events. Apparently, they hear news by word of mouth and feel no need to delve more deeply into the matter because they are sure that further investigation would not change their present perceptions.

All four have an extremely negative view of society. One describes it as "nontolerant, repressive, regimented, cutthroat, capitalistic"; another sees himself as being alienated from "things categorized as 'society' or the 'people' . . . could never get it together to identify with mass movements, mass hysterias, mass diseases . . . just wanted to avoid them as too many people." Another is revolted by the materialism of society, by "the things I come into contact with every day . . . how people act toward you . . . they have no respect for you or anyone else . . . and how this makes you look at yourself."

The rejection of society seems to stem from two related sources— a feeling of political and social impotence, and a disbelief in the viability of the alternatives presented by the radical left. The general feeling of impotence is summarized by a respondent's view of student protest:

saw them [protests] as interesting at first, that so many people wanted to involve themselves in that way . . . my feelings changed to surprise that so many people would allow themselves to get together to realize their impotence, their own inability to do anything about it.

Because of their feeling of impotence, they regard the intense commitment and activity demanded by the radical left as debilitating and frustrating: "Politics is death," or, "In high school I was hoping for social change . . . I'm negative now, bitter."

All have withdrawn into a personalistic life style that focuses on intimate relationships. Although they are not active, all of them are attracted by violence. They speak of it in almost apocalyptic terms, use images of conflagration and revolution, perhaps because they unconsciously realize that they have cut themselves off from any realistic means of achieving a society suitable to their sensibilities.

The twenty-four students interviewed represent a specific population of white, urban and suburban, cosmopolitan middle- and upper-middle-class youth. They were reared in homes insulated from the violence and political machinations of the inner city, protected from witnessing poverty and prejudice. At the same time, their families inculcated them with somewhat lofty and abstract principles—justice, equality, liberty—and they learned to associate these with the American way of life. Unfortunately, reality failed to meet their expectations, and conflict between generations erupted.

However, betrayal of ideals is not in itself enough to radicalize a generation of students. The process of radicalization lies not so much in the subjective consciousness of the students as in the clash of consciousness with a particular set of events. That the political events of the 1960s played a major part in the radicalization of students is undeniable when the general pattern of response to these events is considered. Personal experience of institutional intransigence and societal violence were instrumental in leading to a loss of faith in the existing social order. In turn, loss of faith pushes the students outside of established society and forces them to define themselves in terms other than those provided by the preceding generation.

Generation conflict, however, does not usually manifest itself in a direct struggle between parent and child. In fact, parents were usually instrumental in shaping the core values presently held by their children. The students are aware that even though their parents often support them in principle, they are unwilling to activate their ideological commitment because to do so would jeopardize their pleasant position in the social structure. The students do not harshly condemn their parents but reject instead the established social order with its emphasis on competition, exploitation, individualism, and materialism. Instead they value an enduring commitment to social action and emphasize a way of life that stresses cooperation, community, tolerance, and interdependence.

Notes

1 For a more theoretical discussion of conflict between generations see K. Mannheim, "The Sociological Problems of Generations," in *Essays in the Sociology of Knowledge* (New York: Oxford University Press, 1952); P. Slater, *The Pursuit of Loneliness* (Boston: Beacon Press, 1970); M. Mead, *Culture and Commitment* (New York: Natural History Press, 1970); P. Lauter and F. Howe, *The Conspiracy of the Young* (New York: World, 1970); C. Reich, *The Greening of America* (New York: Random House, 1970); L. Feuer, *The Conflict of Generations* (New York: Basic Books, 1968); P. Altbach and R. S. Laufer, "Youth Protest in Transition," *Annals*, May 1971.

2 This study is the product of a graduate seminar, and we wish to thank the graduate students who freely gave their time, ideas, and energy to this project. The interviews, which took approximately three and a half hours, were administered by the graduate students, and transcriptions of the tapes were also made by them. Without their participation, this study would never have taken place.

3 The background data on these students fit the classic pattern described by Richard Flacks. Despite their upper-middle-class, professionally oriented, and cosmopolitan background, these students do seem to represent sentiments felt by a large portion of the sporadically active student body.

4 Ten fathers and ten mothers were listed as Jews; four fathers and seven mothers as Protestants; two fathers and mothers as Roman Catholics; six fathers

and five mothers as having no religious preference. No answer was given for two fathers. When we take into account the fact that identification with Judaism is often an ethnic rather than a religious identity, the religious identity of this group as a whole seems very weak.

[5] Seven mothers were identified by their children as Protestant, yet only two children identified themselves as such. However, the fact that only four fathers were labeled Protestant probably indicates that religion in these families was relatively weak. The holding power of Judaism seems relatively strong (seven out of ten), but, again, this may be an ethnic rather than a religious identification. One Catholic child retained his religious identity, the other did not. Thus, the dominant shift seemed to be toward a rejection of religion or a switch to one unconnected with the Western tradition.

[6] E. Erikson, *Identity, Youth and Crisis* (New York: Norton, 1968), p. 257.

[7] The Vietnam war was a radicalizing experience for both veterans in the sample. Prior to entering the army, neither was strongly opposed to the war. Although their experience in Vietnam turned them against the war, their rejection was not without qualification. Their baptism in battle both revolted and exhilarated them, and each is fully conscious of the duality of these emotions. "I had expected that after I had seen a battle I would see the results of it in terms of trying to establish who had won the military encounter . . . and all I saw was civilian homes that were ruined . . . the village that was demolished, people coming out of the little bomb shelters they had built . . . at the same time I was developing xenophobia so that the Vietnamese became gooks to me and I hated the goddamn people . . . it was a real schizophrenic kind of thing because I could see how fucked up everything was and . . . I didn't really care." The other veteran also explains what happened to him in the course of battle: "About halfway through . . . when my friends started getting killed, I really got into the war, like I wanted to kill. And all of a sudden it dawned on me . . . like over there, they all call the Vietnamese gooks and they aren't human. And I got to thinking—we're killing people, that guy might have been my friend. And I said, 'I quit, I'm not going to kill anyone anymore.'" After being discharged from the service, both respondents joined Vets for Peace. "Like I really felt on the outside—[I] couldn't identify with students because no matter where they were politically or emotionally, [I] just went through a different experience." Thus, personal experience of the war had radicalizing effect on the two student veterans. Unlike civilian students who experience domestic institutionalized violence, they were emotionally unable to cope with their battle experience through a principled position based on humanitarian and egalitarian values. Their enforced knowledge of man's inhumanity prevented such a straightforward condemnation. Instead, they suffered an agonizing emotional ambivalence toward violence although they were quite clear about their intellectual rejection of the war.

[8] This is the only interview that took place after the Kent State–Cambodia crisis.

[9] See footnote 7.

INDEX

365